TROUT AND SALMON OF NORTH AMERICA

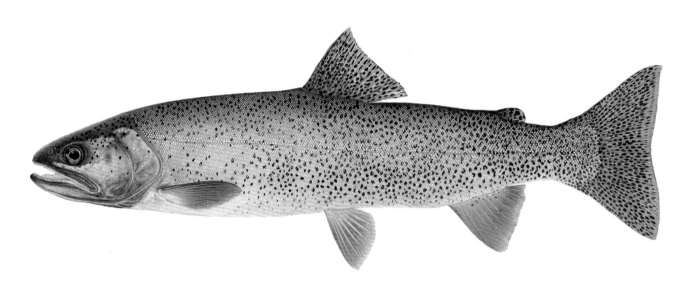

SNAKE RIVER FINESPOTTED CUTTHROAT TROUT
Oncorhynchus clarki behnkei

ROBERT J. BEHNKE

TROUT AND SALMON
OF NORTH AMERICA

ILLUSTRATED BY
JOSEPH R. TOMELLERI

FOREWORD BY
THOMAS McGUANE

INTRODUCTION BY
DONALD S. PROEBSTEL

EDITED BY
GEORGE SCOTT

THE FREE PRESS
NEW YORK · LONDON · TORONTO · SYDNEY · SINGAPORE

A CHANTICLEER PRESS EDITION

THE FREE PRESS
A DIVISION OF SIMON & SCHUSTER INC.
1230 AVENUE OF THE AMERICAS
NEW YORK, NY 10020

PREPARED AND PRODUCED
BY CHANTICLEER PRESS, INC., NEW YORK
AND CHARLES NIX & ASSOCIATES

FIRST EDITION
PUBLISHED OCTOBER 2002

THE FREE PRESS AND COLOPHON ARE
TRADEMARKS OF SIMON & SCHUSTER, INC.

MANUFACTURED IN SINGAPORE
10 9 8 7 6 5 4 3 2 1

LIBRARY OF CONGRESS
CATALOGING-IN-PUBLICATION DATA

Behnke, Robert J.
    Trout and salmon of North America /
Robert J. Behnke ; illustrated by Joseph R. Tomelleri ;
foreword by Thomas McGuane.—1st ed.
        P. CM.
    Includes bibliographical references.
    1. Trout—North America. 2. Salmon—North America.
    I. Tomelleri, Joseph R. II. Title.

    QL638.S2 B432 2002
    597.5'7'097—DC21   2002069256

ISBN: 0-7432-2220-2

FOR INFORMATION ABOUT DISCOUNTS
FOR BULK PURCHASES, PLEASE CONTACT
SIMON & SCHUSTER SPECIAL SALES: 1-800-456-6789
OR business@simonandschuster.com

Contents

Foreword
Thomas McGuane

Trout and Salmon of North America is as much a celebration as a guidebook. The mystery and particularity of so many members of a great family, brilliantly described and handsomely portrayed, enlarge our capacity for wonder: rainbow trout of the Mexican highlands living on terrestrial insects, rainbows of Kodiak Island gorging on sockeye eggs, brown trout in the suburbs of New York, Atlantic salmon born in Connecticut feeding under the pack ice of Greenland, Pacific salmon returning to natal rivers in a kaleidoscope of physical change, brook trout sipping midges in Appalachia or in the pristine waters of Labrador, steelhead from a chaparral-crowded California creek navigating the Gulf of Alaska, Chinook salmon killing wolf eels in the deep North Pacific—are all cousins whether found in boreal forest, tundra, desert, alpine lakes, or mid-ocean. These great and diverse species of fishes with which we live may yet be better understood thanks to this elegant book.

Raising public awareness about fishes is a greater challenge than it is for birds. Fish don't come to the feeder. We can't watch them with binoculars. They don't migrate over our roof or identify themselves through song when they can't be seen. Nevertheless, because most of mankind lives next to seas and rivers, fish subsist in real proximity to us and are, in countless ways, our dependents. Yet they live in great mystery.

Naming, describing, classifying, and, in general, accounting for fish is the business of taxonomy and it is strenuous duty. Driven by such intangibles as philosophy and judgement, taxonomy is not quite, and is more than, a science. Imagine accurately describing

fish that, after half a million years in a specific biome, have by the time of the arrival of Europeans in North America been reduced to one or two museum specimens preserved in a jar. Such miracles of resurrection have actually been achieved in this book.

Glaciation, millennial drought, ancestral invasions, tectonic shift, plate migration, ancient isolation of basins, headwater interbasin transfers, ice dams, lava flows, lakes and landslide ponds, interference by wellmeaning men with mules and milk cans transporting baby trout to places trout had never been—histories of separation and combination often involve co-evolution with other species over timescales of a million years and are only recently beginning to be unwound in the maps of genes. These studies are eternally compromised by the simple fact that even molecular genetics is not a certain predictor of morphologies or life histories.

Evolutionary relationships sometimes contradict external traits. The profusion and placement of spots, numbers of vertebrae, parr marks, bands, colors, fin shapes, run timing, number of scales, and kinds of teeth all can lead the taxonomist toward or away from the truths of a species' history. Is this fish lacustrine, fluvial, resident, or sea-run? Is the steelhead a trout or a salmon? Did the cutthroat give rise to the rainbow? Should we view rare stocks as "heritage" trout? How should we manage a small creek that arises from a spring and vanishes in its own streambed, appearing to the ignorant as an innocuous ditch, but containing a population of trout that has remained uncontaminated for thousands of years? Will we ever thoroughly understand how the magnetite in the noses of trout and salmon supplies geographical data for celestial navigation? How do we quantify the risk of extinction? And where do we place beauty? Or that ghost chorus of departed species?

The very names of our salmonids tie us to other peoples: the Koryak of Kamchatka, the Kootenay, the Inuit. They had the *idea* of these fish first and deserve consultation in their management. When we built Grand Coulee Dam and disfigured our own heritage by destroying a thousand miles of stream-bed salmon habitat, consultation with these forebears as to the eternal aspect of wild things might have played to our long-term advantage and led to a real accounting as to our wealth as a people. We've been thinking about our salmonids for a long time. They were first described by a member of the Coronado expedition; Lewis and Clark first took note of the cutthroat trout; and General Crook chose to angle for them while his colleague Custer fell at Little Big Horn. It's time we embraced them in their bounteous variety.

The rise of mankind has been a calamity for the natural world as there becomes less room for everything *but* man. Loss of habitat comes first, of course; then, the Four Horse-men of the Apocalypse: livestock grazing, logging, mining, and irrigation. Our attempts to overrule evolutionary isolation through fish culture, while well meaning, have abro-gated adaptational strategies and increased vulnerability to disease and event-specific catastrophe. Against a great and stirring

timescape in ancestral headwaters, the diver-sity of fishes has been a cascade of jewels, while indiscriminate hybridization has produced a besetting and assailable unifor-mity. It is urgent that we place value upon diversity so that its loss can be reckoned as cost. Robert Behnke says it here best: "All hereditary changes brought about by artificial selection for more efficient rearing in fish culture are contrary to natural selection, where the sole criterion is survival to repro-duction in the wild." In issues of resource management, the expenditure of diversity should appear on the balance sheet as the gravest entry of all.

Anglers are often activists for aquatic conservation, but their sometimes inadequate skills of discernment have not sufficiently guaranteed diversity. They have occasionally concluded that the struggles of imperiled fish for survival are signs of unfitness. In Idaho, attempts to restore stocks of native cutthroat have been defeated by anglers insisting on their right to fish for hybrids. My home state of Montana has lost more than 90 percent of its westslope cutthroat, the state fish. A local politician suggested that if the state fish was endangered then Montana should pick a more abundant species, thereby avoiding the burdens of protection. A mind thus festooned with ignorance is unlikely to inform itself, but the informed angler will prefer and demand diversity.

Until biodiversity is made tangible, it can never be reckoned as cost. The expensive absurdity of "mitigation" as fish climb ladders,

lose direction in reservoirs, ride barges around dams, and attempt to survive passage through turbines cannot be properly appre-ciated until the tragedy of lost stocks is understood. All salmon, all trout, are not the same. The native cutthroat trout of Pyramid Lake, the largest of all our trouts, reaching more than 60 pounds and representing a millennial horizon of evolutionary deve-lopment, was extinguished forever by an irrigation diversion courtesy of the United States Bureau of Reclamation. This is but the most dramatic of a gloomy whirlwind of shortsighted management decisions possible only in a credulous, misguided, and uninformed public that in surveying its surroundings, has not learned to look closely or acknowledge the complexities of creation. Behnke and Tomelleri have looked closely, and their appreciative readers will find themselves capable of better citizenship than their predecessors in seeing to the well-being of this birthright.

Familiarizing ourselves with elements of the natural world inevitably makes us resist the disappearance of these elements from our lives. Our North American world has been inestimably glorified by its abundant fishes, and, like our birds and mammals, they can never be sufficiently familiar. Robert Behnke has given the trout and salmon of North America a plurality of remarkable voices; Joseph Tomelleri has enabled us, astoundingly, to see them.

Introduction

ORIGINS AND EVOLUTION Fifty million years ago, enormous rivers known today as the Yukons flowed into the Pacific Ocean from a high plateau in the Pacific Northwest. Deep and wide, the Yukons left deposits 600 feet (180 m) high, and buried among these layers of rock were nuggets of gold that would one day drive fortune seekers toward the American West. Surrounded by subalpine vegetation, the Yukons and their tributaries teemed with life. Swarms of fishes including suckers, herring, primitive bonytongues, and hulking 2-ton (1,800-kg) sturgeon swam in these ancient waters. One of these fishes, a nimble trout, would dart after insects and chase smaller fishes, then scurry beneath a log for cover. Perhaps the progenitor of all modern trout and salmon, *Eosalmo driftwoodensis* is the earliest known salmonid fossil. It is considered by the few experts of ancient freshwater fish fossils (paleo-ichthyologists) to be a member of the subfamily Salmoninae. During the time of the Yukons—the Eocene epoch—North America was situated farther north than it is today. Ending its 150-million-year-old union with Greenland, Europe, and Asia, the supercontinent Laurasia was breaking apart and the future basins of the Atlantic and Arctic Oceans were filling with inrushing sea water. The climate was cool near the Pacific coastline where the Eocene Yukon Rivers flowed. We can assume that *Eosalmo* was abundant, but we can only imagine what the other distant relatives of trout and salmon might have looked like. Their fossil remains are waiting to be found.

Inland from the Pacific basin, a number of large lakes known as the Green River Lakes stretched across what is now the central Rocky Mountain region. Lake Uinta, Lake Gosuite, and many others stretched for 100 miles (160 km) in each direction. The climate here was apparently warmer and the fish fauna was quite different from the coastal regions where *Eosalmo* flourished. Warm-water fishes whose descendants are well known today were abundant. No salmonid-like fishes were swimming in these inland lakes of present-day Wyoming, Utah, and Colorado. Their presence in this region of North America would have to wait 30 million years for the Rocky Mountains to emerge, and another 15 million or so for the mountains to slowly rise and the Pleistocene ice ages to come and go, leaving cold mountain streams and alpine lakes. Eventually, about a million years ago, ancestors of all modern cutthroat trout traveled up the Columbia and Snake Rivers; through main stems and tributaries, over waterfalls, up cascading streams and tiny, meandering, alpine meadow creeks; over mountain divides and then only 100,000 years ago, over mountains into the upper Snake and Green Rivers; into the Bonneville basin and the Uinta Mountains; from the Green River into the Colorado River basin; and finally about 10,000 years ago with more headwater transfers to the basins of the Platte, Arkansas, and Rio Grande. By the time Columbus was making his passage across the Atlantic Ocean, these beautiful modern cutthroat trout had found their way into most of the available habitat in the Rocky Mountains, culminating an epic journey of their own through water and time.

To comprehend the evolutionary history of trout and salmon, one must take a perspective completely removed from ordinary human experience. One must think not only in millions of years, but in tens and even hundreds of millions of years. We imagine human beings emerging in the long-distant past, but humans, including our very early ancestors who left footprints in Africa 3.7 million years ago, have been around for a very short time compared to trout; the species *Homo sapiens* has existed for perhaps only 100,000 years. We know that trout-like fishes of the family Salmonidae were swimming in the cool and cold freshwater habitats of the Earth when dinosaurs dominated the planet.

The complete evolutionary history of salmonids and other fishes can only be imagined, based on a limited amount of physical evidence in the form of fossils. What fishes were the progenitors of the 50-million-year-old *Eosalmo*? There is no evidence. A scenario depicting the evolution of salmonid fishes must be regarded as simplified and as a "best estimate" drawing upon limited information.

Origins of Salmonidae
Reconstructing the evolutionary past of trout and salmon is analogous to describing the picture on a 2,000-piece jigsaw puzzle when one has only a few pieces. Yet from very limited evidence, some reasonable conclusions may be drawn. The evolutionary history of salmonids begins with the origin and diversification of bony fishes in the Devonian period of the Paleozoic era (408 to 360 million years ago)—the Age of Fishes. The oldest fossil related to all modern vertebrates, the ostracoderm (a jawless, bony-plated fish), dates to about 490 million

years ago. By the late Devonian—some 100 million years later—enough evolutionary changes had accumulated to allow the separation of not only the major groups of fishes found today, but also the first tetrapods (terrestrial vertebrates) that would later give rise to all reptiles, birds, and eventually mammals.

The two main lines of jawed fishes—the cartilaginous fishes, including modern sharks, skates, and rays, and the bony fishes—had become established by the end of the Devonian period. The bony fishes had branched into three main evolutionary lines that persist today: the lungfishes, the coelocanths, and the more familiar ray-finned fishes. The early ray-finned fishes, ancestors to all bony fishes present today, including trout and salmon, eventually blossomed into the largest of all main vertebrate groups—the Modern Teleosts, which include some 35,000 species, or 95 percent of all living fish species.

Today, the order Salmoniformes includes the families Salmonidae (whitefishes, graylings, trout, salmon, and char), Osmeridae (smelts), and Plecoglossidae (ayu) from the Northern Hemisphere, as well as several families from the Southern Hemisphere. Exactly when the family Salmonidae first appeared on Earth will be known only when more fossils are discovered. Until then, the current assumption is that fishes recognizable as salmonids were present some 100 million years ago.

We can speculate that the beginning of the family Salmonidae was associated with a doubling of the chromosome number of an early ancestor. This event, known as tetraploidization, left all species in the family

Salmonidae with four copies of each chromosome (tetraploid) instead of the typical two (diploid), or about twice the amount of DNA as species from other families in the order Salmoniformes. Thus, whitefishes, graylings, trout, and salmon all have a complexity of genetic material that unites them as a group and distinguishes them from most other fishes.

After *Eosalmo driftwoodensis*, which existed some 50 million years ago, there is a void of about 30 million years in the fossil record of early salmonids resulting in a significant gap of information. However, fossils found in the western United States reveal that by the end of the Miocene epoch (24 to 5 million years ago), the major branches of the subfamily Salmoninae were well established: One branch leads to the Eurasian lenok (*Brachymystax*) and taimen (*Hucho*), one to char (*Salvelinus*) with a Holarctic distribution, another to brown trout and Atlantic salmon (*Salmo*) of the Atlantic Ocean basins, and a fourth to Pacific salmon and trout (*Oncorhynchus*).

Several extinct and extant genera are represented in North American fossils from the middle Miocene and early Pliocene epochs (5 to 2 million years ago), including *Rhabdofario, Paleolox* (or possibly *Hucho*), *Salmo, Oncorhynchus,* and the very unique sabertooth salmon, described as a new genus, *Smilodonichthys.* Most of the fossils from this period represent fish that are very similar to modern trout and salmon. The extinct sabertooth salmon, however, was quite different from any living salmonid. It grew to a length of over 6 feet (1.8 m) and sported a large fang extending beyond the snout. Was this fish a voracious predator like the extinct cat it is named after? The large tooth was probably used more for fighting with other male salmon than for feeding and fossils reveal that it was the species' only tooth. Like some whales and fishes, it fed quite placidly by straining plankton from the water.

The most recent salmonid fossils, those from the later Pliocene through the Pleistocene (2.5 million to 10,000 years ago), emphasize the effects of the dramatic climate changes that occurred during the ice ages and interglacial periods. We know from fossils of the Lake Chapala basin that in the peak glacial episodes when the climate was much cooler, trout in the rainbow lineage existed as far south as southwestern Mexico. This pattern of "recent" southern expansion is also observed in other parts of the world in extant species, notably the masu salmon of Taiwan, the North African brown trout, and the taimen of the Yangtze River basin of central China. The present distribution of Apache and Gila trout, along with that of the Mexican golden trout, also suggests that historically the lower Colorado River basin and northern Mexico were once accessible to cold-water fishes.

There are numerous, interconnected mechanisms and events for this pattern of distribution. Both physical and evolutionary factors have worked together over long periods of time. The physical elements that have contributed to the broad biogeographic patterns include plate tectonics, volcanism and earthquakes, floods, and, of particular importance in the case of salmonids, the effects of climate change. These include gradual but dramatic temperature shifts such as those that have occurred over the last 100 million years—especially the glacial ages of the Pleistocene epoch.

The evolutionary story of trout, salmon, and char is a long volume with many missing chapters. We know that salmonids are among the oldest families of fishes and have graced the waters of the Earth for many millions of years. The ancestral line of ray-finned fishes evolved in very ancient times, giving rise to a fish in the Northern Hemisphere with many unique features. By 100 million years ago or more, this fish was recognizable as a member of the family Salmonidae. By 50 million years ago, the major branching leading to the white-fishes and graylings had probably occurred, thus leading to modern lines of trout, salmon, and char of the subfamily Salmoninae. These lines separated into their present species somewhere between 2 and 5 million years ago. Much of the present diversity, particularly at the subspecies level, is the result of events that occurred in the last one million years and up to about 12,000 years ago, when ice sheets of the last glacial age subsided.

CLASSIFICATION AND TAXONOMY
Classification and nomenclature are an attempt to describe and organize organic diversity and the variability found within similar groups of organisms. The system of classification in use today has its origins in the 1735 first edition of *Systema naturae* by the Swedish botanist, Carolus Linnaeus. Linnaeus's system followed the ancient Greek model of logical division, and in the tenth edition of *Systema naturae* (1758) Linnaeus proposed the now-familiar categories of Regnum (kingdom), Classis (class), Ordo (order), genus, and species. The last two categories are the familiar binomial nomenclature used to formally name a species, such as *Salvelinus fontinalis*. Since Linnaeus, taxonomists have added the categories phylum and family, along with numerous subdivisions such as subclass, superorder, subfamily, subspecies, and others.

Genetics
The current understanding of the "big picture" of salmonid relationships is based primarily on bones. Some authors have incorporated behavioral characteristics such as spawning, anadromy, nest guarding, and territoriality. More recently, genetic methods have been applied to phylogenetic studies. There are a number of ways to make genetic comparisons, such as looking at the number and configurations of chromosomes, evaluating subtle differences in enzymes and directly or indirectly evaluating DNA.

Common ancestry is a critical component in creating an evolutionary picture of trout and salmon. All trout, salmon, and char of the world today can be traced to a time when they shared a common gene pool with white-fishes and graylings—a salmonid progenitor. There are remarkable similarities in the genetic code of modern salmonids—a common genealogy—as well as interesting differences.

However, trout and salmon, like many animals, have about 3 billion nucleotides in their DNA genome and typically only 500 to 2,000 nucleotides are analyzed at one time. Thus DNA analysis relies on making inferences from a small amount of the genome. There is no question, however, that molecular studies in general have contributed much to our understanding of salmonid fishes and will become increasingly powerful in the future. These studies become even more powerful when a holistic approach is applied, one that includes all evidence, including biogeographical information and analysis of morphological attributes.

LIFE HISTORY AND BIOLOGY

Life history is everything a fish does from birth until death. It includes how they grow, mature, reproduce, what they consume, and their patterns of movement and migration. Life histories are determined in part by heredity and in part by the environment— what is commonly called "nature versus nurture." It is impossible to completely separate the genetic components, what salmonids are "born to do," from the environmental factors that affect their lives.

As is emphasized throughout this book, many of the important variations in life histories are found below the lowest levels of taxonomic classification (below the subspecies level), in groupings known as populations, races, and stocks. The subtle adaptations of individual populations are tailored to environmental differences in their native range.

Reproduction

All members of the family Salmonidae share some general characteristics and broad patterns in their reproductive behavior. For example, all begin and end their lives in freshwater habitats. Most reproduce in cold, flowing water by creating excavations in the gravel called redds.

For the majority of salmonids, the female initiates spawning. She prepares a redd by turning sideways near the bottom of the river or stream. She touches her caudal fin to the substrate and rapidly fans gravel with her tail, as if forcefully swimming in place sideways. This movement dislodges gravel and removes fine sediment. The redd is proportional to the size of the fish—the nest of a large Chinook salmon will be many times larger than that of a small brook trout.

Lake trout, grayling, and whitefish do not construct redds. Instead, females scatter eggs during spawning above rocky areas of the substrate, where eggs fall into the spaces between the rocks to develop.

Habitat requirements for successful reproduction are somewhat constant for most trout, salmon, and char. The primary component of a successful redd is the substrate. Suitable gravel is essential to permit the flow of water around the incubating eggs.

Stream- and river-spawning salmonids will often seek riffle areas, or shelves at the head of a pool where the water is accelerating and the gravel is loosely packed. These areas allow ease of redd construction, as well as upwelling through the gravel to maintain adequate oxygen levels. Females will also focus on areas in the river where groundwater is coming in from below. Groundwater is important, especially in more northern regions, as it will prevent freezing during winter. A constant supply of oxygen is critical for egg survival during incubation.

In large natural populations, many male fish will congregate and begin to maneuver for the oppurtunity to spawn long before females appear at the spawning sites. Domi-

nant males will assume aggressive postures, use intricate body language, and will often bite the tail of other males. This sparring can proceed for up to several days, or sometimes weeks. When females arrive, there are intensified aggressive interactions between males, interspersed with courtship behaviors to impress the females.

In nest-building salmonids, the start of redd construction invariably attracts males to the area surrounding the female. Then, the female will send cues via subtle postures of her fins and mouth that she is preparing to release her eggs. Her anal fin will probe the prepared site and males will appear for the final chance at mating. Through some mechanism of male supremacy and female decision, one dominant male will move in alongside the female over the redd.

A dramatic dance in unison of sinuous swimming, gaping mouths, and quivering bodies finally culminates in a stream of eggs enveloped in a cloud of milt (sperm). Usually this involves one male with one female, but sometimes a second male will appear and simultaneously release his milt.

Males may spawn with more than one female during the reproductive cycle. Females generally release their eggs in several sessions over the course of a day or two, and will sometimes create an additional redd in close proximity to their initial spawning site.

The female then covers the redd with a layer of gravel until the eggs are completely buried. In most cases, the female will guard the redd for some time to prevent other fish from disturbing it and consuming the eggs. Pacific salmon females guard the redd until their death, which occurs within one to two weeks of spawning. During their last few days of life, Pacific salmon females and males are weak and listlessly drift downstream.

Compared to many fishes, salmonids have rather large eggs with more yolk material. As a general rule, trout and salmon will lay about 1,000 eggs per 2 ⅕ pounds (1 kg) of body weight. This is not a great number for fishes in general, which can have many hundreds of thousands or even millions of eggs in some of yolk is a salmonid's insurance policy for survival. When a trout or salmon hatches from the egg (called the alevin stage), it retains a significant portion of the yolk attached to the throat region. This yolk-sac allows the alevin to attain a relatively large size in the first month or so of its life and eliminates the total dependence on feeding. By the time the yolk is fully absorbed (about 40 days after hatching, depending upon water temperature), the fish, now called a fry, is about 1 inch (2.5 cm) in length, which is much larger than most fish species at the same age.

Most trout, salmon, and char spawn in response to changes in water temperature and length of daylight hours that correlate to seasonal changes on an annual cycle. Rainbow and cutthroat trout, in general, initiate spawning when the days start getting longer and the daily maximum water temperature becomes warmer. Brook and brown trout initiate spawning when the days get shorter and the maximum daily water temperature begins to fall.

There are many variations on this general theme. For example, mountain streams warm in early spring before snowmelt and can trigger spawning in April. As the weather warms, the snowpack melts, causing high flows and a drop in water temperature that brings spawning to a halt. After peak runoff, a second group of spawning fish will respond to warmer water temperatures and spawn in June or July. This results in two age and size groups of fish born in the same year.

Climatic differences from south to north are an obvious factor in water temperature. Therefore, rainbow and cutthroat trout generally spawn earlier in the milder climates of more southerly or coastal areas and later in more northerly streams and rivers and at higher elevations.

Generally, Pacific trout (rainbow and cutthroat trout) spawn from late winter to early summer, and brook trout, Atlantic salmon, and brown trout spawn from late summer to early winter. There is a tremendous amount of variation in time of spawning in all species of trout, salmon, and char based on local environmental conditions.

Timing of spawning for Pacific salmon is an extremely complicated process and varies widely in different areas or even within the same river basin. For example, Chinook salmon native to the Sacramento River basin are divided into four major runs in each of the seasons of the year. Some spawning of these races occurs in every month.

Age and Growth

Like all aspects of life history, age and growth are determined by interactions of heredity and physical constraints of the environment. Unlike terrestrial vertebrates and other creatures that reach a maximum size at adulthood, salmonids are able to continue to grow throughout their lifetime. Since salmonids are cold-water animals, their body temperature is that of the water that surrounds them. Therefore, rate of growth and longevity are greatly influenced by water temperature. Other environmental factors have an impact on growth, including oxygen level of the water, salinity, competition, and the availability of food.

In most environments, the average life span of a trout is six to seven years, but this can be extended up to 25 years or more in some cold, high-elevation mountain lakes. Some populations of Arctic char can live more than 30 years, and lake trout often live 60 years or longer. The life span of species of salmon rarely exceeds five or six years. While Atlantic salmon are able to spawn more than once, all Pacific salmon native to North America die soon after spawning.

Maximum size is under a strong genetic control, but it is also subject to environmental factors and variation in distinct populations of fish. Many populations reaching a large maximum size—Bear Lake cutthroat trout, Pyramid Lake Lahontan cutthroat trout, and rainbow trout of Kootenay, Eagle, and Crescent Lakes—evolved in large lakes and adapted to eat fish. Over time, nature and nurture have combined to produce these populations of very large fish.

Food and Feeding

When it comes to food, trout and salmon are typically generalists and opportunists—they will feed upon a variety of prey items depending upon what is available at any given time. Most salmonids in fresh water rely heavily on aquatic invertebrates, primarily larvae of aquatic insects. There are several major groups of aquatic insects, and salmonids tend to focus on stoneflies, mayflies, caddis flies, true flies, and at times damselflies and dragonflies. These groups contain vast numbers of species that are specialized to different microhabitats of the stream and are present in varying numbers at different times throughout the year. Terrestrial invertebrates such as grasshoppers, beetles, and ants are also prey items when available. It is very typical for one or two sources of food to dominate the diet at specific times on an annual cycle. Although salmonids are generalists and opportunistic, they often feed in a very selective manner at any one given time. Any serious angler will attest to this!

Trout and small salmon feed on these aquatic insects by taking them from the water column as they drift by, plucking them from the river bottom, or striking adult flying insects on or directly above the water surface.

In some habitats, in addition to the aquatic insect larvae, crustaceans such as freshwater shrimp, crayfishes, and tiny free-swimming "water fleas" are important food items. In lakes, some salmonids, like kokanee salmon and Arctic char, have adapted to the large quantity of the small crustaceans and other zooplankton that bloom in massive numbers at certain times of the year.

As some trout become larger, they prey on smaller forage fishes. These piscivorous (fish-eating) trout are usually able to attain much larger sizes. Since the size of the prey is dictated by the gape of the open mouth, growing past a certain size will open the door to larger prey items and consequently to further growth: The bigger the predator's mouth, the bigger the prey. Salmonids that migrate to the open ocean (salmon, steel-head, and to a lesser degree coastal cutthroat and some char) prey mainly on other fishes, crustaceans (shrimp), and squid.

Feeding times will often follow a pattern of availability of food. In streams where invertebrate drift is greatest just after sunset and just before sunrise, trout feed more actively. Temperature is also known to have a significant effect on feeding behavior. Optimal feeding temperature is generally between 55 and 60 °F (13–16 °C).

The amount of food a fish must consume to maintain its body size is dependent upon the temperature of the water it inhabits. The metabolic rate increases with higher water temperature, and therefore more food must be consumed. Under normal circumstances, a trout or salmon must consume about one percent of its body weight, per day, to maintain its weight; surplus amounts are directed toward growth. This amount is greatly reduced during colder months and the trout and salmon are able to subsist on very little, due to the slowing of metabolic functions associated with a decrease in water temperature.

Movement and Migration
Salmonids are an amazing study in movement and migration. Their ability to move and migrate through complex river systems and open ocean is perhaps their primary evolutionary advantage and the reason they have been able to persist for many millions of years through dramatic changes in climate and geography.

Movements of salmonids include small-scale phenomena such as moving from a prime foraging point behind a rock in a river to open current to snatch a drifting caddis fly larvae, or changing position at the bottom of a lake to the region just below the surface in response to a rush of damselfly larvae beginning to emerge. A trout or salmon will move under a sheltered bank to avoid a foraging bear (or an optimistic angler).

Salmonids are also among the all-time marathon migrators. Migration in salmonids occurs in a regular pattern between two or more distant places, such as from a lake to a river or from a river to the ocean. It involves large numbers or all of a population with a purposeful action influenced by heredity and instinct, such as feeding or spawning, and it is almost always cyclical in nature.

There are major distinctions between trout and salmon that are stream-resident (permanently stream-dwelling), fluvial (making regular migrations within a river system), adfluvial (making regular migrations between a river and a lake), lacustrine (lake-dwelling), and anadromous (migrating from fresh water to the ocean, living a portion of life at sea and returning to fresh water to spawn). Specific examples of each of these various migratory behaviors are described in individual accounts of this book.

A young resident trout, during the first year of life, will often move from an area of high population density to one of low density to avoid competition from older, larger trout and to establish its own territory for feeding. When resident fish reach maturity they are often sedentary, confining movements to short feeding excursions and relocation during spawning season. While this is typical behavior with larger, more dominant fish, recent studies have shown that there is probably more movement in resident trout than previously believed, and better habitats will likely attract more fish for immigration. In rivers where salmon runs occur on a regular basis from early spring to late fall, some resident rainbow trout and Dolly Varden will often move up and down the river and locate in the vicinity of spawning salmon to take advantage of the abundance of salmon eggs as a food source.

At first glance it would seem that migration for a small salmon in fresh water would not be a formula for long-term sustainability. In some cases, such as Chinook salmon and chum salmon of the Yukon River basin, these fish journey more than 1,000 miles (1,600 km) downstream from their spawning sites and face sharks, seals, killer whales, and other predators in the ocean for several years. They then return from the ocean, passing a gauntlet of predators congregated at a river mouth, swim upstream, navigating cascades and small waterfalls, avoiding bears, eagles, and otters, all the while without feeding.

The explanation from an evolutionary standpoint is that the benefits from this migratory strategy must outweigh the costs. Anadromous salmon, trout, and char migrate to the ocean to take advantage of the abundant food in the ocean. The small stream or river where these fish are born does not have the ecological resources to sustain them in great numbers, nor the quantity of prey to allow the kind of growth available in the ocean.

Salmon and anadromous trout and char return to the spawning sites much larger than resident fish from the same stream. The larger size gives them two very significant advantages: They are able to dominate the best spawning locations and they also lay many more eggs than the smaller resident fish.

MORPHOLOGY AND ANATOMY

Salmonid fishes have long been admired for their elegant form and the grace with which they are able to swim through the water and leap over waterfalls. All salmonids share the same basic elongated, streamlined shape. Their power is supplied from compact, highly organized muscles that extend the entire length of the body.

The illustration on this page shows the basic design of a salmonid. There are three major median fins (single fins located along the midline of the body in a vertical plane): the caudal, anal, and dorsal fin. These provide thrust through the water. Stabilization is provided by two sets of paired fins—the pelvic and the pectoral—much like the wings of an aircraft.

The dorsal fin of a salmonid is in the middle of the back. A small, fleshy fin called an adipose fin is found directly behind the dorsal fin in salmonids. The caudal fin can be deeply "forked" as in the lake trout or "square" as in the brook trout. The depth of the indentation in the caudal fin varies somewhat among species.

All salmonids have soft fin rays, except for the adipose fin, which has no rays at all. Each fin ray connects to a free-floating bone that is imbedded in muscles and allows precise control of both the shape and movement of the fins. Salmonids all have a small appendage called the axillary process located at the origin of the pelvic fins on the body.

Salmonid scales are thin and translucent

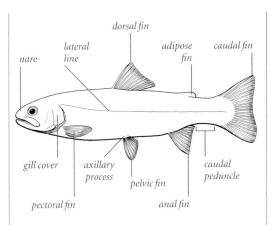

and are categorized as "cycloid," forming concentric rings that may be useful in determination of age, similar to rings of a tree. An experienced scientist can also detect life history characteristics of individual fish, such as number of years in the ocean, spawning times, and other information from subtle markings and spacing features of the rings.

The Skeletal System
The skeletal system of trout and salmon consists of the skull, backbone, a set of bones called the appendicular skeleton, and the ribs and intermuscular bones. The salmonid skull is a complex assemblage of about 50 major bones and many additional smaller ones, including ossified cartilage (cartilage-bones), small bones originating in the skin (dermal-bones), and teeth. Bones of the skull are used in taxonomy, and one of the most important is the basibranchial plate. This is a thin, bony plate in the throat behind the tongue that in some species of fish has tiny teeth. These basibranchial teeth are present in species such as cutthroat trout and char, but absent in other salmonid species, including all Pacific salmon.

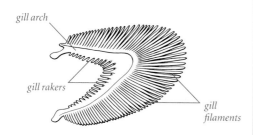

gill arch

gill rakers

gill filaments

Toward the back of the skull are a series of internal bones that support the gills. These consist of many small bones connected by cartilage, allowing for flexibility of movement as water passes through the gills. The gill filaments are attached to bones called the gill arches. The gill filaments are covered by a thin membrane where oxygen is absorbed and carbon dioxide passes back into the water. The gill arches have bony projections called gill rakers, which strain food and particles from the water. Differences in number and morphology of the gill rakers are also often used for taxonomic evaluations and can give clues as to the type of feeding strategies used by the fish. Generally fish that feed by straining plankton from the water will have a higher number of gill rakers, and those that prey more on larger insects and other fish will show a trend toward reduction of gill raker development. For example, kokanee salmon typically have a total of 35 to 40 gill rakers reflecting their specialized diet of zooplankton. Most trout, such as rainbow, cutthroat, and brook trout, that are generalist in their feeding habits have a total of 15 to 20 short, stout, more widely spaced gill rakers.

Functional Morphology

Many features of the functional morphological systems (internal organs, sensory, circulatory, and nervous systems) of trout and salmon are similar to those of most vertebrates. Of course, there are major anatomical differences that are the result of evolutionary adaptation to optimize life in water as opposed to life on land. The greater density of water as compared to air affects movement and the transmission of sound and light. Chemicals, such as oxygen, are influenced by the density of water. The air that humans breathe at sea level has about 200,000 parts per million of oxygen, compared to water at the same elevation, which has at most only 12 parts per million. Sound travels five times faster in water, but light travels more slowly.

Trout and salmon have a heart, kidney, liver, and spleen; a stomach and short, simple intestine; a small urinary bladder; and testes or ovaries. They also have gills—numerous, complex filaments that extend toward the back of the fish on the gill arches. Gill filaments are finely partitioned and filled with blood vessels to handle the relatively low amount of oxygen in water as compared to air. The circulatory/respiratory system functions primarily to pass oxygen in the blood to all parts of the body, and return the deoxygenated blood to the gills where they receive a new complement of oxygen. The heart of a trout, salmon, or char is a simple in-line pump, located directly below the gills in the throat region of the fish.

An organ unique to fishes is the air bladder. The air bladder is a membranous sac that extends the entire length of the body cavity. Filled with gas, it provides buoyancy and stability in the water column.

Food enters the mouth and is swallowed whole. In fish that eat primarily plankton, like whitefishes and kokanee salmon, small food particles are essentially strained from the water by the gill rakers and then funneled into the esophagus and stomach.

Salmonids also have numerous finger-like projections on the intestine just behind the stomach. These sacs, called pyloric caeca, increase the surface area for better absorption and secrete enzymes that assist in digestion. The number of pyloric caeca can be consistently different between some species of trout and salmon and is commonly used as a taxonomic characteristic.

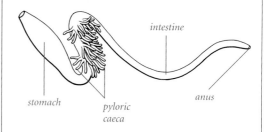

intestine

stomach

pyloric caeca

anus

Trout and salmon are equipped with a sophisticated group of sensory organs that enable them to navigate their aquatic world. The sense of smell is important in many aspects of the fish's life, including feeding, orientation, homing, migration, and probably reproduction. Located between the tip of the snout and the eye on each side of the head are two small openings called the nares (analogous to nostrils). These permit water to pass over the nasal sacs that contain sophisticated chemoreceptor cells. Fish do not "breathe" through their nares; there is no connection to the throat.

Two of the most important aspects of the daily existence of trout and salmon are locating and consuming food. While visual cues are the most important for feeding, the olfactory organs also can play a crucial role in the process. Research has shown that some kinds of chemical compounds elicit a greater response than others. Amino acids and similar compounds appear to play a major role in feeding. (These compounds are actually used in many baits sold to anglers to attract feeding fish.) Pheromones, or special compounds released for the purpose of sending chemical messages, have been found to elicit a wide variety of behaviors, such as schooling or crowding, spawning, predator avoidance, and other social behaviors.

The sense of smell is known to be one of the principle mechanisms that enable homing salmon to accurately locate their natal stream. Pre-smolting salmon are able to imprint the exact chemical fingerprint of the stream in which they were born, and smolting juveniles will in turn record the chemical signature of each tributary as it proceeds to the estuaries and open ocean. When the returning adult encounters a fork in the river, it is able to recall and recognize the smell of the correct tributary, and eventually make its way back to the precise location where it emerged. In the ocean, magnetic orientation is believed to play a major role in movements and migrations. The presence of magnetite crystals in the nares is thought to contribute to the ability of salmon and steelhead to navigate the vast open sea.

Hearing occurs in the inner ear of salmonids. Due to the nature of the movement of sound in water (about five times faster and farther than in air) fishes have no need for an external ear and lack the middle ear found in many terrestrial vertebrates.

Because the density of water is similar to the body density of salmonids, sound passes easily to the inner ear.

Equilibrium and balance in the aquatic world of trout and salmon are aided by the complex inner ear. Inside are tiny bones called otoliths. Otoliths grow continuously throughout the life of the fish and are used by scientists to give accurate estimates of age and other information about individual fish.

Most fish have sense receptors called the lateral line system. This complex sensory mechanism detects movement, slight pressure changes, and chemicals in the surrounding water. Fish are able to detect movement—and even sounds around them—by the water they displace, without the use of their eyes and ears. In trout and salmon, the receptor areas of the lateral line extend along the middle of both sides of the body and are well-developed on the head.

The eye of a salmonid is similar in structure and function to most other vertebrates, except it is enhanced to detect motion and to focus in water. Salmonids can see in cloudy or turbid water that is sometimes nearly opaque. Trout and salmon have very accurate vision over a rather wide range and even possess the ability to focus on objects that are very close, while clearly seeing distant objects at the same time.

Trout and salmon see colors. The cones located in the retina are sensitive to wavelengths associated with ultraviolet, blue, green, and red light. Their perception is greatest toward the blue end of the spectrum.

The location of the eye on the side of the head gives salmonids a great range of vision. In the horizontal field, trout are able to see

objects directly in front of them with both eyes (binocular vision), as well as anything on either side (monocular vision). Only objects directly behind the fish are out of the field of view. Anything that is observed above the water surface, such as a flying insect or predatory bird, is subject to the bending of light waves in water, causing everything but those objects directly overhead to appear slightly closer than their actual location and distorted from their true position. Salmonids have obviously evolved a means of compensating for this phenomenon—they are very adept at leaping out of the water to catch flying insects and at spotting potential predators.

Fish respond to various kinds of environmental stimuli through sensory organs, process the information in the brain, and relay signals or responses to the muscles and glands. The endocrine system includes several glands that secrete hormones into the bloodstream—chemical signals that stimulate a myriad of physiological activities and responses. The endocrine and nervous systems are highly integrated and act in unison to control all basic and complex functions of the fish.

The endocrine system controls metabolism and plays a major role in maturation of sex cells and a wide array of reproductive behaviors. Included in this system are several major glands, the pituitary, thyroid, adrenals, and gonads, along with many smaller glands and less-organized groups of specialized cells.

Salmonids have a central nervous system that includes the brain and spinal cord, and a peripheral nervous system that branches to the organs, muscles, and glands. The salmonid brain has no cerebrum or neocortex, which are responsible for higher thought. Although the brain is comparatively simple, it is capable of very sophisticated tasks and complex behaviors. Salmonids are certainly capable of learning. They are able to "remember" where they spawned. The selectivity of feeding on a specific prey denotes that at least some temporary learning is occurring and predator avoidance in some situations appears to be learned rather than an instinctual response. In catch-and-release fisheries, trout become more difficult to catch after each time they are landed. Trout "learn" from being caught.

This brief introduction gives only an overview of the complex evolution, classification, behavior, and morphology of trout, salmon, and char. It is meant to serve as a basic primer for the main portion of this book, where many of these subjects arise and are often covered in greater detail.

Trout and salmon, indeed, all living things, are richly complex with many functions, systems, and behaviors that are yet to be fully understood. In particular, the phylogeny and various races and subspecies of our native salmonids can be devilishly difficult to understand for experienced scientists, let alone interested non-professionals. Albert Einstein wrote that, "The most incomprehensible fact about Nature is that it is comprehensible." A hopeful comment for anyone interested in learning about the natural world, including the beautiful and intriguing trout and salmon of North America.

A NOTE ABOUT THIS BOOK

The main portion of this book consists of 38 individual accounts covering a species, subspecies, or geographical group. These accounts are divided into four sections: Genus *Oncorhynchus* (Pacific salmon and trout), Genus *Salmo* (Atlantic salmon and brown trout), Genus *Salvelinus* (char), and Other Salmonids (grayling and whitefish).

The text for each account is divided into the following sections: description, biology, distribution, evolution and classification, and conservation.

A life history box is included for each featured fish as well as an illustration pointing out important features. The life history box includes common name, scientific name, other common names, habitat, length and weight, life span, and diet.

Length of the fish is from the tip of the snout to the end of the tail fin and indicates a range for the average size at maturity of the particular form. The given weight is also a range of average size. Maximum lengths and weights as well as angler records are included for some accounts. Diet includes primary sources of food but is by no means comprehensive.

A range map is included in each account and typically shows native historic (late-eighteenth century) distribution. Caption text indicates the particular aspect of each map. Creating completely accurate range maps for trout and salmon is not possible for a variety of reasons, especially due to the extensive stocking of nonnative fishes across North America. Every attempt has been made to reflect the native boundaries of the fishes covered in this book.

Genus *Oncorhynchus*

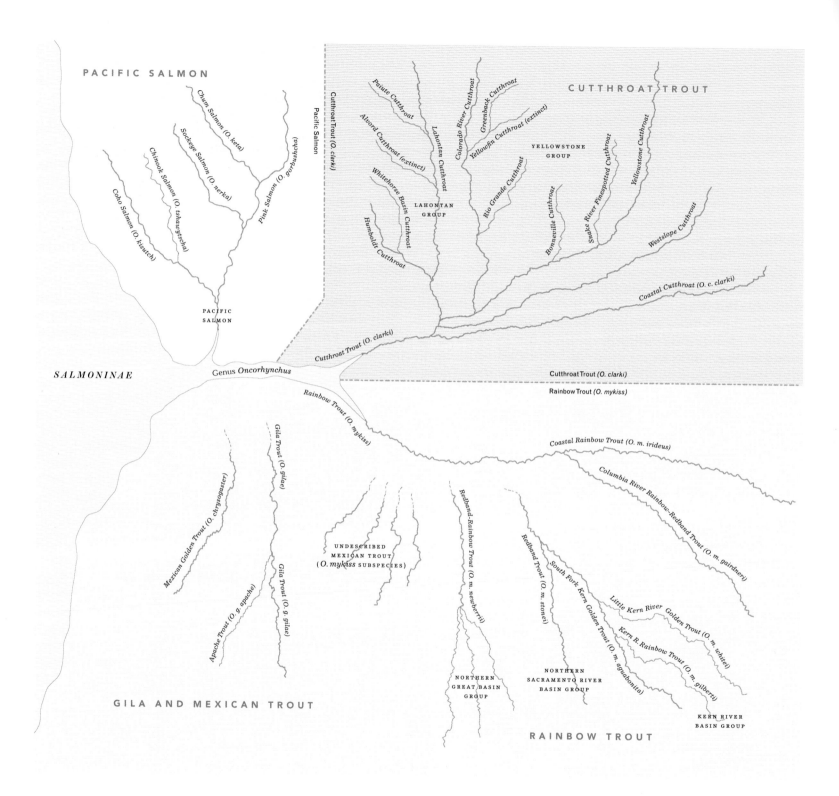

PACIFIC SALMON

Chum Salmon (O. keta)

Sockeye Salmon (O. nerka)

Chinook Salmon (O. tshawytscha)

Pink Salmon (O. gorbuscha)

Coho Salmon (O. kisutch)

Cutthroat Trout (O. clarki)

Pacific Salmon

CUTTHROAT TROUT

Paiute Cutthroat

Colorado River Cutthroat

Greenback Cutthroat

Yellowfin Cutthroat (extinct)

Alvord Cutthroat (extinct)

Lahontan Cutthroat

YELLOWSTONE GROUP

Yellowstone Cutthroat

Snake River Finespotted Cutthroat

Whitehorse Basin Cutthroat

Rio Grande Cutthroat

Bonneville Cutthroat

Westslope Cutthroat

LAHONTAN GROUP

Humboldt Cutthroat

PACIFIC SALMON

Coastal Cutthroat (O. c. clarki)

Cutthroat Trout (O. clarki)

Cutthroat Trout (O. clarki)

SALMONINAE

Genus *Oncorhynchus*

Rainbow Trout (O. mykiss)

Rainbow Trout (O. mykiss)

Gila Trout (O. gilae)

Rainbow Trout (O. mykiss)

Coastal Rainbow Trout (O. m. irideus)

Columbia River Rainbow–Redband Trout (O. m. gairdneri)

Mexican Golden Trout (O. chrysogaster)

UNDESCRIBED MEXICAN TROUT (O. mykiss SUBSPECIES)

Redband–Rainbow Trout (O. m. newberrii)

Redband Trout (O. m. stonei)

South Fork Kern Golden Trout (O. m. aguabonita)

Little Kern River Golden Trout (O. m. whitei)

Kern R. Rainbow Trout (O. m. gilberti)

Apache Trout (O. g. apache)

Gila Trout (O. g. gilae)

NORTHERN GREAT BASIN GROUP

NORTHERN SACRAMENTO RIVER BASIN GROUP

KERN RIVER BASIN GROUP

GILA AND MEXICAN TROUT

RAINBOW TROUT

The genus *Oncorhynchus*

is recognized today to include ten species and some 28 subspecies worldwide. This book covers the nine North American *Oncorhynchus* species, plus some 25 subspecies. All are native to North American waters. Included are the species of Pacific salmon, the rainbow and redband trout, the golden trout, the cutthroat trout, the Gila and Apache trout, the Mexican golden trout, and a group of rainbow-like trout from the Sierra Madre Occidental in Mexico. Also included are the extinct yellowfin cutthroat trout and the Alvord cutthroat trout.

The terms "salmon" and "trout" as used in this book may be confusing. These are terms that enjoy wide use in traditional or popular language. In this context, "salmon" refers to a usually large-bodied fish that lives the bulk of its life in the sea but returns to fresh water to spawn. Five North American species in the genus *Oncorhynchus* have traditionally been called salmon: the Chinook, coho, pink, chum, and sockeye salmon.

"Trout" has traditionally meant a usually smaller-bodied fish that typically resides its whole life in a freshwater stream or lake, and that can spawn more than once. The rainbow trout, the cutthroat trout, and all other members of the genus *Oncorhynchus* discussed in this book's species accounts are named trout in this context, even though two subspecies of rainbow trout and one subspecies of cutthroat trout have forms with a sea-going life history. The sea-run rainbow trout—called steelhead—may, like the five salmon, live most of its life in the sea and can become quite large.

Because of the popular usage of the terms

This somewhat fanciful illustration (left) shows a "map" of all the North American Pacific salmon and trout of the genus Oncorhynchus. *These species and subspecies are part of the large Salmonidae family of fishes and are further divided into the subfamily Salmoninae.*

The map is divided into three regions, Pacific salmon, cutthroat trout, and the rainbow trout, including the Gila, Apache, and Mexican golden trout. The rivers and streams show the many branches that have led to the present diversity of the genus. Some waters do not directly connect to the "main river" of the genus Oncorhynchus, *and this indicates that a direct line of ancestry is not yet understood.*

The length of the rivers and streams in this illustration are not to be taken literally. No precise key exists to measure in years how long it has taken for one trout or salmon to branch off from another into a distinct form.

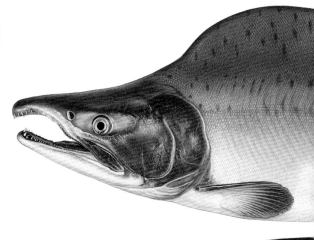

The three species pictured above (top to bottom: pink salmon, sockeye salmon, and redband steelhead) are all male fish showing the elongated upper and lower jaws, called kype. Most mature male trout and salmon develop kype when spawning. It can be particularly pronounced in male salmon, especially the sockeye. Male trout and salmon compete aggressively with one another during spawning, and kype are used almost like a weapon.

salmon and trout, this book uses salmon, or Pacific salmon, to mean the five *Oncorhynchus* species that always die after returning from the sea to spawn, and trout, or Pacific trout, to mean the other members of the genus, whether they migrate to sea or not.

The name *Oncorhynchus* derives from two latinized Greek words meaning "hooked snout." It was proposed in 1861 as a subgenus name by George Suckley, a naturalist-surgeon with the Pacific Railroad Surveys. Suckley did not realize that male and female salmon are sexually dimorphic. This means that at various stages of life they exhibit different physical characteristsics; for example, the hooked jaws that Suckley observed, known as kype, occur only in spawning male salmon. Thus in Suckley's classification, *Oncorhynchus* included only spawning males; females and juveniles were considered to be different species of *Salmo*. Despite this error, *Oncorhynchus* is the first name to be proposed as a genus or subgenus for any Pacific salmon or Pacific trout and is therefore the valid name of the genus.

The hooked jaws of male Pacific salmon result from an unusual form of bone growth when sexual maturity is attained. The premaxillary bone of the upper jaw greatly enlarges and extends downward, while the tip (or apex) of the dentary bone of the lower jaw enlarges and projects upward. This sexually dimorphic trait is found in its most extreme form in male Pacific salmon, but older male Atlantic salmon and brown trout can develop large kype, almost comparable to those of Pacific salmon. And in the genus *Salvelinus*, older males of brook trout and Dolly Varden often develop kype as well.

DESCRIPTION At the purely scientific level, trout and salmon of the genera *Oncorhynchus, Salmo,* and *Salvelinus* are distinguished from one another by differences in dentition and the structure of the bones in the head. For example, vomerine teeth—that is, those on the vomer bone in the center of the roof of the mouth—occur in two well-developed rows along the length of the vomer in *Oncorhynchus* and *Salmo,* but only in a small patch at the front of the vomer in *Salvelinus*. Also, the vomer itself tends to be boat-shaped in *Salvelinus,* but not in *Oncorhynchus* or *Salmo*. According to G.R. Smith of the University of Michigan at Ann Arbor, there are six distinct differences in the structure of the head bones that separate *Oncorhynchus* from *Salmo*. However, these differences require close examination in a laboratory to discern and the process is used solely by scientists.

At a practical level, species in the genus *Oncorhynchus* are characterized by having only black spots on the body. Species in the genus *Salmo* have spots that are either black or red-orange, and most *Salvelinus* species have white or pale yellow spots interspersed with red and orange spots set against a darker background.

BIOLOGY The five species of North American Pacific salmon are all anadromous, which means that they spend a portion of their lives in salt water, returning to fresh water to spawn. In fact, of all salmonid fishes, the five North American Pacific salmon species exhibit the greatest degree of anadromy.

However, Chinook, coho, and pink salmon have also been introduced in the Great Lakes, where they spend their entire lives in fresh water. The kokanee, the freshwater form of sockeye salmon, lives in lakes; some populations spawn in lakes and others run up tributaries to spawn. The life cycle of these fishes does not depend on a period of contact with salt water.

Because salmon occasionally stray from river to river, a degree of continuity, or connectedness, occurs among populations throughout the range of a species. That is, throughout the range of all North American Pacific salmon, no geographic isolation has occurred among populations since the end of the last glaciation, about 10,000 years ago. Since then, all species of North American Pacific salmon have been in continuous contact, unlike the various subspecies of rainbow and cutthroat trout. Many subspecies of rainbow and cutthroat trout evolved in geographically isolated areas where they did not encounter other trout.

The major trend in the evolution of North American Pacific salmon species is a reduction in the freshwater portion of their life history and an increase in their time spent in the ocean. The extreme form of this anadromous life history is found in chum salmon and pink salmon—fry are ready to migrate to the ocean soon after emergence. In these two species, the young smolt when they are barely 1 inch (25 mm) long, allowing great numbers of juvenile salmon to migrate to the ocean from even small areas of fresh-water spawning habitat. Other anadromous salmonid fishes, such as Atlantic salmon, brown trout (sea trout), and rainbow trout (steelhead), spend two or three years in fresh

Chinook Salmon
Oncorhynchus tshawytscha

Chinook salmon once traveled as far as 1,000 miles (1,600 km) up the Columbia River to spawn in their natal waters. Completed in 1941, the Grand Coulee Dam blocked the marathon spawning run of these Chinook and today their numbers in the Columbia River basin are a tiny fraction of their former abundance.

water before smolting at sizes considerably larger than any species of Pacific salmon. (Five to eight steelhead smolts weigh 1 pound, or 0.5 kg, while a pound of pink or chum salmon smolts would consist of several thousand fish.)

This evolutionary trend in species of Pacific salmon for increasing the proportion of their life spent in the ocean means that virtually all feeding and growth occur in the vast expanse of the North Pacific Ocean. Because they are less dependent on fresh water and thus not constrained by its limited habitat volume, Pacific salmon, especially pink and chum salmon, attain by far the greatest natural abundance compared with all other salmonid fishes.

The tracking of marked fish has shown that Pacific salmon (and steelhead) roam great distances, often many thousands of miles, in the Pacific Ocean before returning to their natal ("home") river to spawn. The mechanisms of this homing instinct were long a mystery, but it is now believed that, like migrating birds, these fish use celestial navigation and the detection of Earth's magnetic fields to find their home

river. We now know some of the mechanisms involved—for example, magnitite in the nasal sacs of trout and salmon evidently functions as a built-in geographical information system—but how sensory inputs are integrated to produce a precise navigational system remains unknown. Once in the home river, salmon use their acute sense of smell to find the specific tributary stream in which they were born, and where they will spawn and die.

Homing to the site of their birth allows salmon or trout populations that are associated with different rivers or specific tributary streams to avoid mixing and hybridizing during spawning. This allows for different life histories adapted for specific environments to exist within a species— a phenomenon called adaptive intraspecific diversity. For example, a Chinook salmon population in which young migrate 1,000 miles (1,600 km) to the ocean and breeding individuals return the same distance to the spawning grounds, as once occurred in the Columbia River before Grand Coulee Dam blocked the spawning run, must have a very different life history than a Chinook

salmon population that spawns within 50 miles (80 km) of the ocean.

All individuals of all five species of North American Pacific salmon die soon after spawning. Their carcasses, besides providing food for birds and mammals, fertilize the water and riparian vegetation and nurture the next generation of salmon.

Steelhead, on the other hand, are trout, which means—as discussed above—that they can survive the reproduction cycle to spawn again. Survival to second spawning in most steelhead populations is generally less than 10 percent in their native range. However, introduced into the Great Lakes, where there are no large marine predators, up to 70 percent of steelhead survive their first spawning. They may spawn up to six times, as was found in streams on the north shore of Lake Superior, in Ontario. Up to seven spawnings have been reported in steelhead established in the Río Santa Cruz, in Argentina, but this has yet to be verified.

Pacific trout are considered to be spring spawners, although the range of spawning times extends from late December to mid-July, depending on local conditions.

Lahontan Cutthroat Trout
Oncorhynchus clarki henshawi

Sheepheaven Creek Redband Trout
Oncorhynchus mykiss subspecies

Trout of the genus Oncorhynchus *attain a variety of sizes dictated by habitat, food, and genetics. Trout like the Sheepheaven redband may reach no more than 6 inches (15 cm) and weigh only a few ounces in their native stream. The Lahontan cutthroat once grew to be over 44 inches (1.1 m) long and weighed up to 40 pounds (18 kg).*

All trout are opportunistic feeders and will take a great variety of food items, depending on what is available at any given time in local streams and lakes. Aquatic and terrestrial invertebrates comprise the bulk of a trout's diet in streams. In lakes where they have coexisted with an abundant fish fauna over thousands of years, some trout populations are highly piscivorous (fish eating). Trout in such populations also attain great size compared with their stream-dwelling, invertebrate-eating relatives.

Trout life span may be only three to five years for populations residing in the head-waters of small streams, but about six to seven years is the average maximum age for most environments. The life span may be extended where annual metabolic energy expenditure is low due to cold water, a short growing season, or a sparse food supply. Maximum body sizes vary greatly, depending on local environments. Six to 8 inches (15–20 cm) may be the maximum length in populations residing in small headwater streams, but larger maximum sizes are common among populations dwelling in larger streams and lakes. Notable examples are a 41-pound (18.6-kg) Lahontan cutthroat trout taken from Pyramid Lake, Nevada, which is the hook-and-line record for that species. A massive 52-pound, 8-ounce (24-kg) Gerrard strain Kamloops rainbow trout was recorded from Jewel Lake, British Columbia.

DISTRIBUTION   Worldwide, some species in the genus *Oncorhynchus* are associated with the North Pacific Ocean and occur in both Asia and North America. The northern-most, westernmost, and easternmost distribution of the genus *Oncorhynchus* is that of pink salmon and chum salmon. Both species occur in Arctic Ocean drainages from the Lena River of Siberia to the Mackenzie River of Canada. In the western Pacific, the southernmost continuous distribution is that of chum salmon and masu salmon, which occur to southern Japan. The actual southernmost distribution is on Taiwan, where a subspecies of masu salmon still exists in about 5 miles (8 km) of the headwaters of a mountain stream at about 25° N latitude. As with the distribution of Pacific trout that dispersed from the Gulf of California, the masu salmon of Taiwan attests to glacial periods when ocean temperatures were sufficiently cold for salmon and trout to have extended their range southward.

The easternmost North American native distribution of the genus is shared by the greenback cutthroat trout of Colorado and the Rio Grande cutthroat trout of New Mexico.

In the eastern Pacific, rainbow trout in the Río del Presidio drainage of Mexico (tributary to the Gulf of California) at near 24° N latitude constitute the southernmost known natural distribution of the genus and of the family Salmonidae.

EVOLUTION AND CLASSIFICATION
Before the Pacific trout were transferred from *Salmo* to *Oncorhynchus* (see the box What's in a Name?, page 19), the diagnosis of the genus *Oncorhynchus*—distinguishing the species of North American Pacific salmon from all species of other genera of salmonid fishes—was rather simple and

straightforward. When rainbow trout and cutthroat trout were still classified in the genus *Salmo,* a key to the identification of genera and species in the family Salmonidae would illustrate a characteristic, such as the number of rays in the anal fin, and state "more than 12 anal fin rays (typically 14–18) versus 12 or fewer (typically 9–11)" to distinguish, respectively, *Oncorhynchus* and *Salmo.* A more complete differentiation might note that all individuals of Pacific salmon species die after spawning instead of surviving to spawn again, as trout do.

These older classifications placing rainbow trout and cutthroat trout in the genus *Salmo* were based on a concept known as degree of differentiation, in which species were classified by their physical appearance. In morphological and life history characteristics, the Pacific trout are more similar to brown trout and Atlantic salmon than they are to Pacific salmon. Degree of differentiation, however, is not an accurate indicator of true evolutionary relationships. Diverse lines of genetic evidence demonstrate that Pacific trout are more closely related to Pacific salmon than they are to any species of the genus *Salmo,* such as Atlantic salmon or brown trout. Thus contemporary classification, emphasizing evolutionary relationships rather than degree of differentiation, groups Pacific trout with Pacific salmon in the genus *Oncorhynchus.* The present classification

The various North American species and subspecies of the genus Oncorhynchus *are widely distributed from the Arctic Ocean in the north and southwards on the continent to headwaters in the Sierra Madre Occidental. This map shows the historic range of native populations of Pacific salmon, rainbow trout, cutthroat trout, and other species and subspecies of the genus* Oncorhynchus.

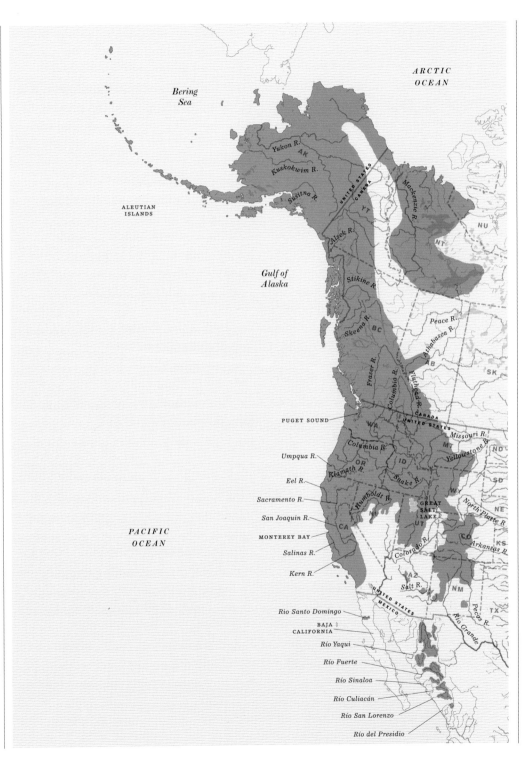

is phylogenetically correct (that is, correct in evolutionary terms), but the diagnosis and description of the genus is no longer as simple as it once was.

Even the older diagnoses of *Oncorhynchus* would be incorrect if the genus's sixth species, the Pacific salmon of Asia (the masu salmon) were included. In morphological and life history characteristics, the masu salmon is more similar to the rainbow trout than it is to other species of Pacific salmon. Genetic evidence of evolutionary relationships places the masu salmon about intermediate between the Pacific trout and the Pacific salmon.

Sometime during the Miocene epoch (perhaps about 15 to 20 million or more years ago), a common ancestor of all the species in the genera *Oncorhynchus* and *Salmo* divided into two groups. One group became isolated in the North Pacific Ocean to become the genus *Oncorhynchus;* the other evolved in the North Atlantic Ocean and gave rise to the genus *Salmo.* Toward the end of the Miocene (about 5 million years ago), species in *Oncorhynchus* were initiating evolutionary divergence into trout-like species and salmon-like species, leading to the present species of Pacific trout and Pacific salmon.

Then about 2 million years ago, toward the end of the Pliocene epoch, a common trout ancestor separated into two evolutionary lines. One line became the cutthroat trout, the other the rainbow trout and its related species.

The species of the genus *Oncorhynchus* vary from "good" (or valid) species, so-called because they generate no controversy concerning their classification, to controversial species on which taxonomists continue to disagree about how many species

and/or subspecies should be recognized. One way to explain the difference between "good" species and controversial species can be explained by their degree of anadromy—that is, how much of a species' life is spent in the ocean—which in turn relates to maintaining continuous variation throughout the range of a species.

For example, there are no subspecies among the five species of Pacific salmon because, without a geographical barrier isolating adjacent populations, a fully anadromous species typically does not partition its diversity into discrete units that might be classified as subspecies. On the other hand, except for one subspecies, the cutthroat trout is restricted to fresh water and is broadly distributed in western North America in many river basins from California to Alaska, and inland to east of the Continental Divide. This distribution has long limited or blocked connections among cutthroat trout of different drainage basins. Some subspecies of cutthroat trout have been isolated from other subspecies for perhaps a million years. This type of evolution, through fragmentation and long isolation as a result of geographical boundaries, allows for intraspecific diversity—that is, for a species to be clearly partitioned into subspecies.

(The coexistence of two subspecies of cutthroat trout in Twin Lakes, Colorado, and of the typical largespotted and finespotted cutthroat trout in the upper Snake River drainage of Idaho and Wyoming are exceptions to the rule of the geographical isolation of cutthroat trout subspecies; this is discussed in more detail in individual accounts for these fish.)

Attempts to classify all the divergences associated with the rainbow trout branch of Pacific trout evolution will lack unanimous agreement. Different people with different species concepts and with different views on classification will offer different classifications of species and subspecies. Any classification of rainbow trout and all of the divergent evolutionary lines associated with it will, to a large extent, be arbitrary. This taxonomic quandary exists because several evolutionary lines branched off and became isolated and strongly differentiated from typical rainbow trout. Several of these evolutionary lines are associated with the Gulf of California, including the Gila and Apache trout of New Mexico and Arizona, the Mexican golden trout, and other rainbow-like trout native to river basins of the Sierra Madre Occidental in Mexico. Classification of these highly diverse forms, which perhaps 500,000 or more years ago diverged from the main evolutionary stem leading to rainbow trout, could be arranged as several full species, comparable in status to rainbow trout, depending on one's philosophy of classification.

In this book, a middle ground is followed. The Gila and Apache trout are considered as two subspecies of the full species *Oncorhynchus gilae.* The Mexican golden trout is classified as a full species, *O. chrysogaster,* and populations north and south of its native range are treated as undescribed subspecies of rainbow trout, or *O. mykiss.* The South Fork Kern and Golden Trout Creek golden trout is also considered a subspecies, *O. m. aguabonita.*

This classification differs from the 2002

edition of the American Fisheries Society's *Common and Scientific Names of Fishes.* The AFS classification recognizes the Gila and Apache trout as two separate species and the South Fork Kern and Golden Trout Creek golden trout as a separate species.

CONSERVATION   In 1991 the American Fisheries Society published a crucial report that focused public attention on issues surrounding diversity. Written by several biologists, the report attempted to define the units of diversity within the five species of Pacific salmon, steelhead, and sea-run coastal cutthroat trout and to determine their risk of extinction. Each species was partitioned into stocks occurring in California, Oregon, Washington, and Idaho. (A "stock" is defined as a population or group of populations of a particular region that share a common life history.) Although the data was incomplete, 106 stocks were classified as extinct, and 214 stocks were considered to have a high (101 stocks), moderate (59), or "special concern" (54) risk of extinction. The blocking of spawning runs by dams was highlighted as the major cause of extinction of stocks.

The Northwest Power Planning Council, charged by Congress to conserve and restore Pacific salmon impacted by the federal hydropower system of the Columbia River basin, estimates that before settlement of the Pacific Coast by European Americans, about 10 to 16 million salmon returned to the Columbia River basin to spawn annually, and that the total annual biomass (total weight) of all salmon ranged from 120 to 160 million pounds. In the 1990s fewer than 2 million salmon and steelhead were returning to the

WHAT'S IN A NAME?

The currently recognized species of Pacific salmon and Pacific trout have been given many different species names. As one example, for most of the twentieth century the rainbow trout was known as *"Salmo gairdneri,"* but it is now known as *Oncorhynchus mykiss.* The transfer in 1989 of rainbow trout, cutthroat trout, and their relatives from the genus *Salmo* to the genus *Oncorhynchus* is based on the fact that there is no reasonable doubt that the species of Pacific trout are more closely related to Pacific salmon than they are to the Atlantic salmon and brown trout of the genus *Salmo.*

The change in the species name of rainbow trout from *gairdneri* to *mykiss* was made in accordance with the International Code of Zoological Nomenclature. When a revision of a species combines two or more species names under one name, the oldest name becomes the valid name. *"Salmo mykiss"* was first used to describe the rainbow trout of the Kamchatka Peninsula in the Russian Far East. The species name *mykiss,* published in 1792, was the first applied to any rainbow trout. The name *"S. gairdneri"* dates to 1836 and described the rainbow trout of the Columbia River. (Although *gairdneri* can no longer be used as a species name for rainbow trout, it can be used as a subspecies name.)

The scientific names of all of the Pacific salmon and rainbow trout are derived in a roundabout way from the common names used for these species by the Koryak ethnic group, the native people of Kamchatka. About 1740, the German naturalist George Wilhelm Steller wrote a manuscript on the natural history of Kamchatka. Included were descriptions of five species of Pacific salmon and rainbow trout. Steller recorded the common names used by native people, in phonetic translations from Koryak into German. Steller died in 1746 before his manuscript was published.

In 1755, a Russian, S.P. Krasheninnikov, translated much of Steller's manuscript from German into Russian. Krasheninnikov's work was translated into English in 1764 and into French in 1768. In 1792, Johann Walbaum first published the names of Kamchatkan salmonid fishes, originally recorded by Steller, as scientific names. This rather convoluted history of the names of salmonid fishes—from the Koryak language to German, to Russian, to English and French, and finally as latinized scientific names—has resulted in some unusual scientific names and tongue-twisting pronunciations: *tshawytscha* (Chinook salmon), *gorbuscha* (pink salmon), *kisutch* (coho salmon), *keta* (chum salmon), *nerka* (sockeye salmon), and *mykiss* (rainbow trout).

Columbia River, and about 70 percent or more of these were hatchery salmon.

Salmon spawning in the streams of Puget Sound were even more abundant than Columbia River salmon. In the early 1900s, the commercial catch of salmon in Puget Sound exceeded that of the Columbia River by four to six times in number of fish and two to three times in weight. Salmon species of Puget Sound have also suffered a roughly 90 percent decline during the past century.

Over the past 50 years or so, the total commercial catch of the five species of Pacific salmon by North American and Asian commercial fisheries has ranged from less than 1 billion pounds to more than 2 billion pounds annually. In most years, the catch consists of mainly chum and pink salmon (60–80 percent of the total) and sockeye salmon (10–20 percent). Coho and Chinook salmon combined make up only a small portion (about 10 percent) of the annual commercial catch but are the most important species for sportfishing.

The maintenance of an array of adaptive intraspecific diversities among many populations requires reproductive isolation (see Biology, above). Much of the original adaptive intraspecific diversity of Pacific salmon species was lost when dams blocked access to upstream spawning grounds, but a large amount was also lost or impaired by artificial propagation in fish hatcheries. Until relatively recently, we did not understand how homing maintains differences in adaptive life history and, in turn, the abundance of a species.

In the late 1800s and early 1900s the leading scientific authorities on fishes rejected the idea of homing in anadromous salmon and trout. After all, they reasoned, how could an organism with such a primitive brain possess a precise navigational system? It was well known that salmon species had different times for their spawning runs from the ocean into rivers. Commercial fisheries were geared to times of runs that had regular patterns year after year; for example, Chinook salmon entering the Columbia River showed trimodal peaks in abundance known as spring, summer, and fall runs.

The simplest explanation at the time was that anadromous salmon and trout, after migrating to the ocean, did not roam great distances in the open ocean but rather remained near the influence of their home river; those that came close to the river mouth would enter the river on a spawning run. Such random movements cannot explain the regular annual patterns of movement, but in the late 1800s there was little in the way of research, experimentation, or life history studies that could show a hereditary basis for homing and adaptive life history differences.

If, as early observers believed, salmon did not home to their natal sites and instead genes were mixed randomly, there was no hereditary basis for local adaptations (upon which abundance depends), such as different life histories attuned to local environments. Local adaptations, or intraspecific diversity, allowed races of anadromous fish to take advantage of a diversity of habitats. Some races would make long runs up specific rivers to spawn, while others traveled only a few miles upstream. This variation in life history traits meant that many types of suitable habitats were used to spawn, and abundance of the species as a whole was maintained. Once certain rivers and streams were impacted by human development, that particular race with a particular life history would be lost.

It took many years of marking juveniles, fishes recovered in the open ocean, and returning adults before homing was conclusively demonstrated. Today we recognize that there is a genetic basis for such a regular and predictable pattern of different life histories governing times of entry into fresh water. Unfortunately, the early lack of knowledge determined the direction of salmon management in the late 1800s.

Early observers considered a species, such as Chinook salmon, to be a single homogeneous entity. They did not realize that Chinook, like other fishes, had a homing instinct and segregated at spawning. Thus they were partitioned into innumerable locally adapted populations in which hereditary distinctions were maintained. To these early observers any population of Chinook salmon, from Alaska to California and from the lowermost to the uppermost parts of the Columbia River basin, was the equivalent of any other population. This erroneous and simplistic concept, which saw a species as so many standardized, homogeneous, and interchangeable parts and thus ignored intraspecific diversity, was the basis for artificial propagation programs that mixed and hybridized different salmon populations with different life histories, especially Chinook and coho salmon of the Columbia River basin.

In the 1870s and 1880s, the U.S. Fish

Commission recognized that overfishing, dams, and pollution were affecting salmon abundance. Since the Commission was powerless to control these consequences, the solution was artificial propagation. The large-scale stocking of salmon that began in the late nineteenth century is a classic example of the naive belief that science and technology can solve all problems and make nature more efficient in serving human society, a belief that seemed to be confirmed by the fact that only 5 to 10 percent of the fish eggs spawned in nature may survive to become emerging fry, while 95 percent survival can be obtained in hatcheries.

The Central Hatchery, constructed in 1909 on the Columbia River in Oregon, had the capacity to rear 60 million salmon eggs. Most of the production was of Columbia River Chinook salmon, but to maintain capacity, the hatchery also reared other salmon species, such as sockeye salmon from Alaska. Chinook salmon from all parts of the Columbia River basin were spawned, from near the mouth of the Columbia to some of its headwaters in the Salmon River of Idaho, and Chinook salmon eggs from many other rivers outside the Columbia basin were also brought to the hatchery. Hatchery management mixed all together indiscriminately and stocked them, also indiscriminately, into the Columbia and many other rivers. Thus began the forced breakdown of intraspecific adaptations and loss of population diversity on a massive scale, through the artificial propagation programs of state and federal agencies— programs driven by ignorance of the homing instinct. The book *Salmon Without Rivers,* by Jim Lichatowich (Island Press, 1999), is a fascinating and highly readable historical account of these cumulative problems, which caused declines of Pacific salmon.

During the past 25 years, the reality of adaptive races or distinct populations of a species has become widely accepted. For application of the Endangered Species Act to a species with considerable intraspecific diversity, such as Chinook salmon or steelhead, the species is partitioned into geographical parts called evolutionarily significant units (ESU). These evolutionarily significant units are neither species nor subspecies as a whole, but are single populations or groups of adjoining populations. The National Marine Fisheries Service considers ESU to be segments of the species in which all individuals within the segment share the same evolutionary legacy. The U.S. Fish and Wildlife Service employs the same concept for Pacific trout and for bull trout but uses the term distinct population segment (DPS) instead of ESU.

The goal of the Endangered Species Act is to preserve the significant units of diversity— in other words, to preserve as many parts of the whole species as possible. Thus, although no species of Pacific salmon as a whole is protected under the act (in 1999, about 2 billion pounds of Pacific salmon were harvested in commercial fisheries in the North Pacific Ocean), 26 ESU of Chinook, coho, sockeye, and chum salmon and steelhead are protected under the Endangered Species Act to prevent further loss of adaptive intraspecific diversity. Considerable controversy has been generated by this protection. The Gila trout is the only *Oncorhynchus* species as a whole that is protected by the Endangered Species Act. (The Gila trout is listed as endangered and the Apache trout as threatened.)

At the subspecies level, three subspecies of cutthroat trout are listed as threatened, including the Lahontan, Paiute, and greenback cutthroat. Several other cutthroat trout subspecies have recently been petitioned for listing. Declines in these fishes have been attributed to habitat loss due to overgrazing in rangeland areas, poor logging practices in forested areas, poor mining practices where mineral extraction has occurred, and water withdrawals for irrigation and water supplies. The introduction of nonnative fishes—such as brook trout, brown trout, and rainbow trout—has resulted in replacement of many native populations and hybridization of others.

The listed ESU and DPS represent a range of life history adaptations that have evolved in specific geographical areas. The total diversity of a species would be significantly diminished if these life history forms were lost. The greater the range of diversity, the greater are the options for a species' continued existence and evolution into the future as it is exposed to changing environments.

Chinook Salmon
Oncorhynchus tshawytscha

Chinook Salmon
Oncorhynchus tshawytscha

Chinook Salmon
SPAWNING MALE

28–40"

The Chinook salmon, also known as the king salmon, is the least abundant of the five species of North American Pacific salmon, but it attains the largest size by far. A commonly cited maximum size is 126 pounds (57 kg), for a Chinook caught in 1949 by a commercial fisherman near Petersburg, Alaska, and there have been unverified reports of Chinook 60 inches (1.5 m) long and weighing as much as 135 pounds (61 kg). The rod-and-reel angler-caught record is 97 pounds, 4 ounces (44 kg) for a Chinook landed in Alaska's Kenai River in 1986. However, the average size of most Chinook returning to spawn is much smaller, in the range of 28 to 40 inches (71–102 cm) and 10 to 25 pounds (4.5–11.3 kg).

The other contender for the title of world heavyweight champion of salmonid fishes is the Siberian huchen, also called taimen, for which undocumented weights of more than 200 pounds (91 kg) have been reported. The official rod-and-reel angler-caught record for taimen is 92 pounds, 8 ounces (42 kg). Sportfishing for trophy taimen is a relatively new phenomenon.

Although the Chinook salmon is a minor commercial species within the context of the total catch of all Pacific salmon—it accounts for about 5 percent—it was and is of great importance to Native Americans. The Chinook is named for the Chinook people of the Columbia River, once great traders, who for thousands of years depended on salmon and sea-run trout.

Chinook salmon are the basis for popular sport fisheries in the Pacific Northwest. Farther east, Chinook are a particularly

CHINOOK SALMON

SCIENTIFIC NAME
Oncorhynchus tshawytscha

OTHER COMMON NAMES
King salmon, tyee salmon, quinnat salmon

HABITAT
Coastal streams and rivers, intertidal areas, and open ocean; introduced in Great Lakes

LENGTH AND WEIGHT
28–40" (71–102 cm) and 10–25 lb (4.5–11.3 kg); maximum 126 lb (57 kg)

LIFE SPAN
3–6 years; maximum known 8 years

DIET
Aquatic and terrestrial invertebrates and salmon eggs in freshwater; amphipods, insects, and fish larvae in intertidal areas; fishes, large crustaceans, and squids in open ocean. Spawning fish do not feed.

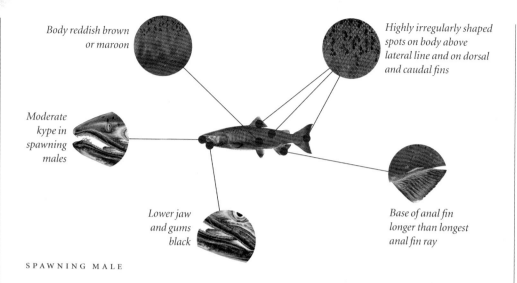

Body reddish brown or maroon

Highly irregularly shaped spots on body above lateral line and on dorsal and caudal fins

Moderate kype in spawning males

Lower jaw and gums black

Base of anal fin longer than longest anal fin ray

SPAWNING MALE

important game fish in the Great Lakes, where their abundance is maintained by large-scale artificial propagation. Under certain conditions, Chinook in the Great Lakes can attain a great size. A Great Lakes record of 47 pounds, 13 ounces (22 kg) was landed in 1991 in the Salmon River, a tributary to Lake Ontario.

Chinook salmon is a high-quality food fish much prized for its flavorful and attractively colored bright pink to red flesh. Far less abundant than it once was, it is now artificially propagated and raised in pens in marine waters of the Pacific to meet consumer demands. In the southern Pacific, Chile has become a commercial center for the raising of Chinook salmon. Pen-reared Chinook now supply most of the retail and restaurant trade of Chinook salmon (and depress the price paid for wild-caught Chinook).

DESCRIPTION Characteristic differences in size and in the timing of spawning runs distinguish adults of Pacific salmon species.

In addition, the anal fin readily distinguishes all North American species of Pacific salmon from all rainbow and cutthroat trout. The anal fin of Chinook salmon has 14 to 19 fin rays (versus typically 10–12 in rainbow and cutthroat trout), and its base is longer than the longest anal fin ray. The anal fin of trout (and Atlantic salmon) has a relatively shorter base, and the longest fin ray is equal to or longer than the base.

In Chinook salmon, black spots, restricted to above the lateral line and to the dorsal and caudal fins, are highly irregular in size and shape.

As in all Pacific salmon (and anadromous trout) species, Chinook in marine waters are brilliant silver. In fresh water, with the onset of the final stages of sexual maturation, coloration darkens to reddish brown or maroon on the sides of the body, and males develop kype. Transformation in coloration and body shape before spawning is not as pronounced in Chinook salmon as it is in pink, chum, and sockeye salmon.

BIOLOGY Because Chinook salmon exhibit a great diversity of life histories, any life history aspect characterized as "the rule" is subject to many exceptions. For example, as is typical of Pacific salmon species, most Chinook salmon spawn in the fall—in September, October, and November. However, in every month of the year there is at least one Chinook life history form that is spawning.

The Sacramento River basin has four major races of Chinook salmon—known as spring, summer, fall, and winter races, or runs—based on the time when the adults return to fresh water on their spawning runs. (Race and stock are terms used for a group of the same species, in this case Chinook salmon, that share similar life history traits that distinguish it from other groups of the same species. The time of spawning runs is the most important factor in the identification and classification of stocks or races of salmon.) The winter-run race enters the river mainly in January and February, and spawning peaks in May. The winter-run Chinook of the Sacramento River is the only Chinook known to spawn in spring (like rainbow and cutthroat trout) in its native range.

Columbia River Chinook have three major runs: spring, summer, and fall. Each of these runs is further subdivided into numerous subgroups, each associated with spawning in different areas of the basin and with different life history characteristics. It is not known how many distinct populations of Chinook salmon occurred in the Columbia River basin before human development of the area, but we can

Chinook Salmon
OCEAN FORM

28–40"

gain some insight by looking at the Chinook salmon native to the Nanaimo River, on Vancouver Island, British Columbia. The river, only 30 miles (50 km) long, is home to three races of Chinook salmon, which differ mainly in the time the young migrate to sea. The young of one race migrate within weeks after they emerge from the redds in early summer. The young of the second race, which emerge at the same time, migrate in late summer, while young of the third race remain in the river over the winter and migrate the following spring.

When salmon are introduced outside their native range into new environments with different environmental cues, strange things can happen. One such oddity is observed in the spring spawning by some Chinook salmon in Lake Superior. In some

tributaries to the lake, introduced Chinook salmon spawn in spring, mainly during May. These spring-spawning salmon are derived from parental stocks that may have spawned in November and December in their native rivers, but in the Lake Superior tributaries the temperature would be too cold to initiate embryonic development of Chinook eggs in November and December. Although the Chinook are ready to spawn in the fall, evidently they are able to maintain a physiological status quo during the winter and to initiate spawning when tributaries warm (to around 42 °F, or 5 °C) in the spring. As all species of North American Pacific salmon die soon after spawning (no matter where they are), the spring-spawning Chinook of Lake Superior prolong their normal life span by about six months.

Chinook salmon are commonly divided into two types—stream type or ocean type—based on the age the young enter the sea. This is determined by analysis of the circuli (growth rings) on their scales. Stream-type Chinook exhibit close spacing of first-year circuli, the result of slow growth in rivers. Much more rapid growth in the ocean produces more widely spaced circuli. Chinook that go to sea in their first year of life are ocean type; all of their circuli are widely spaced—that is, laid down in the ocean. Those that migrate in their second year of life are stream type; the circuli up to the first annulus (annual marks) on their scales are closely spaced, having been laid down in fresh water.

Migration to the ocean during the first year of life is characteristic of Chinook salmon of the southern part of the species' range, although migration in the second year is relatively common in some populations of the Columbia River basin. Northward, where there is a shorter growing season, more Chinook migrate in the second year. Almost all the Chinook salmon of Alaska migrate in their second year of life, and some Yukon River Chinook do not go to sea until their third year.

Chinook salmon that spawn in the headwaters of the Yukon River basin probably undertake the longest migration known for any anadromous species. Documentation of the precise distance to the uppermost Yukon spawning site is not known exactly but is commonly stated to be an astounding 1,500 to 2,000 miles (2,400–3,200 km) from the sea. Before Grand Coulee Dam blocked migration in the Columbia River, Chinook salmon spawned in headwater areas of British Columbia, about 1,000 river miles (1,600 km) from the ocean.

After entering marine waters, growth is rapid. Feeding habits vary in different areas of the ocean and from year to year. Fishes typically make up most of the Chinook diet (60–70 percent), and species of large crustaceans the rest. As Chinook grow they can feed upon larger and larger prey organisms. Chinook salmon roam over thousands of miles in the ocean feeding and growing for two to five years before they mature sexually and return to their home river to spawn. Once in fresh water, Chinook, like all Pacific salmon, cease feeding. Their stomachs atrophy, creating room for eggs in females and sperm (milt) in males, and they exist only to reach their natal waters to reproduce.

The various populations of Chinook salmon have widely different counts of characteristics such as gill rakers (18–30), pyloric caeca (90–240), and vertebrae (66–75). Although average numbers for these traits can be significantly different among populations, the differences are not associated with discrete geographical areas. Rather, the important intraspecific differentiation in Chinook salmon concerns life history. Groups of populations with similar life histories—races or stocks—are specifically adapted to different parts of a drainage basin and can coexist in the same river system. These individual populations display microspecializations that are important to maximizing the abundance of the species.

Throughout much of the range of Pacific salmon, all five species often occur in the same river. Each species—in fact, each race of a species—utilizes different areas for spawning and/or spawns at different times, so hybridization does not occur among the species or among the races of the same species. However, even though hybrids are unknown in the native range of the species, hybrids between introduced Chinook and introduced pink salmon have been documented in Lake Superior. These hybrids occur because of overlaps in spawning times and because the relatively small spawning streams do not provide adequate segregation of the two species. Also, hybrids between Chinook and coho salmon have been found, especially in the Klamath River basin of California; this hybridization is attributed to large-scale artificial propagation of both species, in which small Chinook and large coho might be confused with each other and

spawned together in a hatchery. Also, mixing different populations of one or both species during hatchery propagation can break down hereditary barriers to hybridization. The precision in time and place of spawning that permits native populations to maintain their reproductive isolation is lost when different populations are mixed in a hatchery stock.

DISTRIBUTION   Historically, the natural range of Chinook salmon in North America extended from Point Hope, Alaska, southward to the Ventura River, in southern California. The southernmost distribution of any Pacific salmon species in the eastern Pacific was the former occurrence of Chinook salmon in the Ventura River of southern California. Presently, Chinook salmon breeding populations in North America are not found south of the Sacramento River. In Asia, their distribution extends from northern Japan (Hokkaido) northward to the Anadyr River in the Bering Sea basin.

Chinook salmon are more abundant in North America than in Asia. The main center of abundance is the Columbia River basin, where during periods of optimal ocean conditions, Chinook spawning runs likely were at one time on the order of 4 to 6 million fish with a total biomass of up to 100 million pounds (45 million kg). Before the effects of human development, the Sacramento–San Joaquin basin of California may have had spawning runs of Chinook salmon numbering up to about 2 million fish. More than half of the total abundance of the species was derived from the Columbia and Sacramento River basins. Today, however, dams, diversions, pollution, and degraded watersheds have eliminated a significant part of their spawning and juvenile rearing habitat.

Abundance in the Columbia and Sacramento River basins has been greatly reduced and is now largely dependent on artificial propagation. The Chinook salmon was the first species of Pacific salmon propagated by the U.S. Fish Commission, beginning in 1872 on the McCloud River in the Sacramento River basin. The offspring of McCloud River Chinook were distributed to many states and foreign countries. Beginning in 1875, Chinook eggs were shipped to New Zealand, first from the McCloud River and later from the Battle Creek hatchery, both in the Sacramento basin. In 1907, adult Chinook salmon were observed returning from the sea in a river on South Island of New Zealand. They spread to other rivers, and today self-sustaining Chinook salmon populations exist in several rivers on South Island. The New Zealand Chinook represent the only long-term establishment of self-sustaining anadromous populations introduced outside the species' native range.

Chinook salmon commercially raised in pens in Chile frequently escape and have reproduced in Chilean rivers. In January 2001, I observed adults (assumed to be on a spawning run) and smolts from the previous

The native range of Chinook salmon in North America extends from northern Alaska south to the Sacramento River basin. Chinook have been introduced in the Great Lakes for sportfishing; although these are reproducing populations, as much as 90 percent of their abundance depends on the stocking of hatchery Chinook.

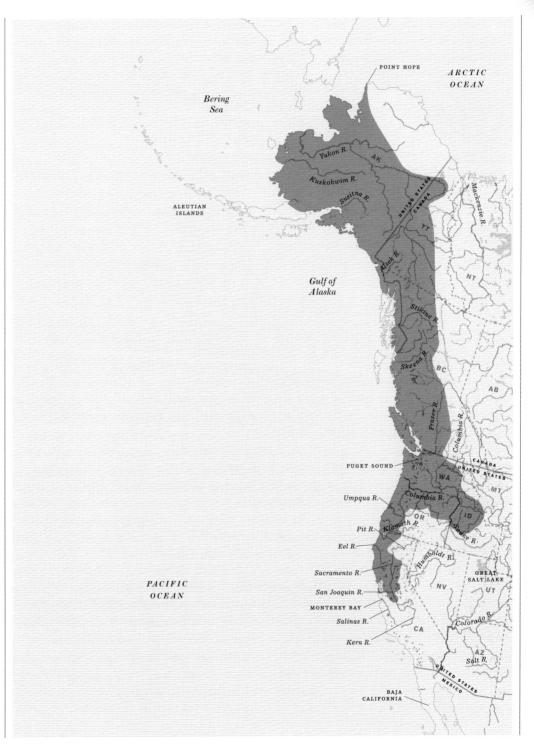

year's spawning in the Río Simpson, near Coihaique, about 30 miles (50 km) from the mouth of the river. The fate of these offspring of escaped pen-raised salmon is yet to be determined. Will they establish self-sustaining populations that migrate to sea and return to the river to spawn? Natural reproduction of introduced Chinook salmon is now widespread in tributaries of all the Great Lakes. Most of the abundance of Great Lakes Chinook, however, is maintained by artificial propagation.

EVOLUTION AND CLASSIFICATION

The Chinook earned its original scientific name, "*Salmo tshawytscha*," in 1792. This name persisted to the late nineteenth century, when the Chinook was classified as part of the genus *Oncorhynchus*. The species name *tshawytscha* ("cha-*vee*-cha") came about in the same roundabout way as the other scientific names for the Pacific salmon: from the Koryak languages of the Kamchatka Peninsula, to German, to Russian, to English and French, and finally a Latinized species name. (See the box What's in a Name?, page 19.)

The ancestral lines of all the Pacific salmon and trout—genus *Oncorhynchus*—diverged from an unknown common ancestor during the late Miocene epoch, more than 5 million years ago. During the past 5 million years much divergence and extinction occurred in both the evolutionary lines leading to the present diversity of salmon and trout. By the late Pliocene–early Pleistocene epochs (approximately 2 million years ago), one surviving trout ancestor diverged to give rise to the cutthroat trout and to the rainbow trout and its derived subspecies. The ancestor of salmon gave rise to the five present species of Pacific salmon.

As with other species of Pacific salmon, Chinook salmon have not evolved differentiated geographical groupings that are recognized as subspecies. During the last glacial epoch, the species was probably separated by isolation in two glacial refugia (unglaciated areas): one associated with the Bering Sea (Berengia) and one in southern parts of the Columbia River basin and southward.

After the end of the glacial epoch about 11,000 years ago, distribution of the species became essentially continuous, although the Aleutian Islands now separate the Asian from the North American populations. Despite the fact that Chinook salmon possess a strong homing instinct to return to the river of their birth, fish occasionally wander to adjacent rivers. Such occasional mixing among populations results in continuous variation throughout the range, in contrast to the long periods of geographic isolation that have given rise to subspecies of cutthroat trout.

CONSERVATION

Native populations of Chinook salmon have suffered great declines across their range, particularly in their former centers of abundance, the Columbia and Sacramento Rivers. Mining impacted the Sacramento populations of Chinook in the second half of the nineteenth century, particularly when industrial-size placer mining began, which tremendously increased sediment loads. Placer mining (placer is derived from the Spanish word meaning "sandbank") involved extensive stream diversion to expose streambeds in order to access gold deposits. By 1900, gold mining companies, using large dredges, tore up entire river valleys and completely destroyed many Chinook spawning tributaries.

Livingston Stone, a pioneer fish culturist and a minister of the Unitarian church, began the first artificial propagation of Chinook salmon for the U.S. Fish Commission on the McCloud River in 1872. He observed the terribly degraded environment in other parts of the Sacramento basin and sought to preserve a pristine area in the McCloud River drainage. Stone befriended the only inhabitants of the drainage, the Winton Indians, and he proposed that the McCloud River drainage be set aside as a national sanctuary for the native salmon and the Native Americans. The site of Stone's salmon hatchery now lies under 300 feet (90 m) of water in the McCloud River arm of Shasta Lake. Created by a dam between 1935 and 1945, it is the largest man-made reservoir in California, with the second-tallest concrete dam in the United States.

Over the past 150 years, dams of all sizes have been constructed on most of the larger North American rivers to power mills, divert water for irrigation, store water, and generate power. The conversion of watersheds to agriculture, livestock grazing, and urbanization has further degraded or eliminated spawning habitat.

Grand Coulee Dam on the Columbia River (begun in 1935 and completed in 1941) blocked access to about 1,000 miles (1,600 km) of spawning and juvenile rearing habitat utilized by Chinook and sockeye salmon and steelhead. Hells Canyon Dam on the Snake River blocked access to the upper parts of the main Snake River and tributaries to below Shoshone Falls, the natural barrier that historically limited upstream distribution of anadromous fishes. The large Owyhee River drainage, before access was blocked by Hells Canyon Dam, had Chinook spawning runs that extended all the way into its headwaters in Nevada.

To reach the present uppermost spawning sites in the Columbia River, adult Chinook and sockeye salmon and steelhead must ascend fish ladders over nine dams, and smolts migrating to the ocean must pass over the dams or go through turbines, then migrate through reservoirs. These unnatural environments delay migration and increase the risk of predation on smolts by larger fishes. To reach the Salmon River, in Idaho, historically the most productive tributary for Chinook salmon and steelhead in the Columbia River basin, the fish must traverse eight dams and reservoirs, four on the Columbia River and four on the Snake River.

When large-scale artificial propagation of Chinook salmon began, the reality and the significance of intraspecific diversity was not understood. Populations and races of a species were considered as so many interchangeable parts. Although the peaks of Chinook spawning runs of the spring, summer, and fall races were apparent, they were considered to be of no biological importance, and often all races were randomly mixed and spawned together. In 1909, the Central (or Bonneville) hatchery on the Columbia River, in Oregon, was constructed to hatch 60 million Chinook salmon eggs. Eggs were procured from all races throughout the Columbia basin and from outside it in order to operate the hatchery at full capacity. The newly hatched fry, of mixed and diverse ancestry, were widely stocked in and outside the Columbia basin. This forced mixing of races in artificial propagation acts to break down the reproductive isolation that is necessary for wild populations to maintain their adaptive life history traits. Such hatchery practices propagating mixed, generic stocks of Chinook salmon continued into the modern era but are now being reviewed with the objective of reducing adverse impacts on wild populations.

Because of the cumulative impacts that affected Chinook salmon in the Columbia and Sacramento River basins, the species as wild, native populations now exist at only a fraction of its historical abundance. These populations once produced more than half of the total world abundance of the species.

For the purpose of Endangered Species Act protection, the Chinook salmon species is partitioned into evolutionarily significant units (ESU) based on individual races or geographical groupings. In late 2001, the following ESU were listed: Sacramento River winter run (as endangered), Snake River spring and summer runs (combined; threatened), Snake River fall run (threatened), upper Columbia River spring run (endangered), lower Columbia spring and fall runs (threatened), upper Willamette River spring run (threatened), and all Puget Sound runs (threatened).

In the late 1990s, biological productivity in the North Pacific Ocean improved as a result of cyclical changes in temperature, currents, and upwelling. This increased the food supply for foraging salmon and greatly improved the survival and abundance of the salmon during their spawning runs compared to the early to mid-1990s. During 2001, more than 3 million salmon and steelhead returned to the Columbia River. The runs consisted of about 1.3 million Chinook salmon, 1.1 million coho salmon, and more than 700,000 steelhead. Hatchery fish made up 75 percent of the Chinook and steelhead runs and almost 95 percent of the coho run. Compared to recent years, the 2001 Columbia River salmon and steelhead runs were at bonanza levels. In relation to the abundance of wild, native Chinook, however, the 325,000 or so wild salmon in the run represent only about 5 to 10 percent of what their abundance might have been 150 years ago with comparable ocean conditions.

Coho Salmon
Oncorhynchus kisutch

Coho Salmon
Oncorhynchus kisutch

Coho Salmon
SPAWNING MALE

24–28"

The coho salmon, also known as silver salmon, is the second least abundant species of Pacific salmon, after Chinook. It typically makes up 7 to 10 percent of the total commercial salmon catch of Asia and North America; about two-thirds of the coho catch comes from North American waters mainly off the shores of British Columbia.

The flavorful bright pink or orange-red flesh of coho makes it a favorite food fish. As a sport fish, it is the most popular species of Pacific salmon among American and Canadian anglers due to its ubiquitous distribution and its willingness to take flies and lures near the surface. Coho have spawning runs, sometimes large ones, in the smallest coastal streams, whereas Chinook spawning is associated with larger rivers.

Also, the feeding of coho in marine waters as they grow to maturity is mainly associated with inshore areas along the continental shelf, where they are accessible to commercial fishermen and anglers trolling bait or lures.

Coho feed intensively in marine waters, but, as with other species of Pacific and the Atlantic salmon, feeding ceases once they move from marine waters into fresh water. Like other salmon species, coho strike at flies and lures cast by anglers during their fresh-water spawning migration. Why they do this is not known, but the behavior may be associated with rising hormone levels that cause increased aggression. Whatever the cause, bright, silvery coho, which average 6 to 9 pounds, 8 ounces (2.7–4.3 kg) as they return to their home stream to spawn, are spectacular fighting fish much prized by anglers.

COHO SALMON

SCIENTIFIC NAME
Oncorhynchus kisutch

OTHER COMMON NAMES
Silver salmon, silverside

HABITAT
Coastal streams (pool habitats preferred) and rivers, intertidal areas, and inshore marine waters; introduced in Great Lakes

LENGTH AND WEIGHT
24–28" (61–71 cm) and 6–9½ lb (2.7–4.3 kg); maximum 39" (99 cm), world record 33 lb, 4 oz (15.1 kg)

LIFE SPAN
2–4 years; maximum known 6 years

DIET
Aquatic and terrestrial invertebrates in fresh water; fishes, crustacean larvae, shrimps, and squids in salt water. Spawning fish do not feed.

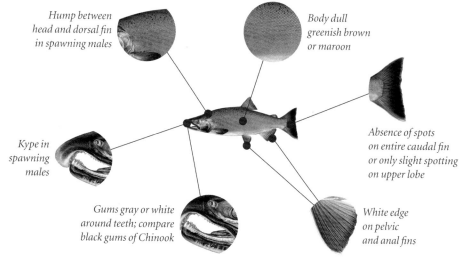

Hump between head and dorsal fin in spawning males

Body dull greenish brown or maroon

Kype in spawning males

Absence of spots on entire caudal fin or only slight spotting on upper lobe

Gums gray or white around teeth; compare black gums of Chinook

White edge on pelvic and anal fins

SPAWNING MALE

DESCRIPTION In inshore marine waters, coho and Chinook salmon often occur together, and small Chinook can be mistaken for coho. A distinguishing trait is the gums around the teeth, which are black in Chinook and gray with white at the crown of the gum in coho. Also, Chinook salmon have black spots or markings on both the upper and lower lobes of the caudal fin, while coho have such markings only on the upper lobe.

Coloration in marine waters is bright silver. On spawning runs in fresh water, coloration darkens, and as spawning time approaches, dull greenish brown or maroon coloration predominates. Males develop a red stripe that can spread over most of the body. Male coho develop kype upon entering fresh water to spawn.

Gill raker numbers range from 18 to 26 and anal fin rays typically number 13 to 16, averaging one or two fewer than is typical of Chinook salmon. Pyloric caeca typically number 50 to 100 and vertebrae 62 to 68. These number ranges overlap with those of Chinook salmon, but average values among coho populations are lower than those of Chinook, especially for pyloric caeca.

BIOLOGY Coho salmon exhibit less diversity in life history types than is found in Chinook salmon. From central British Columbia southward, coho populations follow a rather consistent pattern. Spawning runs enter rivers typically in September and October, and spawning occurs in small coastal streams or small tributary streams of larger rivers from November into January and even February. The young hatch the following March and April, and spend at least one full year in the river before smolting and migrating to the ocean in April and May, at typical lengths of 4 to 5 inches (10–13 cm). Growth in the ocean is rapid.

In general, coho do not roam thousands of miles in the open ocean as do other salmon. Feeding fish typically concentrate along inshore areas, often within sight of the coast. Migrations may cover long distances—coho that originate in Oregon and Washington forage in the ocean from California to Alaska—although some coho may not migrate more than 100 miles (160 km) or so from their home river. Of 235 coho tagged south of Adak, in the Aleutian Islands, eight were subsequently recovered in Alaska and two in Kamchatka.

With the onset of sexual maturation, coho return to their home rivers after 16 to 18 months of ocean growth, at average lengths of 24 to 28 inches (61–71 cm) and weighing about 6 to 9 pounds, 8 ounces (2.7–4.3 kg).

There are numerous exceptions to this generalized life history. In the northern parts of the species' range—in northern British Columbia and Alaska, where there is a short growing season—it often takes two years before the young smolt and migrate to the ocean. In some northern populations, spawning runs may be in July and August, with spawning in August and September. The Columbia River has both early- and late-run coho populations, which are now maintained mainly by artificial propagation. The early run enters the Columbia from late August to mid-September, the late run mainly in October.

A common phenomenon in coho spawning populations is the occurrence of "jacks." Jack coho—all or virtually all males—mature sexually and return to their home river in spawning runs after only a few months of ocean life, at lengths typically of 12 to 16 inches (30–41 cm). Jack coho die after the spawning period even if they do not actually spawn. The proportion of jack coho in spawning runs varies among populations and within the same population from year

Coho Salmon
OCEAN FORM

24–28"

to year. In this respect, jack coho salmon are comparable to grilse in spawning populations of Atlantic salmon, except that Atlantic salmon grilse spend one year (one winter) at sea before returning to spawn. Also, grilse do not necessarily die after their "early" spawning attempt and may return again to spawn in subsequent years.

As with coastal cutthroat trout, coho salmon do not generally migrate far inland for spawning—typically no more than 100 to 200 miles (160–320 km). Exceptions are long-distance migrations in the Columbia, Skeena, and Yukon Rivers. In the Columbia basin, spawning runs of coho were known from the Grande Ronde River, tributary to the Snake River, and from the Wenatchee River, tributary to the upper Columbia; both sites are about 500 miles (800 km) from the Columbia River estuary. And in the Yukon River basin, spawning coho have been found about 1,400 miles (2,250

km) from the river's mouth. Long-distance cohos have a distinct morphology: They are slimmer and more streamlined compared to the typical coastal coho.

Coho are opportunistic feeders at sea, consuming fishes, squids, and crustaceans. They will consume whatever is most abundant and available, but some reports indicate that squids and species of herring in particular make up a significant portion of their diet.

DISTRIBUTION In North America, the original distribution of coho spawning runs extended from Monterey Bay, in California (the San Lorenzo River), northward to Point Hope, Alaska, including some of the larger islands in the Aleutian chain. In Asia, in a distribution pattern similar to that of Chinook salmon, the range of coho extends from Hokkaido, in northern Japan, to the Anadyr River in the Bering Sea basin. In Asia,

however, the distribution of coho spawning populations is sporadic and disjunct. As with Chinook salmon, North American distribution and abundance is much greater than in Asia, where pink and chum salmon are the overwhelmingly dominant salmon species.

Coho have always been extremely rare in the Sacramento River basin, and all attempts to establish runs with hatchery coho have failed. It is not clear why the coho salmon niche is so ill-fitted for the salmonid habitat of the Sacramento basin.

In 1966, coho salmon were introduced into the Great Lakes at a most opportune time. The parasitic sea lamprey, native only to Lake Ontario among the Great Lakes, attaches to the body of larger fish, rasps a hole, and sucks out blood and body fluids, eventually causing the death of its host. The sea lamprey invaded Lake Erie after the construction of the Welland Canal in 1829, which allowed boat passage around Niagara

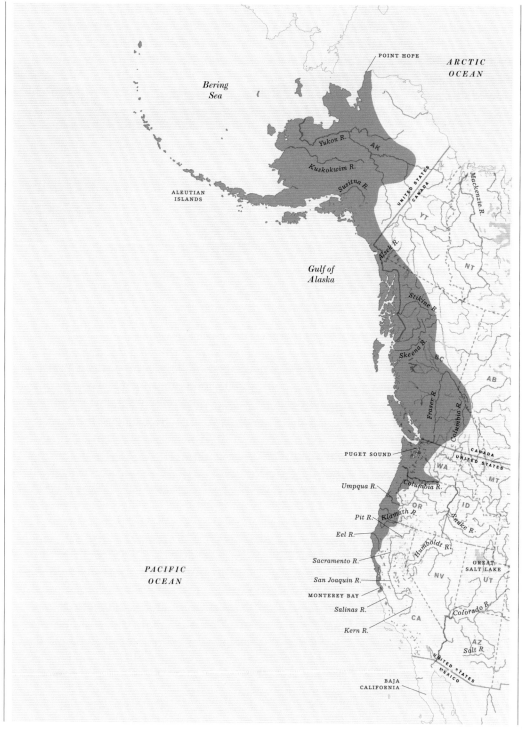

Falls. Over time and after improvements to the canal in 1919, even more sea lamprey gained easy access and subsequently invaded the remaining Great Lakes. They were discovered in Lake Erie in 1921, in Lake Huron in 1932, in Lake Michigan in 1936, and in Lake Superior in 1946. In Lake Michigan, the lamprey exterminated the lake trout, the top predator among the native Great Lakes fish fauna. The result was an explosion in the abundance of another nonnative fish, the alewife, a species of the herring family preyed upon by the lake trout. This phenomenon produced an estimated total biomass of 200 million pounds (91 million kg) of alewives. The nonnative alewife entered the Great Lakes in a similar way to the sea lamprey, through the Welland and Erie Canals, and the extension of the Hudson River to Lake Ontario completed in 1825.

With an essentially unlimited food supply, the coho salmon stocked during the first few years after 1966 exhibited growth and survival that exceeded all expectations. Within a few years, the fisheries of Lake Michigan, and later of the other Great Lakes, changed from commercial fisheries for lake trout and whitefishes to sport fisheries for salmon, with considerably greater economic benefits.

As the coho matured, spawning traps were installed on tributary streams to take their eggs and expand the propagation program. The average size of coho on spawning runs from Lake Michigan was in the range of 10 to 12 pounds (4.5–5.4 kg), and anglers took

Coho salmon spawn in North American rivers from Point Hope, Alaska, south to Monterey Bay, California. Many wild, native populations in Washington, Oregon, and California are now protected under the Endangered Species Act.

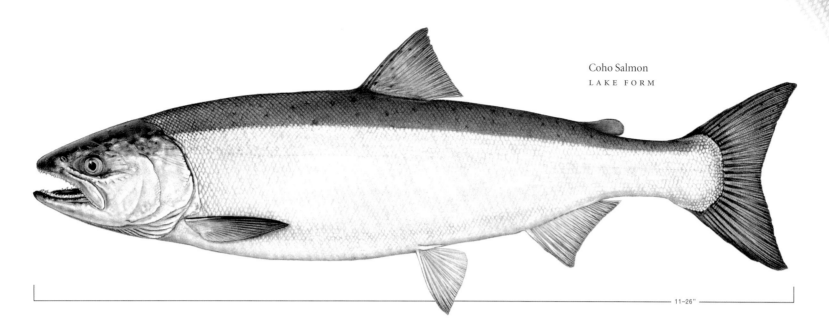

Coho Salmon
LAKE FORM

11–26"

coho weighing 30 to 33 pounds (13.6–15 kg), considerably larger than they grow in their native range. As stocking rates increased and as Chinook salmon became the main salmon species stocked in the Great Lakes, the alewife population crashed. There was no longer a plentiful supply of food for all the salmon being stocked. By 1979, the average size of spawning coho in Lake Michigan declined from 10 to 12 pounds (4.5–5.4 kg) to 4 pounds (1.8 kg).

Natural reproduction of coho salmon occurs in some Great Lakes tributaries, but coho abundance is dependent on the stocking of hatchery fish. Since roughly 1980, the Chinook salmon has replaced the coho salmon as the species most commonly raised in hatcheries and stocked in the Great Lakes. The coho salmon is still a popular Great Lakes sport fish, and individuals occasionally attain a great size. In 1989, the world-record coho of 33 pounds, 4 ounces (15.1 kg)

was caught in the Salmon River, a New York tributary to Lake Ontario.

Coho salmon have been stocked all over the world and are commonly raised in pens from which they frequently escape. Except for the Great Lakes, however, long-term establishment of self-reproducing coho populations outside of the species' native range has not been documented. Coho salmon that had escaped from pens ran up some rivers tributary to the Atlantic Ocean in eastern Canada. The presence of juvenile coho in these streams showed that natural reproduction had occurred. While some observers expressed a fear that coho could replace the native Atlantic salmon, self-sustaining populations of coho salmon did not develop in Atlantic Ocean rivers. As with Chinook salmon, escapes of pen-reared coho are common in Chilean rivers, but whether they can establish populations naturally and on a long-term basis is not known.

EVOLUTION AND CLASSIFICATION

The exact origin of the common name for the coho is somewhat mysterious. Some linguistic sources attribute it to an alteration of *cohose* from a Pacific Northwest Native American language, Halkomelem, which is part of a group of languages known as Salish from southwestern British Columbia. Other references point to its first appearance in English as *co-hue*, stemming from Native American dialect names such as *kwahult* and *kuchuks*. A precise source will probably never be known, but there is no doubt that the name derived from a Native American word for this particular salmon, which was adopted and transliterated by early European traders and explorers.

The coho earned its original scientific name, "*Salmo kisutch*," in 1792 and this name persisted to the late nineteenth century when it was classified as part of the genus *Oncorhynchus*. The species name *kisutch* ("keez-*utch*") came about in the same circuitous way as the scientific names for the other Pacific salmon originating from the Koryak languages of the Kamchatka Peninsula.

The evolution of the coho parallels the development of the other Pacific salmon. An unknown common ancestor of both Pacific salmon and trout existed about 5 million years ago. Over time, salmon branched off from the ancestral trout, resulting in the present diversity of five distinct species: Chinook, coho, pink, chum, and sockeye. The coho is most closely related to Chinook salmon, sharing some life history patterns and genetic markers.

CONSERVATION The dependency of coho on small streams and tributaries for spawning makes them vulnerable to the impacts of civilization, such as clear-cutting of watersheds, dams, waterway diversions, and urbanization. Numerous small coastal streams north and south of San Francisco that once had spawning runs of coho salmon are now encased in culverts or transformed into cement-lined drainage ditches. Coho spawning populations virtually disappeared from the Columbia River basin east of the Cascade Range even before large dams were constructed because of degradation and dewatering of their spawning tributaries.

Coho salmon are more easily raised in fish hatcheries (to smolt size at one year old) than are other species of Pacific salmon. The relative ease of mass-producing many millions of coho smolts for stocking (mainly in Oregon and Washington) has had both positive and negative aspects. The good news—or what was good news in the 1970s—was great early success in stocking some 60 million coho smolts from hatcheries during a period of high productivity of marine waters. The artificially produced coho increased the sport and commercial catch by three- and fourfold by the mid-1970s. But the euphoria surrounding the coho boom was short-lived. When the cycle of marine productivity reached a period of decline, an inverse relationship became apparent: More coho were stocked from hatcheries, but fewer adults returned. Catches dropped to below 10 percent of previous highs.

The reason technological fixes—such as the artificially produced boom in coho abundance—often fail is "You can't fool Mother Nature." Large corporations that invested in the "ocean ranching" of salmon, such as British Petroleum and Weyerhaeuser, used advanced technologies in an attempt to make quick profits, in the process releasing massive numbers of artificially produced coho smolts. The success of ocean ranching depends on the released salmon fattening in the ocean and being captured and sold when they return as adults. It was assumed that for every pound of smolts released, 10 to 15 pounds (4.5–6.8 kg) of adults would return and be harvested. Such an excellent return on investment seemed too good to be true—and it was. The underlying assumption driving corporate salmon ranching was that ocean conditions are stable and an unlimited food supply is available for unlimited numbers of salmon. As it turned out, when ocean productivity declined, all of the corporate salmon ranches went out of business.

Worse than the economic losses associated with the bust in coho abundance was the fact that during the period of reliance on artificial reproduction, the natural reproduction of wild coho and the maintenance of intra-specific life history diversity among wild stocks was given short shrift. Hatchery stocks of coho were derived from many different wild populations. Thorough mixing during hatchery propagation produced "bastardized" generic hatchery populations that were stocked in such great numbers that the returning hatchery coho overwhelmed wild coho in many small spawning streams. Here the hatchery coho hybridized with wild coho populations and compromised long-evolved, site-specific adaptive life histories.

In the Columbia River basin, once the greatest producer of coho salmon, wild coho populations virtually vanished. For many years, almost the entire run (more than 90 percent) of coho in the Columbia has consisted of hatchery fish of mixed background. It is doubtful that a pure coho population, uncontaminated by hatchery coho, remains anywhere in the whole Columbia River basin.

Wild, self-sustaining, native populations (excluding hatchery coho) have been greatly depleted in Washington, Oregon, and California. Many are now protected under the Endangered Species Act. ESA-listed coho include three groupings of evolutionarily significant units (ESU): populations along the central California coast, the northern California and southern Oregon coast, and the remaining Oregon coast. Other groupings have been proposed. 🐟

Pink Salmon
Oncorhynchus gorbuscha

Pink Salmon
Oncorhynchus gorbuscha

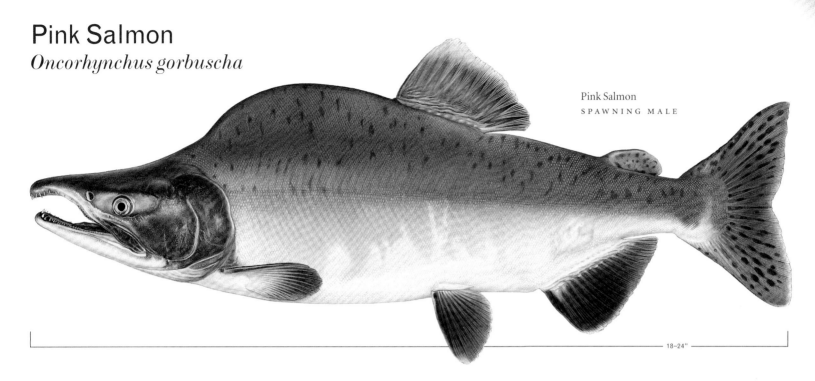

Pink Salmon
SPAWNING MALE

18–24"

The pink salmon, also known as the humpback salmon, is the most abundant of the salmon species. It has the least variable life cycle, in which essentially all individuals mature, spawn, and die at two years of age. This results in the phenomenon known as even-year and odd-year classes of pinks. Populations that spawn in one year do not mix with populations spawning the following year. Pink salmon reach sexual maturity at the smallest size in comparison to the other species of Pacific salmon.

Pink salmon, as with chum salmon, have a lower commercial value compared to Chinook, coho, and sockeye because of the relatively low fat content of their pale pink flesh. However, pink salmon are an important fish for canneries, and canned pink salmon is sold extensively in markets all over the world.

Because of their relatively smaller size compared to other salmon, pink salmon are not a particularly popular sport fish. However, early in spawning runs, pink salmon will aggressively strike flies and lures, making them good sport on light tackle.

DESCRIPTION   In the ocean, pink salmon are distinguished from other Pacific salmon by relatively large black spots or markings along the body above the lateral line and on both the upper and the lower lobe of the caudal fin.

The sexual maturation and secondary sexual characteristics of pink salmon come on rapidly as the fish return to their spawning streams. The back of the male just behind the head abruptly rises, forming a hump—hence the alternate name humpback salmon, or "humpy."

PINK SALMON

SCIENTIFIC NAME
Oncorhynchus gorbuscha

OTHER COMMON NAMES
Humpback salmon, humpy

HABITAT
Coastal streams and rivers, intertidal areas, and open ocean

LENGTH AND WEIGHT
18–24" (46–61 cm) and 3–5½ lb (1.4–2.5 kg); maximum 30" (76 cm), world record 13 lb, 1 oz (5.9 kg)

LIFE SPAN
2–3 years

DIET
Aquatic invertebrates in fresh water and intertidal areas; variety of zooplankton, fish larvae, squids, and fishes in open ocean. Spawning fish do not feed.

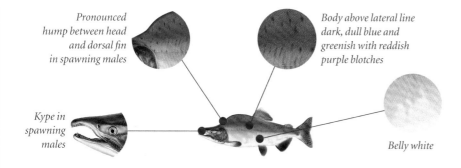

Pronounced hump between head and dorsal fin in spawning males

Body above lateral line dark, dull blue and greenish with reddish purple blotches

Kype in spawning males

Belly white

SPAWNING MALE

In the ocean, before prespawning colors develop, pink salmon are silvery, like other salmon species. During the onset of sexual maturation, which culminates in spawning and ultimately death, coloration darkens. The upper half of the body develops dark, dull blue and greenish colors. Dull reddish purple blotches extend from the middle of the body to the ventral area. At similar stages of sexual maturity females are similar to males in coloration but lack the kype and highly humped back.

Anal fin rays number 13 to 19, gill rakers 25 to 35, and pyloric caeca about 100 to more than 200.

The size of returning spawners varies from year to year, from area to area, and between even- and odd-year classes, but in most areas of their range pink salmon rarely grow longer than about 24 inches (61 cm) or larger than 5 pounds, 8 ounces (2.5 kg).

BIOLOGY The spawning and early life history of pink salmon, up to migration into the open ocean, are virtually identical to chum salmon. Spawning typically occurs in small rivers near the coast, often in intertidal zones at the mouths of streams. In larger

rivers, some pink salmon spawning runs occur relatively far inland, but not as far as chum salmon and other species of Pacific salmon. The longest recorded migration occurs in the Amur River basin of Asia, where fish travel about 460 miles (750 km) from the Sea of Okhotsk. In North America, the longest-distance spawning migration is in British Columbia, in the Skeena River basin into the Babine River, about 300 miles (500 km) from the mouth of the Skeena.

In general, in northern parts of the range, prespawning pink salmon move into inshore waters in July and August, and then into fresh water for spawning during August to early September. Farther south, spawning migrations and spawning occur one to two months later. The eggs incubate in redds over the winter and hatch in late winter or early spring. Pink salmon fry are physiologically prepared to enter marine waters in bays and estuaries as soon as they emerge from redds at lengths of about 1¼ inches (30 mm). Depending on the temperature regime of the spawning rivers, fry migrate seaward as early as March or as late as July. Fry that migrate to marine waters in April and return to spawn in September of the following

year would spend 16 months feeding in the ocean.

Because the life history of pink salmon in their native range is "fixed" for a two-year life cycle, populations spawning in one year are completely isolated from populations spawning the following year, giving rise to even-year and odd-year runs: Pink salmon in 2002 are even-year runs, while those spawning in 2003 are odd-year runs.

Pink salmon can migrate over thousands of miles during their relatively short sojourn in the ocean. Different stocks (geographical groupings) of pink salmon utilize different areas of the North Pacific. Generally North American stocks tend to occur in the eastern North Pacific Ocean and Asian stocks in the western North Pacific, but some stocks from both continents commingle in feeding areas around the Aleutian Islands.

In the ocean, the diet of the pink salmon is comparable to other Pacific salmon, all of which feed opportunistically on available invertebrates and fishes. When they return to fresh water to spawn, they cease feeding altogether, a behavior shared by all Pacific salmon.

The size attained during 14 to 18 months of ocean feeding varies among populations in different regions, between even- and odd-year runs, and among fish born in years with varying ocean productivity. In commercial catches of "small" pink salmon, the average fish is about 3 pounds (1.4 kg). Catches of "large" pink salmon average about 5 pounds, 8 ounces (2.5 kg). The largest pink salmon are taken in the fishery along the coast of northern California. In 1971, the California catch averaged 7 pounds, 5 ounces (3.3 kg).

Pink Salmon
OCEAN FORM

18–24"

The parental source of these extra-large pink salmon is not known, but the largest size is generally attained by pink salmon spawning in the Fraser River and streams tributary to Puget Sound in British Columbia and Washington. Some coastal areas have popular sport fisheries for pink salmon where boat anglers troll with artificial lures.

Natural hybrids between pink and chum salmon are known, but hybrid populations are not self-sustaining, and both species maintain their species-specific integrity in rivers where hybridization occurs. Although pink salmon and Chinook salmon have never been known to hybridize in their native range because of differences in the times and places of spawning, pink × Chinook hybrids occur in some Lake Superior tributaries. These hybrids are mostly first generation, but some back crosses and second-generation hybrids are produced. Back crosses are the offspring of hybrids with either of their parent species, and second-generation hybrids are the progeny of male and female hybrids. Most of the pink × Chinook hybrids are the result of male pink salmon fertilizing the eggs of female Chinook salmon.

DISTRIBUTION Pink salmon are noted for straying. Spawning runs might suddenly appear where they were never noted before and outside of the "normal" range. Perhaps the straying is due to ocean conditions that lure schools of feeding pink salmon beyond the range of their normal feeding migration. If sexual maturation comes on rapidly, some of these pink salmon—far from their home spawning streams—might try to make do with the nearest available stream.

Long-distance straying is the likely explanation for the range of pink salmon in North America, which is often cited as extending southward to the Sacramento and San Lorenzo Rivers (Monterey Bay) of California. Although small, self-sustaining populations of pink salmon may have occurred historically in the Sacramento and Russian Rivers of California, recent records are most likely based on strays, not self-sustaining populations.

Self-sustaining populations of pink salmon occur from Puget Sound northward, around Alaska up to (but not including) the Mackenzie River. Pink salmon also have spawning populations on several of the Aleutian Islands. Pink salmon populations do not maintain consistently high commercial abundance north of Norton Sound, in the Bering Sea basin of west-central Alaska.

In Asia, the distribution of spawning populations extends from North Korea northward to the Arctic Ocean and then westward, at least sporadically, to the Lena

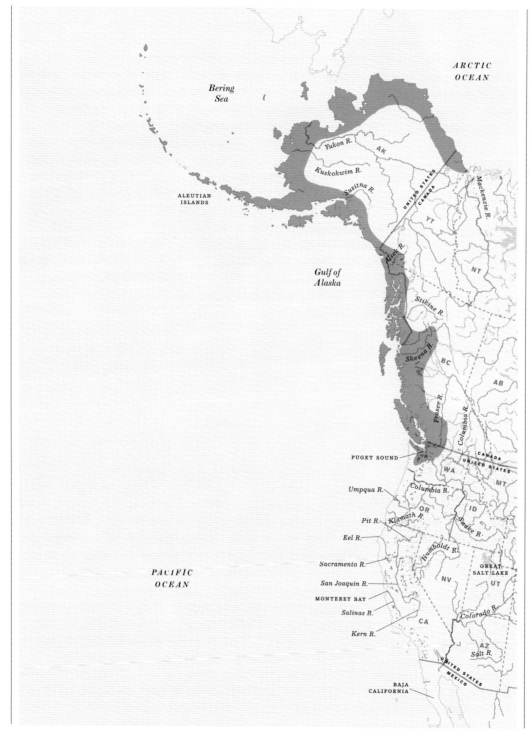

River. The northern limit of commercial abundance is the Gulf of Anadyr, at about the same latitude as Norton Sound, Alaska. The Asian distribution of abundant spawning populations is considerably greater than in North America. Based on commercial catch records from various fisheries for the past 50 to 75 years, the annual Asian catch of pink salmon averages two to three times the North American catch, 70 to 80 percent of which occurs in marine waters of central and southeastern Alaska.

Beginning in the nineteenth century, pink salmon from many parental sources were widely stocked outside of their native range. In Atlantic Ocean drainages of eastern Canada and New England, some of these transplants of newly hatched fry resulted in spawning runs, often to other rivers besides the ones stocked. Some were taken in commercial fisheries and evidently sold as Atlantic salmon. In the 1960s, spawning runs of several thousand pink salmon appeared in Newfoundland rivers. After a few generations, however, populations of spawning pink salmon in North Atlantic rivers declined and eventually vanished.

The only present example of long-term, self-sustaining transplanted pink salmon is in the Great Lakes, an accidental by-product of a failed attempt to establish pink and chum salmon in Hudson Bay. In 1956, pink salmon fry were being transported from Thunder Bay in Ontario (Lake Superior), to Hudson Bay. A few fry—probably only about

Self-sustaining populations of pink salmon in North America spawn in rivers from northeastern Alaska south to Puget Sound.

100—escaped, and some matured and spawned in Lake Superior tributaries in 1957 (the parental stock was an odd-year class from the Lakelse River, in British Columbia, that spawned in 1955).

Slow growth in nutrient-poor Lake Superior resulted in pink salmon spawning at 14 to 18 inches (36–46 cm) long and weights of 1 to 2 pounds (0.45–0.9 kg). And some of the slow-growing fish did not spawn until age three, initiating even-year spawning runs in addition to the odd-year runs. Because of the penchant of pink salmon for straying, self-sustaining populations of pink salmon now occur in all five of the Great Lakes. In 1992, the Great Lakes produced the world-record pink salmon of 13 pounds, 1 ounce (5.9 kg).

EVOLUTION AND CLASSIFICATION

The scientist Johann Walbaum first published the scientific name of the pink salmon "*Salmo gorbuscha*" in 1792, which subsequently became *Oncorhynchus gorbuscha,* retaining the transliteration of a Kamchatkan language word for the species.

The evolutionary line of the pink salmon is most closely related to the chum. What the pink and the chum particularly share is a minimal dependence on fresh water for feeding and growth, much less than the other three North American Pacific salmon. This allows them more time to feed and grow in the fertile waters of the ocean. This evolutionary specialization in their life history has resulted in making the pink salmon the most numerous of all species of salmon.

CONSERVATION

There are great fluctuations in the abundance of pink salmon, especially between even- and odd-year classes and among different regions. The loss of pink salmon spawning streams has been minimal compared to the Chinook salmon, whose main centers of abundance are the greatly impacted Columbia and Sacramento River basins, and the coho salmon, which has experienced major losses of spawning streams.

Changes in the abundance of pink salmon are associated with ocean productivity cycles, not large-scale loss and degradation of spawning habitat. No population of pink salmon is protected by the Endangered Species Act.

Chum Salmon
Oncorhynchus keta

Chum Salmon
Oncorhynchus keta

Chum Salmon
SPAWNING MALE

24–31"

The chum salmon, also known as the dog salmon and the calico salmon, is the most widely distributed and most abundant in terms of total biomass of all Pacific salmon. Pink salmon are more numerous but are the smallest of the Pacific salmon species. Chum salmon, on the other hand, attain a maximum weight second only to Chinook; there have been undocumented reports of chum 43 inches (1.1 m) long and weighing as much as 46 pounds (21 kg). The world-record angler-caught chum salmon, taken in British Columbia in 1995, weighed 35 pounds (15.9 kg).

Chum salmon are commonly caught in sport fisheries, especially in rivers, where they typically migrate for 50 to 100 miles (80–160 km) for spawning. Even though such prespawning chums are rapidly deteriorating and often have patches of fungus on the body, they strike flies and lures and put up a strong, determined, dogged fight. However, they do not leap clear of the surface when caught, as coho salmon do.

Chum salmon is the dominant species used for artificial propagation in ocean ranching, because of its minimal dependency on fresh water and freshwater feeding and its enormous weight increase from fry to adult. Several billion fry are released annually in Asia and Alaska with expectations of a highly favorable return on investment. If comparable results could be achieved with Chinook and coho, they would be the primary salmon propagated for ocean ranching. Chum have a lower fat content in their pale pink flesh and their wholesale value is considerably less than that of Chinook and

CHUM SALMON

SCIENTIFIC NAME
Oncorhynchus keta

OTHER COMMON NAMES
Dog salmon, calico salmon

HABITAT
Coastal streams and rivers, intertidal areas, and open ocean

LENGTH AND WEIGHT
24–31" (61–79 cm) and 6½–12½ lb (3–5.7 kg); undocumented maximum 43" (1.1 m) and 46 lb (21 kg)

LIFE SPAN
3–4 years south of central British Columbia; 4–5 years in western Alaska and Asia; maximum known 7 years

DIET
Aquatic invertebrates in fresh water and intertidal areas; variety of zooplankton, fish larvae, squids, and fishes in open ocean. Spawning fish do not feed.

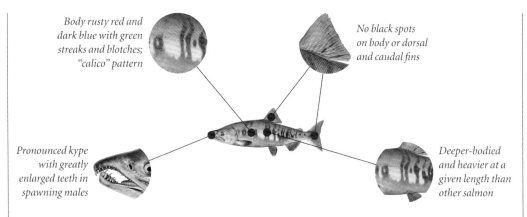

Body rusty red and dark blue with green streaks and blotches; "calico" pattern

No black spots on body or dorsal and caudal fins

Pronounced kype with greatly enlarged teeth in spawning males

Deeper-bodied and heavier at a given length than other salmon

SPAWNING MALE

coho. Nevertheless, chum are still an important commercial fish and their popularity is increasing.

DESCRIPTION Chum salmon are distinguished from other species of Pacific salmon by the absence of black spots on the body and on the dorsal and caudal fins. Gill rakers number from 18 to 26, similar to coho and Chinook salmon, but the gill rakers of chum salmon typically are shorter in length. The number of rays in the anal fin varies from 13 to 17, and pyloric caeca number from 120 to more than 200.

On average, chum salmon have deeper bodies than other species of salmon and, at a given length, are heavier. For example, at lengths of 24 to 25 inches (61–63 cm) chum typically weigh about 6 to 7 pounds (3 kg) compared to about 5 to 6 pounds (2.5 kg) in other species. As with other species of Pacific salmon, males tend to be larger than females of the same age.

During their life in the ocean, chum salmon are bright silver in color, similar to other salmon species. Within days of entry into fresh water for spawning, chum that spawn in small coastal streams show signs of deterioration that are associated with an advanced state of sexual maturity. Proteins have begun to break down, turning the flesh from firm to mushy. Coloration has darkened, and streaks and blotches of dark red and dark hues of blue and green have appeared, giving rise to one of the common names "calico salmon." In males, the teeth greatly enlarge, especially near the tip of the lower jaw—thus the common name "dog salmon." These spawning fish are not prime fish for human consumption, but native people in Canada and Alaska dry and smoke them to feed their dogs.

BIOLOGY Chum salmon and pink salmon have the least dependency on fresh water of all anadromous species of the family Salmonidae. With chum and pink salmon, successful reproduction can occur in intertidal zones at the mouth of streams, where developing eggs are subjected to varying levels of salinity during each tidal cycle.

Newly emerged fry are ready to enter bays and estuaries as soon as they absorb their yolk sacs, when they are about $1\frac{1}{5}$ inches (30 mm) long and weigh about $\frac{9}{1,000}$ ounce (250 mg). At this size, 4,000 of these tiny fry would weigh a little more than 2 pounds (1 kg)—1 million fry would weigh 550 pounds (250 kg). If, three and four years later, only 1 percent were to survive to return as adults and average from 8 to 10 pounds (3.6–4.5 kg), a spawning population of 10,000 chum salmon would have a biomass ranging from 80,000 to 100,000 pounds (36,000–45,000 kg).

Chum salmon populations are broadly divided into summer and fall races according to the time they return to their spawning streams. This dichotomy between summer and fall races is more clearly separated in Asia than in North America. Only a few of the larger North American rivers, such as the Columbia and the Yukon, have both races. Summer chums return to spawning rivers mainly during June and July. Early runs are characteristic of the northern part of the range. Southward, chum populations return to spawn typically from September through December. Large variation occurs in run times among the thousands of individual populations.

Spawning sites in areas of flow from springs that maintain more stable temperatures and warmer water during winter can extend the time of spawning over many months. Young chum salmon emerge from the redds in late winter to early spring and like coho and Chinook smolts are physiologically ready to enter bays and

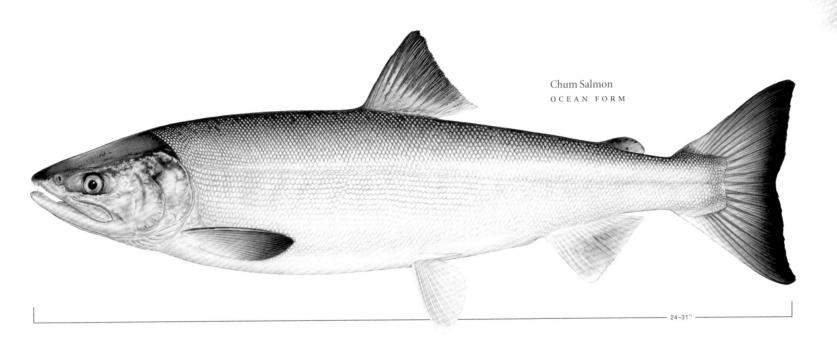

Chum Salmon
OCEAN FORM

24–31"

estuaries. A distinct smolt transformation in coloration and body shape does not occur in chum or pink salmon.

Chum fry commonly feed on small invertebrates while in fresh water, especially chum that migrate longer distances to marine waters from the spawning grounds. A critical feeding period occurs during the first month in bays and estuaries, where the young chum feed mainly on crustaceans in brackish water and grow rapidly in preparation for a long ocean journey.

Chum salmon fry migrating from their natal stream into marine waters in April likely came from eggs spawned the previous October or November, making them six to seven months old. Time spent in the ocean by chum salmon varies from about 30 to 66 months before they return to fresh water or intertidal zones to spawn. This long period of ocean feeding explains the fact that mature

chum are relatively large, although their growth rate in the ocean is less than that of coho and Chinook salmon. Essentially no chum salmon sexually mature and return to spawn after one year, unlike all pink salmon.

Some chum salmon, especially in southern parts of their range, mature and return to spawn three years after their parent generation spawned. If this spawning run occurs in October, the actual time spent in marine waters would be 30 months.

In most populations spawning in southern parts of the range, the dominant ages of chum spawners are three and four years old. Spawning at age four or five becomes more prevalent in northern populations, with even an occasional fish spawning at six years of age.

In the ocean, chum salmon feed opportunistically on invertebrates and fishes, but in general, there is a greater proportion of

invertebrate animals in their diet than in the diets of coho and Chinook salmon. Like all Pacific salmon, chum do not feed once they return to fresh water to spawn.

Chum salmon and pink salmon commonly spawn in the same stream. Typically when the two species occur together, they avoid hybridization by spawning at different times and/or at different spawning grounds. However, natural hybrids between chum and pink salmon are occasionally found. Despite having the most extreme numbers of chromosomes in the genus *Oncorhynchus* (74 in chum salmon and 52 in pink salmon), chum and pink salmon are more closely related to each other than they are to any other species, and their hybrids (with 63 chromosomes) are fertile. Strong natural selection must prevent the hybrids from surviving long enough to spawn: No self-sustaining hybrid population is known that is comparable to rainbow × cutthroat trout hybrid populations.

Chum salmon begin to rapidly deteriorate, both internally and externally, as spawning time nears. These changes begin while the salmon are still in marine waters and as they congregate to enter fresh water and accelerate rapidly thereafter. Bright, silvery chum salmon taken in commercial fisheries are caught before the prespawning changes occur. Even then, chum salmon have a lower commercial value than Chinook, coho, or sockeye salmon. Chum salmon have the lowest fat content of all the salmon species, and their flesh is pale pink, not the bright pink, red, or orange-red preferred by consumers. In North America, most of the catch of chum salmon is canned. Despite its low fat content and pale flesh, if chum salmon are taken before prespawning deterioration sets in, they are good-tasting fish and are sometimes sold fresh or frozen in markets as "silver bryte salmon," a name that sounds much more appetizing to consumers than their more common names, chum or dog salmon.

The Bering Sea had a period of high productivity in the early 1990s; its cycle is typically inversely related to the cycles of productivity in the North Pacific Ocean. During this time, ocean ranching of pink and chum salmon naturally coincided with great increases of wild pink and chum populations. At first these increases were welcomed and considered a "boom," but what could be done with some 100 million pink and chum salmon returning to spawn? Canneries reached capacity, whole-sale prices dropped to five cents a pound,

salmon were given away on the streets of Anchorage, and boats were hired to dump the excess carcasses at sea. It was too much of a good thing.

In Japan, where the species' common name is "sake," people use and appreciate chum salmon more fully than in North America. Chum is by far the main species of salmon used there in raw fish dishes such as sushi and sashimi, and chum salmon eggs (red caviar) have a high value. The ranching of chum salmon has reached its most advanced level in Japan. Because the skin of chum salmon thickens and toughens with sexual maturity, even spawned-out chum can produce a commercial commodity known as salmon leather. Salmon leather is used in making wallets, purses, and handbags.

Newly hatched fry are raised for a few weeks, fed an artificial diet, and then released from ocean ranching operations when they are about 2¾ inches (7 cm) long and weigh ⅒ ounce (3 g). The survival of these "advanced" fry to returning adults is about 2 percent and higher, as compared with about 1 percent for unfed fry. At this rate, 2 billion fry released annually from Japanese facilities can result in the return of 40 to 50 million adults.

DISTRIBUTION In North America, historically chum salmon were recorded as far south as the San Lorenzo River (Monterey Bay, California), northward along the Pacific Coast around Alaska (including the larger Aleutian Islands), and eastward in Arctic Ocean drainages to the Mackenzie River of Canada. They were never sufficiently abundant to sustain commercial fishing

south of Tillamook Bay, Oregon, about 40 miles (65 km) south of the mouth of the Columbia River. Today, records of chum salmon in the Sacramento and San Lorenzo Rivers are sporadic and consist of few fish, suggesting that they are strays from more northern populations rather than self-sustaining populations. Self-sustaining populations consistently producing relatively large numbers (approximately 1,000 or more) of spawning chum salmon do not occur south of northern Oregon (Tillamook Bay). It is likely, however, that before potential spawning tributaries in the Sacramento River basin were badly degraded in the last half of the nineteenth century, some spawning runs of chum salmon were present. The occurrence of chum salmon 200 miles (320 km) upriver in the Sacramento basin indicates that a small remnant of a native population persisted for some time. In small coastal rivers, chum salmon spawn near the coast typically within days of entering the river. Chum salmon with such a life history could not likely survive a river journey of 200 miles (320 km). Most populations of chum salmon, like pink salmon, enter small streams at an advanced state of sexual maturation, spawn within days, and die within a week of completing spawning.

Some populations, however, have a distinctly different life history associated with long-distance spawning migrations requiring survival for two or three months after the salmon enter fresh water. As with coho and Chinook salmon, the longest known migration distance is in the Yukon River, where chum salmon have been observed 1,750 miles (2,820 km) from the sea.

In the Mackenzie River, chum salmon spawn in the Slave River after migrating through Great Slave Lake, about 1,000 miles (1,600 km) from the Arctic Ocean.

Chum salmon have not been established outside their native range. The stocking of pink and chum salmon fry in tributaries to Hudson Bay, which has no native Pacific salmon, failed to establish spawning populations.

Attempts to develop ocean ranching of chum salmon in Chile have failed. Virtually none of the many millions of fry released were ever seen again, except in the stomachs of brown trout that feasted on them during their seaward migration.

EVOLUTION AND CLASSIFICATION

The scientific name of the chum salmon was published in 1792 by Johann Walbaum as "*Salmo keta*." This name eventually changed to *Oncorhynchus keta*. Like the other Pacific salmon, the second part of the name comes from a Russian transliteration of a Kamchatkan language word. Specifically, it is from the Nanai people and in their language simply means "fish." The common name chum derives from the Native American Chinook language word for "striped" or "variegated" and is descriptive of the streaks and blotches found on the body of a chum as it nears spawning time.

The species known today as the chum

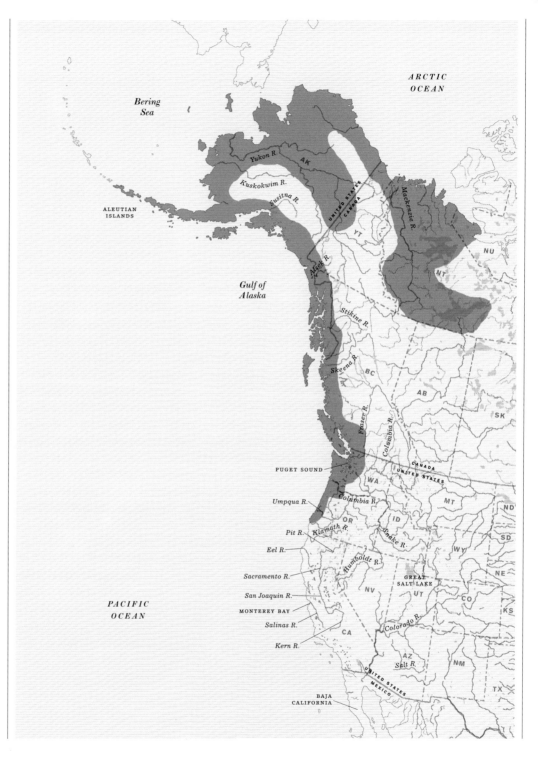

North American chum salmon spawn in waters from the Arctic Ocean drainages in the north to Tillamook Bay, Oregon, in the south. All wild populations of chum salmon in the Columbia River basin and the Hood Canal (Puget Sound) population are protected under the Endangered Species Act.

salmon is most closely related to the pink salmon. Chum and pink salmon are the most specialized species of salmon. They share a common lack of dependence on freshwater periods for feeding and growth. This specialization explains the greater abundance and distribution of chum among the other salmon species. A life history linked more to the vast Pacific Ocean with its enormous supply of food is a distinct advantage when compared with the relatively limited food and foraging opportunities of rivers and streams.

CONSERVATION   Chum salmon populations are characterized by great natural variation in abundance. In areas affected by watershed degradation from logging, grazing, dams, diversions, and urbanization, abundance is severely depressed, and many populations have been lost.

How many spawning chum salmon once occurred in the Columbia River is not known. Commercial fisheries for chum salmon did not begin until the early 1900s, after the more valuable spring and summer Chinook salmon were severely depleted. The maximum commercial catch of Columbia River chum salmon was about 1 million fish totaling about 10 million pounds (4.5 million kg) in the late 1920s, about 80 years after chum salmon spawning tributaries began to feel the impact of European American settlements.

Chum salmon spawn in downstream areas of tributary streams in the Columbia River basin, where the quality and even the existence of spawning habitat are affected by upstream factors such as logging, pollution, and water diversions. By the 1950s, chum salmon had experienced a great decline in the Columbia basin. Since 1955, the number

of chum salmon entering the Columbia River on spawning runs has ranged from less than 1,000 to about 5,000 fish.

The 2001 Columbia River chum salmon spawning run (both summer and autumn runs) reached 10,000 for the first time in 46 years, the result of habitat protection and enhancement, and, especially, improved ocean productivity.

All wild populations of chum salmon in the Columbia River basin are protected under the Endangered Species Act. The Hood Canal (Puget Sound) population of chum salmon is also protected under the Endangered Species Act.

Sockeye Salmon
Oncorhynchus nerka

Sockeye Salmon
Oncorhynchus nerka

Sockeye Salmon
SPAWNING MALE

21–26"

The sockeye is the most important commercial salmon species in North America. Highly prized for its delicious red flesh, it is the most valuable salmon caught for canning and is sold throughout the world typically as "red" salmon.

When sockeye salmon return to fresh water to spawn, they become aggressive and, at least in some places at some times, can be readily caught by anglers even though they do not feed during spawning runs. Kokanee, the lake-resident form of sockeye salmon, is an extremely popular game fish and is stocked in great numbers in deep, cold lakes in western North America.

The species' common name has nothing to do with the eyes of the fish. The name is actually an anglicized version of various Native American words for the sockeye, spelled phonetically as "sukkai." The scientific name, *nerka,* derived in a roundabout way from the Koryak languages of the people of the Kamchatka Peninsula, now part of the Russian Federation. The name of the freshwater form, kokanee, is from a word meaning "red fish" in the language of the Kootenay Native Americans, who knew the kokanee from Kootenay Lake, in British Columbia.

DESCRIPTION   In the ocean, sockeye salmon have bright, silvery sides and a steely blue dorsal surface. The head is conical, and the snout is blunt. Smallish, well-developed teeth line both the upper and lower jaws. The caudal fin is moderately forked and dark, with no spots. There are 10 to 12 rays in the dorsal fin, 12 to 18 in the anal fin, approximately 16 in the pectoral fins, and 11 in the pelvic fins.

As sexual maturation approaches and

SOCKEYE SALMON

SCIENTIFIC NAME
Oncorhynchus nerka

OTHER COMMON NAMES
Big redfish, red salmon, blueback

HABITAT
Coastal streams and rivers, lakes, intertidal areas, and open ocean

LENGTH AND WEIGHT
21–26" (53–66 cm) and 4–7 lb (1.8–3.2 kg); maximum 33" (84 cm) and 15½ lb (7 kg)

LIFE SPAN
4–6 years; maximum known 7 years

DIET
Variety of invertebrates (including amphipods and euphausiids), fishes, and squids in salt water. Spawning fish do not feed.

Head greenish gold

Kype in spawning males

Pronounced hump between head and dorsal fin in spawning males

Body brilliant red

SPAWNING MALE

sockeye begin to enter fresh water on their spawning runs, dramatic changes occur. The body becomes bright red, sometimes with a dark green dorsal surface. The head of the male undergoes grotesque changes: The jaws and teeth enlarge, and the jaws curve into a hook-like shape (kype). The male's body deepens behind the head, so that the sockeye male presents a humpback profile like that of a pink salmon. Females lack the pronounced hump and kype but exhibit the same brilliant coloration. Sexual maturation changes at spawning also occur in the freshwater kokanee, but to a lesser degree. Prior to spawning, kokanee resemble a smaller version of the ocean form of sockeye.

Sockeye salmon are relatively small; of the North American species of Pacific salmon only pink salmon are smaller. After two or three years of ocean feeding, sockeye returning to spawn typically range from 21 to 26 inches (53–66 cm) and from about 4 to 7 pounds (1.8–3.2 kg). Average size varies by region. Extreme size is about 33 inches (84 cm) and 15 pounds, 8 ounces (7 kg).

Stunted kokanee populations commonly attain sexual maturity at about 7 to 9 inches (18–23 cm) and 4 ounces (113 g). The size of kokanee varies from lake to lake, but generally a 14-inch (36-cm) fish is common, while a 20-inch (51-cm) fish is considered "trophy" size. Extreme size for kokanee is about 26 inches (66 cm) and 6 pounds, 8 ounces (3 kg). These landlocked fish never attain the maximum size of the ocean-going form.

BIOLOGY Of all species of Pacific salmon, the sockeye salmon exhibits the greatest diversity of life history types. Besides resident freshwater kokanee and anadromous sockeye forms, sockeye salmon subdivide into life history types that spend different amounts of time (up to three years) in fresh water before smolting and migrating to the ocean, and have different times of spawning runs from the ocean and different times of spawning (from July into October). Some populations spawn within two or three weeks after leaving the ocean, some within two or three months.

Commonly, two or more populations of anadromous sockeye occur together in the same lake; such populations also occur together with kokanee. Among populations occurring together, hybridiza-

tion is avoided because the populations spawn at different times and/or at different spawning grounds.

Sockeye and kokanee typically spawn in streams that are tributaries to lakes, but spawning along shorelines on lake bottoms is also common. Fertilized in the fall, the eggs incubate over the winter, and the young emerge in late winter or early spring, depending on the water temperature. All adults die within a few weeks after spawning. During and after spawning, sockeye, and indeed all Pacific salmon, become an important food source for bears, other mammals, and birds throughout their range. The millions of dead fish that remain in rivers after spawning add to the nutrient base of the water system. This affects the nitrogen levels, which in turn aid the growth of algae, a source of food for zooplankton. Sockeye salmon fry are dependent on aquatic zooplankton as a source of food. The fry grow into their next juvenile life history stage, then smolt and migrate to their life at sea, and then return to spawn in their natal waters.

Young sockeye and kokanee feed in lakes mainly on crustacean zooplankton, especially "water fleas" of the genus *Daphnia* that are about 1/16 inch (1–2 mm) in size. Because *Daphnia* abundance is cyclical, the salmon must be flexible and opportunistic in feeding. When zooplankton is sparse they supplement their diet by taking insect larvae and pupae in the water column.

After one or two (rarely three) years spent growing in a lake, sockeye juveniles undergo the smolting process in preparation for life in the ocean. Most sockeye smolt and migrate

Sockeye Salmon
OCEAN FORM

21–26"

to the ocean when they are 3 to 6 inches (8–15 cm) long. Migration of smolts occurs in the spring.

After two or three years of ocean feeding, mature sockeye reenter their home river, then travel on to their home lake within the river basin, and finally return to the precise spawning tributary or lake-bottom spawning grounds where they were born. (Like all other Pacific salmon, sockeye cease feeding when they return to fresh water to spawn.) Their refined homing instinct allows for sockeye and kokanee and different populations of both life history forms to coexist in the same watershed without hybridizing.

It was long believed that the sockeye salmon was an obligatory lacustrine species; that is, it was thought that the juvenile stage was completely dependent on lakes for feeding on zooplankton. We now know that some popula-

tions of sockeye do not use lakes. After the eggs hatch in rivers, the young of these fluvial populations feed in flooded areas along a river's floodplain and backwaters. They smolt and enter marine waters at only a few months of age, as pink and chum salmon do.

This fluvial type of life history is common for sockeye of the Kamchatka River of Russia and is also known to occur in some populations of a few North American rivers.

The characteristic that clearly identifies sockeye and kokanee salmon from all other Pacific salmon and from all other species in the genus *Oncorhynchus* is the number of gill rakers on the first gill arch. *O. nerka* is the only species in the genus that has more than 30 gill rakers. This characteristic, discerned solely by biologists, reflects its zooplankton feeding specialization.

DISTRIBUTION   In North America, the distribution of viable populations of sockeye salmon extends from the Columbia River to the Yukon River in northern Alaska. Sporadic reports of sockeye farther south and farther north are based on strays and not on established populations.

Although widely distributed, sockeye abundance is concentrated in three major centers: the Bristol Bay region of Alaska, the Fraser River basin in British Columbia, and the Kamchatka Peninsula of Russia. Sockeye spawned in the fresh waters of these three regions supply most of the world's commercial catch. In Asia, sockeye occur from Hokkaido, in Japan, to the Anadyr River, in Russia.

Before the completion of Grand Coulee Dam in 1941, the most inland North American natural distribution of sockeye

Kokanee Salmon
SPAWNING MALE

14–20"

occurred in the Arrow Lakes, in the head-waters of the Columbia River in British Columbia, about 1,200 miles (1,900 km) from the sea.

Kokanee are derived from anadromous sockeye salmon. Their natural distribution is associated with the distribution of sockeye salmon, and both anadromous sockeye and resident kokanee commonly occur together in the same lake without hybridizing. Some kokanee populations, such as those of Kootenay Lake, in British Columbia, were established from sockeye before free access to the ocean was blocked.

After access to the sea is lost, the anadromous sockeye is lost, and only the resident kokanee remain. Kokanee have been widely stocked as sport fish in lakes and reservoirs outside their native range, especially in the western United States.

EVOLUTION AND CLASSIFICATION

When large sockeye and small kokanee salmon were first observed and described in the nineteenth century, they were commonly called "big redfish" (sockeye) and "little redfish" (kokanee). Before it was firmly established that all Pacific salmon die after spawning, some observers believed that the "little redfish" were fish that were spawning for the first time and that "big redfish" were repeat spawners.

When it was confirmed that "big redfish" and "little redfish" were two distinct life history forms, observers assumed that they must represent different species. The species name *nerka* was given to anadromous sockeye (big redfish) and the name *kennerlyi* to kokanee (little redfish).

Today biologists do not give separate species status to sockeye and kokanee because kokanee have been derived from sockeye salmon many times and in many different areas. Refined genetic analyses have clearly demonstrated that the closest—in fact, virtually identical—relationships are between kokanee and sockeye of the same river basin or lake system, rather than between similar kokanee and sockeye life history forms in other river basins. Thus kokanee are considered to be polyphyletic, which means they are a life history form of sockeye salmon that has arisen many times independently.

CONSERVATION
Although sockeye salmon is the most important commercial salmon species in North America—more than 100 million pounds (45 million kg) are harvested during a peak in an abundance cycle—about 95 percent of former popula-

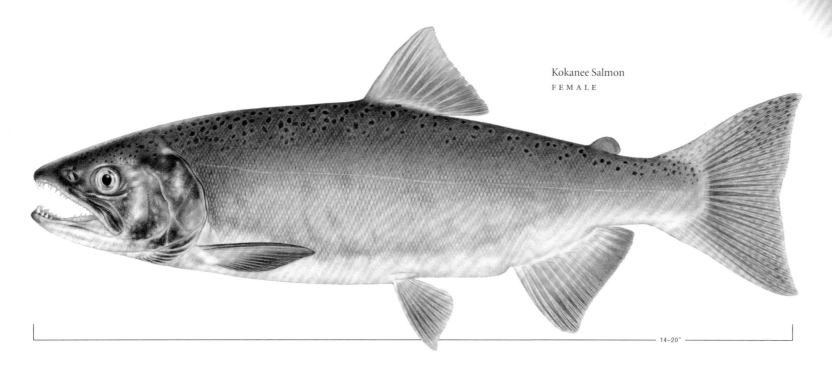

Kokanee Salmon
FEMALE

14–20"

tions in the Columbia River basin have been lost following the construction of dams. The farthest inland population (in the Arrow Lakes of British Columbia) was lost when Grand Coulee Dam was constructed, blocking upstream migration into Canada. Construction of the dam began in 1935 and by the time it was completed in 1941 over 1,000 miles (1,600 km) of stream spawning and rearing habitat for salmon and steelhead were lost.

The next-longest spawning migration of sockeye occurred historically in five lakes in the headwaters of the Salmon River drainage of Idaho, part of the Snake River division of the Columbia River basin. Only one of the Salmon River populations (in Redfish Lake) remained in recent times. After the fourth dam on the Snake River was completed in 1976, the Redfish Lake sockeye

rapidly declined toward extinction. Overcoming four dams on the Columbia River and four more on the Snake River proved too much for the Redfish Lake sockeye.

The Redfish Lake sockeye, along with Snake River Chinook salmon and steelhead, which also must pass dams on both their upstream spawning migrations and downstream smolt migrations, are now listed as endangered species under the Endangered Species Act. The Redfish Lake sockeye salmon is maintained by a captive breeding program, but the wild, native population is functionally extinct.

The protection of endangered populations of salmon under the Endangered Species Act has generated considerable controversy. The Redfish Lake sockeye salmon is not a species in its own right; it is part of the species *Oncorhynchus nerka*, and as a whole, *O. nerka*

KOKANEE SALMON

SCIENTIFIC NAME
Oncorhynchus nerka

OTHER COMMON NAMES
Little redfish, landlocked sockeye, silver trout, Kennerly's salmon, blueback

HABITAT
Deep, cold lakes; some populations spawn in tributaries

LENGTH AND WEIGHT
14–20" (36–51 cm) and 1–3 lb (0.45–1.4 kg); some stunted populations mature at 7–9" (18–23 cm) and 4 oz (113 g); maximum 26" (66 cm) and 6½ lb (3 kg)

LIFE SPAN
3–4 years

DIET
Variety of aquatic invertebrates, especially "water fleas" of genus *Daphnia*

is not endangered. It and the pink salmon are the most abundant species in the genus *Oncorhynchus* in North America; a can of sockeye (or red) salmon can be purchased at any grocery store.

Why then, if the species is so common, is a single population of the species endangered? The answer concerns the intent of the Endangered Species Act and the definition of "species" that qualify for protection under law. The Endangered Species Act is designed to protect biodiversity rather than formally recognized species, reflecting the fact that there are no universally accepted criteria for recognizing "species" and, especially for invertebrate animals, that many more species exist than have been formally described.

One goal of the Endangered Species Act is to protect all the parts of a species—the separate races and populations that have evolved to adapt to different environmental conditions in different parts of a species' range. The result is that, for vertebrates such as salmon, the Endangered Species Act defines a species as including all the parts down to the level of a single population. As the population of *O. nerka* occurring farthest inland, the Redfish Lake sockeye represents a unique part of the biodiversity of *O. nerka* and qualifies for protection from extinction under the Endangered Species Act. ◀━🐟

The North American distribution of sea-run sockeye salmon extends from the Yukon River in northern Alaska south to the Columbia River. In North America, the sockeye's abundance is concentrated in Bristol Bay, Alaska, and the Fraser River basin, British Columbia.

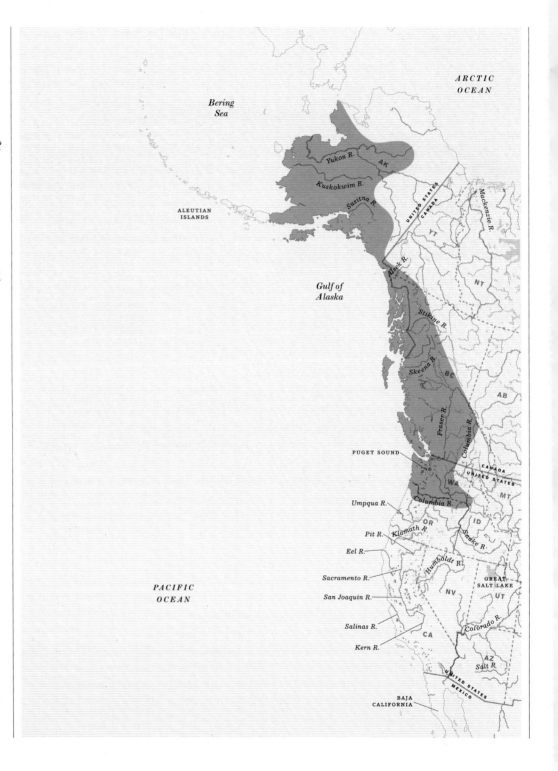

Rainbow Trout
Oncorhynchus mykiss

The rainbow trout is the best-known species of trout in the world. Its renown as a sport fish has led to its introduction worldwide into virtually all suitable cold-water habitats, and it is by far the most important species of trout raised commercially for markets and the restaurant trade. Beautiful iridescent colors, most vivid during spawning times, have given rise to this species' common name.

The different names used for rainbow trout (as in the general terms "trout" and "salmon") can be confusing. The sea-going, or anadromous, form of rainbow trout is known as steelhead, and the term redband trout is used to describe distinctive forms of rainbow trout, native to particular regions of North America. Redband trout are named for the brick red colors along their flanks, and the sea-going form of rainbow trout are called steelhead because of their metallic silvery color in salt water. A certain type of redband trout also has a sea-going life history and is called a redband steelhead. As confusing as this may be for the non-expert, the important consideration is that no matter whether correctly called redband, steelhead, or redband steelhead, they are all rainbow trout and are classified as subspecies of the full species *Oncorhynchus mykiss.*

This opening section on the rainbow trout is an introduction to the forms, life histories, and classifications of the various subspecies of *O. mykiss,* including a group of unclassified rainbow-like trout found only in Mexico. Six subsequent chapters describe the various subspecies that make up the group. The characteristics that categorize each form of rainbow trout are covered in the following accounts:

1. coastal rainbow trout *(O. m. irideus)*

2. redband trout of the mid- and upper Columbia and Fraser River basins *(O. m. gairdneri)*

3. redband trout native to six internal basins of the Northern Great Basin, plus the Upper Klamath Lake basin, *(O. m. newberrii)*

4. redband trout of the northern Sacramento River basin (the scientific name *"O. m. stonei"* is often used for this group)

5. three subspecies of trout native to the Kern River basin *(O. m. aguabonita, O. m. gilberti,* and *O. m. whitei)*

6. rainbow-like trout native to the Río Yaqui, Río San Lorenzo, and Río del Presidio drainages of Mexico (tributaries to the Gulf of California)

DESCRIPTION   The various forms that make up the whole of the rainbow trout species exhibit a great range of variation in all characteristics used in classification. The literature and keys on the subject of species identification that attempt to differentiate all rainbow trout from, for example, all cutthroat trout might list characteristics such as color patterns, the presence or absence of cutthroat marks under the jaws, the presence or absence of basibranchial teeth (tiny teeth found in the throat between the gill arches), and the number of scales along the lateral line. Such differential diagnoses are valid for some geographical regions. However if the total variation of rainbow trout and cutthroat trout throughout the ranges of both species is considered, no unambiguous characteristics, except genetic markers as detected in laboratory analysis, can positively distinguish all rainbow trout from all cutthroat trout.

The problem of overlap of characteristics between rainbow trout and cutthroat trout is apparent in the older literature, in which certain subspecies of rainbow trout, including redband trout, Kern River drainage golden trout, and the Apache trout of Arizona, were all wrongly identified as cutthroat trout.

Scientists have observed an evolutionary trend of transition in characteristics— coloration and number of scales, among others—from more primitive forms of rainbow trout, such as the redband trout and the Kern River drainage subspecies, to the most evolutionarily advanced subspecies, the coastal rainbow trout.

BIOLOGY All wild rainbow trout have a hereditary (genetic) basis for spawning in the spring when water temperatures are rising. The time of spawning, which depends on water temperature, can be as early as January or February in moderate climates along the Pacific Coast and as late as May or June in colder climates. But, in general, spawning is initiated when the daily water temperature exceeds 42 to 44 °F (6–7 °C), regardless of geographical area. Rainbow trout introduced into the Southern Hemisphere, where the seasons are reversed, spawn in the Southern Hemisphere spring, from September to November.

Artificial selection has developed domesticated rainbow trout that spawn in the fall in fish hatcheries. (This diversity in spawning

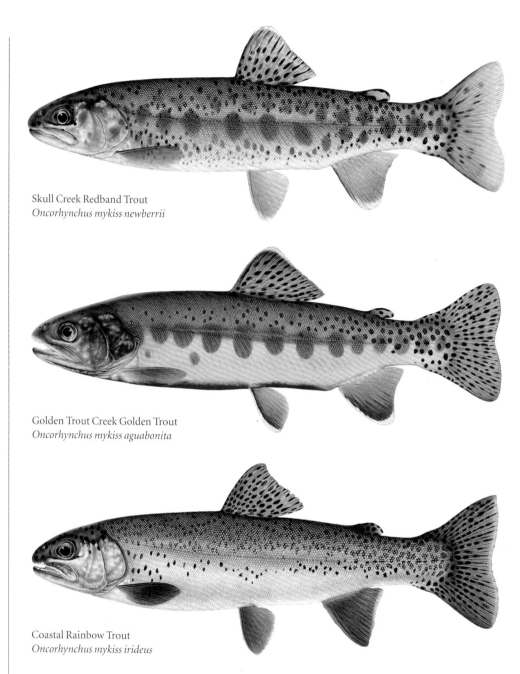

Skull Creek Redband Trout
Oncorhynchus mykiss newberrii

Golden Trout Creek Golden Trout
Oncorhynchus mykiss aguabonita

Coastal Rainbow Trout
Oncorhynchus mykiss irideus

Scientists have observed an evolutionary trend in characteristics of rainbow trout based on coloration, number of scales, chromosome counts, and other qualities. The most primitive forms of rainbow trout include redband and golden trout. Scientists recognize the coastal rainbow subspecies as the most evolutionarily advanced form of rainbow trout.

The first hatchery rainbow trout propagated by the U.S. Fish Commission in the late 1800s was a mixture of McCloud River steelhead and stream-resident (non-anadromous) McCloud River redband trout from California.

McCloud River Redband Trout
Oncorhynchus mykiss stonei

times allows hatcheries to produce rainbow trout of specific sizes on a year-round basis.) Also, some rainbow trout introduced outside their native range, such as the Firehole River in Yellowstone National Park and the North Platte River in Nebraska, spawn in the fall. Evidently spawning is triggered when the trout move from colder water into warmer tributary streams.

In small-stream populations, spawning may occur at two or three years of age (males often mature a year before females), and spawning may be repeated in successive years.

The most dramatic difference in life histories occurs between the inland, stream-resident forms of rainbow trout, and the anadromous forms. Anadromous forms occur in two subspecies of rainbow trout, *Oncorhynchus mykiss irideus* and *O. m. gairdneri*. Whereas stream-resident rainbow trout may complete their life cycle in a limited area of a small stream and attain a length of only 8 inches (20 cm) or so, steelhead may spend half their lives at sea, roaming for thousands of miles in the North Pacific Ocean. Steelhead return to spawn at

sizes ranging from about 24 inches (61 cm) and 5 pounds (2.3 kg) to about 36 to 40 inches (90–100 cm) or more and 20 pounds (9 kg) or more.

Different steelhead populations vary in the time they initiate spawning runs from the ocean into rivers, the time of spawning, the number of years juveniles spend in fresh water before smolting and going to sea, and the number of years in the ocean before first sexual maturation. Throughout their range, some steelhead enter rivers on their spawning runs in every month of the year, but spawning runs are grouped, for simplification, into winter runs and summer runs, depending on when the majority of the fish enter fresh water. Generally, summer run refers to fish entering fresh water from May through October and winter run includes fish entering rivers from November through April. In early summer-run steelhead, the male testes and female ovaries are not mature because they come into fresh water many months before they will spawn, in the following spring. In winter-run fish, the male testes and female ovaries are

near maturity because these fish spawn shortly after freshwater entry. Unlike Pacific salmon, some steelhead continue to feed after entering fresh water, but at a much reduced rate.

All but one of the *Oncorhynchus mykiss gairdneri* steelhead populations migrating east of the Cascade Range are characterized as summer-run steelhead (entering the Columbia River from May into the early fall in October); the one exception is a winter-run steelhead spawning in Fifteenmile Creek, which drains the eastern side of the Cascades in Oregon. The genetic traits of Fifteenmile Creek steelhead make it intermediate between the subspecies *irideus* and *gairdneri*. Steelhead of the subspecies *irideus* are mainly winter-run fish, but *irideus* also has summer runs. Considering the entire range of *irideus* from California to Alaska, steelhead can be found entering one river or another in every month of the year.

Juvenile steelhead generally spend two years in fresh water (the parr stage) before smolting and migrating to the ocean at lengths of about 6 to 8 inches (15–20 cm).

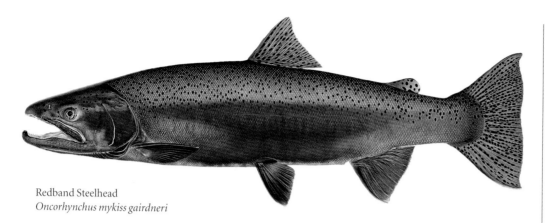

Redband Steelhead
Oncorhynchus mykiss gairdneri

Steelhead
Oncorhynchus mykiss irideus

Throughout their range steelhead populations enter fresh water to spawn in nearly every month of the year. Unlike Pacific salmon, they do not necessarily die after spawning. Numbers of steelhead return to spawn again in some populations. Repeat spawning is particularly successful in the tributaries of the Great Lakes where steelhead are introduced. Without large marine predators such as seals, sea lions, sharks, and killer whales, the Great Lakes offer steelhead a much better chance to spawn a second time— up to 70 percent in some populations.

In the northern part of their range, however, steelhead commonly smolt at three years of age. Most steelhead return to their home rivers for spawning after about 15 to 30 months of ocean life.

Unlike Pacific salmon, steelhead do not all die soon after spawning, but the rate of survival to repeat spawning is generally low—about 10 percent or less. Highest survival occurs in steelhead introduced into the Great Lakes that have no large marine predators. In such cases, survival to repeat spawning has been reported to range from about 20 percent to 50 percent and higher. On the north shore of Lake Superior, up to 70 percent of steelhead survive after the first spawning and may spawn up to six times. Both figures are higher than those known for any steelhead in their native range.

The anadromous life history found in the steelhead of the two subspecies *O. m. irideus* and *O. m. gairdneri* differs from the anadromy found in the coastal cutthroat trout, the only cutthroat trout subspecies that enters marine waters. *O. mykiss* steelhead can be considered fully anadromous in that they spend from one to three years feeding in the open ocean, far from shore, before returning to their natal river for spawning. Coastal cutthroat trout, by comparison, spend 60 to 90 days during summer feeding in estuaries and coastal zones. Despite their relatively short stay in salt water, coastal cutthroat are silvery and can be confused with small steelhead.

The life history differences that distinguish steelhead from stream-resident rainbow trout (as discussed above) are so striking that the two forms were once classified as separate

Hatchery Rainbow Trout
Oncorhynchus mykiss

8–16"

species. However, modern genetic analysis has confirmed not only that steelhead and rainbow trout belong to the same species, but also that the two different life history forms from one river basin are more closely related to each other than they are to similar life history forms in other river basins. It is clear that the hereditary basis for the different life history forms is slight and, in some cases, reversible.

The extreme closeness of the relationship between a resident rainbow trout that may spend all its life within a few-hundred-yard area of a stream and a steelhead that may spend half its life roaming thousands of miles in the North Pacific Ocean has caused problems for identifying or proving the hereditary (genetic) basis for the two strikingly different life history forms. Unless there are strong differences in time and/or place of spawning to separate steelhead and resident rainbow trout, complete reproductive isolation is not likely, and occasional hybridization between resident rainbow trout and steelhead can

occur—for example, when male juvenile steelhead mature sexually before they smolt and go to sea (these trout are called residual steelhead). Small residual steelhead most probably will spawn with resident female rainbow trout of approximately similar size. And a sexually mature resident rainbow trout male, if it is in the vicinity of a pair of spawning steelhead, may dart in during the spawning act, release sperm, and fertilize some of the steelhead eggs (such males are known as "sneakers").

The hereditary basis for migratory behavior and the timing of steelhead runs from the ocean is even more complex when summer-run steelhead, winter-run steelhead, and resident rainbow trout all spawn in the same river. Although hybridization among the different life history forms is rare, even a slight amount of genetic interchange will obscure attempts to document a genetic or hereditary basis for steelhead versus resident life history or between winter- and summer-

Rainbow trout are raised in hatcheries by the millions every year across North America and are stocked worldwide for sportfishing and for food. Over the many years of their propagation, hatchery rainbow trout have influenced native populations with some devastating results—native rainbow, redband, and cutthroat trout have been extirpated from much of their historic range across western North America.

run steelhead. Several studies using the most modern methods of genetic analysis have failed to find evidence of genetic distinctions between steelhead and resident rainbow trout or between winter-run and summer-run steelhead spawning in the same river. These studies often reach the erroneous conclusion that there is no hereditary basis for the different life histories. Before such a conclusion is implemented into fisheries management programs, other methods should be used to address the question of hereditary basis. The basic question is: Do resident rainbow trout give rise to resident rainbow trout and steelhead to steelhead, at least in the overwhelming majority of cases?

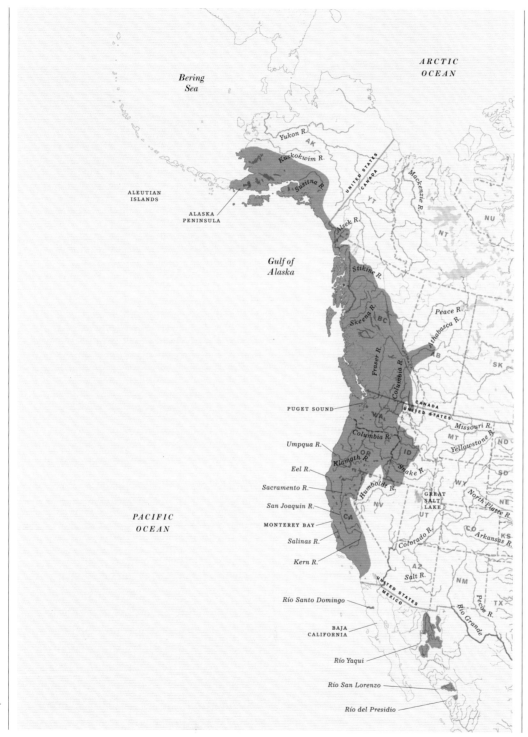

One way scientists address this question is through analysis in a laboratory. They examine the calcium-strontium ratio in the nucleus of otoliths. Otoliths are tiny bones in the inner ear of a fish. Results of the analysis can identify whether the fish's female parent is a steelhead or a stream-resident rainbow trout. If the female parent is a steelhead, its life in the ocean results in a calcium-strontium ratio distinct from that of a female living its entire life in fresh water. This signature ratio is passed on from the female to its young and is retained throughout the life of the fish.

When the otoliths from 20 steelhead and 38 resident rainbow trout from the Deschutes River, in Oregon, were tested, it was found that all 20 steelhead came from steelhead mothers and all 38 rainbow trout had resident rainbow trout mothers. In the Babine River, in Canada, one of 24 steelhead had a resident rainbow trout mother, and two of nine resident rainbow trout came from a steelhead mother. (The Babine River is in the Skeena River basin, home to the largest steelhead in the world.) Obviously, the Skeena River basin cannot maintain both steelhead and resident rainbow trout if the two forms freely hybridize into a single population. Reproductive isolation, although not complete, must be sufficient to maintain the integrity of the hereditary basis that separates steelhead and resident rainbow trout.

The native distribution of all subspecies classified within Oncorhynchus mykiss *ranges from southwestern Alaska to the Sierra Madre Occidental in Mexico.*

In other words, the populations remain distinct from one another—one population runs to the sea and returns to spawn in its natal rivers and one population maintains a stream-resident life history.

In the late nineteenth and early twentieth centuries, the U.S. Fish Commission propagated both rainbow trout (identified at the time as *"Salmo irideus"*) and steelhead (*"S. gairdneri"*) under the mistaken notion that they were two different species. The first hatchery rainbow trout propagated by the U.S. Fish Commission (as *"S. irideus"*) and shipped to most states and many foreign countries were a mixture of a steelhead population that spawned in the McCloud River and resident McCloud River redband trout living in tributary streams. Thus the first rainbow trout shipped by the U.S. Fish Commission consisted of both steelhead and resident redband trout that were indiscriminately mixed for propagation.

Although steelhead ancestry influenced the development of the hatchery rainbow trout that were introduced all over the world, the true steelhead life history (in which the trout spend more than one year roaming the open ocean) has developed only rarely outside their native range. For example, virtually all New Zealand rainbow trout are derived from eggs taken in 1883 from steelhead native to Sonoma Creek, a tributary to San Francisco Bay, and shipped to New Zealand. Rainbow trout are widespread in New Zealand, where they are all resident populations that spend all of their lives in fresh water; no anadromous steelhead ever became established. In North America, steelhead introduced into the Great Lakes

have given rise to descendants with typical steelhead life histories, except that they spend their entire lives in fresh water.

A recent publication on both steelhead and resident rainbow trout in the Río Santa Cruz, in Argentina, is of interest in relation to the hereditary basis for anadromous and resident life histories and the parental sources used in the early propagation of rainbow trout. According to the 1908 report of the U.S. Bureau of Fisheries, 25,000 eggs of rainbow trout (*"Salmo irideus"*) and 300,000 steelhead eggs (*"S. gairdneri"*) were shipped to Argentina, and the fish that hatched were stocked into the Río Santa Cruz. Although genetic analysis could find no distinction between steelhead and resident rainbow trout in the Río Santa Cruz, it is likely that other methods, such as the calcium-strontium ratio in otoliths, will demonstrate that in the overwhelming majority of spawnings among the two life history forms, steelhead give rise to steelhead and resident rainbow trout to resident rainbow trout. This situation is worthy of further research.

DISTRIBUTION After the final retreat of the last glacial era (about 10,000 years ago), the subspecies *Oncorhynchus mykiss irideus* extended the northernmost range of rainbow trout species to the southern tributaries of the Kuskokwim River, in Alaska, the first major river south of the Yukon.

In the Far East, *O. mykiss* occurs on the Kamchatka Peninsula of Russia. The Kamchatkan rainbow trout is virtually identical to North America's coastal rainbow trout, especially those in Alaska.

Kamchatkan and Alaskan *O. mykiss* were probably isolated from one another only after the last ice melted and the land bridge over the Bering Sea was submerged. The Kamchatkan *O. mykiss* is represented by both steelhead and resident rainbow trout. In Alaska, steelhead occur to the north side of the Alaska Peninsula. Northward and eastward from there, only stream-resident rainbow trout occur.

Inland, the natural distribution of *O. m. gairdneri* in the Columbia River basin extends to barrier falls on the Kootenay River, in Montana. The southernmost natural distribution of the species is found in the Río del Presidio of Mexico, near 24° N latitude. In fact, these rainbow-like trout represent the southernmost known native occurrence of any trout or salmon.

EVOLUTION AND CLASSIFICATION

The great diversity found in *O. mykiss,* as defined in this book, is geographically fragmented into groups of varying degrees of differentiation. There are diverse opinions about which of these groups should be included in *O. mykiss.* Some taxonomists have considered some groups to be subspecies, while others recognize them as full species. Perhaps unanimous consensus among taxonomists should not be expected on the best way to classify this species. New information on genetic relationships occurs continually, and future changes in the classification used here are anticipated.

Classification of rainbow trout and their relatives has always been difficult for scientists. The crux of the problem is ancient and stretches back toward the end of the

Pliocene epoch, around 2 million years ago. At about that time, a common ancestor divided, with one branch leading to the cutthroat trout and the other eventually to the rainbow trout. Along the long evolutionary path leading toward the modern rainbow trout, some highly divergent lines arose. Much of the taxonomic controversy concerns how to classify these distinctive groups. This guide uses a compromise between taxonomic "lumping" and "splitting," and recognizes the two most divergent groups—Gila trout *(O. gilae)* and the Mexican golden trout *(O. chrysogaster)*—as full species. *O. gilae* has two subspecies: the Gila trout of New Mexico and Arizona *(O. g. gilae)* and the Apache trout of Arizona *(O. g. apache)*. The Mexican golden trout is native to three river basins that are tributary to the Gulf of California.

All other evolutionary branches along the path to the modern rainbow trout are included in *O. mykiss.*

CONSERVATION   A report published in 1991 by the American Fisheries Society found that 214 stocks of anadromous *Oncorhynchus* species were to some extent at risk of extinction. Within *O. mykiss,* there were 75 at risk stocks, more than for any species of Pacific salmon. For consideration for protection under the Endangered Species Act, *O. mykiss* was divided into 15 evolutionarily significant units (ESU), 12 for *O. m. irideus* and three for *O. m. gairdneri.* Nine of these (six *irideus* and three *gairdneri*) were listed for protection.

Inland resident redband trout of the Columbia and Sacramento River basins, the Northern Great Basin, and the three subspecies of the Kern River basin all have suffered great declines due to introductions of nonnative trout and loss of habitat. The obstacles these populations face and their current conservation status is discussed in the individual accounts that follow.

Coastal Rainbow Trout
Oncorhynchus mykiss irideus

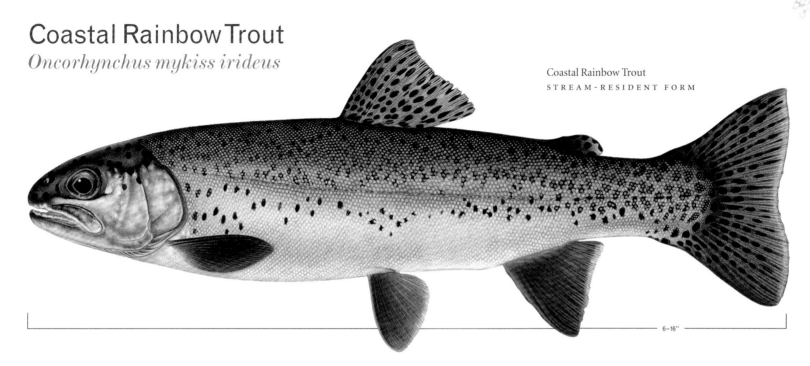

Coastal Rainbow Trout
STREAM-RESIDENT FORM

6–16"

There are two basic forms of the coastal rainbow trout: the sea-run (anadromous) form and the stream-resident form, which spends its life entirely in fresh water. The sea-run form is commonly called steelhead. The exact derivation of the name is unknown, but it is most likely a combined reference by anglers to its bright, steel blue coloration when fresh from the sea and its rather blunt, bony skull. The subspecific name, *irideus,* is from the Latin word for rainbow and the Greek goddess of the rainbow *(iris)* and refers to the bright red-pink band along the lateral line and gill covers, especially prominent in spawning males.

There is a great range of variation in both physical appearance and life history in the North American coastal rainbow trout from its southernmost range in California north to Alaska. There are also transitional zones of overlap in characteristics between this subspecies and *Oncorhynchus mykiss gairdneri,* the stream-resident redband trout of the Columbia River basin.

The coastal rainbow trout subspecies is the most typical form of the rainbow trout raised in fish culture, and has been introduced in waters all over the world. The combination of its hardiness, iridescent coloration, and hard-fighting qualities as a game fish make it a favorite with anglers and fishery managers.

DESCRIPTION Coastal rainbow trout are generally heavily spotted with irregularly shaped spots both above and below the lateral line. Spots are small and are profusely scattered over the sides of the body, on top of the head, and on the dorsal and caudal fins. The body coloration is generally silvery or

COASTAL RAINBOW TROUT

SCIENTIFIC NAME
Oncorhynchus mykiss irideus

OTHER COMMON NAMES
Rainbow

HABITAT
Clear, cool streams and rivers; lakes

LENGTH AND WEIGHT
Typically 6–8" (15–20 cm) and 2 oz (57 g) in small streams. 12–16" (30–41 cm) and 1–1½ lb (0.45–0.68 kg) or larger in rivers and lakes

LIFE SPAN
3–4 years in small streams; 6–8 years in rivers and lakes; maximum known 10 years

DIET
Aquatic and terrestrial invertebrates, salmon eggs, and fishes

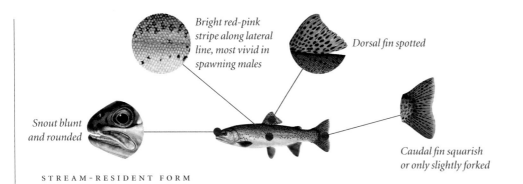

Bright red-pink stripe along lateral line, most vivid in spawning males

Dorsal fin spotted

Snout blunt and rounded

Caudal fin squarish or only slightly forked

STREAM-RESIDENT FORM

brassy. Bright silver coloration is characteristic of steelhead fresh from the ocean, while darker colorations are characteristic of resident freshwater fish. The back can be dark greenish brown to steely blue to emerald green in steelhead and some lake-dwelling rainbow trout. The band of color along the lateral line and on the cheek can vary from pink to deep red. Mature males have the brightest colors. The caudal fin is squarish and often shows only a slight fork. Parr marks on juveniles fade as the fish mature.

There are no diagnostic characteristics, morphological or genetic, that can positively separate all coastal rainbow trout from all other subspecies or geographical populations or races of rainbow trout. Nevertheless, although far from absolute, there are some distinctions between coastal rainbow trout and the redband trout subspecies *(Oncorhynchus mykiss gairdneri)* that shares its range. Coastal rainbow trout typically have fewer scales: about 120 to 140 scales counted along the side of the body about two scale rows above the lateral line, versus about 140 to 170 in redband trout. Coastal rainbow trout tend to have more pyloric caeca (appendages on the intestine) than are characteristic of the redband trout: 50 to 60 versus 35 to 45.

The size of steelhead and stream-resident coastal rainbow trout varies from population to population and is dependent on a variety of factors, including length of time spent at sea, in steelhead, and availability of food. In small streams, coastal rainbow trout, like all subspecies and races of rainbow trout, typically mature at 6 to 8 inches (15–20 cm) in length. In rivers and lakes, they attain a length of 12 to 16 inches (30–41 cm) and an average weight of up to 1 pound, 8 ounces (0.68 g). Some steelhead measure only 18 inches (46 cm) at spawning, while others reach a maximum length of 43 inches (1.1 m). The subspecies coastal rainbow trout *(irideus)* and redband trout *(gairdneri)* attain the largest sizes of any subspecies of *Oncorhynchus mykiss.* The world-record angler-caught rainbow trout, 43 inches (1.1 m) long and weighing 42 pounds (19.1 kg), was an *irideus* steelhead returning to the Skeena River basin in British Columbia. The Skeena River is home to the world's largest steelhead.

BIOLOGY Within the genus *Oncorhynchus,* the *irideus* steelhead has the greatest variety of life histories. Some populations of steelhead travel great distances from salt water into the upper reaches of freshwater rivers and

streams to spawn, while others travel only a few miles upstream.

The timing of spawning runs also varies widely: Summer-, fall-, and winter-run populations occur throughout the coastal rainbow trout's range. It is likely that steelhead enter fresh water somewhere in their range every month of the year. However, typically spring- and summer-run populations enter fresh water from May through August and reside in their natal stream through the winter to spawn the following spring. Fall-run populations enter fresh water from September through November and also spawn in the spring. In some rivers winter runs occur between December and March, and spawning begins soon after the fish enter fresh water. Steelhead populations introduced into fresh water, such as the Great Lakes, run in tributaries to spawn in the gravel beds of faster-moving water. Depending on location throughout the steelhead's range, spawning occurs in fresh water from January through June.

Steelhead typically spend two to three years in fresh water before smolting and migrating to salt water. After one to three years in the ocean, steelhead migrate to their natal streams to spawn. Unlike Pacific salmon, steelhead do not die after spawning and may return to their home waters a second time after another period of marine migration. The average return rate of steelhead for a second spawning ranges from less than 10 percent in some populations in some years to as high as 20 percent in others. Land-locked steelhead runs are highly successful by comparison, with reports of repeat spawning reaching 60 to 70 percent. The

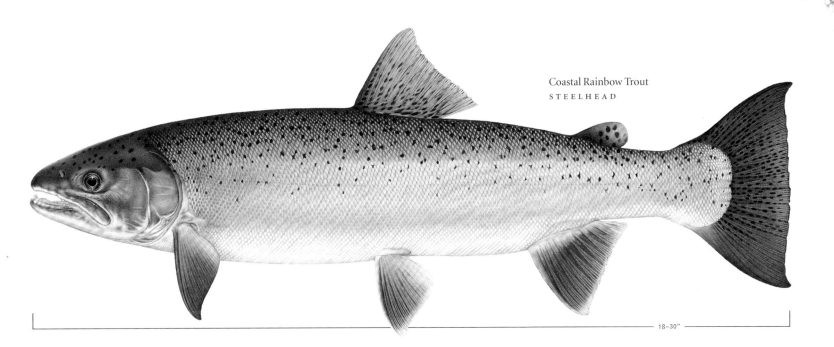

Coastal Rainbow Trout
STEELHEAD

18–30"

majority of repeat spawners of both sea-run and landlocked steelhead are female.

An unusual life history stage—known as the "half-pounder"—occurs in most steelhead populations of the Klamath and Rogue Rivers of northern California and southern Oregon. Klamath and Rogue steelhead smolts enter marine waters in late spring, as is typical for all steelhead, but in late summer they return again to the rivers. They measure about 12 or 13 inches (30–33 cm) weighing about a half-pound (230 g), to overwinter in fresh water. The following spring, the half-pounders again migrate to the ocean, but this time they become full-fledged steelhead and spend the next 18 months (some spend 30 months) at sea before maturing and returning to their home river to spawn.

From northern California to southern Alaska, the coastal rainbow trout and the coastal cutthroat trout occur together in many waters. Hybridization between the two species has always occurred, but the incidence of hybridization has increased as a result of two factors: the stocking of hatchery fish of both species, and human-induced changes in environmental regimes that act to break down reproductive barriers. One such alteration is the building of dams, which block historic spawning runs and alter water flow and water temperature.

While at sea, steelhead grow quickly because of the abundance of food and unrestricted habitat. Studies show that smolts entering salt water grow 1 inch (2.5 cm) in length per month and can continue at this rate until they return to their natal fresh water to spawn. Thus, the longer a steelhead

STEELHEAD RAINBOW TROUT

SCIENTIFIC NAME
Oncorhynchus mykiss irideus

OTHER COMMON NAMES
Steelhead

HABITAT
Clear, cool streams and rivers; lakes; intertidal areas and open ocean

LENGTH AND WEIGHT
18–30" (46–71 cm) and 2½–12 lb (1.1–5.4 kg); maximum 43" (1.1 m) and 42 lb (19.1 kg)

LIFE SPAN
4–7 years; maximum known 9 years

DIET
Aquatic and terrestrial invertebrates, salmon eggs, squids, and fishes; spawning fish rarely feed

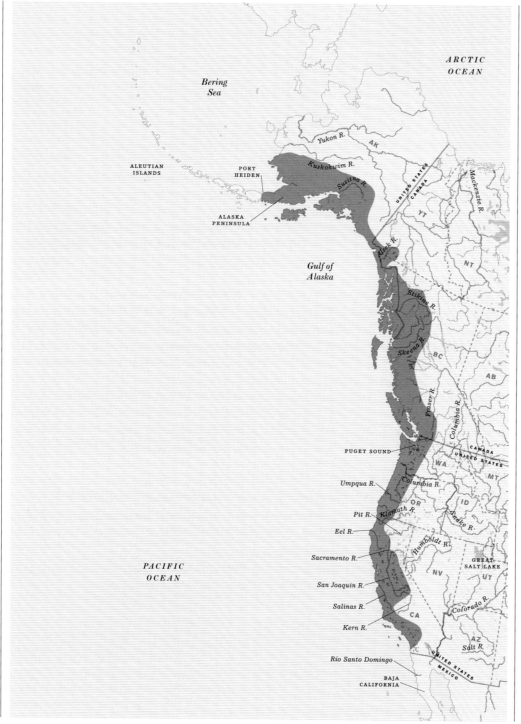

remains in salt water, the larger it grows.
During their life at sea, steelhead eat
a variety of foods including squids, other
fishes, and crustaceans (amphipods).
Steelhead overwintering in fresh water
prior to spawning feed very little, if at all.
However, food is found in the stomachs of
some steelhead in fresh water, in contrast
to Pacific salmon and Atlantic salmon that
do not feed after returning to fresh water.
Newly hatched fry feed on tiny invertebrates,
such as insect larvae; after a few months
as fingerlings (parr), they graduate to
larger prey.

DISTRIBUTION The southernmost
natural distribution of *Oncorhynchus
mykiss irideus*, as here defined, is the Río
Santo Domingo, in Baja California. The
Santo Domingo trout is sometimes classified
as the subspecies *nelsoni*.

Continuous historical distribution in the
native range of the coastal rainbow trout
begins in the Otay River drainage southeast
of San Diego and extends northward to the
southern tributaries of the Kuskokwim River,
in Alaska. In the Sacramento River basin,
coastal rainbow trout occur inland to the
McCloud and Pit Rivers, where a transition
is found between coastal rainbow trout
and interior redband trout, *O. m. stonei*, of
the northern Sacramento River basin.

In the Columbia River basin, the coastal
rainbow trout is native inland to the Cascade
Range. The redband trout is native east of

*The continuous native range of the coastal rainbow
trout extends from the Kuskokwim River, Alaska, south
to the Otay River drainage, in California.*

the Cascades, and a transition in genetic and morphological traits between the two subspecies is found toward the eastern side of the Cascades. Similarly, in the Fraser River basin *irideus* occurs upstream to Hell's Gate and *gairdneri* occurs above this area. Where the two subspecies overlap, intermediate populations blur any clear-cut distinction or precise demarcation of their distributions.

Steelhead occur throughout most of the range of the coastal rainbow trout from southern California to Alaska. The northern and western limits of steelhead distribution are in a few streams on the northern side of the Alaska Peninsula near Port Heiden. Eastward and northward to the Kuskokwim River only resident rainbow trout are known.

EVOLUTION AND CLASSIFICATION

In the late nineteenth and early twentieth centuries, it was common to name varieties or forms now classified as *Oncorhynchus mykiss irideus* as new species. Some of these older names, which are now considered synonyms of *O. m. irideus,* include: "*Salmo regalis,*" the royal silver trout of Lake Tahoe; "*S. smaragdus,*" the emerald trout of Pyramid Lake (these first two names were based on introduced hatchery rainbow trout); "*S. beardslei*" (a lake-adapted form of *irideus* that is a predator on kokanee salmon) of Crescent Lake in Washington ; "*S. rivularis,*" the Sacramento River steelhead; and "*S. masoni,*" the Oregon brook trout. Because "*Salmo irideus*" was named in 1855, and all of the names for coastal rainbow trout

mentioned above were published between 1860 and 1917, *irideus* is the valid name for what is now classified as a single subspecies. (See the box What's in a Name? in the *Oncorhynchus* genus account, page 19.)

In 1870, in San Francisco, the California Acclimatization Society began artificial propagation of coastal rainbow trout, the first rainbow trout subspecies to be artificially propagated. For the next several years, eggs from several coastal rainbow trout populations around the San Francisco Bay area were used for propagation. From 1880 to 1888, a federal hatchery on the McCloud River propagated rainbow trout; coastal *irideus* steelhead running up the McCloud River apparently provided most of the eggs and sperm, but resident McCloud River redband trout ("Shasta" trout) were also used at the federal hatchery.

After 1888, brood stocks of the McCloud River hybrids (steelhead × redband) were established in some federal hatcheries for shipment of eggs to most states and to foreign countries. The late nineteenth and early twentieth century shipments were identified as "rainbow trout, *Salmo irideus.*" In 1894, the U.S. Fish Commission began propagation of steelhead (identified as "*S. gairdneri*") from several rivers of northern California and Oregon, for distribution to other states and abroad.

Thus, the earliest propagation of rainbow trout was based on diverse parental sources, although most were of the subspecies *irideus,* and had a large measure of steelhead ancestry from the start. For more than 100 years,

the commonly held belief that the origin of all hatchery rainbow trout could be traced to resident "Shasta" rainbow trout of the McCloud River has been repeated over and over in the literature, but it is simply not true.

CONSERVATION We can only speculate about the abundance of these fish under more pristine conditions—that is, before Europeans settled North America—but there is no doubt that steelhead and, in many areas, stream-resident rainbow trout of the subspecies *irideus* have greatly declined from their former abundance.

In 1996 the National Marine Fisheries Service published a review of the status of steelhead populations in Washington, Oregon, Idaho, and California. Steelhead of the subspecies *irideus* were divided into 12 geographical groups of evolutionarily significant units (ESU) in relation to protection under the Endangered Species Act. Six ESU were found to have suffered such great declines that they were listed for protection under the act.

Of the coastal steelhead populations currently protected by the Endangered Species Act, four are in California: along the central California coast, along the south-central California coast, in southern California, and in the Central Valley (Sacramento River basin). The remaining two are in the Columbia River basin: in the lower Columbia River and in the upper Willamette River. The Klamath River Province ESU is currently under review for Endangered Species Act listing.

Redband Trout of the Columbia River Basin
Oncorhynchus mykiss gairdneri

Redband Trout
STREAM-RESIDENT FORM

6–18"

In the late nineteenth and early twentieth centuries ichthyologists identified the trout we now call redband trout either as cutthroat trout or as intermediate between cutthroat and rainbow trout. This confusion is not surprising because, especially in the stream-resident (non-anadromous) redband trout, the larger spots on the body, the yellowish coloration, and the frequent presence of an orange cutthroat mark under the jaws create a stronger resemblance to a cutthroat trout than to a coastal rainbow trout. The subspecies *Oncorhynchus mykiss gairdneri* and other subspecies of Pacific trout earned their common name "redband" for the distinctive red coloration along the lateral line. This coloration can be quite pronounced in spawning males. In rivers of the Columbia River basin, local anglers call the fish "redsides." Sea-run populations, known as redband steelhead, lose this characteristic in salt water but regain the brilliant red stripe when moving back into fresh water to spawn. An inland form of redband trout native to lakes in British Columbia is known as Kamloops trout. Larger stream-resident and the sea-run form are excellent sport fish.

DESCRIPTION Stream-resident redband trout best exemplify this subspecies' distinctive spotting pattern—large profuse spots on the body—and its typical coloration: a brick red lateral band, often with tints of yellow or

INLAND REDBAND TROUT

SCIENTIFIC NAME
Oncorhynchus mykiss gairdneri

OTHER COMMON NAMES
Redside, redband

HABITAT
Small, cool streams and rivers; lakes

LENGTH AND WEIGHT
6–10" (15–25 cm) and 1.5–7 oz (43–198 g) in small streams; 14–18" (36–46 cm) and 1–3 lb (0.45–1.4 kg) in rivers and lakes

LIFE SPAN
3–10 years

DIET
Aquatic and terrestrial invertebrates; larger fish in lakes become piscivorous

orange on the ventral region. Steelhead, along with Kamloops trout found in large lakes, typically have a silvery sheen that masks the spotting pattern and coloration found in stream-resident redband trout. Interior redband trout, especially stream-resident populations, often exhibit a yellow or orange cutthroat mark. Spawning steelhead exhibit a crimson red stripe along the lateral line. The deep red coloration extends into the mid-ventral region and into the pelvic fins. The gill covers can also be brilliant red.

The official angler-caught world record for rainbow trout—42 pounds (19.1 kg)—is of the subspecies *irideus,* but *gairdneri* trout are known to have attained even larger sizes. Kamloops trout can grow to 25 pounds (11.3 kg) and 40 inches (1 m) long or more, and records of trout weighing more than 50 pounds (23 kg) exist from the 1930s (see the box The Giant Gerrard Kamloops Trout, page 85).

BIOLOGY The most distinctive biological attribute of *gairdneri* is the adaptation of Kamloops trout for life in large lakes of the upper Fraser and upper Columbia River basins. Kamloops trout prey on other fishes, especially kokanee salmon. These lake-adapted trout generally do not attain sexual maturity and spawn for the first time until they are four to six years old, and they can attain a life span of eight to ten years. In comparison, stream-resident populations of redband trout typically spawn at two or three years of age and generally have a relatively short life span of three or four years.

The redband trout of streams and rivers reach a smaller maximum size than the

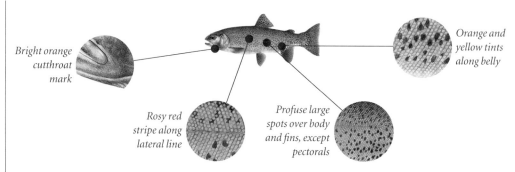

Bright orange cutthroat mark

Orange and yellow tints along belly

Rosy red stripe along lateral line

Profuse large spots over body and fins, except pectorals

STREAM-RESIDENT FORM

historical 50-pound (2.3-kg) behemoths of the lakes. Small-stream populations are typically 6 to 10 inches (15–25 cm) long. Those inhabiting larger bodies of water often grow to 18 inches (46 cm) and 3 pounds (1.4 kg); steelhead are known to attain lengths of 40 inches (1 m) and weights up to 25 pounds (11.3 kg).

O. m. gairdneri steelhead spend two to three years in fresh water, smolt, and migrate to salt water. After 18 to 30 months in the ocean, steelhead migrate to their natal streams to spawn. Like other steelhead, *gairdneri* steelhead do not die after spawning as do Pacific salmon and may return to their natal waters again. However, redband steelband rarely survive in the Columbia and Snake Rivers to spawn again. Only one percent or less make the long journey to reach their redds for a second time. They usually live about four to six years.

All *gairdneri* steelhead are summer-run fish entering the Columbia River, mainly from May through September. Steelhead of the subspecies *gairdneri* migrate much farther inland than *irideus* steelhead. Because of the numerous large lakes in the upper Fraser and Columbia River basins, specialized

lake-adapted populations are much more common in the subspecies *gairdneri* than in the subspecies *irideus.*

DISTRIBUTION Inland redband trout occur east of the Cascade Range in the Columbia River basin upstream to Kootenay Falls on the Kootenay River in western Montana. They also occur to Albeni Falls on the Pend Oreille–Clark Fork drainage in western Idaho, to Spokane Falls on the Spokane River in eastern Washington, and to Shoshone Falls on the Snake River in southern Idaho. Above these falls cutthroat trout and bull trout are the only native trout, except for the Snake River above Shoshone Falls, which lacks bull trout. Above Hell's Gate on the Fraser River, redband trout are native to the entire upper basin.

Inland rainbow trout are native to upper sections of the Peace River and Liard River drainages of the Mackenzie River basin, in British Columbia. It is not known if their origin is from coastal rainbow trout via inter-basin transfers from the Stikine River (that is, the *irideus* subspecies) and/or the Skeena River or from a Fraser River redband trout (*gairdneri*). As with the origins and ancestors

Redband Steelhead
SPAWNING MALE

25–36"

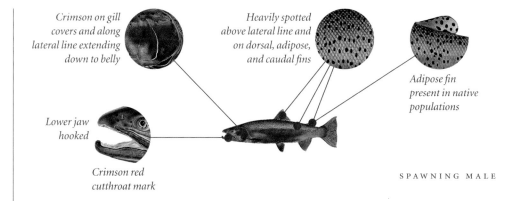

Crimson on gill
covers and along
lateral line extending
down to belly

Heavily spotted
above lateral line and
on dorsal, adipose,
and caudal fins

Adipose fin
present in native
populations

Lower jaw
hooked

Crimson red
cutthroat mark

SPAWNING MALE

REDBAND STEELHEAD TROUT

SCIENTIFIC NAME
Oncorhynchus mykiss gairdneri

OTHER COMMON NAMES
Steelhead, redband

HABITAT
Clear, cool streams and rivers; lakes; intertidal areas and open ocean

LENGTH AND WEIGHT
25–36" (64–91 cm) and 6–18 lb (2.7–8.2 kg); maximum 40" (1 m) and 25 lb (11.3 kg)

LIFE SPAN
4–6 years

DIET
Aquatic and terrestrial invertebrates and fishes

of the upper Klamath River redband, the Peace and Liard rainbows could have come from coastal or interior sources, or perhaps both.

A peculiar form of rainbow trout is native to the upper parts of the Athabasca River system (part of the Mackenzie River basin), in Alberta. It is assumed that the ancestor of the Athabascan rainbow trout came from the Fraser River basin before the beginning of the last glacial epoch about 70,000 years ago,

or perhaps earlier. The Athabascan rainbow trout is heavily marked with large, coarse spots over the body overlying a dark brassy coloration. Genetic studies on Athabascan rainbow trout show distinctions from both coastal rainbow trout and redband trout. That is, after some 70,000 years or more of isolation, its genetics are distinct from the present Fraser River redband trout.

At the southern extreme of the range of

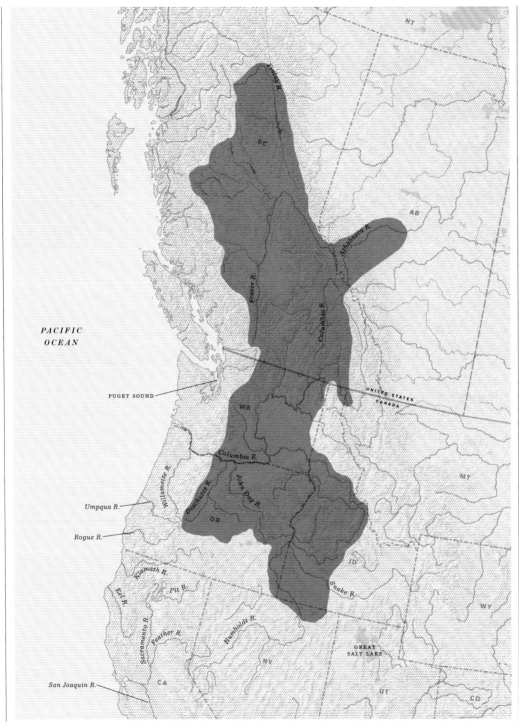

the rainbow trout, a form of rainbow trout is found that closely resembles *Oncorhynchus mykiss gairdneri* in appearance and in the number of scales and vertebrae. It is not known if this similarity is the result of a direct ancestor-descendant relationship or independent convergent evolution.

EVOLUTION AND CLASSIFICATION

In the 1940s, well-known nature author Ted Trueblood published an article in *Outdoor Life* entitled "Cutthroats of the Cattle Country." The "cutthroats" featured in the article were Columbia basin redband trout caught in small streams tributary to the Snake River, in southeastern Idaho, where the redband trout is the only native trout. Many other early descriptions of the redband trout of the Northern Great Basin, the northern Sacramento River basin, and the Upper Klamath Lake basin also confused inland redband with the cutthroat species.

In the 1970s, considerable interest surrounded the question "What is a redband trout?" The 1980 edition of the American Fisheries Society's *Common and Scientific Names of Fishes* includes this annotation for rainbow trout (called "*Salmo gairdneri*" at the time): "The redband trout has been recognized as a species distinct from rainbow trout and has been included on recent published lists. The systematic status of this species is unresolved, and no specific scientific name was applied to it by the authors cited above."

Inland distribution of redband trout of the Columbia River basin includes populations east of the Cascades in the upper Columbia and upper Fraser Rivers. Redband steelhead once migrated from the sea to the Snake River below Shoshone Falls.

However, modern genetic analysis leaves no doubt that all of the forms of redband trout are part of the rainbow trout species *Oncorhynchus mykiss,* and that all *O. mykiss* trout native to the Columbia River basin east of the Cascade Range and to the upper Fraser River basin above Hell's Gate—steelhead, Kamloops, and stream-resident redband trout—are closely related to each other and comprise the subspecies *O. m. gairdneri.*

The common name of the lake-adapted populations of the *gairdneri* subspecies was derived from the Kamloops region of British Columbia, where in 1892 this trout was originally described as a distinct species—first as "*Oncorhynchus kamloops,*" under the mistaken belief that it was derived from a coho salmon, and later as "*Salmo kamloops.*"

CONSERVATION Historically, steelhead of the subspecies *gairdneri* were more abundant than *irideus* steelhead in the Columbia River, a result of the much larger area for spawning and rearing in the Columbia basin east of the Cascade Range compared to the area of the basin west of the Cascades. Before the building of Grand Coulee Dam (from 1935 to 1940), runs of *gairdneri* steelhead migrated to the headwaters of the Columbia in British Columbia and to Shoshone Falls on the Snake River in Idaho. The Columbia had by far the most abundant steelhead (both *irideus* and *gairdneri*) of any river. Records from the Columbia River commercial fishery for steelhead (the only reliable early records) say that the largest commercial catch, in 1892, was 4.92 million pounds (2.3 million kg). It's estimated that under optimal conditions for survival in both fresh water (juveniles) and

Kamloops Trout

THE GIANT GERRARD KAMLOOPS TROUT

Some of the larger lakes of British Columbia are home to a form of trout known as Kamloops. *Kamloops* is a Shuswap Native American word meaning "meeting of the waters" and Kamloops Lake is the meeting place of the North and South Thompson Rivers. Native Americans knew the Kamloops trout and fished for it in lakes and tributaries across British Columbia.

Most Kamloops trout are not known today for extraordinary size. However, in Kootenay Lake a particular strain of Kamloops trout, the Gerrard strain, has a genetic predisposition to grow to enormous size under certain conditions. In 1924, the Gerrard Kamloops trout was stocked in Jewel Lake, in British Columbia, a body of water that had an abundance of forage fishes. In 1932, a specimen of 52 pounds, 8 ounces (24 kg) was caught; this giant was probably eight years old. Gerrard Kamloops trout were stocked in the United States in Lake Pend Oreille, Idaho, in 1942. Here they were exposed to a superabundance of kokanee salmon, their preferred food. Four years later in 1946, a four-year-old

Kamloops was caught that weighed 32 pounds (14.5 kg). In 1947, a five-year-old fish was taken that weighed 37 pounds (17 kg) and was 40 ½ inches (103 cm) long, with a girth of 28 inches (71 cm).

Kamloops trout in Kootenay Lake occur in at least three races (distinct populations): one associated with the lake's west arm, another with the south arm, and a third with the north arm. The north arm race originally spawned in the Lardeau River and its tributary the Duncan River. A dam on the Duncan River eliminated that original spawning site, and now all Gerrard Kamloops trout spawn in the Lardeau River near the town of Gerrard. Thus the name, Gerrard Kamloops trout.

While large Kamloops exist in some lakes, none come close to the giants that once cruised the deep cold waters gorging themselves on forage fishes. Declines in the number of prey fishes, such as the kokanee salmon in Lake Pend Oreille, have resulted in a much smaller overall size. Kamloops weighing 15 pounds (7 kg) are caught, but these are the exception, not the rule.

the ocean (adults) and before the impact of European American settlers, about 1 million or more steelhead may have entered the Columbia River during annual spawning runs. Of this total, based on relative areas of habitat available for spawning and for the rearing of juveniles, about 75 percent or more should have been *gairdneri* steelhead spawning east of the Cascades and about 25 percent *irideus* steelhead spawning from the Cascades westward.

Although nine main stem dams on the Columbia River and four on the Snake River have fish ladders, the upstream migration of adults through fish ladders and reservoirs and the downstream migration of juveniles over dams and through turbines has increased mortality rates well above those of the pre-dam era. During the past 50 years, steelhead abundance has become dependent on artificial propagation and the annual stocking of 10 to 15 million trout—both *irideus* and *gairdneri*—in the Columbia River basin.

Beyond the effect of dams, the abundance of wild steelhead has declined also under pressures from pollution, habitat degradation, and altered water flow and temperatures.

While conditions on the river and its tributaries continue to put pressure on the trout, overall abundance of adults strongly depends on the survival rate in the ocean. Ocean survival began improving in the late 1990s, and some 275,000 *gairdneri* steelhead passed Bonneville Dam on the Columbia River in 2000. In 2001, a historical record run of 630,200 steelhead passed Bonneville Dam, 75 percent of which were hatchery steelhead. The *gairdneri* steelhead population, which spawns east of the Cascade Range in the Columbia basin, now consists mainly (approximately 75 percent) of hatchery fish, the result of stocking many millions of hatchery-reared juveniles each year.

The National Marine Fisheries Service has delineated three groupings, evolutionarily significant units (ESU), of *gairdneri* steelhead in the Columbia River basin: those in the middle Columbia River, the upper Columbia, and the Snake River. Because of the low numbers of wild, native steelhead in proportion to hatchery-reared individuals, only wild, native steelhead of these three groupings are protected by the Endangered Species Act.

All hatchery steelhead have their adipose fin removed. Anglers catching steelhead without an adipose fin are allowed to keep them. By law, all wild steelhead must be released.

In most drainages of the Columbia River basin east of the Cascade Range, a long history of stocking hatchery rainbow trout of the subspecies *irideus,* superimposed on the native resident *gairdneri,* has resulted in hybridization between the two subspecies. Pure populations of *gairdneri,* uncontaminated by hatchery rainbow trout, are now relatively rare.

Redband Trout of the Northern Great Basin
Oncorhynchus mykiss newberrii

Skull Creek Redband Trout
of the Catlow Basin

6–8"

The Great Basin covers a vast area in the western United States. In the southern part of its extent it comprises much of the land east of the Sierra Nevada and west of the Colorado River in southern California and most of Nevada. In the north it extends to south-central Oregon. The Great Basin comprises roughly 200,000 square miles (518,000 sq km) or nearly one-fifth of the western United States.

The Great Basin itself consists of many separate basins in which all drainages are internal and no water reaches the ocean. The cutthroat was the first trout to invade this expanse and fossils of cutthroat trout more than 600,000 years old have been found in the Lahontan basin in the central region

of the Great Basin. Today different subspecies of cutthroat trout are the native trout of the Lahontan, Alvord, Whitehorse, and Bonneville basins—all areas within the Great Basin.

Redband trout invaded several segments of the Northern Great Basin at a much later time, beginning roughly 70,000 years ago. The group designated as Northern Great Basin redband trout includes the trout native to six internal basins of south-central Oregon. These six basins are the Harney–Malheur, Catlow, Fort Rock, Chewaucan, Warner, and Goose Lake basins. Based on its fish fauna and former interior connections, the Upper Klamath Lake basin is also considered part of the Northern Great Basin. Although Upper Klamath Lake now drains to the Pacific via the

Klamath River, the ancestors of most of its native fish species came from interior connections, not coastal ones.

The redband trout of the Northern Great Basin have diverse ancestral origins— they exemplify the difficulties involved in attempting to divide the species *Oncorhynchus mykiss* into subspecies in a neat and orderly manner. Some biologists, as a matter of convenience, classify these trout as members of the subspecies *O. m. newberrii.*

DESCRIPTION   Northern Great Basin redband trout generally exhibit the spotting and coloration typical of the stream-resident redband trout of the Columbia River basin. In most populations a rosy red to brick red band runs along the lateral line, earning them the name redband. They are profusely spotted both above and below the lateral line with the number of spots decreasing gradually toward the ventral region. Their bodies contain varying tints of green, yellow, gold, and pink. A series of elliptical purplish parr marks runs along the sides from the gill plates to the caudal peduncle. Residents of small streams retain these parr marks through adulthood. The caudal fin is slightly forked and spotted. A white tip is frequently present on the dorsal, pelvic, and anal fins.

Lacustrine (lake-adapted) forms, such as populations from Goose Lake and Upper Klamath Lake, are significantly less spotted and show a subdued (if present at all) pinkish lateral stripe. Faint parr marks may be present especially in younger fish. The overall body coloration varies by habitat but is generally dark green or purplish blue on the top of the body becoming increasingly light along the sides to the ventral region. The caudal fin is only slightly forked and is heavily spotted. Populations of *Oncorhynchus mykiss newberrii* found in Upper Klamath Lake and the adjacent Williamson River bear a striking outward resemblance to *O. m. irideus* steelhead: a stout body, steely blue coloration, a bullet-shaped head, and darkish pectoral, pelvic, anal, and caudal fins. These fish are commonly called rainbow trout and not redband trout for their similarity in appearance to sea-run rainbow trout.

Because of their diverse ancestral origins, there is no unique diagnostic trait that distinguishes all Northern Great Basin redband trout from all other forms of *O. mykiss,* but they do share a common evolutionary

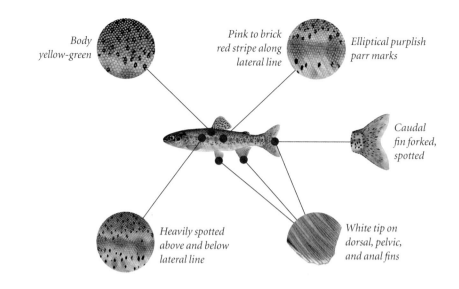

Body yellow-green

Pink to brick red stripe along lateral line

Elliptical purplish parr marks

Caudal fin forked, spotted

Heavily spotted above and below lateral line

White tip on dorsal, pelvic, and anal fins

POISON CREEK REDBAND TROUT

heritage from the last glacial epoch. About 10,000 to 50,000 years ago there were large lakes in these basins, and the ancestral trout in each basin independently acquired lacustrine specializations.

Compared to other forms of rainbow trout, Northern Great Basin redband trout have more gill rakers. The average number of gill rakers on the first gill arch varies from 21 to 23 in the Northern Great Basin redband trout versus 18 to 20, which is typical for all other forms of rainbow trout. There is one exception to the trend for a higher number of gill rakers. The Upper Klamath Lake basin is the only basin that has maintained a continuous large lake environment since the end of the last glacial epoch, and its native redband trout has maintained a separation into a lacustrine form that typically has 20 to 22 gill rakers and a stream-adapted (fluvial) form that typically has 18 to 20 gill rakers.

Body size of redband trout of the

Northern Great Basin, as in all forms of trout, is dictated by a number of factors including size of environment and availability of food. Typically, redband trout range in size from 6 to 8 inches (15–20 cm) and 4 ounces (113 g) in small streams to 20 inches (51 cm) and 3 pounds (1.4 kg) in rivers. In larger rivers, especially those adjacent to a lake, such as Goose Lake, much larger sizes are recorded. In Upper Klamath Lake and the Williamson River with their abundance of forage fishes and aquatic invertebrates, trout may reach 36 inches (91 cm) and 20 pounds (9.1 kg).

BIOLOGY Just as steelhead and resident rainbow trout of the subspecies *irideus* and *gairdneri* share a drainage basin and maintain their separate identities, the large lacustrine form of redband trout of Upper Klamath Lake and the stream-resident form use different parts of the basin for spawning and thus avoid hybridizing. In late winter and

Poison Creek Redband Trout
of the Malheur Basin

6–8"

spring, trout on spawning runs leave Upper Klamath Lake and migrate up the Wood and Williamson Rivers. Their offspring migrate to Upper Klamath Lake to feed and grow. Members of the stream, or fluvial, form of Upper Klamath basin redband trout spend their whole lives in small tributary streams.

The other basins within the Northern Great Basin with native redband trout have not maintained a continuous large lake environment over the past several thousand years, comparable to the one that exists in the Upper Klamath Lake basin. In most years, Malheur Lake, Goose Lake, and the Warner Valley lakes retain sufficient water volume for stream-resident trout from tributary streams to utilize these lakes for foraging and rapid growth. But then there are years when these lakes recede to the point that they

cannot be used by trout. In the harsh and unstable environments characteristic of the Great Basin, it is beneficial for fishes to have flexible life histories that allow them to take advantage of opportunities when they arise.

An evolutionary heritage reflecting selection for survival in the harsh environment of the Great Basin was revealed when the redband trout of Catlow Valley was subjected to experiments in the 1980s at the Fish Technology Center of the U.S. Fish and Wildlife Service in Bozeman, Montana. In the experiments, the Catlow Valley redband was tested for the influence of temperature on feeding and growth. All other forms of *Oncorhynchus mykiss* tested exhibited maximum feeding and maximum growth rate at temperatures of 55 to 61 °F (13–16 °C). Maximum feeding and growth of the Catlow

REDBAND TROUT OF THE MALHEUR BASIN

SCIENTIFIC NAME
Oncorhynchus mykiss newberrii

OTHER COMMON NAMES
Redband

HABITAT
Small, often warm, unstable streams; rivers

LENGTH AND WEIGHT
6–8" (15–20 cm) and 4 oz (113 g) in small streams.
Maximum 20" (51 cm) and 3 lb (1.4 kg) in rivers

LIFE SPAN
Probably 3–5 years

DIET
Aquatic and terrestrial invertebrates

Goose Lake Redband Trout
STREAM-RESIDENT FORM

6–14"

Valley redband trout peaked at 66 °F (19 °C), the highest temperature used in the test. Given the sometimes adverse stream conditions of the Northern Great Basin, redband trout are well served by a flexible life history.

DISTRIBUTION The Harney–Malheur basin is the largest basin within the Northern Great Basin. During historical times, the continued existence of trout in the Harney–Malheur basin has depended on habitat in the basin's three drainage systems: Silver Creek, Silvies River, and Donner und Blitzen River. Silver Creek drains from the north to Harney Lake. The Silvies River drains from the north to Malheur Lake, and the Donner und Blitzen River feeds Malheur Lake from the south.

Until about 18,000 years ago the

Harney–Malheur basin drained to the Snake River of the upper Columbia basin via the Malheur River. A lava flow blocked the outlet, isolated the basin, and created a large lake. With the climate changing toward increased aridity about 8,000 to 10,000 years ago, the large lake declined into two lakes, Harney Lake and Malheur Lake, which still connect during prolonged periods of above-normal precipitation. Harney Lake is presently too alkaline for fish life, but redband trout from the Donner und Blitzen River utilize Malheur Lake for foraging. During prolonged droughts, Malheur Lake desiccates to a point that it cannot be used by trout.

The Catlow basin borders the southwestern part of the Harney–Malheur basin. Trout native to the Catlow basin closely resemble the Harney–Malheur basin trout

and probably were derived from a headwater stream transfer from the Donner und Blitzen drainage. Since the desiccation of the ancient lake in the Catlow basin, trout have been restricted to four small streams: Threemile Creek, Skull Creek, and Home Creek drain the eastern side of the basin, and Rock Creek drains the western side.

Three perennial streams in the Fort Rock basin drain to Silver Lake, an alkaline body of water that is barren of fish. Around the turn of the twentieth century, trout were collected from Silver, Bridge, and Buck Creeks and preserved in museums, and these museum specimens have been compared with the trout in these streams today. It appears that the native redband trout of Silver Creek have been replaced by introduced eastern brook trout. However, native redband trout are still

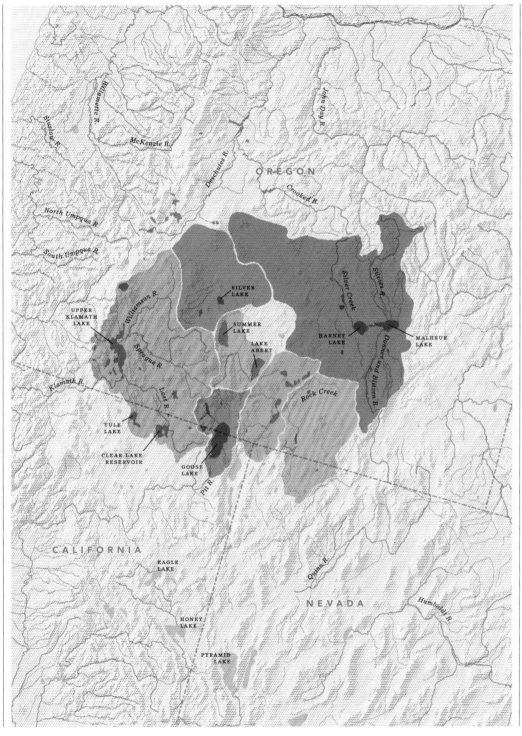

found in the headwaters of Bridge and Buck Creeks that are virtually identical to the trout found in these creeks almost 100 years ago. They appear to have been little influenced by the stocking of nonnative strains of hatchery rainbow trout in these two drainages.

The ancestral origin of the trout native to the Fort Rock basin most probably was from the Upper Klamath Lake basin. Only a slight divide separates the Fort Rock basin from Sycan Marsh, in the Upper Klamath basin, and the native trout of both basins share some diagnostic genetic markers.

The redband trout native to the Goose Lake, Warner, and Chewaucan basins are highly similar and share a common origin. Several distinctive genetic markers are shared by the native trout of these three basins.

During prolonged wet periods in historical times, Goose Lake has overflowed at its southern end and connected to the Pit River in the Sacramento River basin of northern California. The distinctive genetic markers diagnostic for the Goose Lake, Warner, and Chewaucan basin redband trout are also found in the redband trout in streams

Redband trout of the Northern Great Basin are native to seven separate areas. Because of the introduction of hatchery rainbow trout, there are few remaining pure populations of these fish.

- FORT ROCK BASIN
- HARNEY-MALHEUR BASIN
- CATLOW BASIN
- WARNER LAKES BASIN
- GOOSE LAKE BASIN
- CHEWAUCAN BASIN
- UPPER KLAMATH LAKE BASIN

Goose Lake Redband Trout
LAKE FORM

12–36"

tributary to the upper Pit River, downstream to the confluence with the Fall River. Downstream from the Fall River, the genetic profile of the native trout in the Pit River drainage clearly differs from that found in the trout upstream from Fall River and in the Goose Lake, Warner, and Chewaucan basins.

EVOLUTION AND CLASSIFICATION
There are no hard and fast rules for recognition of taxonomic categories for the redband trout of the Northern Great Basin, and many possibilities exist for classifying the various forms. The options, described below, range from "lumping" all the forms in a single subspecies to "splitting" the different forms into several subspecies.

A lumping perspective, based on shared evolutionary histories in large lakes during the last glacial epoch, would emphasize similarities in evolutionary ecology rather than a tracing of ancestral evolutionary lines. Such a classification could include all redband trout native to the Northern Great Basin as the subspecies *newberrii*. This would reflect the fact that the only Great Basin redband trout ever to be formally described with a scientific name was the lacustrine form of Upper Klamath Lake, named "*Salmo newberrii*" in 1858.

Scientists who favor classification strictly according to phyletic (evolutionary) relationships are likely to object to the *newberrii* subspecies name, because at least three evolutionary lines of *Oncorhynchus mykiss*—Upper Klamath, Columbia River, and upper Sacramento (Pit River) ancestral trout—gave rise to Northern Great Basin redband. Thus, the Northern Great Basin redband would be considered polyphyletic rather than monophyletic, meaning that it has more than one evolutionary lineage. However, since the International Code of Zoological Nomenclature does not rule out polyphyletic subspecies, grouping all Northern Great Basin redband trout as the subspecies *newberrii* remains an option. "Lumping" these forms creates a practical subspecies classification. It groups all Northern Great Basin redband trout as *newberrii* based on a geographical boundary and a common evolutionary heritage for life in the large, late Pleistocene lakes that existed in this basin for perhaps 40,000 to 50,000 years.

A "splitting" classification based on ancestral relationships would begin with the

Deming Creek Redband Trout of the Upper Klamath Lake Basin

6–8"

three ancestral lines that gave rise to all of the Great Basin redband trout. Thus *O. m. newberrii* would be restricted to the Upper Klamath Lake trout and to the redband trout of the Fort Rock basin whose ancestors came from the Upper Klamath basin. Alternatively, the Fort Rock basin redband trout could be split off from *newberrii* and described as a new subspecies.

The Harney–Malheur basin directly drained to the Columbia River basin via the Snake River until about 18,000 years ago, and the native trout of the Harney–Malheur basin are most closely related to the Columbia River basin inland redband trout (*O. m. gairdneri*). The Harney–Malheur redband trout could be classified as *gairdneri* or described as a new subspecies. The Catlow

Valley redband trout could be "lumped" with the Harney–Malheur redband trout or described as a new subspecies.

The redband trout native to the Goose Lake, Warner, and Chewaucan basins are very similar to each other, while also highly differentiated from all other Great Basin redband trout. Together, they constitute the most divergent of the Great Basin redband groups. Thus a convincing case, based on common ancestry, could be made for the native trout of those basins to be recognized as a new subspecies. This subspecies could also include the redband trout native to the upper Pit River drainage downstream to the confluence with the Fall River, which share common genetic markers.

Taxonomy blends art and science. Different

schools of thought advocate different methods and philosophies that often cause conflicts that remain unresolved. This review of options for classifying the redband trout of the Northern Great Basin illustrates the problems faced by any attempt to partition a highly variable species such as *O. mykiss* into subspecies. Because of differences in how evidence is interpreted and evaluated by different taxonomists, no universal agreement is likely to be reached on the matter.

Upper Klamath Lake redband most likely came—via internal waterways before the last glacial epoch—from a common ancestor that also gave rise to the Columbia River redband. However, after a long period (perhaps 100,000 years) of isolation, the two are now quite distinct.

Williamson River–Upper Klamath Lake
Redband Trout

12–36"

CONSERVATION Millions of hatchery rainbow trout of the subspecies *irideus* have been stocked in Northern Great Basin waters during the past 100 years. Hatchery trout continued to be stocked on top of native redband trout in popular trout streams of the Chewaucan basin until 1999, when the emphasis in Oregon shifted to one favoring the preservation of native trout.

Few existing populations of Northern Great Basin redband trout have remained pure, uncontaminated by hybridization with these introduced hatchery rainbow trout. Comparisons of museum specimens collected about 100 years ago with current specimens from the same locality have generally found close similarity, but not complete identity. Thus in most present populations the original redband trout of the Northern Great Basin still exists with only a slight hybrid influence from hatchery rainbow trout, suggesting that the native redband's superior adaptations to harsh environmental conditions favor them over nonnative hatchery rainbow trout.

In the arid lands of the West, much—in some cases, most or all—of the water in a stream is diverted for irrigation, and the original distribution and abundance of Northern Great Basin redband trout has been considerably reduced as a result of the dewatering of streams. In addition, watersheds in arid regions are particularly susceptible to degradation from livestock grazing. Intense grazing eliminates most vegetative cover that holds the soil in place, resulting in accelerated erosion and arroyo cutting, a common phenomenon in the Great Basin.

WILLIAMSON RIVER– UPPER KLAMATH LAKE REDBAND TROUT

SCIENTIFIC NAME
Oncorhynchus mykiss newberrii

OTHER COMMON NAMES
Rainbow

HABITAT
Rivers and lakes

LENGTH AND WEIGHT
12–18" (30–46 cm) and 1–3 lb (0.45–1.4 kg); maximum 36" (91 cm) and 20 lb (9.1 kg)

LIFE SPAN
Probably 6–7 years

DIET
Aquatic and terrestrial invertebrates and fishes

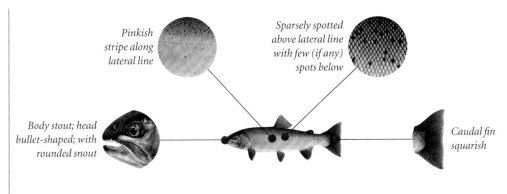

Pinkish stripe along lateral line

Sparsely spotted above lateral line with few (if any) spots below

Body stout; head bullet-shaped; with rounded snout

Caudal fin squarish

WILLIAMSON RIVER—
UPPER KLAMATH LAKE REDBAND TROUT

Northern Great Basin watersheds are owned by federal agencies (the U.S. Forest Service and the U.S. Bureau of Land Management) and by private individuals, who mainly own large ranches. In recent years, the federal agencies have placed greater emphasis on environmental concerns and native species in their multiple-use management programs. The restoration of riparian vegetation and the improvement of aquatic habitats have increased the abundance of redband trout in most Great Basin streams compared to 10 to 20 years ago.

Cooperative agreements between private ranchers and the federal agencies have led to revised grazing management strategies, called prescription grazing, that are designed to restore and protect watersheds and aquatic habitat. The results generally have been favorable for Northern Great Basin redband trout populations. Because of this trend for improving conditions, in 2000 the U.S. Fish and Wildlife Service decided not to list the redband trout of the Northern Great Basin for protection under the Endangered Species Act, but rather to continue to monitor the success of restoration efforts.

Redband and Rainbow Trout of the Northern Sacramento River Basin

McCloud River Redband Trout
Oncorhynchus mykiss stonei

6–20"

The Sacramento River

basin contains the greatest natural diversity of native trout of any large river system. The basin is noted for its high percentage of endemic fishes with 16 species found there and native to no other place. This endemism reflects the long geographic isolation of the area and its ancient connections to other basins. Ancient connections of the Sacramento River basin to other basins brought in a diverse number of fishes, which are ancestors of the present species in the basin.

Redband and golden trout groupings of more primitive forms of rainbow trout occur in the basin's northern and southern parts, respectively. The redband type of rainbow trout occurs to the north and is tied

to the headwaters of the Sacramento River, the McCloud and Pit Rivers, and the Feather River drainages, in three prominent forms: the northern Sacramento redband trout *(Oncorhynchus mykiss stonei)*, which includes the population referred to as the McCloud River redband trout; the Eagle Lake rainbow trout *(O. m. aquilarum);* and the Sheepheaven Creek redband trout, a peculiar redband found in the headwaters of the McCloud River above the upper barrier falls.

The Sacramento River basin also hosts native populations of coastal rainbow trout, which occur throughout a substantial portion of the basin. Coverage of that subspecies, provided in a previous account, is not repeated here, except to note genetic

McCLOUD RIVER REDBAND TROUT

SCIENTIFIC NAME
Oncorhynchus mykiss stonei

OTHER COMMON NAMES
Redband

HABITAT
Clean, cool streams and rivers

LENGTH AND WEIGHT
6–12" (15–30 cm) and 2–12 oz (57–340 g) in small streams. 12–20" (30–51 cm) and up to 2–3 lb (0.9–1.4 kg) in larger streams and rivers

LIFE SPAN
3–7 years

DIET
Aquatic and terrestrial invertebrates

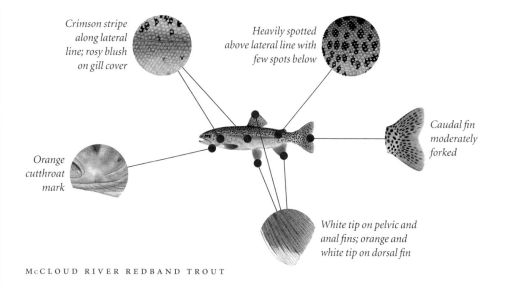

Crimson stripe along lateral line; rosy blush on gill cover

Heavily spotted above lateral line with few spots below

Caudal fin moderately forked

Orange cutthroat mark

White tip on pelvic and anal fins; orange and white tip on dorsal fin

McCLOUD RIVER REDBAND TROUT

analysis indicating that at least two forms of coastal rainbow trout (and steelhead) are native to the Sacramento basin. Rainbow trout native to San Francisco Bay tributaries show the closest relationships to rainbow trout of coastal drainages south of the bay, and they also differ from the coastal rainbow trout and steelhead of the Central Valley region of the Sacramento–San Joaquin basin. (The Central Valley is the area drained from the north by the Sacramento River and from the south by the San Joaquin River.) Thus, even in the coastal rainbow subspecies, there is evidence of two and probably more slightly differentiated ancestors invading the Sacramento basin.

The group including the golden trout and related forms—three recognized subspecies restricted to the Kern River drainage, the southernmost extreme of the Sacramento–San Joaquin River system—are discussed in the following account.

DESCRIPTION Distinctions of coloration and spotting pattern are not clear-cut among the northern Sacramento River basin redband trout. In general, northern Sacramento redband trout adults have varying degrees of yellowish background colors on the sides of the body, as is characteristic of other forms of primitive rainbow trout, and a brick red lateral band that is present to some extent. Spotting patterns typically differ from coastal rainbow trout. In northern Sacramento redband trout, the black spots tend to be larger, sparser, and more confined to the area above the lateral line. Also, in northern Sacramento redband the dorsal, anal, and ventral fins typically have pronounced white, yellow, or orange tips. Coloration is most intense in mature males.

However, great variation is found among northern Sacramento basin redband, and zones of transition with coastal rainbow trout blur clear-cut boundaries of distinction.

The spotting pattern and coloration of

the Eagle Lake rainbow trout, which is native to the eponymous California lake, is more similar to coastal rainbow trout than to any form of redband trout. Some traits, such as the number of scales along the body, are intermediate between a typical coastal rainbow trout and a typical redband trout. Eagle Lake is an isolated subbasin of the Lahontan basin of the Great Basin, but its trout are derived from the Pit River drainage, part of the northern Sacramento system. The connection from the Pit River drainage to Eagle Lake for this interbasin dispersal of trout came from the lower Pit River, an area where redband trout and coastal rainbow trout would be expected to have come into contact and mixed to produce a trout intermediate between coastal rainbow and northern Sacramento redband trout.

The Sheepheaven redband trout is clearly differentiated from all other forms of the northern Sacramento River basin redband trout. It averages only 16 gill rakers (the lowest number in the genus *Oncorhynchus*) and half of the specimens possess basibranchial teeth, which are otherwise characteristic of cutthroat trout and are only occasionally found in other primitive forms of rainbow trout.

The size attained by resident redband trout of the northern Sacramento River basin is determined by their environment. Maximum size in small streams rarely exceeds about 12 inches (30 cm) and 12 ounces (340 g); trout in larger streams and rivers are known to reach a length of 20 inches (51 cm) and a weight of 3 pounds (1.4 kg). The Eagle Lake rainbow trout, which includes the tui chub in its diet, commonly exceeds 24 inches (61 cm) and 5 pounds (2.3 kg), with exceptional specimens to 30 inches (76 cm) and 10 pounds (4.5 kg).

BIOLOGY All trout of the northern Sacramento River basin, with the exception of Eagle Lake rainbow trout, are stream-resident fish and occur in fresh water throughout their life history. They occur mostly in small streams, but a few larger riverine habitats support populations in the upper Sacramento River, the lower McCloud River, and the Pit River, including its major tributary, the Fall River.

Typical of life histories of all trout in small streams, the northern Sacramento redband trout grows slowly, matures early (typically at two years old), and has a short life span, generally of three to four years, with a maximum of six to seven years. It feeds opportunistically on whatever small aquatic and terrestrial invertebrates it encounters. In most streams, all or almost all of the invertebrate food consists of insects, mainly aquatic insects such as mayflies, caddis flies, and midges. Especially during summer months, terrestrial insects such as beetles, ants, and grasshoppers can make up a considerable portion (to 50 percent or more) of their diet.

In larger rivers with greater habitat volume and food supply, redband trout can attain a much larger size. In sections of low-gradient rivers, beds of aquatic vegetation provide habitat for crustaceans, particularly scuds and the aquatic sowbug. When

Diverse forms of redband and rainbow trout are native to the upper Sacramento River basin, including the McCloud, Pit, and Feather Rivers, and Eagle Lake.

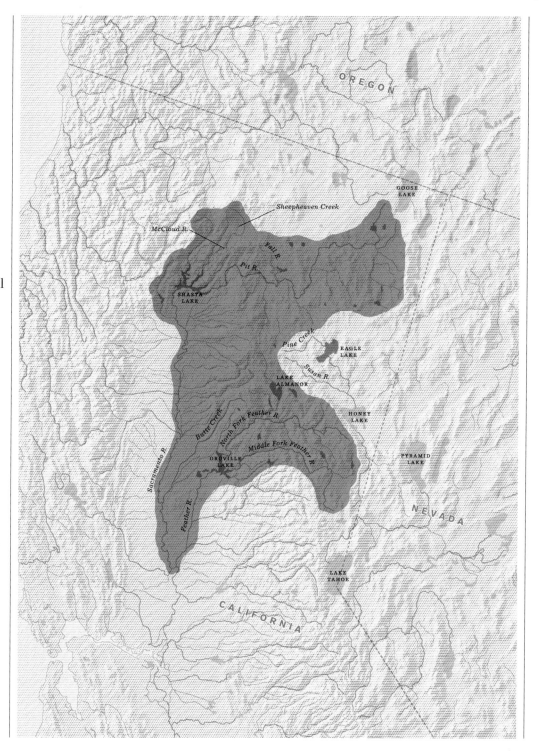

Sheepheaven Redband Trout
Oncorhynchus mykiss subspecies

6–8"

available, crustaceans can be an important item in a trout's diet, and their carotenoid pigments impart a red or salmon color to the flesh.

Small-stream habitat is found in its extreme form in Sheepheaven Creek, which arises in a series of small springs and flows not much more than 1 mile (1.6 km) before its flow sinks into the streambed. The volume of flow is only about 0.8 cubic feet (25–30 liters) per second. It is difficult to believe that, with such restricted habitat, the small population of redband trout inhabiting this tiny rivulet has existed there, as it has, for untold thousands of generations. This confined habitat, completely isolating Sheepheaven Creek from invasion after the original ancestor gained access from the upper McCloud drainage, has allowed the continuation of the ancestral evolutionary line, free from mixing with later invasions

of other redband trout. Sheepheaven Creek's minuscule amount of trout habitat also discouraged the stocking of nonnative hatchery trout. This extremely limited and isolated habitat has so far saved this ancient relict trout from extinction. Their growth is related to the amount of habitat volume, and as is common with other trout species and subspecies living their whole lives in small streams, the trout of Sheepheaven Creek attain a maximum size of only about 8 inches (20 cm) and 3.2 ounces (91 g).

The Eagle Lake rainbow trout has a physiological adaptation to high alkalinity that distinguishes it from all other rainbow trout. The precise mechanisms of this adaptation are not known, but high levels of carbonate, bicarbonate, and sulfate ions associated with high alkalinity destabilize the pH of the blood of fishes that lack the adaptive response to high alkalinity.

SHEEPHEAVEN CREEK REDBAND TROUT

SCIENTIFIC NAME
Oncorhynchus mykiss subspecies

OTHER COMMON NAMES
Redband

HABITAT
Small, intermittent Sheepheaven Creek, California

LENGTH AND WEIGHT
6–8" (15–20 cm) and 3.2 oz (91 g)

LIFE SPAN
3–4 years

DIET
Aquatic and terrestrial invertebrates

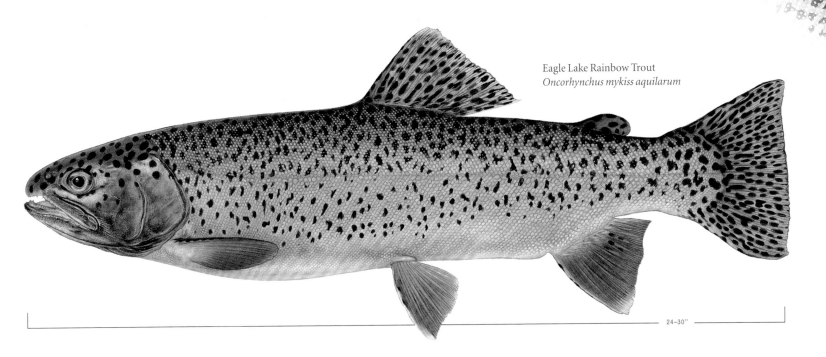

Eagle Lake Rainbow Trout
Oncorhynchus mykiss aquilarum

24–30"

DISTRIBUTION Northern Sacramento redband trout are native to the upper Sacramento River and to the McCloud, Pit, and Feather Rivers. Within this range, a variety of different forms of diverse ancestry are found. Because of mixing among the ancestral redband trout and with coastal rainbow trout, transitions in diagnostic traits occur that preclude the drawing of precise boundaries separating distinctive population groups, except for the unique population of Sheepheaven Creek. This is particularly true for the McCloud River. The upper McCloud River falls has long isolated the most distinctive redband trout above the falls from contact with coastal rainbow trout below the falls. Great diversity occurs in this lower area representing degrees of intermediacy between the redband and the coastal rainbow trout.

The Pit River drainage also contains a mosaic of diversity. The Goose Lake redband trout of the Northern Great Basin (see the previous account) extends its distribution in the upper Pit River drainage downstream to the confluence with the Fall River. Although there is no physical barrier separating the Pit River above and below the Fall River, there is an ecological barrier. Above the confluence with the Fall River, the Pit River is characteristic of a desert stream and is thus inhospitable for trout except in the colder upper reaches of tributary streams; the native trout is virtually identical genetically to the Goose Lake redband trout. Below the Fall River and extending to the Pit River's confluence with the Sacramento River (now submerged under Shasta Lake), the genetic profiles of redband trout abruptly change, and several distinctive groups of populations are found. Some more closely resemble cutthroat trout than rainbow trout, but genetically they are part of *Oncorhynchus mykiss*.

EAGLE LAKE RAINBOW TROUT

SCIENTIFIC NAME
Oncorhynchus mykiss aquilarum

OTHER COMMON NAMES
Rainbow

HABITAT
Eagle Lake, California

LENGTH AND WEIGHT
24–30" (61–76 cm) and 5–10 lb (2.3–4.5 kg)

LIFE SPAN
Probably 6–7 years

DIET
Aquatic and terrestrial invertebrates; larger fish become piscivorous and feed primarily on tui chub

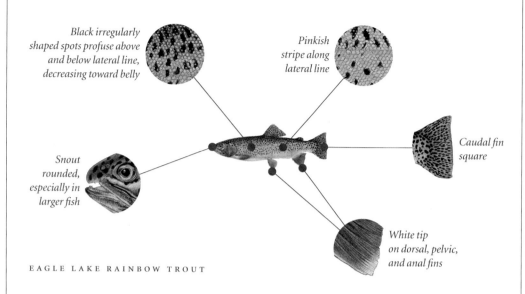

Black irregularly shaped spots profuse above and below lateral line, decreasing toward belly

Pinkish stripe along lateral line

Snout rounded, especially in larger fish

Caudal fin square

White tip on dorsal, pelvic, and anal fins

EAGLE LAKE RAINBOW TROUT

The Eagle Lake rainbow trout has an anomalous distribution. Eagle Lake is an isolated part of the Lahontan basin that in turn is part of the Great Basin. All native fishes of Eagle Lake, except for the trout, are Lahontan basin species. It is probable that, in late Pleistocene times (10,000 to 20,000 years ago), the original trout of Eagle Lake was the Lahontan cutthroat trout (*O. clarki henshawi*). The warmer and drier climate that prevailed from about 4,000 to 10,000 years ago likely resulted in modified flows and temperatures in Pine Creek, the only tributary to Eagle Lake, making it unsuitable for natural reproduction, and the cutthroat trout became extinct. A subsequent cooler, wetter climate allowed for a headwater connection to a segment of the Pit River drainage and the invasion of a redband trout. By about 1940, irrigation diversions from Pine Creek had depleted the flows to a point that the Eagle Lake rainbow trout could no longer reproduce naturally. Extinction of the present Eagle Lake rainbow trout was averted through artificial propagation (see the box Artificial Propagation, page 103).

Sheepheaven Creek, isolated by falls in the headwaters of the McCloud River drainage, contains the most distinctive form of northern Sacramento River basin redband trout and probably best represents the earliest ancestor that invaded the northern Sacramento basin.

EVOLUTION AND CLASSIFICATION

The redband trout found in the northern section of the Sacramento basin occur in a medley of diverse forms, suggesting that several differentiated ancestors invaded the basin at different times. The present diversity reflects mixing of the ancestral forms with each other and with later-invading coastal rainbow trout. The resulting pattern of diversity is chaotic and precludes the drawing of geographic boundaries that neatly categorize subspecies.

The apparent transition from cutthroat-like to typical coastal rainbow trout observed in the trout of the McCloud River and the golden trout of the main Kern River to the south (see the following account) could easily lead to the conclusion that the Sacramento River basin was where an ancestral cutthroat trout evolved into the rainbow trout. But looks can be deceiving. Modern genetic analysis of proteins, DNA sequences, and chromosomes leaves no doubt that the full range of variation among all redband and golden trout of the Sacramento River basin falls within the limits of *Oncorhynchus mykiss*. They are all very distinct from any form of cutthroat trout.

The names "*shasta*" and *stonei* were given to McCloud River redband trout in 1894. In my 1992 monograph *Native Trout of Western North America*, I used the subspecies name *O. m. stonei* to designate all of the northern Sacramento redband trout, qualifying that classification with this statement: "I use *O. m. stonei* only as a practical catchall category to group the great variability found in the McCloud and Pit River drainages. The redband trout native to Sheepheaven Creek is sufficiently differentiated to justify recognition as a new subspecies, but the name would only be applicable to the Sheepheaven population." This usage of *stonei* is similar to applying the name *O. m. newberrii* to all Northern Great Basin redband trout, despite the fact that at least three different ancestral evolutionary lines gave rise to that form. *O. m. stonei* denotes the trout of mixed ancestry native to an approximate geographical region rather than a grouping that can be traced to a single common ancestor.

The Eagle Lake rainbow trout is derived from an ancestral headwater transfer from the Pit River drainage. Not a typical redband trout, this form may have been influenced by a mixing of coastal rainbow trout in its ancestry. Eagle Lake is now a closed basin, with alkaline waters that are lethal to most other trout, and this trout is noted for its tolerance of high alkalinity.

The Sheepheaven Creek trout is a pure form of redband trout that probably represents the earliest ancestral invasion that gave rise to the northern Sacramento redband trout. The first mention of the Sheepheaven Creek trout in the literature, in 1939, suggested it might be an introduced population of South Fork Kern and Golden Trout Creek golden trout; other early references to these trout identified them as cutthroat trout or as a new species or subspecies. Evidently the Sheepheaven Creek trout have been long isolated from contact with other forms of redband trout and coastal rainbow trout. Sheepheaven Creek redband are sufficiently differentiated to merit recognition as a new subspecies.

CONSERVATION   Although the Eagle Lake rainbow trout evolved for life in a large lake, it was dependent on stream habitat for reproduction. In the 1940s the flow in Pine Creek, the only spawning tributary stream to Eagle Lake, became so depleted from irrigation diversion and siltation that the trout could no longer spawn naturally. Its extinction was prevented by artificial

ARTIFICIAL PROPAGATION

The rainbow trout is the trout species most commonly raised for human consumption and for stocking waters for sportfishing. The diverse ancestry of parental sources used in the founding of domesticated strains of hatchery rainbow trout provided a broad base of genetic diversity and allowed for rapid domestication, based on such factors as efficient utilization of artificial diet, rapid growth, early sexual maturation, and high fecundity. Domestication is also based on artificial selection for behavioral modifications, such as the ability to tolerate crowding and a willingness to come to humans for feeding. However, all hereditary changes brought about by artificial selection for more efficient rearing in fish culture are contrary to natural selection, where the sole criterion is survival to reproduction in the wild.

The origins of domesticated strains of rainbow trout are diverse. There has long been a belief, commonly expressed in the world literature on trout, that the origin of all hatchery rainbow trout was the McCloud River. This error has been repeated for so long that it has become accepted as fact. The truth is that the first rainbow trout used in artificial propagation came from the San Francisco Bay area seven years before eggs were taken from McCloud River redband trout; artificial propagation of rainbow trout began in 1870 in San Francisco, conducted by the California Acclimatization Society.

For the first several years, the parental sources used in propagation were the San Francisco Bay form of coastal rainbow trout.

Beginning in 1877, eggs taken from McCloud River trout were added to the California propagation program. From 1880 to 1888, the U.S. Fish Commission propagated and indiscriminately mixed McCloud River redband trout and steelhead (probably the Central Valley form of coastal rainbow trout). After 1888, the Commission (which later became the U.S. Fish and Wildlife Service) added steelhead from northern California and southern Oregon for the artificial propagation of rainbow trout. Several federal hatcheries maintained brood stock derived from the mixture of steelhead and resident redband trout of the McCloud River but could have included other parental sources. In the late nineteenth and early twentieth centuries, shipments to other states and foreign countries were identified as steelhead *"Salmo gairdneri"* or rainbow trout *"S. irideus."*

Because of its evolutionary history of coexistence with and feeding on nongame fishes, the Eagle Lake rainbow trout is now propagated in hatcheries and stocked into lakes and reservoirs in several western states. Especially in waters with nongame fishes (mainly minnows and suckers), the survival of Eagle Lake rainbow trout two and three years after stocking can be several times that of domesticated strains of hatchery rainbow trout. Evidently many generations of artificial selection for domestication have resulted in a loss of the ability of domesticated strains of rainbow trout to compete with nongame fishes for a common food supply.

propagation. Currently, efforts are being made to restore Pine Creek and its watershed with a goal of restoring natural reproduction of Eagle Lake rainbow trout.

All of the redband trout (and golden trout, covered in the following account) native to the Sacramento River basin can hybridize with any form of rainbow trout and also with cutthroat trout. The hybrids are fertile. Loss of genetic integrity from hybridization with introduced hatchery rainbow or cutthroat trout is a serious threat to maintaining the purity of the original diversity of the native trout.

Some natural mixing occurred between coastal rainbow trout and northern Sacramento redband trout wherever the ranges of coastal rainbow steelhead overlapped with redband trout, such as the upper Sacramento, McCloud, and Pit Rivers (before Shasta Dam blocked steelhead and salmon runs in 1940).

The greatest threat to redband trout, especially those populations isolated from contact with coastal steelhead, has been the introduction of nonnative trout. Brown trout and brook trout have replaced redband trout in many waters, and hatchery rainbow trout have hybridized with some redband populations.

During the past 20 years, in an era of increased environmental awareness and recognition of the importance of preserving the biodiversity of native species, the California Department of Fish and Game has established a committee of biologists to manage native trout, especially native trout considered as threatened. A transplant was made of Sheepheaven Creek trout into a larger neighboring stream, after chemical treatment to remove a population of hatchery rainbow trout, to ensure the perpetuation of this unique form of redband trout.

The redband trout of the upper Sacramento River tributaries are far removed from the redband trout of Sheepheaven Creek. Their evolution would have consisted of contact and some hybridization with coastal steelhead prior to the building of Shasta Dam. The redband trout found in the headwater drainages of the Sacramento River still retain some of the redband trout ancestry—as can be seen in their bright coloration, with tints of golden yellow and orange—distinguishing them from hatchery rainbow trout. However, the continued stocking of hatchery rainbow trout for some 100 years must have further compromised their evolutionary heritage.

In the early 1990s, a train derailment spilled a tank car full of a toxic herbicide into the uppermost headwaters of the Sacramento River. Virtually all the fish downstream to Shasta Lake were killed. Until this accidental "chemical treatment" occurred, the fishery in the upper Sacramento was based on the stocking of catchable-size hatchery rainbow trout. After much controversy and local opposition (many business people believed the stocking of large numbers of hatchery trout was necessary to attract anglers to the area), the California Department of Fish and Game decided to cease stocking hatchery trout and allow the native trout from tributaries to populate the upper Sacramento River.

The change in fisheries management from the stocking of catchable-size hatchery rainbow trout, for a "put-and-take" fishery, to a fishery based on wild, native trout is an example of a changing philosophy among natural resource agencies that makes the preservation of biodiversity of native species a high priority in their management programs.

Golden Trout of the Kern River Drainage

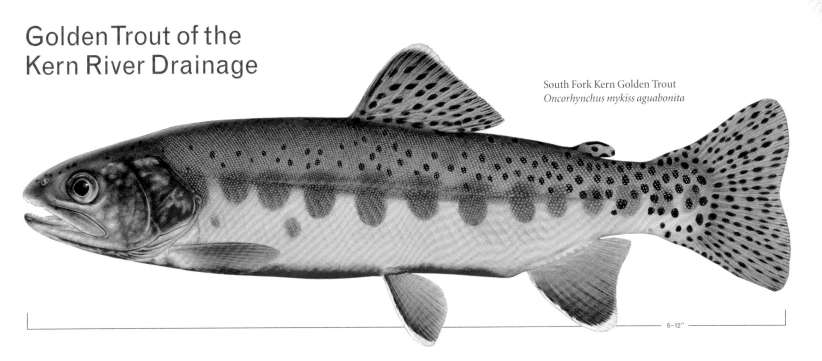

South Fork Kern Golden Trout
Oncorhynchus mykiss aguabonita

6–12"

Long isolated, though with ancient connections to other basins, the Sacramento River basin has the greatest natural diversity of rainbow trout of any large river basin. Redband and golden trout groupings of relatively primitive forms of rainbow trout occur in the basin's northern and southern parts, respectively.

The redband type of rainbow trout that occurs to the north in the upper parts of the Sacramento River, the McCloud and Pit Rivers, and the Feather River drainages is covered in the preceding account. The group including the golden trout and related forms discussed here consists of three recognized subspecies: the South Fork Kern and Golden Trout Creek golden trout (*Oncorhynchus mykiss aguabonita*), the Little Kern River golden trout (*O. m. whitei*), and the Kern

River rainbow trout (*O. m. gilberti*). All are restricted to the Kern River drainage of California, the southernmost extreme of the San Joaquin River system.

DESCRIPTION   Compared to the redband trout of the northern Sacramento basin, the three subspecies native to the Kern River drainage are more sharply differentiated from coastal rainbow trout, especially the South Fork Kern and Golden Trout Creek golden trout and the Little Kern River golden trout.

The South Fork Kern and Golden Trout Creek golden trout is the most distinctive of the Kern subspecies and probably represents the most ancient of the ancestral invaders, which arrived some 70,000 years ago or earlier, prior to the last glacial epoch. In the evolution of the South Fork Kern and

Golden Trout Creek golden trout, trends in coloration, spotting, and meristic (countable) traits characteristic of northern Sacramento basin redband trout have been taken to extremes. When these traits are expressed in their full glory, specimens of South Fork Kern and Golden Trout Creek golden trout can be described as spectacularly brilliant, and it is easy to see why this subspecies has been called the most beautiful trout in the world.

The color of the back is brassy or copper, becoming a bright golden yellow just above the lateral line. A deep red stripe runs along the lateral line and the golden yellow body color intensifies below. A deep crimson color suffuses the ventral region from the anal fin to beneath the lower jaw; the intensity of this color is influenced by age, sex, and diet.

Golden Trout Creek Golden Trout
Oncorhynchus mykiss aguabonita

6–12"

Parr marks are typically retained into the adult stage and for the entire life of the fish. When introduced in some lakes, older and larger individuals may lose parr marks. The fins of this subspecies are infused with orange and yellow colors, and the pelvic, anal, and dorsal fins have a pronounced white tip, framed by a dark border. The spots are large, rounded in outline, and mainly confined to the caudal peduncle. Above the lateral line anterior to the caudal peduncle, the spots become smaller and sparser and, in some specimens, disappear completely.

The outward characteristics—the bright colors, the size, shape, and arrangement of spots, and the number of scales along the sides of the body—of the South Fork Kern and Golden Trout Creek golden trout are remarkably similar to those of the Colorado River cutthroat trout, so much so that in the late nineteenth century, it seemed logical that the South Fork Kern and Golden Trout Creek golden trout was derived from a cutthroat trout.

Despite the fact that the distinctive traits of this golden trout are more typical of the cutthroat trout, the chromosomes and DNA of the South Fork Kern and Golden Trout Creek golden trout clearly demonstrate that its true evolutionary relationship is with the rainbow trout.

In the golden trout, the average number of vertebrae (59–60) and pyloric caeca (30–32) are the lowest found in any rainbow trout, and the number of scales along the lateral line (170–200) the highest.

In the Little Kern River golden trout and, especially, the Kern River rainbow trout,

GOLDEN TROUT CREEK GOLDEN TROUT

SCIENTIFIC NAME
Oncorhynchus mykiss aguabonita

OTHER COMMON NAMES
California golden trout

HABITAT
Small, cool, high-altitude streams; adaptable to high lakes

LENGTH AND WEIGHT
6–12" (15–30 cm) and 12 oz (340 g) in streams. Larger in lakes; world record 11 lb (5 kg)

LIFE SPAN
Maximum known 9 years

DIET
Aquatic and terrestrial invertebrates

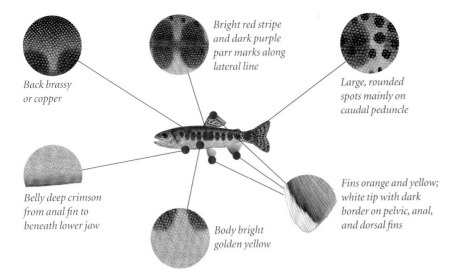

Back brassy or copper

Bright red stripe and dark purple parr marks along lateral line

Large, rounded spots mainly on caudal peduncle

Belly deep crimson from anal fin to beneath lower jaw

Body bright golden yellow

Fins orange and yellow; white tip with dark border on pelvic, anal, and dorsal fins

GOLDEN TROUT CREEK GOLDEN TROUT

there is a gradual transition from the extreme characteristics of the South Fork Kern and Golden Trout Creek golden trout toward the typical rainbow trout, the coastal rainbow trout. The Little Kern River golden trout resembles a slightly subdued version of the South Fork Kern and Golden Trout Creek golden trout, though with more numerous spots, especially anterior to the caudal peduncle. Compared with the South Fork Kern and Golden Trout Creek golden trout, the Little Kern River golden trout has fewer scales along the body (typically 155–160), more pyloric caeca (35–40), and more vertebrae (60–61).

The Kern River rainbow trout has characteristics intermediate between the two forms of golden trout and the coastal rainbow trout. The golden yellow and orange-red colors are further reduced in the Kern River rainbow trout, and the spots are much more profuse and occur over the entire sides of the body. The spots also are smaller and more irregular in outline, as compared with the rounded spots in the two golden trout. Some of the more "typical rainbow trout" appearance of Kern River rainbow trout could be natural and not entirely the result of the influence of hatchery rainbow trout. It is most likely the result of an invasion of coastal rainbow trout from the San Joaquin River through Tulare Lake and into the Kern River during the late Pleistocene epoch (10,000–20,000 years ago) or later.

BIOLOGY In their native range, South Fork Kern and Golden Trout Creek golden trout and Little Kern River golden trout are restricted to small-stream habitat. As with other trout living in similar environments, this influences their life history and limits their growth. These trout rarely exceed a length of 12 inches (30 cm) and a weight of 12 ounces (340 g), and a fish longer than 10 inches (25 cm) is considered large.

The Kern River rainbow trout exists in a large-river environment, and thus has a more rapid growth and much larger maximum size. In the main Kern River, these trout have been known to attain lengths of up to 28 inches (71 cm), and specimens weighing up to 8 pounds (3.6 kg) were reported in the early 1900s.

There are no feeding specializations in Kern River drainage trout: All three subspecies feed opportunistically on invertebrates, mainly insects, and like most trout species, they are generalists. When stocked in lakes with crustaceans, the South Fork Kern and Golden Trout Creek golden trout demonstrates its generalist-opportunistic feeding by consuming crustacean zooplankton in addition to insects such as caddis flies and chironomid midges that inhabit the lakes.

The life history of trout of the southern Sacramento River basin is similar to that of any other species of trout living in similar environments. All of the Kern River basin subspecies spawn in the spring when water temperatures rise to 43 to 49 °F (6–9 °C). These temperatures are reached in April and May at lower elevations and in June or even July at higher elevations. Spawning first occurs when fish are two to four years old; males typically mature at a younger age than females.

Spawning is rarely successful in lakes, unless a lake has a gravel bar, generally in the outlet zone, where sufficient flow circulates through the gravel to maintain oxygen levels at 5 parts per million or greater for the embryonic development of eggs. Otherwise the Kern River drainage trout, along with all forms of rainbow and cutthroat trout, can be considered as obligatory stream spawners.

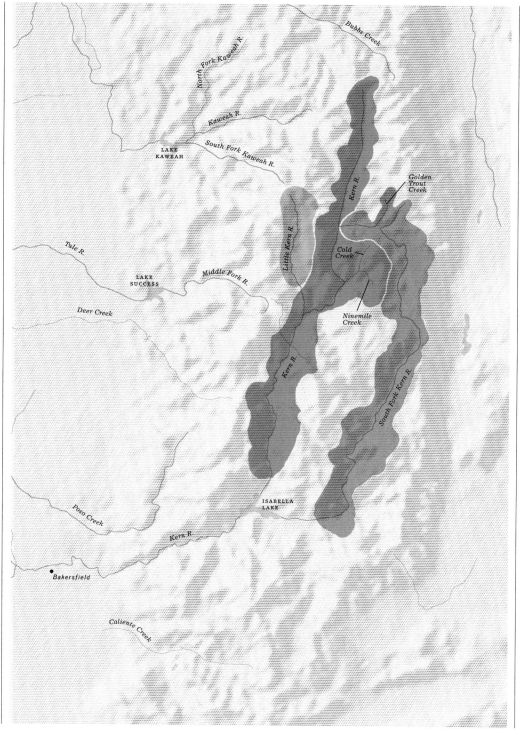

Lakes without suitable tributary streams for spawning must be continually stocked every two or three years. The stocking of mountain lakes was once carried out by a pack train of horses or mules carrying milk cans or canisters of baby trout. Now stocking is done by dropping the small trout, which are generally stocked at less than 2 inches (5 cm) long, from aircraft.

The South Fork Kern and Golden Trout Creek golden trout have been stocked in numerous mountain lakes outside their native range. About 300 lakes in California are stocked with them, as are lakes in other western states. As with other trout with an evolutionary history of life in small-stream habitat, the South Fork Kern and Golden Trout Creek golden trout adapts well to lake habitat and can attain a much larger size than in its native range. The world-record South Fork Kern and Golden Trout Creek golden trout—11 pounds (5 kg)—was caught in 1948 from a lake in Wyoming.

DISTRIBUTION The original distributions of the three subspecies of the Kern River drainage are as follows: *aguabonita* in the South Fork Kern River and Golden Trout Creek (tributary to the main Kern River), *whitei* in the Little Kern River, and *gilberti* in the main Kern River.

The Kern River drainage, part of the San Joaquin River basin of California, is the original native range of three subspecies of rainbow trout.

◼ Little Kern River golden trout (*O. m. whitei*)

◼ Kern River rainbow trout (*O. m. gilberti*)

◼ South Fork Kern and Golden Trout Creek golden trout (*O. m. aguabonita*)

Little Kern River Golden Trout
Oncorhynchus mykiss whitei

6–12"

The original ranges of the South Fork Kern and Golden Trout Creek golden trout and the Little Kern River golden trout have been greatly reduced due to stocking of nonnative trout. By the 1960s South Fork Kern and Golden Trout Creek golden trout were replaced by brown trout in most of their original range, pushed back toward the headwaters above a barrier. Pure populations of Little Kern River golden trout were also restricted to about 8 miles (13 km) of habitat in three small headwater streams above barriers that protected them from nonnative trout and hybrids.

A long history of stocking hatchery coastal rainbow trout in the main Kern River has compromised the integrity of the *gilberti* subspecies.

EVOLUTION AND CLASSIFICATION

As with the redband trout of the northern Sacramento River basin, there have been changing opinions and confusion about the classification and evolutionary relationships of the trout in the southern part of the basin.

Before Tulare Lake was drained in the 1870s and the area converted to agriculture, the ancient lake was a large, shallow body of water. The original terminus of the Kern River, Tulare Lake once connected to the San Joaquin River during prolonged wet cycles. Although these temporary connections of the Kern to the San Joaquin could allow movement of trout from the San Joaquin into the Kern, such movement would have been highly restricted due to the warm waters of the low-elevation Tulare Lake. However, the isolation of the Kern River and its inter-mittent connections via Tulare Lake to the San Joaquin River can explain the diversity found in the three subspecies of Kern River drainage trout. During glacial periods and the short-term interglacial wet cycles in the late Pleistocene (10,000–20,000 years ago) or later, Tulare Lake overflowed, and the resultant connections between the San Joaquin and Kern Rivers provided opportunities for trout to gain access to the Kern. How many ancestral invasions occurred to give rise to the three subspecies is not known, but the earliest of these invasions would have been of an ancient redband trout similar to the earliest redband trout invading the northern Sacramento basin, and the most recent invasions (up to about 10,000 years ago or later) would have been of coastal rainbow trout.

In 1878, the first mention in the literature of the South Fork Kern and Golden Trout Creek golden trout identified it as *"Salmo pleuriticus,"* the Colorado River cutthroat trout, now classified as *Oncorhynchus clarki pleuriticus*). Subsequently, the golden trout was described as a subspecies of cutthroat trout in 1892. In 1894, the apparent degrees of intermediacy (from South Fork Kern and Golden Trout Creek golden trout to Little Kern River golden trout to Kern River rainbow trout to "typical" rainbow trout) led to a revised opinion on the classification of the South Fork Kern and Golden Trout Creek golden trout; instead of a subspecies of cutthroat trout, it was classified as a subspecies of rainbow trout, *"S. gairdneri aguabonita."* At that time, it was believed that this subspecies represented a transitional form whereby an ancestral cutthroat trout gave rise to the rainbow trout species.

Consulting the authority of the time, Jordan and Evermann—authors of *Fishes of North and Middle America* (1896–98) and *American Food and Game Fishes* (1902), works on which most other contemporary accounts of trout classification were based— we find that in 1896 the South Fork Kern and Golden Trout Creek golden trout was changed from a subspecies of *"S. gairdneri"* to a subspecies of *"S. irideus"* under a mistaken belief that steelhead were *"S. gairdneri"* and resident rainbow trout *"S. irideus."* (The U.S. Bureau of Fisheries retained this classification into the 1900s for the propagation and distribution of *O. mykiss.*)

A practical resolution to the uncertainty about the most correct classification of the South Fork Kern and Golden Trout Creek golden trout was to declare it a full species, as was done in 1902, when the form was classified as *"S. aguabonita."* The American Fisheries Society continued to recognize the South Fork Kern and Golden Trout Creek golden trout as a full species (since 1989 as *"O. aguabonita"*), but in my 1992 monograph on western trout, I reduced it to subspecies status as *O. m. aguabonita.*

Modern genetic analysis and the total number of chromosomes (58, versus 64–68 in cutthroat trout) leave no doubt that the South Fork Kern and Golden Trout Creek golden trout is part of the rainbow trout species. A full species classification for this trout would create a problem if the goal of a classification is to best reflect evolutionary relationships. The three Kern subspecies *aguabonita, whitei,* and *gilberti* are most closely related to each other, and genetically all are part of the species *O. mykiss.* Elevating the South Fork Kern and Golden Trout Creek golden trout to full species status would distort its true ancestral origin and evolutionary relationships. And if *"O. aguabonita"* as a full species were to include both *"O. a. aguabonita"* and *"O. a. whitei"* (the Little Kern River golden trout), with the Kern River rainbow trout remaining classified as a subspecies of rainbow trout (*O. m. gilberti*), true relationships among the three subspecies would become even more distorted. The Kern River rainbow trout is more closely related to the Little Kern River golden trout than it is to any other form of coastal rainbow trout.

Historically, there has been some confusion between Golden Trout Creek and Volcano Creek. Current U.S. Geological Survey maps designate the main drainage as Golden Trout Creek, with a southern tributary named Volcano Creek, but in 1906 the main drainage was called Volcano Creek. In 1906, the "Volcano Creek golden trout" was named as a new species (*"S. rooseuelti"*) in honor of President Theodore Roosevelt, who commissioned a survey of the trout of the Kern River drainage by the U.S. Bureau of Fisheries. Although there are some genetic distinctions between the golden trout of Golden Trout Creek–Volcano Creek and the South Fork Kern golden trout, as would be expected because of their long isolation, they are similar in appearance, and both are classified today as *O. m. aguabonita.*

Common names abound for the golden trout of the Kern River drainage. This can be confusing because they tend to either pinpoint a fish to a particular stream, such as "Volcano Creek golden trout," or encompass a diversity of forms under one name, such as "California golden trout." The dozen or so common names for what are really two subspecies (*aguabonita* and *whitei*) of rainbow trout reflects the passion that so many have for this pair of jewel-like fish.

Kern River Rainbow Trout
Oncorhynchus mykiss gilberti

6–28"

The South Fork Kern and Golden Trout Creek golden trout probably represents the first invasion, and the Kern River rainbow trout is probably most influenced by the most recent invasion or invasions.

Although Golden Trout Creek is now a tributary to the main Kern River, it was once a tributary to the South Fork Kern. Thousands of years ago, a lava flow blocked Golden Trout Creek from its connection to the South Fork and diverted it to the main Kern River. The trout of Golden Trout Creek are obviously derived from the South Fork Kern and closely resemble the South Fork Kern golden trout. As such, the golden trout of Golden Trout Creek are classified with the golden trout of the South Fork Kern as the subspecies *O. m. aguabonita.*

The Little Kern River golden trout more closely resembles the South Fork Kern and Golden Trout Creek golden trout than it does the Kern River rainbow trout. It may represent another ancestral line of an early redband invasion or the same line that gave rise to South Fork Kern and Golden Trout Creek golden trout, with a slight influence from coastal rainbow trout.

The golden trout of the South Fork Kern and Golden Trout Creek and of the Little Kern River evolved in isolation from other fishes and lack an evolutionary history of coexistence with other fish species, except for the Sacramento sucker, which overlaps with the South Fork Kern and Golden Trout Creek golden trout in the South Fork Kern River. In addition to their susceptibility to hybridization with other forms of rainbow trout, the golden trout are replaced by brown trout

KERN RIVER RAINBOW TROUT

SCIENTIFIC NAME
Oncorhynchus mykiss gilberti

OTHER COMMON NAMES
Rainbow

HABITAT
Kern River, California

LENGTH AND WEIGHT
6–12" (15–30 cm) and 4–11 oz (113–312 g); maximum 28" (71 cm) and 8 lb (3.6 kg)

LIFE SPAN
Unknown

DIET
Aquatic and terrestrial invertebrates

Red stripe and faint parr marks along lateral line

Irregularly shaped spots profuse above and below lateral line; decreasing toward belly

Orange tints along belly

White tip on dorsal, pelvic, and anal fins

KERN RIVER RAINBOW TROUT

and nonnative brook trout where they have come into contact.

There is little doubt that at least some of the present characteristics of the Kern River rainbow trout have been influenced by the introduction of hatchery coastal rainbow trout in the Kern over the past 100 years. For example, the coloration and spotting pattern of Kern River rainbow trout is more similar to that of coastal rainbow trout. Museum specimens of Kern River rainbow trout collected in 1893 and 1904 have the same meristic characteristics as specimens of Little Kern River golden trout collected at the same time. Specimens from the main Kern River collected after 1950 show higher numbers of vertebrae and pyloric caeca and a

lower number of scales, compared to the 1893 and 1904 specimens. Such changes in meristic characteristics would be expected from a hybridization with hatchery rainbow trout.

Almost all South Fork Kern and Golden Trout Creek golden trout introduced outside their native range are derived from the golden trout of Golden Trout Creek. In about 1872, according to an old newspaper account, a transplant was made from Golden Trout Creek into the headwaters of Mulkey Creek. Although Mulkey Creek is a tributary to the South Fork Kern, a natural barrier prevented invasion of its upper reaches by South Fork Kern golden trout, and its waters were fishless until the 1872 transplant. In 1876, thirteen golden trout from Mulkey Creek were put into a coffee pot, carried over a divide, and stocked into Cottonwood Creek; twelve survived the trip. Cottonwood Creek drains from the eastern side of the Sierra Nevada to Owens Valley (part of the Great Basin) and was fishless at the time. Later, trout from Cottonwood Creek were transplanted into Cottonwood Lakes. Almost all subsequent propagation and distribution of the South Fork Kern and Golden Trout Creek golden trout has been from Cottonwood Lakes.

It is interesting to note that the number of scales, vertebrae, and pyloric caeca in the Sheepheaven Creek redband trout, which occurs near Mount Shasta in the northern Sacramento basin, are virtually identical to Little Kern River golden trout. Both the Mount Shasta region and the Kern basin served as glacial refugia during the last glacial epoch. Both regions share some "glacial relict" species of animals and plants, such as the foxtail pine.

CONSERVATION   In 1904, President Theodore Roosevelt at the urging of naturalist Stuart Edward White had the U.S. Bureau of Fisheries send an exploratory expedition to study the trout of the Kern River drainage. At the time the only serious perceived threat to the preservation of the native subspecies of the southern Sacramento River basin was the presence of human "fish hogs." The indiscriminate introduction of nonnative species was not seen, at that time, as a cause for alarm. Overexploitation by fish hogs may reduce the abundance of a population, but abundance rebounds once effective catch regulations are imposed. A much more serious threat to the continued existence of the diversity of native trout is posed by the introduction of nonnative species that replace or hybridize with native trout.

All trout native to the Sacramento River basin can hybridize with any form of rainbow or cutthroat trout, and the hybrids are fertile. Loss of genetic integrity from hybridization with introduced hatchery rainbow or cutthroat trout is a serious threat to the purity of the native trout's original diversity. For example, the South Fork Kern and Golden Trout Creek golden trout has been widely propagated and stocked in western states for the past 70 years, and there is not a single example of an introduced population of South Fork Kern and Golden Trout Creek golden trout that was not lost to hybridization if rainbow trout or cutthroat trout were later stocked with the golden trout.

In 1973, the Little Kern River golden trout was given Endangered Species Act protection as a threatened species. The Little Kern River golden trout has benefited from California Department of Fish and Game programs for wild trout, native trout, threatened trout, and "heritage" trout. These benefits include cooperative ventures with federal agencies and private landowners to improve habitat and water quality, as well as special angling regulations whereby all or most of the trout caught must be released. Such measures have greatly reduced angling exploitation rates. In addition, small streams above barrier falls are chemically treated to eliminate nonnative species and hybrids, and then pure Little Kern River golden trout are stocked to start a new population. The distribution of this subspecies has now been increased, and its future is much brighter.

A petition to list the South Fork Kern and Golden Trout Creek golden trout for Endangered Species Act protection was submitted in 2000. The battle to maintain the purity and expand the range of this trout has been a continual struggle, including barrier construction and reconstruction, and chemical treatments to eliminate brown trout and hybrids. More than 100 years of stocking nonnative trout in lower reaches of the South Fork Kern drainage resulted in hybridization between the golden trout and hatchery rainbow trout and in the establishment of brown trout. Pure South Fork Kern and Golden Trout Creek golden trout were restricted to the headwaters of the South Fork Kern above a falls at Ramshaw Meadows. In 1969, brown trout were found up to Ramshaw Meadows, and within a few years they outnumbered the golden trout 50 to 1 below the falls.

In the 1970s, a barrier at Ramshaw

Meadows was enlarged to ensure against upstream movement of brown trout and hybrids, and two additional barriers—the Templeton barrier and the Schaeffer barrier—were constructed downstream. Chemical treatment of the South Fork Kern between the Ramshaw barrier and the Schaeffer barrier has been carried out several times in attempts to eliminate brown trout and hybrids. However, by 1994 brown trout were again above the Schaeffer barrier, and pure golden trout were restricted to the headwaters of the South Fork Kern above the Templeton barrier. Also in the late 1990s, a tributary stream between the Schaeffer and Templeton barriers was found to contain a population of golden × rainbow trout hybrids.

Some environmental organizations believe Endangered Species Act protection is needed also to eliminate livestock from the upper South Fork Kern watershed. Since the 1870s, three native Kern River subspecies have suffered from the effects of overgrazing, first by sheep and later by cattle. Despite the fact that the upper South Fork Kern watershed is in the Golden Trout Wilderness Area on U.S. Forest Service lands, meaningful changes in the Service's livestock management program—intended to restore terrestrial vegetation and aquatic habitat for the golden trout—have occurred only in recent years.

Livestock can devastate trout habitat in a variety of ways. Allowed to roam freely in and around streams, cattle and sheep will trample banks and pass through streambeds, resulting in heavy siltation and loss of water-cooling shade vegetation. Bank erosion also destroys niche habitats favored by trout,

such as deep undercut sections along the edges of streams.

The South Fork Kern and Golden Trout Creek golden trout, the California state fish, is stocked in about 300 mountain lakes in the state, and the subspecies has been widely placed outside its native range in many western states. Such an active propagation and distribution program would suggest that, although the subspecies' distribution and abundance is greatly reduced in its native range, the abundance of the populations introduced outside the native range should be greater even than historical abundance in the native range. The reasons this assumption is wrong relate to a hybrid influence in the source population for all South Fork Kern and Golden Trout Creek golden trout used for artificial propagation and stocking.

In 1997, genetic analysis demonstrated the influence of hatchery rainbow trout in the wild brood stock of golden trout in Cottonwood Lakes. Although apparently slight, this hybridization may have been taking place for 40 years or longer. Hatchery rainbow trout may have been inadvertently mixed with fingerling South Fork Kern and Golden Trout Creek golden trout in a hatchery prior to stocking the fingerlings back into Cottonwood Lakes, but this is only speculation. In any event, the brood stock of South Fork Kern and Golden Trout Creek golden trout in Cottonwood Lakes is contaminated by hybridization. Some of these hybrids have been stocked into lakes in the Golden Trout Creek drainage and have gained access to Golden Trout Creek. In the Golden Trout Creek drainage, only the population in Volcano Creek remains isolated from the threat of hybridization. Consideration of all of the threats discussed above led to the petition in the fall of 2000 to list the South Fork Kern and Golden Trout Creek golden trout for protection under the Endangered Species Act.

Stuart Edward White, for whom the subspecies *whitei* is named, sounded a warning in his 1904 book, *The Mountains*, in regards to indiscriminate stocking of hatchery trout in the southern Sierras. White wrote that "care should be taken lest the two species become hybridized [golden trout and hatchery rainbow trout], as has occurred following certain misguided efforts in the South Fork of the Kern." Unfortunately White's warning went unheeded.

The Kern River rainbow trout probably no longer exists in its pure form. From 1904 to the 1950s and continuing even into the 1990s, the main Kern River and its major tributaries were continually stocked with nonnative trout, mainly hatchery rainbow trout. Although the trout found in the main Kern River today are not typical of hatchery rainbow trout and probably retain a large measure of the original Kern River rainbow trout, all collections of Kern River rainbow trout specimens from the main Kern River made in the 1950s through the 1970s have higher numbers of vertebrae and pyloric caeca and lower numbers of scales compared to specimens collected in 1893 and 1904. Such modification of meristic characteristics would be expected from a hybrid influence from hatchery rainbow trout, which were continually stocked in the main Kern and its tributaries for more than 90 years.

Rainbow Trout of Mexico
Oncorhynchus mykiss subspecies

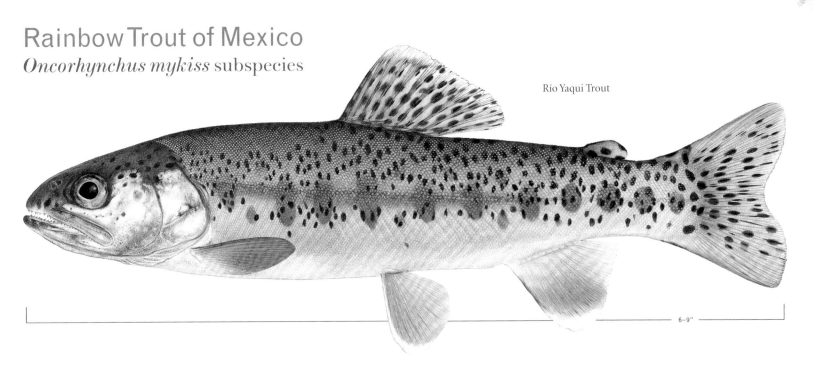

Río Yaqui Trout

6–9"

Trout native to rivers

draining from the Sierra Madre Occidental to the Gulf of California (also known as the Sea of Cortés) make up the most diverse and least known trout of western North America. Uncertainties surround the classification of these fish. This guide recognizes the two most divergent groups as full species and discusses them in separate sections. The first such group—Gila trout and Apache trout— probably represent the earliest radiation from the Gulf of California. After an ancestor of the Gila and Apache trout entered the Colorado River and dispersed up the Gila River, perhaps about 500,000 years ago, a divergence occurred in the western (Salt River system) and eastern parts of the Gila River basin. This divergence gave rise to the Apache trout in the west and Gila trout in the east.

The second clearly divergent form also recognized as a full species is the Mexican golden trout. This colorful fish is derived from an ancestor that may have become established around 500,000 years ago in three river drainages: the Río Fuerte, Río Sinaloa, and Río Culiacán.

In this section, three other distinctive groups of trout are considered as undescribed subspecies of *Oncorhynchus mykiss*. The first group is found in the Río Yaqui and the Río Mayo, north of the range of the Mexican golden trout. A very similar trout is found in the headwaters of the Guzmán basin, which drains from the east side of the mountains; the Guzmán basin once connected to the Rio Grande but is now an internal desiccating basin. It is most likely that trout are not native to the Guzmán basin and that the trout found there were transplanted by humans from the Río Yaqui basin.

RAINBOW TROUT OF MEXICO

SCIENTIFIC NAME
Oncorhynchus mykiss subspecies

OTHER COMMON NAMES
Trucha nativa (in Mexico)

HABITAT
Small, high-elevation headwater streams

LENGTH AND WEIGHT
6–9" (15–23 cm) and 4 oz (113 g)

LIFE SPAN
3–4 years

DIET
Aquatic and terrestrial invertebrates

Río Mayo Trout

6–9"

The second group occurs in the Río San Lorenzo drainage, south of the range of the Mexican golden trout. The third form, which occurs in the Río del Presidio drainage, closely resembles a typical rainbow trout, especially the Columbia River basin redband trout. It probably represents the most recent invasion from the Gulf of California, perhaps during the last glacial period of the late Pleistocene epoch, about 10,000 to 60,000 years ago.

No species or subspecies names have been published for the trout of the Río Yaqui and Río Mayo, the Río San Lorenzo, or the Río del Presidio.

DESCRIPTION Although great variation is found among the Mexican trout classified under *Oncorhynchus mykiss,* they have spotting patterns and general body colors similar to the redband forms of rainbow trout found in the upper Sacramento River basin, the mid–Columbia River basin, and the Northern Great Basin. The trout of the Río Yaqui, Río Mayo, and Río San Lorenzo drainages are characterized by yellowish background colors and a pink rainbow band in mature fish. They have oblong or elliptical parr marks, often with supplemental blotch-like markings above and below the main row of parr marks. Compared with coastal rainbow trout, spotting is more sparse and mainly above the lateral line.

The Río del Presidio trout clearly resembles the stream-resident Columbia River basin redband trout, *O. m. gairdneri.*

BIOLOGY No unique attributes in life history or ecology are known for any of the Mexican trout that would distinguish them from any other form of rainbow trout or cutthroat trout.

During interglacial periods, trout of Mexico were restricted to life in small streams. The small amount of habitat in small streams consequently influenced their life history traits, especially growth.

All Mexican trout spawn in the spring when water temperatures begin to rise. The southern latitudes are associated with earlier warming, and there are reports of Mexican trout spawning from January to March.

There were no natural lakes in the range of Mexican trout, throughout their evolutionary history, so they never developed lake-adapted populations. For many thousands of years the Gulf of California has been too warm for anadromous, steelhead-like populations to exist. Perhaps the trout longest isolated in fresh water, the Gila and Apache trout, have lost or greatly reduced the physiological processes that allow for osmoregulation (maintenance of a stable salt and water balance in the blood) in marine waters. The

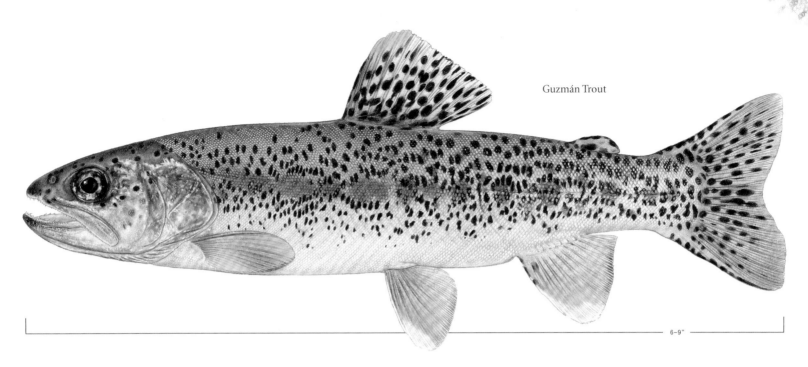

Guzmán Trout

6–9"

Río del Presidio trout probably was the most recently isolated from an ancestor that swam in the Gulf of California, and it might still retain the potential to give rise to anadromous forms if the opportunity arose.

As is typical of other rainbow (and cutthroat) trout of this size in small streams, the Mexican trout feed mainly on aquatic insects and terrestrial insects that fall onto the water.

Because of the small-stream habitat in which all of the Mexican trout live, they do not attain a large size. Typically, sexually mature fish are about 6 to 9 inches (15–23 cm) long and weigh about 4 ounces (113 g). Their typical life span is three or four years.

DISTRIBUTION   The trout in the Río del Presidio drainage, just north of 24° N latitude (the Tropic of Cancer), reflect the southern-most natural distribution of any species of the family Salmonidae, but questions have been raised concerning the genealogy of these trout. Are they native or were they introduced by humans? The occurrence of trout in the Río del Presidio drainage was documented in 1898, ten years after the U.S. Fish Commission first sent rainbow trout to Mexico. The rainbow trout sent to Mexico in 1888 came from the McCloud River, in California. The trout propagated by the U.S. Fish Commission on the McCloud River in the 1880s were sufficiently distinct (based on museum specimens) from the Río del Presidio trout to strongly indicate that the distribution of trout in the Río del Presidio is a natural distribution and not the result of an introduction of McCloud River rainbow trout.

In 2000, a trout was documented to occur in the Río Baluarte drainage, the next drainage south of the Río del Presidio.

Historical records are lacking, but it is likely that the Baluarte trout is introduced and not native. Comparisons of Baluarte trout with Río del Presidio trout and with rainbow trout raised in Mexican hatcheries will have to be made before any firm conclusions can be reached on the current southernmost natural distribution of salmonid fishes.

However, there is no doubt that trout distribution did extend farther south at some ancient time. A fossil trout named "*Salmo australis*" (now classified as *Oncorhynchus australis*), perhaps of the middle or later Pleistocene epoch, was found in the Lake Chapala basin, about 250 miles (400 km) south of the present distribution of trout in the Río del Presidio.

The Pleistocene epoch covers the past 2 million years up to about 10,000 years ago and includes four major glacial periods. During a glacial period, the climate, even far

Río San Lorenzo Trout

6–9"

south of the glacial front, is colder and often involves higher precipitation. During these periods of colder climates, ancestral trout must have used the Gulf of California to disperse into rivers from the Río del Presidio to the Colorado River, giving rise to the present diversity that occurs in these drainages.

During warmer, drier interglacial periods, trout could persist only in colder, mountain headwater parts of the drainages. The headwaters of rivers draining the Sierra Madre Occidental originate from elevations of about 8,000 to 10,000 feet (2,400–3,000 m) and maintained environments for trout to persist during interglacial periods.

In 1975, trout were first documented in the headwaters of the Río Mayo drainage above Basaseachic Falls. The Río Mayo trout, which is very similar to the Río Yaqui trout, could have originated from a natural head-water transfer from the Río Yaqui drainage. In one possible scenario, a landslide could have disconnected a Yaqui tributary and its fishes, changing the direction of flow and connecting to the Río Mayo drainage. Another possibility is that humans may have transplanted trout from the Yaqui to the headwaters of the Mayo drainage above the barrier falls. It can be assumed that an ancestral trout invaded the Río Mayo and moved inland until blocked by falls. As with the Río San Lorenzo drainage, trout derived from more than one ancestor might occur in the Río Mayo.

Trout found on the western side of the Sierra Madre Occidental in the headwaters of the Guzmán basin appear identical to Río Yaqui trout. The headwaters of the Guzmán basin are in close proximity to the headwaters of the Yaqui drainage, and a natural head-water transfer could have occurred. However, the Guzmán basin once connected to the Rio Grande. If the Guzmán basin contained a native trout, it would be expected to be a cutthroat trout derived from the Rio Grande. More likely, the Guzmán basin contained no native trout, and trout from the Río Yaqui drainage were transplanted into the Guzmán basin by early settlers.

EVOLUTION AND CLASSIFICATION

The trout associated with the Gulf of California are more closely related to the evolutionary line leading to rainbow trout than they are to cutthroat trout. However, the classification of the diversity of these trout is in a rudimentary stage. Based on the current state of knowledge, conclusions about how many distinct ancestors gave rise to the present diversity as well as the degrees of relationships among the trout of different drainage basins can only be a matter of speculation.

Arroyo la Sidra Trout
FEMALE

6–9"

Arroyo la Sidra Trout
MALE

6–9"

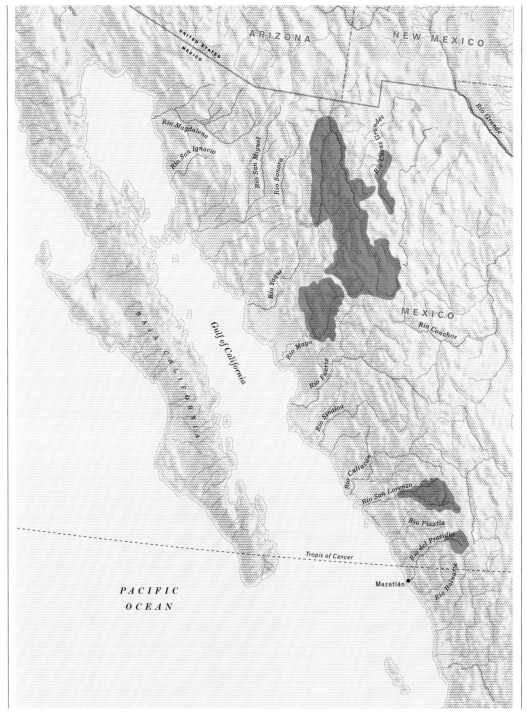

In coloration and spotting patterns, and in their meristic characteristics, the Yaqui and Mayo trout resemble the Gila trout, which might suggest they were derived from the same ancestor. However, genetic analysis to date shows that Yaqui and Mayo trout are strongly differentiated from Gila and Apache trout—about equidistant between coastal rainbow trout *(Oncorhynchus mykiss irideus)* and Gila trout *(O. gilae)*. The total chromosome number in Yaqui and Mayo trout is 64, versus 56 in *O. gilae.* (The number of chromosomes found in other rainbow trout varies from 58 to 64.)

The number of vertebrae can also be useful for assessing divergence. Some fish species that have a north–south distribution show a cline in number of vertebrae, with the lowest numbers found in southernmost populations and the highest numbers in northernmost populations. This is not true for *Oncorhynchus* trout. The southernmost rainbow trout, found in the Río del Presidio drainage, average more than 64 vertebrae, the typical number found in the Columbia River redband trout some 1,750 miles (2,816 km) to the north. Yaqui and Mayo trout average about 60 vertebrae (the range is 58–62). The Mexican golden trout typically has between 56 and 58 vertebrae, which is six to eight fewer than the number found in the Río del Presidio trout.

The Río San Lorenzo drainage is south of

High-elevation areas of the Sierra Madre Occidental in Mexico are home to various forms of rainbow trout. The southernmost known native occurrence of any trout or salmon is found in the headwaters of the Río del Presidio just above the Tropic of Cancer.

Río del Presidio Trout

6–9"

RÍO DEL PRESIDIO TROUT

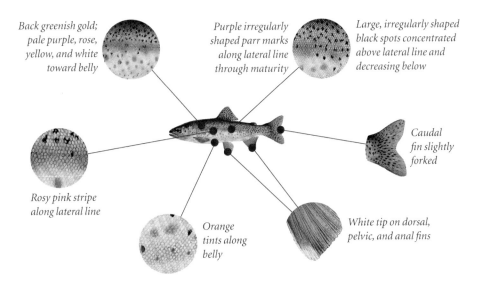

Back greenish gold; pale purple, rose, yellow, and white toward belly

Purple irregularly shaped parr marks along lateral line through maturity

Large, irregularly shaped black spots concentrated above lateral line and decreasing below

Caudal fin slightly forked

Rosy pink stripe along lateral line

Orange tints along belly

White tip on dorsal, pelvic, and anal fins

the Río Culiacán, where the Mexican golden trout is found, and north of the Río del Presidio. A headwater tributary to the Río San Lorenzo, the Río Truchas, contains trout with an average of 61 vertebrae. In a lower tributary to the Río San Lorenzo, the Arroyo la Sidra, seven trout collected there in October 2000 averaged more than 64 vertebrae. These specimens came from below waterfalls, a natural barrier to upstream migration. However, there is a trout hatchery above this barrier, the Granja Truticola del Ejido Vencedores. Trout collected above the falls in proximity to the hatchery averaged 62 vertebrae.

What can be inferred from the vertebrae counts from these locations? If Arroyo la Sidra trout are native and not introduced by humans, the difference between Arroya la Sidra trout below the falls (64 vertebrae) and

THE SOUTHERNMOST NATIVE TROUT

In the late 1890s the naturalist E.W. Nelson traveled to the Sierra Madre Occidental at the behest of the Smithsonian Institution. Nelson wrote the scientist B.W. Evermann describing trout he had observed in the headwaters of the Río del Presidio drainage: "I regret exceedingly that I failed to get specimens of these Sierra Madre trout, but that does not help us any now." Indeed, if he had collected the fish he observed, they would have been the first specimens of trout ever recorded from this area. The following year, the United States vice-consul to Durango, Walter C. Bishop, an outdoorsman and avid angler, sent Nelson five specimens of Mexican trout from the headwaters of the Río del Presidio. Unfortunately these early specimens of trout were lost. Were these fish native to these remote headwater streams or were they stocked? Ninety-five years later, Walter C. Bishop's son recalled that his father made several trips by mule from Durango to Mazatlán in the Río del Presidio drainage, fishing along the way: "I remember him telling me the trout were native and do not recall him mentioning anything about anyone planting eggs or fry." The younger Mr. Bishop has also fished much of the Río del Presidio headwaters and in 1946 guided Ralph G. Miller to several streams. Miller sent his specimens to the U.S. National Museum in Washington, D.C., where they exist today as the earliest extant specimens of trout from the Río del Presidio drainage.

the Río Truchas trout (61 vertebrae) and the trout collected on the Arroyo la Sidra above the falls (62 vertebrae) indicates that two distinct ancestors invaded the Río San Lorenzo at different times. Low vertebrae counts (60–62) are assumed to be ancestral, from an earlier occupation. Higher numbers of vertebrae (64–65) are assumed to reflect a more recent entrance from the Gulf of California into these headwaters.

In 1898, naturalist E.W. Nelson recorded trout in the Río del Presidio drainage near the town of El Salto. Nelson did not name the stream where he observed the trout, but it was probably La Rosilla (El Salto Creek). Nelson's mention of trout he observed in Río del Presidio in 1898 is the first United States recording of trout from this region of Mexico. R.G. Miller collected trout from the Río del Presidio drainage in 1946, and these specimens are the "official" southernmost record of the natural distribution of any member of the family Salmonidae.

The first published report of trout in the Río Yaqui drainage was in 1904, when the trout were mentioned, though not described or further commented on, in a publication on fishes of Mexico by S.E. Meek. Until the 1950s little new information appeared on Mexican trout.

During the 1950s, Paul R. Needham of the University of California, Berkeley, conducted field trips to collect specimens from the drainages of the Río Yaqui, Río Fuerte, Río Sinaloa, Río Culiacán, Río San Lorenzo, and Río del Presidio. Complete morphological descriptions of the specimens were given

in a 1959 publication "Rainbow trout in Mexico and California" (*University of California Publications in Zoology*: 67), coauthored by Needham and Richard Gard.

It remains to be seen if the trout reported in recent times from the Río Baluarte and the Río Acaponeta drainages, south of the Río del Presidio, are native or introduced by humans. The lack of historical record would suggest that the Baluarte and Acaponeta trout are introduced and not native, but the question remains open.

CONSERVATION

Little is known about the status of the populations in all of the drainages. It is known that trout are exceedingly rare near villages and roads. All the drainages have areas, such as deep canyons, that are virtually inaccessible to humans and that serve as refugia from overfishing.

There are environmental threats from logging, mining, road construction, and pollution, but the major threat to maintaining the continued existence of pure populations of the native trout in Mexico is hybridization with introduced hatchery rainbow trout. There is no evidence that hybridization has been a problem to date, but with many hatcheries in Mexico raising domesticated rainbow trout, escapes from fish culture operations and the stocking of hatchery trout in private waters and in reservoirs could result in large-scale hybridization and loss of genetic purity of the native trout, similar to what has occurred over much of the western United States.

Gila and Apache Trout

Oncorhynchus gilae gilae and
Oncorhynchus gilae apache

Gila Trout

5–9"

Trout have long been known to occur in the Gila and Salt River basins of New Mexico and Arizona. Early settlers to the region called the trout they found in the headwaters of the Little Colorado and Salt Rivers "yellow bellies" for their distinctive coloration. Specimens of Apache trout were collected by a U.S. Geographical Survey in 1873 and identified as a variety of Colorado River cutthroat trout. The Gila trout and the Apache trout were not described with scientific names until relatively recently. Even so, recognition of *Oncorhynchus gilae* as a full species with two subspecies is a judgment call, as discussed in Evolution and Classification, below.

DESCRIPTION   The basic yellowish golden body coloration of both the Gila trout and the Apache trout is probably a primitive trait. It is also found in more primitive forms of rainbow trout, such as the diverse groups of redband trout found in the northern Great Basin and the upper Columbia, Klamath, and Sacramento River basins; the undescribed rainbow trout of the Sierra Madre Occidental; and the Mexican golden trout.

The yellowish coloration is typically more restricted to the ventral region in Apache trout and extends farther up the sides of the body in Gila trout. The most apparent distinction between Gila trout and Apache trout is their spotting patterns. Apache trout have larger and fewer spots, making them similar in this regard to interior subspecies of

GILA TROUT

SCIENTIFIC NAME
Oncorhynchus gilae gilae

OTHER COMMON NAMES
None known

HABITAT
Small, cool, relatively unstable streams

LENGTH AND WEIGHT
5–9" (13–23 cm) and 1–6 oz (28–170 g)

LIFE SPAN
Typically 4 years; maximum known 6 years

DIET
Aquatic and terrestrial invertebrates

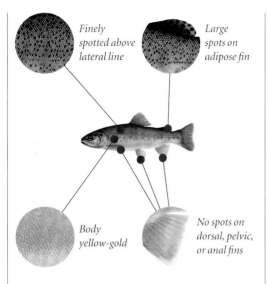

Finely spotted above lateral line

Large spots on adipose fin

Body yellow-gold

No spots on dorsal, pelvic, or anal fins

GILA TROUT

cutthroat trout. The small, profuse spots on the Gila trout are more suggestive of coastal rainbow trout.

Another diagnostic trait is the great reduction or absence of parr marks in Gila and Apache trout. Parr marks, dark blotches that occur along the sides of the body in most salmonid fishes, are most pronounced in the juvenile (parr) stage and typically fade as a trout matures. Parr marks are absent or extremely rare in all life history stages of the Apache trout. Faint parr mark–like blotches are sometimes found in Gila trout.

Mature Gila trout often have a faint rose coloration along the lateral line, like rainbow trout. The Apache trout lacks rose or red colors on its body in all life history stages. The fins of Gila and Apache trout can be bronze-yellow to yellow-orange, and the dorsal, pelvic, and anal fins have a light-colored leading edge with a white or yellow to orange tip.

Pure populations of Apache trout have a

black pigment spot in front of and just behind the pupil, likened to a mask. This trait is absent in many hatchery-reared fish.

The main diagnostic feature for scientific differentiation of Gila and Apache trout from all other *Oncorhynchus* species is their chromosomal profile (karyotype). The Gila trout and the Apache trout both have a total of 56 chromosomes and 106 chromosomal arms. Rainbow trout have 58 to 64 chromosomes, and the chromosome number in cutthroat trout varies from 64 to 68. The karyotypes of rainbow trout and cutthroat trout contain 104 chromosomal arms.

BIOLOGY   The habitat characteristic of the small, unstable streams where pure populations of both Gila and Apache trout exist severely limit opportunities for growth. During low flow periods, when the populations must survive in pools fed by groundwater seeps, dense numbers of trout, rarely larger than 8 inches (20 cm), are crowded into a limited space, and the small trout are in survival mode.

Because Gila and Apache trout face an environmental regime of greatly increased habitat during wetter than normal years and greatly diminished available habitat during drought years, their population abundance may fluctuate by tenfold over a period of a few years. Their evolutionary heritage has adapted them for the perpetuation of a population in extremely harsh and unstable environments.

Gila and Apache trout, as with rainbow and cutthroat trout, spawn in the spring when water temperature is rising and runoff flows are declining. Temperature appears

to be the key factor to initiate spawning, which begins when daily temperatures rise to 46 or 47 °F (8 °C). At lower elevations, up to about 7,000 feet (2,100 m), spawning typically begins in April. At higher elevations, temperatures initiating spawning typically occur in May. In small streams where growth is severely limited, Gila and Apache trout typically spawn for the first time at three years of age, at which point the slow-growing trout are only about 5 inches (13 cm) long. A 5-inch female spawns about 70 eggs, a 9-inch (23-cm) female about 300.

The maximum known age for Gila and Apache trout is six years, but few live beyond the age of four. No natural lakes occurred in the range of Gila and Apache trout throughout their evolutionary history, so there are no lake-adapted populations with specialized life histories for longer life spans and large maximum size, as is found in some populations of rainbow and cutthroat trout.

The small adult size of Gila and Apache trout is mainly a reflection of habitat and food limitations. Apache trout stocked in lakes constructed for recreation have attained weights of 5 pounds (2.3 kg). Yet the species' evolutionary heritage, which emphasizes survival in harsh and unstable environments, probably imposes limits on maximum size. Most likely, a 20-pound (9-kg) Apache or Gila trout will never occur, regardless of environment and food availability.

DISTRIBUTION   It is estimated that in the mid- to late nineteenth century about 600 miles (970 km) of streams were inhabited by each of the two subspecies, mostly at

Apache Trout

5–9"

elevations between about 6,000 to 9,000 feet (1,800–2,700 m). The 600 stream miles for Apache trout included the Black and White River drainages (headwaters of the Salt River) draining the western and southern parts of the White Mountains and a few high-elevation headwater tributaries of the Little Colorado River, draining from the White Mountains to the east. The 600 stream miles estimated for the original distribution of Gila trout included the upper Gila River drainage of New Mexico (the East, West, and Middle Forks of the Gila River), and parts of the San Francisco River, which enters the Gila River in eastern Arizona.

The only remaining pure population of Gila trout in the San Francisco drainage, isolated from nonnative trout above barrier falls in tiny Spruce Creek, is the most differentiated population of Gila trout,

indicating a long period of isolation from other populations.

A native trout also occurred in high-elevation tributaries to the Verde River, a tributary to the Salt River, south of Flagstaff, Arizona. All that is known of the Verde trout is based on a few faded museum specimens collected from Oak Creek Canyon in 1888 and 1889. The spotting pattern of the Oak Creek Canyon specimens indicates that they are Gila trout, but other characters are indicative of Apache trout. Gila and Apache trout may have come together in the Verde River during the last glacial period and hybridized to produce an intermediate form.

While the distribution of Gila and Apache trout 100 years ago is not known for certain, we do know that after 1900 the widespread introduction of brook, brown, and rainbow trout and loss of habitat due to livestock

APACHE TROUT

SCIENTIFIC NAME
Oncorhynchus gilae apache

OTHER COMMON NAMES
Arizona trout, yellow belly

HABITAT
Small, cool, relatively unstable streams; stocked in lakes

LENGTH AND WEIGHT
5–9" (13–23 cm) and 1–6 oz (28–170 g); maximum in lakes 5 lb (2.3 kg)

LIFE SPAN
Typically 4 years; maximum known 6 years

DIET
Aquatic and terrestrial invertebrates

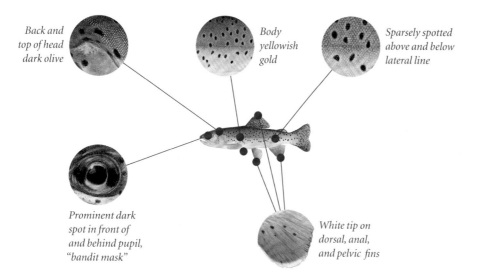

Back and top of head dark olive

Body yellowish gold

Sparsely spotted above and below lateral line

Prominent dark spot in front of and behind pupil, "bandit mask"

White tip on dorsal, anal, and pelvic fins

APACHE TROUT

grazing, logging, road construction, and diversion of water from streams have drastically affected their former native range.

In the second half of the twentieth century, the Gila and Apache trout were officially named and restoration efforts began. By that time, however, pure populations of Apache trout were restricted to a few small headwater streams that provided, in total, about 30 miles (50 km) of habitat. The remnant populations of Gila trout also inhabited about 30 total miles of stream. Thus, in stream miles, the distribution of both subspecies had diminished by about 95 percent to only 60 miles (100 km).

However, the loss of habitat and the associated loss in abundance of Gila and Apache trout was greater than 95 percent because the few refuge streams holding pure populations are very small headwater tributaries. In downstream areas, the streams increase in size and habitat volume. These larger streams are now inhabited mainly by brown trout, rainbow trout, and hybrid mixtures between rainbow trout and the two native subspecies.

When enhancement and restoration efforts began for Gila trout in the 1960s, Main Diamond Creek in New Mexico held the largest population, which consisted of about 4,000 fish, the largest measuring 9 inches (23 cm) long. Main Diamond Creek held more than half of all the pure Gila trout existing at the time. The rest were distributed among four other small streams that also contained pure populations. The high abundance of Gila trout in Main Diamond Creek was attributed to numerous pools formed by log dams constructed by Civilian Conservation Corps workers in the 1930s.

EVOLUTION AND CLASSIFICATION

Oncorhynchus gilae represents probably the earliest living branch of ancestral trout associated with the Gulf of California. During one of the earlier glacial periods, an ancestor from the Gulf of California moved into the Colorado River and ascended the Gila River basin of Arizona and New Mexico. A period of a colder, wetter climate allowed dispersal from the marine environment of the Gulf of California to the uppermost headwaters of the Gila River basin. It is speculated, based on degrees of differentiation, that invasion of the ancestral Gila and Apache trout in the Gila River basin may have occurred in mid-Pleistocene times or somewhat later—between 500,000 and 1 million years ago.

At a later time, a warmer, drier interglacial period greatly reduced the amount of habitat where trout could survive and resulted in the separation and long isolation of the ancestral trout into two groups. The group isolated in the Salt River segment of the Gila basin evolved into the Apache trout, and the group restricted to the upper Gila River drainage became the Gila trout.

Unlike terrestrial animals, fishes cannot leave their habitat and migrate over land to survive periods of drastic changes in climate. To survive the warmest, driest periods, trout must find a refuge area that has suitable habitat, mainly a sufficient supply of cold water to meet all their life history needs. During the most recent postglacial period the Apache trout found its refuge in the headwaters of the Salt River drainage of the White Mountains of east-central Arizona. The Gila trout found refuge in the various branches of the upper Gila River draining the Mogollon Mountains (pronounced mow-*guy*-yon) and the Black Range of west-central New Mexico. Elevations in the White Mountains occur to over 11,000

Apache Trout
HATCHERY BROOD STOCK

12–18"

feet (3,350 m), and the Mogollon Mountains attain a similar elevation.

During glacial epochs the range of freshwater and terrestrial organisms was reduced in northern regions. On the other hand, in southern regions, such as the Gila River basin and watersheds draining to the Gulf of California, the cooler, wetter climate of glacial periods allowed for range expansions, particularly in more cold-adapted species of fishes, such as trout. During interglacial periods, the range of species in the north expanded into regions once covered by ice, whereas in southern regions the range of cold-adapted species contracted to refuge areas in the mountains. This is exemplified by the Gila and Apache trout and other trout native to tributaries to the Gulf of California.

The short-term and long-term shifts in temperature and precipitation that took place during glacial and interglacial periods lasted from a few years or decades to hundreds of years. In addition to the long-term influences on the distribution and abundance of Apache and Gila trout, short-term effects have been observed. During a year or two with above-normal precipitation, a small stream may maintain trout habitat for 15 to 20 miles (24–32 km), whereas during droughts most of the 15 to 20 miles of streambed are dry. The trout that survive persist in pools maintained by spring-fed groundwater.

The Gila trout was named *"Salmo gilae"* in 1950 and the Apache trout *"S. apache"* in 1972. Since then, genetic analyses have demonstrated that the Gila trout is much more closely related to rainbow trout than it is to cutthroat trout. Analyses have also confirmed that the Apache and Gila trout are closely related to each other and are, in fact, subspecies within the same species. The recognition of the species *O. gilae* is a compromise between taxonomic "splitting" (treating both Gila and Apache trout as full species) and "lumping" (including both as subspecies of *O. mykiss*).

CONSERVATION   The great natural contraction of the range of the Gila and Apache trout pales in comparison to the "unnatural" contraction during the past 100 years, which has resulted from resource exploitation, water development, and, especially, the introduction of nonnative species of trout.

The rapid decline of Apache and Gila trout began about 100 years ago when introductions of nonnative brook, brown, and rainbow trout began. Gila and Apache trout

TROUT HABITAT IN THE DESERT

The lower elevations of the Gila River basin of Arizona and New Mexico are Sonoran Desert country. Suitable habitat for trout has not existed there for thousands of years. However, a transition occurs as one moves toward the mountain headwaters with their cooler climate and higher precipitation. Vegetation shifts from cactus and sage to mesquite, pinyon and juniper, oak, sycamore, and aspen that merge into conifer forests at the higher elevations. Especially in the White Mountains, high-elevation wet meadows called *cienegas* act as giant sponges that retain snow melt and rain, which are gradually released to feed cold water into the headwaters of trout streams. Streams of the Mogollon Rim and the Central Highlands of Arizona, such as the Iron, McKenna, and Spruce Creeks in the Gila Wilderness and the Main and South Diamond Creeks in the Aldo Leopold Wilderness, provide suitable habitat for the endangered Gila trout.

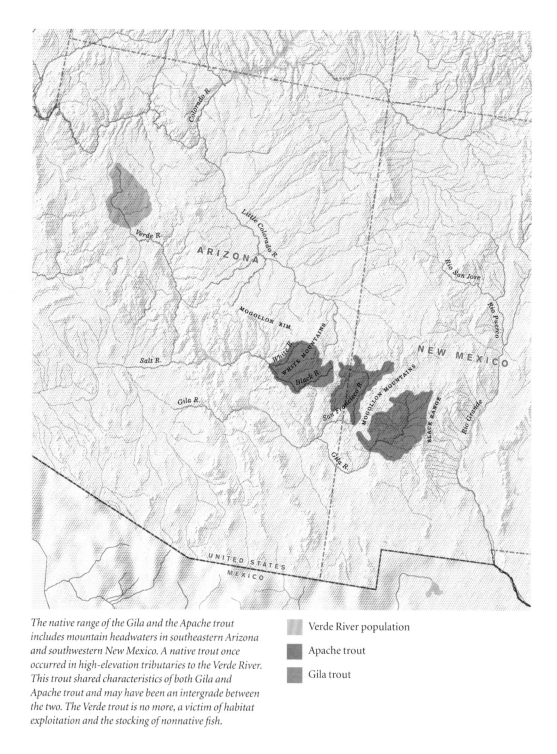

The native range of the Gila and the Apache trout includes mountain headwaters in southeastern Arizona and southwestern New Mexico. A native trout once occurred in high-elevation tributaries to the Verde River. This trout shared characteristics of both Gila and Apache trout and may have been an intergrade between the two. The Verde trout is no more, a victim of habitat exploitation and the stocking of nonnative fish.

Verde River population

Apache trout

Gila trout

hybridize with rainbow trout, which spawn at the same time and at the same sites as the native trout. There are no reproductive barriers, such as reduced fertility of hybrids. When hybridization begins it spreads throughout a population generation by generation, and pure populations of the native Gila and Apache trout are hybridized out of existence. This scenario has occurred throughout most of the original range of both subspecies.

Negative impacts on Gila and Apache trout from brown trout and brook trout are mainly due to competition for food and space. Fall-spawning brown and brook trout may have an advantage because their young have already emerged from the redds and have occupied territories by the time the Gila and Apache trout spawn in the spring.

Fall-spawning species are likely to also have an advantage over spring-spawning species in watersheds degraded by livestock grazing, logging, and roads, all of which greatly increase erosion and sediment input into streams during spring runoff. Sediment can fill redds and cause high or complete mortality of developing eggs.

Most of the original range of the Apache trout is on the Fort Apache Indian Reservation of the White Mountain Apache tribe. The reservation, about the size of Yellowstone National Park, is about 100 miles (160 km) from Phoenix, Arizona. All of the remnant pure populations of Apache trout (except one, in the Apache-Sitgreaves National Forest) once occurred on the Fort Apache reservation. The White Mountain Apache tribe long ago realized that a distinctive native trout was rapidly disappearing. In the 1940s they began closing streams to angling that contained Apache trout.

In the 1960s artificial propagation began at the Alchesay and Williams Creek National Fish Hatcheries on the Fort Apache reservation. By the 1990s about 500,000 Apache trout were being produced annually by the hatcheries for stocking lakes constructed on the reservation, a popular recreation area for camping and fishing. About half of the hatchery production is fingerling fish, and about half are stocked at the catchable size of 8 inches (20 cm) or larger. The White Mountain Apache tribe derives considerable economic benefits from its recreational programs, and the Apache trout is now an integral part of the attractions.

The Apache trout is listed as threatened under the Endangered Species Act. Regulated angling is permitted for fishes in the threatened category, but not if the fish is listed as endangered, as is the case with the Gila trout.

Many restoration projects for these trout have occurred over the past 35 years. Restoration consists of chemically treating a small stream above a barrier to eliminate all nonnative trout and then introducing pure Gila or Apache trout to start a new population. Several restored populations of Apache trout exist on the Fort Apache reservation and on National Forest lands. Restoration of Gila trout was progressing according to plan, and in 1989 a change in status from endangered to threatened was considered. However, in that same year, a series of natural disasters hit much of the range of the natural and restored populations. A prolonged drought was followed by fire and subsequent heavy rains that caused floods to wash ash and debris from fire into streams. The result was a significant loss of Gila trout, which resulted in the subspecies retaining its endangered status.

Mexican Golden Trout
Oncorhynchus chrysogaster

Mexican Golden Trout
SPAWNING MALE

5–10"

Found only in the highest elevations of the Sierra Madre Occidental, the Mexican golden trout is the only formally described salmonid south of the U.S.–Mexico border. The recognition of the Mexican golden as a full species, as with the Gila and Apache trout, is a judgment call based on the degree of differentiation from all other rainbow trout species. Whether considered a distinct species or not, its isolated habitat, primitive lineage, and particular beauty make it one of the more fascinating members of the family Salmonidae.

DESCRIPTION The scientific name *chryso-gaster* means "golden belly." It is an accurate descriptive name for the Mexican golden trout because the yellowish coloration on the sides of the body intensifies to golden orange along the ventral region of the body. The Mexican golden trout's fins also are yellow or orange. The pelvic, anal, and dorsal fins have lighter-colored leading edges, and the dorsal fin has a yellow to orange tip.

In the Mexican golden trout, the greatest differentiation from all other rainbow trout species is found in meristic (countable) characteristics, such as number of scales, fin rays, and pyloric caeca. The average number of vertebrae and the average number of pyloric caeca are lower in Mexican golden trout than those found in any form of rainbow or cutthroat trout. The average number of vertebrae counted in more than 100 specimens from several populations of Mexican golden trout is about 57 to 58, as

MEXICAN GOLDEN TROUT

SCIENTIFIC NAME
Oncorhynchus chrysogaster

OTHER COMMON NAMES
None known

HABITAT
Small headwater streams

LENGTH AND WEIGHT
5–7" (13–18 cm) and 3 oz (85 g); maximum 9–10" (23–25 cm) and 6–7 oz (170–198 g)

LIFE SPAN
Probably 4–6 years

DIET
Aquatic and terrestrial invertebrates

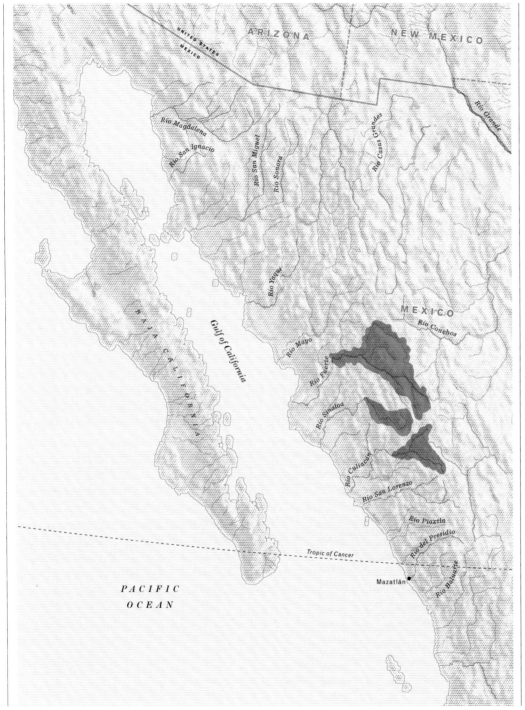

compared with the lowest average number of vertebrae in *Oncorhynchus mykiss* (59–60), found in South Fork Kern and Golden Trout Creek golden trout (*O. m. aguabonita*). The highest average number of vertebrae, 64 or 65, is found in Columbia River redband and the trout native to the Río del Presidio drainage.

The number of pyloric caeca in Mexican golden trout ranges from 10 to 30, averaging from 21 to 23 among several populations. Pyloric caeca number in all subspecies of both rainbow trout and cutthroat trout is variable but none have such low numbers as found in Mexican golden trout.

The total number of chromosomes (the karyotype) of the Mexican golden trout is 60 (versus 56 in the Gila and Apache trout, and 64 in Río Mayo and Río Yaqui trout). Such diversity of karyotypes attests to the ancestral diversity that must have occurred at various times in the Gulf of California; one of these ancestors became the present-day Mexican golden trout.

BIOLOGY   There are no indications that Mexican golden trout utilize habitat differently than other species of trout, and although no life history studies have been conducted on Mexican golden trout, it is unlikely that they have unique attributes distinct from other species of trout. The Mexican golden trout spawns in the spring.

Mexican golden trout live in the higher-elevation headwaters of the Río Fuerte, Río Sinaloa, and Río Culiacán drainages, from about 6,000 to 9,000 feet (1,800–2,700 m).

Mexican Golden Trout
FEMALE

5–10"

Probably similar to Gila and Apache trout, spawning would be initiated when daily water temperatures reach 46 to 47 °F (8 °C). Because of the southern distribution of this species, this temperature might be attained as early as January or February at lower elevations and as late as March and April at higher elevations.

Most Mexican golden trout exist as slow-growing populations inhabiting small streams under a harsh and highly fluctuating environmental regime. The fish mature sexually and spawn first when they are 5 to 7 inches (13–18 cm) long. In its typical small-stream habitat, the species' maximum size is about 9 or 10 inches (23–25 cm). It is believed that these trout live for four to six years.

There are no natural lakes in the range of the Mexican golden trout, so no lake-adapted life histories have evolved. Reservoirs have been constructed in the range of the Mexican golden trout, but there are no published reports of Mexican golden trout growing to a large size in these reservoirs. As with Apache trout, however, it is likely that Mexican golden trout, given optimal environmental conditions and an abundant food supply, could grow to a size severalfold greater than that imposed by the limitations of the harsh environment they inhabit.

DISTRIBUTION   The highest elevations of the Sierra Madre Occidental form a plateau interspersed with ridges that allow snow and rain to collect and supply flow to the

headwaters of tributaries to the Gulf of California. Tributary networks come together to form larger rivers that have cut deep canyons through the mountains as they descend to lower elevations. Except for the highest elevations that receive more precipitation, especially in the form of snow, the watersheds draining the Sierra Madre Occidental are set in an arid landscape subjected to extremes of flood and drought, similar to the habitat of Gila and Apache trout.

Mexican golden trout live in the higher-elevation headwaters of the Río Fuerte, Río Sinaloa, and Río Culiacán drainages, from about 6,000 to 9,000 feet (1,800–2,700 m). The headwaters of all three rivers drain from Mount Mohinora, the highest elevation

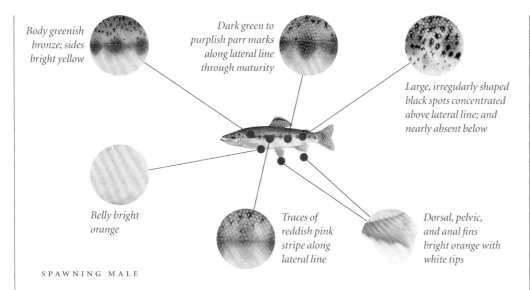

Body greenish
bronze; sides
bright yellow

Dark green to
purplish parr marks
along lateral line
through maturity

Large, irregularly shaped
black spots concentrated
above lateral line; and
nearly absent below

Belly bright
orange

Traces of
reddish pink
stripe along
lateral line

Dorsal, pelvic,
and anal fins
bright orange with
white tips

SPAWNING MALE

in the Sierra Madre Occidental range, at 10,984 feet (3,350 m). Currently there are no estimates as to the amount of habitat inhabited by Mexican golden trout.

The close similarity among populations of Mexican golden trout in the three drainages and the close proximity of their headwaters suggest that headwater transfers of trout have occurred among the drainages as a result of natural events such as lava flows and landslides. If, on the other hand, the populations of each river drainage were isolated from each other since their common ancestor became established, perhaps about 500,000 years ago or so, considerable evolutionary differentiation into three distinct groups, comparable to the divergence of Apache trout and Gila trout in the Gila River basin, would be expected. However, populations of the Mexican golden trout throughout its range in the three river drainages appear to be quite uniform, with little intraspecific variation. This indicates that they have

not been isolated from contact with each other for a long period of time—perhaps only since the end of the last glacial period (about 10,000–12,000 years ago), when a warmer climate prevailed forcing the trout into headwater refugia where water temperatures were colder.

It is also possible that movement from river mouth to river mouth occurred during the last glacial period. This scenario, which requires movement in the Gulf of California, must assume that the Mexican golden trout had retained the capability to osmoregulate in marine waters.

EVOLUTION AND CLASSIFICATION

The first published account of trout in Mexico was in 1886, when a short note by E.D. Cope appeared in the journal *American Naturalist* entitled "The most southern salmon." The note mentions that a Professor Lupton collected and preserved two small specimens from streams at an elevation of

7,000 to 8,000 feet (2,100–2,400 m) in the "southern part of the state of Chihuahua near the boundaries of Durango and Sinaloa." The specimens had "…teeth on the basihyal bone, as in *Salmo purpuratus,* which they otherwise resemble." ("*Salmo purpuratus*" was the name then used for the cutthroat trout species now called *Oncorhynchus clarki.*) "Basihyal teeth" probably refers to what we now call basibranchial teeth.

Some salmonid species, such as cutthroat trout, are characterized by small teeth on the basibranchial plate, a thin bony structure that lies between the gill arches. Typically rainbow trout lack basibranchial teeth, but they do occur in some populations of redband trout. Basibranchial teeth have been found, at very low frequencies, in some populations of Gila and Apache trout but in no other trout associated with the Gulf of California, including the Mexican golden trout. The two specimens collected by Lupton evidently were lost and their identification as cutthroat trout could not be verified or refuted.

The naturalist E.W. Nelson reported in 1906 that in 1898 he observed trout in a small stream draining the slopes of Mount Mohinora. This stream visited by Nelson was in the Río Sinaloa drainage, and the trout he observed would have been Mexican golden trout. Perhaps the two specimens collected by Professor Lupton were Mexican golden trout from either the Río Sinaloa or Río Verde drainage.

The precise locations of these collections of fish are unknown, but there is an intriguing possibility that the trout came from the headwaters of the Río Conchos, part of the Rio Grande basin. If so, there is a possibility that the fish were cutthroat trout, never known to exist in Mexico. However, no trout of any kind have been collected in the Río Conchos, so this first published record of Mexican trout remains a mystery.

Paul R. Needham of the University of California, Berkeley, conducted field trips to collect specimens from various Mexican drainages during the 1950s. This work led to a 1964 publication in the journal *Copeia* by Needham and Richard Gard describing the Mexican golden trout as a new species, *"Salmo chrysogaster"* (now *Oncorhynchus chrysogaster*).

CONSERVATION   The human population increase in Mexico during the past 50 years has negatively affected the Gulf of California watershed through increases in exploitation of natural resources, erosion and sediment input, and pollution from towns and villages. The virtually inaccessible canyon areas that all of the rivers pass through should create refuge areas where Mexican golden trout are protected from overexploitation and the human impacts that occur in upstream areas.

The greatest threat, as observed in the great declines in distribution and abundance of Gila and Apache trout, is the introduction of nonnative trout, especially hatchery rainbow trout, which almost certainly would hybridize with Mexican golden trout if they occurred together. According to Dean Hendrickson of the University of Texas, there are now a number of trout hatcheries in the Río Fuerte basin. It is not known if these hatchery trout have been stocked in streams with Mexican golden trout. There are also small reservoirs and private lands where the stocking of hatchery rainbow trout might seem to be an attractive proposition, and many hatcheries throughout Mexico raise rainbow trout. The highest priority of any program to protect Mexican golden trout should be preventing the establishment of rainbow trout in the Fuerte, Sinaloa, and Culiacán drainages.

Cutthroat Trout
Oncorhynchus clarki

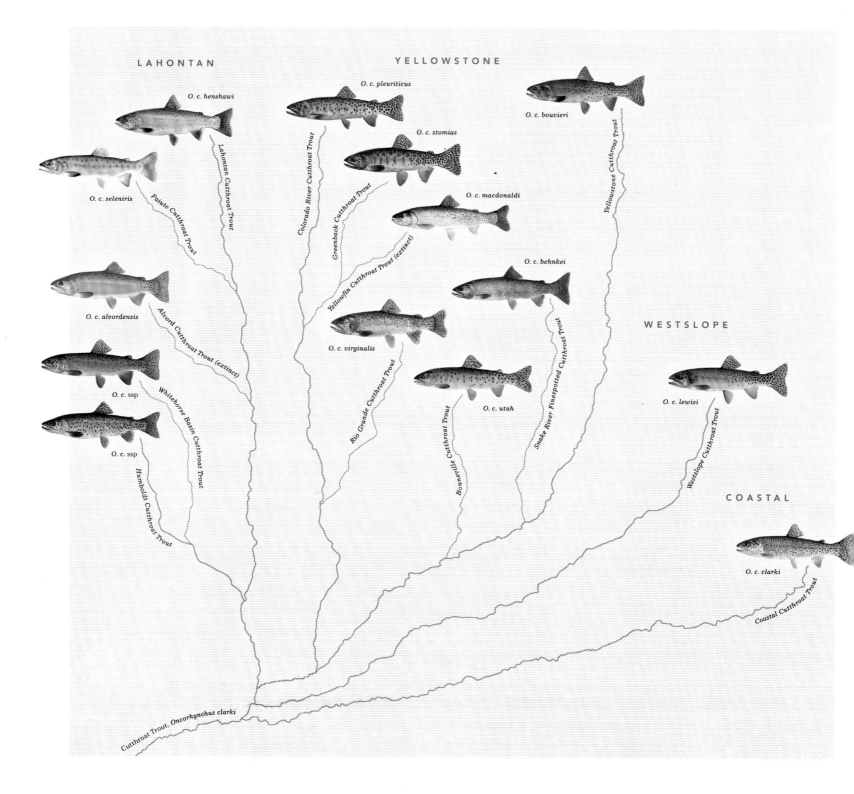

LAHONTAN

YELLOWSTONE

WESTSLOPE

COASTAL

O. c. henshawi

O. c. pleuriticus

O. c. bouvieri

O. c. seleniris

O. c. stomias

O. c. macdonaldi

O. c. alvordensis

O. c. behnkei

O. c. lewisi

O. c. virginalis

O. c. ssp

O. c. utah

O. c. clarki

O. c. ssp

Lahontan Cutthroat Trout

Paiute Cutthroat Trout

Colorado River Cutthroat Trout

Greenback Cutthroat Trout

Yellowfin Cutthroat Trout (extinct)

Yellowstone Cutthroat Trout

Alvord Cutthroat Trout (extinct)

Whitehorse Basin Cutthroat Trout

Rio Grande Cutthroat Trout

Bonneville Cutthroat Trout

Snake River Finespotted Cutthroat Trout

Westslope Cutthroat Trout

Humboldt Cutthroat Trout

Coastal Cutthroat Trout

Cutthroat Trout, *Oncorhynchus clarki*

The cutthroat trout was the first North American trout recorded by Europeans. In 1541, Francisco de Coronado's expedition in search of a mythical city of gold came across the Rio Grande cutthroat trout in the upper Pecos River, south of present-day Santa Fe, New Mexico. The cutthroat trout was also the first trout encountered by the Lewis and Clark expedition, who recorded the westslope cutthroat trout in 1805 below the Great Falls of the Missouri River. Subsequently the westslope cutthroat earned the name *Oncorhynchus clarki lewisi* in honor of both Meriwether Lewis and William Clark.

Compared with that of the rainbow trout, diversity in the cutthroat trout is more neatly segregated by the geographical boundaries of river basins that isolate subspecies. Such isolation, which eliminates the areas of overlap and transition found among subspecies of rainbow trout, allows for clearer definition of cutthroat trout subspecies.

Cutthroat trout subspecies diversity can be traced to four major evolutionary divergences, ancestral lines that have been separated from each other for up to 1 million years. These four lines have, in turn, given rise to four major subspecies. Two of these have given rise to additional subspecies. In all, this book recognizes 14 cutthroat subspecies, of which two are unnamed and two extinct.

DESCRIPTION In cutthroat trout, the cutthroat mark beneath the jaws is an intense color and is typically bright red, whereas in rainbow trout populations that exhibit a cutthroat mark, such as some redband trout, it is a more subdued yellow or orange.

However, because of the great range of diversity found in both cutthroat trout and rainbow trout, no single character except molecular genetic markers can positively distinguish all cutthroat trout from all rainbow trout.

In pure populations of cutthroat trout, at least 90 percent of specimens have basibranchial teeth—minute teeth that exist in the base of the throat between the gill arches and are not readily detected by the naked eye. In rainbow trout, the occurrence of basibranchial teeth is sporadic; when these teeth are present in a population of rainbow trout, it is extremely rare to find them in more than 10 percent of specimens. Thus the presence or absence of basibranchial teeth is not an absolute trait for distinguishing all cutthroat trout from all rainbow trout.

There is only a slight overlap between the cutthroat trout and the rainbow trout in chromosome numbers. In cutthroat trout, chromosome numbers vary from 64 to 68. In rainbow trout, the most common numbers are 58 to 60, but a few populations of coastal rainbow trout of northern California and the undescribed subspecies of rainbow trout in the Río Yaqui and Río Mayo, in Mexico, have 64 chromosomes.

A characteristic that works well to identify inland subspecies of cutthroat trout (but not coastal cutthroat trout) from all forms of rainbow trout and from cutthroat × rainbow trout hybrids is the presence or absence of spots on the top of the head. In the rainbow trout and hybrids, the top of the head is heavily spotted. Inland subspecies of cutthroat trout have no spots or only minute black specks on the top of the head.

This phylogenetic "map" shows the four major groups of cutthroat trout: coastal, westslope, Yellowstone, and Lahontan. The Yellowstone group has the most diversity, with seven derived subspecies, one of which is extinct. The Lahontan group consists of five subspecies, including one that is extinct. All cutthroat trout share a common ancestor, which branched off from rainbow trout at the end of the Pliocene epoch, about 2 million years ago.

Rio Grande Cutthroat Trout
Oncorhynchus clarki virginalis

Pedro de Castaneda of Najara, a member of the 1541 Coronado expedition into southwestern North America, recorded: "There is a little stream which contains very good trout and otters, and there are very large bears and good falcons hereabouts." The little stream, a tributary to the Pecos River, was filled with Rio Grande cutthroat trout. These handsome fish were the first North American trout encountered by Europeans.

Compared with rainbow trout, cutthroat trout typically have more scales along the sides of the body, and they express brighter coloration. These traits are effective in separating cutthroat trout from coastal rainbow trout (and hatchery rainbow trout), but the scale counts and the coloration of Columbia River redband trout and several subspecies of Sacramento basin redband trout can be confused with those of cutthroat trout. There is a long history of misidentification of Columbia and Sacramento basin redband and rainbow trout as cutthroat trout.

Some subspecies of cutthroat trout can develop brilliant colorations of golden yellow and crimson red. There is a hereditary basis for the expression of color, but the intensity of the expression is influenced by gender, degree of maturity, and diet. For example, greenback cutthroat trout from a small stream in Colorado were introduced into Bear Lake in Rocky Mountain National Park as part of the recovery program for this rare subspecies. The greenback cutthroat in their small stream had rather somber hues of pink and yellowish brown. Fish from this population transplanted into Bear Lake fed on crustaceans containing carotenoid pigments. This change in their diet resulted in intense coloration, especially in mature males, whose ventral region became suffused with brilliant crimson. These Bear Lake greenback cutthroat could easily be mistaken for the most gaudily colored Arctic char.

BIOLOGY The most significant aspect of cutthroat trout life history, ecology, and biology that can be offered to explain their great decline in distribution and abundance concerns the cutthroat trout's susceptibility to hybridization with rainbow trout and to replacement by brown trout and brook trout in streams and by lake trout in large lakes.

Both rainbow and cutthroat trout spawn in the spring. They respond identically to environmental cues that lead to spawning, and the two species utilize similar spawning habitat. Thus when rainbow trout are introduced into a population of cutthroat trout, hybridization almost always occurs.

An exception to this is found in coastal cutthroat trout and part of the westslope cutthroat subspecies, both of which coevolved with rainbow trout and maintain reproductive isolation. The barrier to hybridization in these subspecies has nothing to do with the sterility of hybrids, as they are fully fertile. Instead, in the river basins where the two species have coexisted and coevolved for thousands of years they have evolved differences in their selection of spawning sites and habitat that result in segregation. The cutthroat trout spawn in small headwater tributaries, and rainbow trout spawn in larger streams.

This reproductive isolation often breaks down with the introduction of hatchery rainbow trout, which have life histories and spawning site preferences similar to those of the native cutthroat trout. For example, in the Salmon and Clearwater River drainages of Idaho, the native redband trout has the seagoing steelhead life history. Large steelhead spawn in the main river and in the larger tributaries and are completely segregated from the native cutthroat. From spawning to adulthood, the two species have evolved life history differences that maintain segregation. The native steelhead typically spend two years in rivers before smolting and migrating to the ocean, and the native cutthroat are virtually never found in the same habitat at the same time with juvenile steelhead. Their coevolved life histories not only maintain reproductive isolation but also avoid competition. However, when hatchery rainbow trout are stocked, they spend their whole life in fresh water and will likely hybridize with the cutthroat trout. Thus, even in areas where rainbow trout and cutthroat trout have coevolved and maintain reproductive isolation, the introduction of hatchery rainbow trout has caused serious hybridization problems.

Although hybridization between introduced rainbow trout and native cutthroat trout is the major cause of the decline of all subspecies of cutthroat trout, including the extinction of two subspecies, the hybrids can be popular sport fish. They can attain a large size and are excellent fish to catch on a hook and line. Ashley Lake, near Kalispell, Montana, originally had a native cutthroat trout, the westslope cutthroat. Many years of stocking nonnative rainbow trout and nonnative Yellowstone cutthroat trout predictably resulted in hybridization. Ashley Lake has become noted for the large trout it produces. Genetic analysis of tissue from a 30-pound (13.6-kg) angler-caught trout from Ashley Lake revealed its diverse ancestry: part native trout (the westslope subspecies), part rainbow trout, and part Yellowstone cutthroat trout. There are no hybrid sterility barriers among these hybrids, so once hybridization begins, the native cutthroat population is lost.

Cutthroat trout are spring spawners, spawning during rising water temperatures and increasing daylight hours. In the moderate climate along the Pacific Coast spawning can peak in February and March, while in the coldest inland waters at high elevation spawning is delayed until June or July. The cutthroat trout can be considered as an almost obligatory stream spawner, but it can reproduce successfully in lakes where

Westslope Cutthroat Trout
Oncorhynchus clarki lewisi

Bull Trout
Salvelinus confluentus

Northern Pikeminnow
Ptychocheilus oregonensis

The westslope cutthroat trout rarely preys on fishes. Its coevolution in the upper Columbia River basin with another salmonid predator, the bull trout, and a large species of minnow, the northern pikeminnow, likely influenced its feeding habits in the course of evolutionary programming. Westslope cutthroat trout thrived because it specialized in consuming invertebrates.

there are suitable gravel beds and adequate water circulation. The deciding factor for successful reproduction is the amount of dissolved oxygen in the water surrounding the developing eggs. The oxygen demand of the embryo is highest as the time of hatching draws near. About 6 to 8 parts per million of oxygen in the water surrounding the eggs should ensure a high percentage of hatch.

Depending on temperature, it takes about four to five weeks from fertilization for the eggs to hatch, and about another three weeks for the juvenile trout to emerge from the gravel of the redd. There is often high mortality during this period; survival of 50 percent or more from spawning to emergence indicates good spawning habitat and good water quality. In watersheds exposed to high erosion, such as clear-cut areas with logging roads, a storm can overburden streams with high sediment loads that clog the gravel of a trout redd, reducing water circulation and oxygen content. The sediment can also be a barrier to emergence of the newly hatched trout.

Compared to other trout of the genera *Oncorhynchus* and *Salmo,* cutthroat prefer colder water, but spawning temperatures and incubation times, as influenced by water temperature, are similar for all species.

The cutthroat trout is the species most often stocked in the coldest high-elevation lakes in western states. In these cold environments, spawning temperatures of about 43 to 46 °F (6–8 °C) may not be reached until July, and continuing cold water prolongs incubation and delays emergence time until well into September. By then, winter-like conditions have arrived, and the baby trout do not have the time to feed and accumulate sufficient energy to survive the long period under ice cover. In such situations, even with optimal spawning habitat, the stocked trout may survive for many years but leave no surviving offspring.

As with other trout species, cutthroat trout living their whole lives in small streams rarely reach more than 10 inches (25 cm) in length. Under these conditions, sexual maturity and first spawning occur at age two or three, and the trout typically survive for only three or four years. Maximum age to ten years has been reported in some populations of sea-run coastal cutthroat trout and in some lake populations of other subspecies. The maximum age can be greatly extended when cutthroat trout are stocked in the coldest lakes, which are at high elevations and have a short growing season. In such lakes, where the ice-free season is only 60 to 90 days, life span can be extended to about 20 years. This is because long periods of cold temperatures result in a lower metabolic rate and the fish therefore use less energy over the course of their lives, which extends their life span considerably.

Growth and maximum size are also influenced by heredity, habitat type, food availability, and life span. The largest of all cutthroat trout, and perhaps the largest North American trout, the Lahontan cutthroat trout of Pyramid Lake, Nevada, was specialized (before it was extirpated there) to feed on the abundant forage fish of the lake, the tui chub. Likewise the Bonneville cutthroat trout, native to Bear Lake, in Utah and Idaho, is a specialized predator on sculpins and whitefishes.

The feeding habits of most cutthroat trout are no different than those of other species of trout living in similar habitat. They mainly consume whatever invertebrate prey is available. Coastal cutthroat trout living in rivers with spawning runs of species of Pacific salmon will opportunistically take advantage of seasonal bonanzas of prey when great numbers of juvenile salmon are migrating to the ocean.

As a general rule, cutthroat trout prey more on fishes than do rainbow trout. The westslope cutthroat trout, however, rarely preys on fishes. Its coevolution in the upper Columbia River basin with another salmonid predator, the bull trout, and a large species of minnow, the northern pikeminnow, likely influenced its feeding habits in the course of evolutionary programming. Westslope cutthroat trout thrived in waters among fish-hungry species because it specialized in consuming invertebrates.

An historical example demonstrating this dietary habit of westslope cutthroat is found in the stocking of a nonnative fish into Lake Pend Oreille, in Idaho, where westslope cutthroat trout and bull trout are the native trout species. After the landlocked form of sockeye salmon, called kokanee, was introduced and became abundant in the lake, the world-record bull trout of 32 pounds (14.5 kg) was caught in 1949. The introduced kokanee obviously became a primary food source for the highly predatory bull trout. Also in the 1940s, during the peak of kokanee abundance, Kamloops rainbow trout from Kootenay Lake, in British Columbia, a specialized predator on kokanee in its native lake, was introduced to Lake Pend Oreille and attained weights to 32 pounds (14.5 kg) four years after stocking and to 37 pounds (16.8 kg) after five years. During this period no larger than normal westslope cutthroat trout occurred (a large normal specimen is about 2 pounds/1 kg), indicating that the westslope cutthroat trout had made no use of the abundant new source of protein in their native lake.

DISTRIBUTION The original distribution of cutthroat trout is greater than for any other salmonid species in North America with the exception of the lake trout. Although the distribution of the rainbow trout extends farther north and farther south, cutthroat trout ancestors had dispersed inland in the Columbia River basin before barriers formed that blocked greater inland access for the later-invading rainbow trout. Cutthroat trout dispersed even farther eastward, crossing the Continental Divide and establishing subspecies in upper sections of the South Saskatchewan, Missouri, South Platte, Arkansas, and Rio Grande River basins.

There is still some confusion surrounding the southernmost distribution of cutthroat trout. An 1875 report of cutthroat trout in Arizona was actually based on Apache trout, as discussed in the account on the Gila and Apache trout (page 123). An 1886 report of cutthroat trout in Mexico is likely another case of mistaken identity—probably based on observation of Mexican golden trout, as discussed in the account on trout native to the Gulf of California (page 115). These two reports on the southernmost

With the exception of lake trout, the original distribution of cutthroat trout is greater than that of any other form of North American trout or salmon.

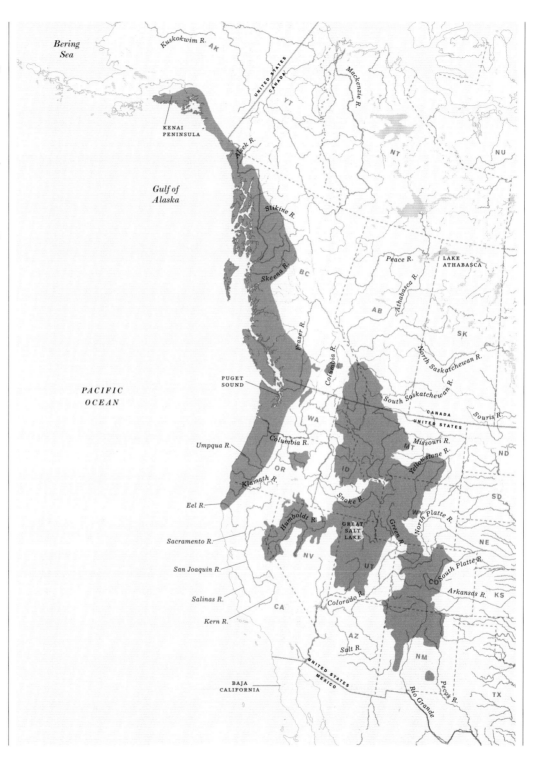

distribution of cutthroat trout were repeated in Jordan and Evermann's classic work *The Fishes of North and Middle America* (1896–98), the authority in its time on fish classification and distribution. The errors became incorporated into the popular literature on trout and persisted for some time. In fact, a popular two-volume book entitled *Trout* (second edition published in 1984) states that the distribution of cutthroat trout extends to the Sierra Madre Occidental of Mexico.

An apparently authentic Civil War account claimed that trout occurred in streams of the Davis Mountains of western Texas, in Jeff Davis County. It is likely that in the 1860s the watersheds at higher elevations in western Texas (about 4,000–5,000 feet / 1,200–1,500 m) were in a pristine condition and maintained flows of cool water suitable for Rio Grande cutthroat trout. If so, the Davis Mountains of western Texas would be the actual southernmost historical distribution of cutthroat trout.

In any event, cutthroat trout in Texas are long gone. Similarly, the cutthroat have disappeared from sites reported in early records, such as the Pecos River, noted by members of Coronado's expedition in 1541, or below the Great Falls of the Missouri River, where Lewis and Clark first encountered cutthroat trout. Only nonnative brown trout and rainbow trout are found there today.

An idea of the greatly diminished range of the cutthroat trout can be gained by a look at what has happened in the "type localities," the sites that produced the type specimens for the original descriptions of the presently recognized subspecies.

The Lahontan cutthroat trout was named "*Salmo henshawi*" in 1872, based on a specimen from Lake Tahoe. By 1940, cutthroat trout were extirpated in Lake Tahoe because of the blockage of spawning tributaries and an introduced predator, the lake trout. The Truckee River drains from Lake Tahoe into Pyramid Lake, which produced the largest cutthroat trout in the world and perhaps the largest trout native to North America, including the official angling record of 41 pounds (18.6 kg) and unauthenticated reports from tribal commercial fisheries of fish weighing to 62 pounds (28 kg). An irrigation diversion dam blocked access to spawning grounds in the Truckee River, the only spawning tributary to Pyramid Lake, and the cutthroat trout of Pyramid Lake was extinct by 1940.

The subspecies name *bouvieri,* now designating the Yellowstone cutthroat trout, named in 1883, was based on specimens from Waha Lake, Idaho. The cutthroat trout native to Waha Lake have been extinct for some 70 years or more due to the introduction of nonnative fishes. "*Salmo utah*" (*utah* is now the subspecies name for the Bonneville cutthroat trout) was used for the name of the cutthroat trout of Utah Lake in 1874. The native cutthroat trout of Utah Lake, where in the 1860s a commercial fisherman claimed to have taken more than 3,000 pounds (1,360 kg) of trout in a single haul of his net, has been extinct since the 1930s as a result of diversion of inflow that radically degraded the water quality of the lake. Utah Lake is now dominated by nonnative warm-water fishes.

In 1891, the yellowfin cutthroat trout was named from Twin Lakes, Colorado.

A collection of fishes from Twin Lakes in 1903 failed to find the yellowfin trout. About half of the 1903 collection of greenback cutthroat trout, which coexisted with yellowfin trout in Twin Lakes, were hybridized with rainbow trout. By 1903, the nonnative rainbow trout was the dominant trout of Twin Lakes; the yellowfin cutthroat was extinct and the greenback cutthroat was gone from Twin Lakes soon after. Because the yellowfin cutthroat trout was found only in Twin Lakes, the whole subspecies became extinct. The greenback cutthroat trout persisted in the upper Arkansas and South Platte River drainages, but by the 1930s it was so rare it was believed to be extinct. (The coexistence of two subspecies of cutthroat trout in Twin Lakes and of the typical largespotted cutthroat trout in the upper Snake River drainage of Idaho and Wyoming are exceptions to the rule of the geographical isolation of cutthroat trout subspecies; this is discussed in more detail in individual accounts.)

Rainbow trout were originally absent throughout most of the range of the cutthroat trout. However, the coastal cutthroat trout coexists and coevolved with the coastal rainbow trout throughout its range from northern California to southern Alaska. Also, while rainbow trout are not native to most of the range of the westslope cutthroat trout in Idaho and Montana, the westslope cutthroat has an evolutionary history of coexistence with interior Columbia River basin redband trout in the John Day River drainage of Oregon, the Salmon and Clearwater drainages of Idaho, and the Yakima, Wenatchee, and Methow River drainages of Washington.

Coevolution between rainbow and cutthroat trout implies a high degree of reproductive isolation between the two species; otherwise they could not maintain their species identity. In most of the range of the cutthroat trout, rainbow trout were absent, and reproductive isolating mechanisms did not evolve. When hatchery rainbow trout are introduced into these cutthroat trout populations hybridization almost always occurs, with eventual loss of the native cutthroat. This can be observed in the best-known trout streams of the West, such as the upper Colorado, South Platte, and Gunnison Rivers of Colorado, and the Madison and Bighorn Rivers of Montana, where anglers now fish for nonnative brown trout and rainbow trout, but where the cutthroat trout, now long gone, is the only native trout.

Unlike the rainbow trout, which has been introduced and established in cold-water habitats all over the world, cutthroat trout have rarely become established outside of their native range. However, anglers and backpackers are familiar with cutthroat trout in many high-elevation lakes in the western United States. Almost all of these mountain lakes, which have barriers in their outlets that block natural upstream dispersal, were originally devoid of fish. The cutthroat trout now in these lakes have been introduced, formerly by pack trains of horses and mules, and more recently by aerial stocking.

EVOLUTION AND CLASSIFICATION

The cutthroat trout species has ancient roots and began divergences leading to the present diversity of subspecies perhaps 1 million years ago. The earliest divergences resulting

Coastal Cutthroat Trout
Oncorhynchus clarki clarki

Cutthroat diversity can be traced to four evolutionary divergences. These ancestral lines have remained separated from each other for up to 1 million years.

Westslope Cutthroat Trout
Oncorhynchus clarki lewisi

Lahontan Cutthroat Trout
Oncorhynchus clarki henshawi

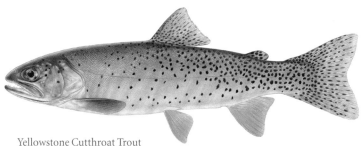

Yellowstone Cutthroat Trout
Oncorhynchus clarki bouvieri

in the four major subspecies (the most ancient evolutionary lineages) are connected to geographic isolation and reduction in the number of chromosomes.

Coastal cutthroat trout have 68 chromosomes. It can be hypothesized that a change to 66 chromosomes occurred in the interior Columbia River basin, east of the Cascade Range. The 66-chromosome group persisted in the northern part of the Columbia basin, becoming the westslope cutthroat trout. In the southern segment of the Columbia basin, probably in the Snake River system, the chromosome number changed to 64. The ancestor with 64 chromosomes soon separated, with one branch gaining access to the Lahontan basin of the Great Basin and evolving into the Lahontan cutthroat trout, and the other remaining in the Snake River system and becoming the Yellowstone cutthroat trout. Although the transfer of trout from the Snake River drainage—across the Continental Divide into the Yellowstone River drainage—occurred only about 6,000 years ago, after the glacial ice left the Yellowstone Plateau, the cutthroat trout of Yellowstone Lake became famous with anglers and in fish culture, and the common name Yellowstone cutthroat trout is used for the subspecies as a whole. (In the older literature, the name Yellowstone cutthroat trout was commonly applied to all of the interior subspecies of cutthroat trout.)

Similarly, the westslope cutthroat trout also crossed the Continental Divide in postglacial times to become established in the headwaters of the South Saskatchewan and Missouri River basins. Thus, even though there are native eastern-slope populations of westslope cutthroat trout, as with the common name of Yellowstone cutthroat, the use of the name westslope cutthroat trout has become well established. The antiquity of the ancestral divergences resulting in the four major subspecies—the coastal, westslope, Lahontan, and Yellowstone cutthroat trout—can be gauged by cutthroat trout fossils more than 600,000 years old found in the Lahontan basin.

The 68-chromosome and 66-chromosome evolutionary lineages each have only one subspecies—the coastal cutthroat trout and the westslope cutthroat trout, respectively. The 10 "minor" subspecies, all with 64 chromosomes, have their origins within about the last 100,000 years. Four of the minor subspecies are derived from the Lahontan cutthroat trout, and six are derived from the Yellowstone cutthroat trout.

As might be expected from the great range of diversity found in the cutthroat trout, which often overlaps with the many forms of rainbow trout, early attempts to classify cutthroat trout were chaotic. Returning to the often-cited 1896 publication of Jordan and Evermann, all western trout were classified in the genus *Salmo;* the cutthroat species was "*S. mykiss,*" under the mistaken belief that the Kamchatkan trout, named "*S. mykiss*" in 1792, was a cutthroat trout. After recognizing that Kamchatkan trout were not cutthroat trout, in 1898 Jordan and Evermann classified the cutthroat trout species as "*S. clarki,*" the first name proposed for any member of the species in 1836. The name *clarki* is based on the coastal cutthroat trout; thus when the species is divided into subspecies the coastal cutthroat becomes *Oncorhynchus clarki clarki* because this subspecies is the "type" (first described) of the species.

In 1896, besides the coastal cutthroat trout, Jordan and Evermann recognized the following eight subspecies of cutthroat trout:

1. "*lewisi,*" which then included both the present westslope cutthroat and the Yellowstone cutthroat

2. "*gibbsi,*" which was based on an inland redband trout of the mid–Columbia River basin, now classified as *O. mykiss gairdneri*

3. *henshawi,* the Lahontan cutthroat trout

4. "*virginalis,*" mistakenly used for the Bonneville cutthroat trout (it was later learned that the type specimen for the name *virginalis* came from the Rio Grande basin and not the Bonneville basin; *virginalis* thus became the subspecies name for the Rio Grande cutthroat, and the subspecies name *utah* was given to the Bonneville cutthroat)

5. *pleuriticus,* for the Colorado River cutthroat trout

6. *bouvieri,* restricted to the cutthroat trout of Waha Lake, Idaho

7. *stomias,* for the greenback cutthroat trout of the headwaters of the South Platte and Arkansas River basins

8. "*macdonaldi,*" for the now-extinct yellowfin cutthroat trout found only in Twin Lakes, Colorado (the upper Arkansas River basin)

Jordan and Evermann freely admitted to the inadequate state of knowledge on which they based their classification, writing: "It is not unlikely that when the waters of the Northern Hemisphere are fully explored, it will be found that all the black-spotted trout of America, Europe, and Asia are forms of one species, for which the oldest name is 'Salmo trutta.'" Such a classification would be an extreme example of "lumping." In 1902, Jordan and Evermann published a popular version of fish classification in their book *American Food and Game Fishes;* in this work they became "splitters," classifying all of the 1896 subspecies as full species. They also added new species described between 1896 and 1902. "*S. bathoecetor*" was named for the coastal cutthroat trout native to Crescent Lake, Washington. (Jordan had previously named the Crescent Lake cutthroat trout "*S. gairdneri crescentis*," a mistaken species identity based on the fact that the type specimen of *crescentis* lacked basibranchial teeth, although all six of the other "*crescentis*" specimens collected in 1896 with the type specimen and six collected in 1899 have these teeth. In the 1902 classification, "*S. crescentis*" was considered to be part of the "steelhead" group of species.) "*S. jordani*" and "*S. declivifrons*" were named in 1899 for the coastal cutthroat trout of Lake Sutherland, a neighboring lake to Crescent Lake.

Modern classification considers "*crescentis*," "*bathoecetor*," "*jordani*," and "*declivifrons*" as synonyms of *Oncorhynchus clarki clarki*—that is, names published for the same species or subspecies after the first or original description of the name *clarki* in 1836. During the period when it was popular for taxonomists to describe every slight variation, real or imagined, as a new species, it is difficult to imagine how many species of cutthroat and rainbow trout might have been described if there were more taxonomists actively engaged in studying western North America trout.

In part 2 of the *1928 Report of the U.S. Fish Commission,* published in 1930, Jordan and Evermann, along with their coauthor, Howard Walton Clark, published their last classification. The 1930 classification lists 16 full species of cutthroat trout. The species recognized in the 1930 report and not mentioned above include: "*Salmo tahoensis*" from Lake Tahoe, based on a large specimen of Lahontan cutthroat trout, and "*S. eremogenes*" of Crab Creek, Washington, now considered to be part of the Yellowstone subspecies.

Granted, the history of classification of cutthroat trout (and of rainbow trout) is muddled and confusing, but many of the names discussed above were commonly used in the earlier literature on trout and trout fishing.

CONSERVATION   The cutthroat trout is highly sensitive to environmental changes, especially the introduction of nonnative species of trout. The species' present distribution and abundance is only a small fraction of what it was before the impacts of western settlement, and two of 14 subspecies are extinct.

Cutthroat trout can be compared to the "canary in a coal mine" once used by miners to detect deadly gases or lack of oxygen underground. Cutthroat trout are very sensitive to changes in water quality, especially increases in sediment and water temperature resulting from logging, road building, and livestock grazing. The greatest negative impact, however, has been introductions of nonnative trout, especially rainbow trout, with which the cutthroat trout hybridize, but also brown trout, which replace native cutthroat trout in larger streams; brook trout, which have commonly replaced cutthroat trout in small streams; and lake trout, which replace cutthroat in large lakes.

The yellowfin trout, found only in Twin Lakes, Colorado, was extinct by about 1905. The Alvord cutthroat trout quickly hybridized with rainbow trout first stocked in the late 1920s and early 1930s. Although a small population of relatively pure Alvord cutthroat were found in an isolated portion of Virgin Creek in the 1980s, these fish did not survive preservation attempts and the Alvord cutthroat trout is no more. Other interior subspecies became so rare that in the 1930s and 1940s scientists believed that Lahontan cutthroat trout, Bonneville cutthroat trout, and greenback cutthroat trout were extinct as pure populations. Fortunately, a few populations of each of these subspecies persisted, and they are the basis for present-day recovery and restoration programs.

The Lahontan cutthroat trout, the Paiute cutthroat trout, and the greenback cutthroat trout are protected by the Endangered Species Act (ESA) as threatened species. The protection of the Lahontan subspecies also extends to undescribed subspecies derived from and closely related to the Lahontan group. These include the cutthroat trout native to the Humboldt River drainage of the Lahontan basin, and the cutthroat trout of the Whitehorse basin, immediately north of the Lahontan basin.

During the past decade, environmental organizations have drafted petitions to add most of the other interior subspecies—Yellowstone, westslope, Bonneville, Colorado River, and Rio Grande—to the ESA list of protected species and subspecies. Those ESA petitions have caused controversy, but they do encourage federal and state natural resource agencies to intensify efforts to restore and protect native trout through better management of logging and roads (the major sources of sediment input into western rivers) and revised management of livestock grazing designed to restore and protect riparian vegetation, which is vital for the stability of stream channels and for cooler water temperatures.

The distribution and abundance of native cutthroat trout have been increased by reintroductions into waters of the cutthroat's native range. Reintroductions are typically initiated by finding a small stream above an impassable barrier to upstream movement of fish; such streams are mostly inhabited by nonnative trout, especially brook trout. Before cutthroat trout can be introduced to a restoration stream to establish a new population, all nonnative trout must be eliminated, which is accomplished through chemical treatment. However, even in small streams with flows of only 1 or 2 cubic feet per second, a complete kill of all nonnative trout is difficult, and it may take two or three treatments before all are eliminated. Because of this difficulty, restorations are small-scale and restricted to small headwater tributary streams.

Chemical treatment to kill nonnative game fish and the cessation of the stocking of nonnative hatchery rainbow trout in waters where they have the possibility of mixing and hybridizing with native trout have generated concern and anger among some anglers and outdoor writers. Their typical argument follows an ersatz Darwinian theme of survival of the fittest. If cutthroat trout are so susceptible to extinction, then they must be "unfit" and humans should not interfere with the "natural" extinction process. What good are these fish?

Of course, cutthroat trout extinction *is* unnatural; they were doing just fine before European Americans came upon the scene. Insensitivity toward preservation of biodiversity in general and of cutthroat trout in particular demonstrates the need for public education that leads to a deeper understanding and appreciation of nature. Aldo Leopold, the pioneer ecologist, wrote that to ask "What good is a species?" is the height of ignorance, and that the first rule of intelligent tinkering is not to throw away a part because you do not understand where it goes or what it does.

There are also very practical values associated with the preservation of the diversity of cutthroat trout. Lake trout were illegally introduced into Yellowstone Lake, in Yellowstone National Park. By 1994, when the introduction was discovered, lake trout had become relatively abundant. After reaching a size in the range of 14 to 18 inches (36–46 cm), the diet of lake trout consists almost entirely of the native cutthroat trout. Without human intervention to remove thousands of lake trout each year, which is now the practice, the cutthroat trout of Yellowstone Lake would become extinct or reduced to a small fraction of its abundance and the role of fish in the Yellowstone ecosystem would change drastically. Cutthroat trout commonly occur in relatively shallow water, where they are the principal food of fish-eating birds such as pelicans, osprey, and bald eagles, and for spawning they run up tributary streams, where they are an important food for grizzly bears. In contrast, the lake trout spends its entire life in deep water, completely unavailable as prey for birds and mammals. If the lake trout is allowed to eliminate the cutthroat trout from Yellowstone Lake, the effects would reverberate throughout the ecosystem.

Also, angling for the native cutthroat trout in Yellowstone Lake and in the river below the lake would be lost. Presently this is one of the most outstanding public trout fisheries in the world in terms of average size of fish caught and catch rate; on average, about one 16-inch (41-cm) trout is caught per hour of angling. One study demonstrated that in the Yellowstone River, where "no kill" fishing regulations are in place and all trout caught must be released, the average native cutthroat trout is caught (and released) 9.7 times during the angling season. No other species of trout is so susceptible to angler catch as is the cutthroat trout. If the famous Yellowstone River cutthroat trout fishery in Yellowstone National Park were to be replaced by a brown trout fishery, the catch rate of the Yellowstone fishery would decline greatly. Based on many studies, brown trout are much more difficult to catch than cutthroat trout, by a factor of at least ten. For successful results in special-regulation trout fisheries, where all or most of the trout are released, no species of trout compares with cutthroat trout. Also, many anglers find great joy and satisfaction in the pursuit of fish that are native to the region where they are fishing.

If the philosophical, theoretical, and practical values associated with cutthroat trout were better understood, insensitivity and opposition to their restoration and protection would greatly diminish.

Coastal Cutthroat Trout
Oncorhynchus clarki clarki

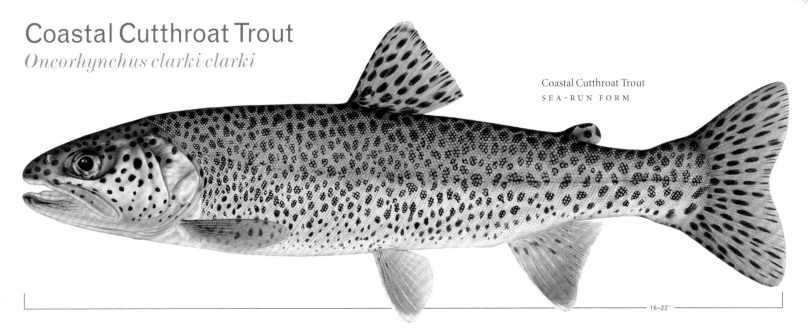

Coastal Cutthroat Trout
SEA-RUN FORM

16–22"

Four life history types are found in coastal cutthroat trout: sea-run (or semi-anadromous) forms, resident (non-migrating) stream populations, fluvial populations that feed and grow in large rivers but migrate to small tributaries to spawn, and lake-adapted (lacustrine) populations. The coastal cutthroat trout is the only subspecies of cutthroat trout that utilizes the marine environment. It does not roam the open ocean and typically spends only two or three months in salt water; the terms "sea-run" and "semi-anadromous" are used to distinguish the sea-run coastal cutthroat trout life history from the fully anadromous life histories of coastal rainbow trout (steelhead) and Pacific salmon.

The coastal cutthroat also is the only cutthroat trout subspecies, as a whole, that has coevolved with the rainbow trout (the coastal subspecies) throughout its entire range from northern California to southern Alaska. The westslope cutthroat subspecies coevolved with the inland redband trout in parts of the mid–Columbia River basin downstream from barrier falls, but most of the natural distribution of the westslope cutthroat did not overlap with the range of any form of rainbow trout before the introduction of hatchery rainbows.

DESCRIPTION Compared with some of the brightly colored inland subspecies of cutthroat trout, the coloration of the coastal cutthroat is more subdued. Body tints of yellow and pink, and pectoral, pelvic, and anal fins that are yellow to orange-red are often seen, especially in populations living their whole lives in small streams.

Sea-run coastal cutthroat, after spending 60 to 90 days in marine waters, return to fresh water with a bright silver coloration; such trout resemble small steelhead, the anadromous form of the coastal

COASTAL CUTTHROAT TROUT

SCIENTIFIC NAME
Oncorhynchus clarki clarki

OTHER COMMON NAMES
Speckled trout (stream-resident form); harvest trout, salter, blueback trout (sea-run form); silver trout (population in Crescent Lake, Washington)

HABITAT
Small, cool headwater streams and larger rivers; ponds and lakes; sea-run form in intertidal areas and inshore marine waters

LENGTH AND WEIGHT
5–8" (13–20 cm) and 0.4–3.2 oz (11–91 g) in small streams. Fluvial and sea-run forms maximum 16–22" (41–56 cm) and 2–5 lb (0.9–2.3 kg); Washington state sea-run record 6 lb (2.7 kg). Lake form may grow heavier: Washington state record 12 lb (5.4 kg); 17 lb (7.7 kg) reported from British Columbia

LIFE SPAN
3–5 years in small streams; 7–9 years for fluvial and lake forms; 7–10 years for sea-run form

DIET
Aquatic and terrestrial invertebrates in small streams; invertebrates and fishes for fluvial and lake forms; crustaceans and fishes for sea-run form

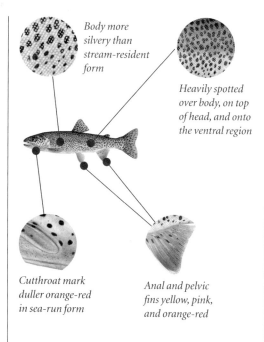

Body more silvery than stream-resident form

Heavily spotted over body, on top of head, and onto the ventral region

Cutthroat mark duller orange-red in sea-run form

Anal and pelvic fins yellow, pink, and orange-red

SEA-RUN FORM

rainbow trout. Coastal cutthroat trout living in large lakes, such as the "silver trout" of Crescent Lake, Washington, can also exhibit a silvery coloration.

The spotting pattern of coastal cutthroat trout differs from that of all other subspecies in the profusion of spots over the body, on top of the head, and often onto the ventral region. In contrast, spots of inland cutthroat subspecies are often concentrated toward the back of the body and above the lateral line; no spots are found on the surface of the head except in populations influenced by hybridization with rainbow trout.

The size of the spots of coastal cutthroat trout range from tiny, dot-like speckles to relatively large spots that are similar in size to those of some inland subspecies.

There should be no confusion in distinguishing coastal cutthroat trout from other subspecies, as distributions of cutthroat trout subspecies are mutually exclusive. While historically the westslope and Yellowstone subspecies were stocked, particularly in lakes, within the range of coastal cutthroat trout, rarely have any of the nonnative subspecies become established.

Unlike leopards and other mammals that can't change their spots, all species of trout can change the presence or absence and the size, shape, and distribution of spots; this ability is directly related to the environment in which they live.

Scale counts along the side of the body average about 155 to 160 in sea-run coastal cutthroat trout. However, small-stream populations often exhibit great variation, from average counts of about 125 (typical of coastal rainbow trout) to about 180 (typical of inland cutthroat subspecies).

The total number of chromosomes (68) in coastal cutthroat differs from all other subspecies of cutthroat trout and from all rainbow trout.

BIOLOGY Sea-run populations of coastal cutthroat trout spend only part of the year feeding in marine waters; they return to fresh water for overwintering. In the marine environment, these trout do not roam in the open ocean, as do typical anadromous species of salmonid fishes. Most studies show that sea-run coastal cutthroat do not venture far from shallow shore zones, generally remaining in bays or along the coastline and making excursions of less than 50 miles (80 km) from their home river.

In the sea-run life history there is great variation among populations in age and size at smolting and at first marine migration (the range is from two to five years of age, and from 6 to 10 inches, or 15–25 cm, in length), time of entry into salt water (from March into June), and time of return to fresh water (from July into January–February). Considerable diversity in life history types is found even among populations in the same region, such as Puget Sound. The sea-run cutthroat trout of the Stillaquamish River, Washington, are divided into two run times from the sea to fresh water; the early run returns to the river mainly in September and October, and the late run returns mainly in December and January. To maintain the hereditary basis for all of the different life history types of sea-run coastal cutthroat, there must be a high degree of homing to natal spawning areas to ensure reproductive isolation among populations.

Sea-run cutthroat trout generally do not roam in the open ocean, but a specimen tagged along the coast in northern Oregon was later recaptured in the Umpqua River after traveling a distance of about 180 miles (290 km). Also, sea-run cutthroat trout have been found in the Columbia River plume. These fish were 40 miles (60 km) from shore over depths of more than 100 feet (30 m). These observations demonstrate that much is yet to be learned about life history diversity in sea-run coastal cutthroat trout.

While in the sea, coastal cutthroat trout feed mainly on small fishes and crustaceans, and grow about 1 inch (2.5 cm) per month. Sea-run females rarely spawn before four years of age, while males can spawn by age three. Survival to repeat spawning can be relatively high, up to about 40 percent in

Coastal Cutthroat Trout
STREAM-RESIDENT FORM

5–8"

some populations. The maximum life span is generally seven to nine years, but a maximum age of ten, with five spawnings during a lifetime, has been documented.

Despite their predatory feeding habits and relatively long life span, sea-run cutthroat trout rarely attain a large size. Those found in small streams reach lengths of 5 to 8 inches (13–20 cm), while the fluvial and sea-run forms reach a general maximum size of 16 to 22 inches (41–56 cm) and 2 to 5 pounds (0.9–2.3 kg). Sea-run fish may attain an extreme maximum of about 6 pounds (2.7 kg).

It is common to find resident stream populations of coastal cutthroat trout isolated in small streams above waterfalls. In these populations, the maximum life span is rarely more than three years, and maximum size may be only about 7 inches (18 cm). If rainbow trout are introduced into a resident popula-tion of coastal cutthroat trout in a small stream, hybridization into a single hybrid population (a "hybrid swarm") can be expected because the limited volume and complexity of habitat does not allow for habitat partitioning and reproductive isolation between the two species.

Fluvial populations of coastal cutthroat trout occur in many of the larger coastal rivers, often upstream of natural barriers to upstream migration from the sea, such as Oregon's Willamette River above Willamette Falls and Washington's Snoqualmie River above Snoqualmie Falls. However, a fluvial population has also been documented in Oregon's Rogue River where no natural barrier exists, so other large coastal rivers may harbor fluvial as well as anadromous coastal cutthroat trout. Where they occur, fluvial coastal cutthroat trout use the main river much as sea-run coastal cutthroat trout use salt water—that is, they reside in the main stem to feed and grow, then migrate to small tributaries to spawn. Data from the Willamette River suggest that juveniles of fluvial populations move downstream from spawning areas during their first year of life, then spend two to three years feeding and growing in the main stem before attaining sexual maturity and migrating back to their natal tributaries to spawn. The life span of fluvial coastal cutthroat trout is about the same as that of the anadromous form—that is, seven to nine years—and fluvial fish can attain about the same maximum size.

Lake-adapted populations of coastal cutthroat trout occur in many lakes along the Pacific Coast. In some of these lakes native coastal rainbow trout occur along

Roundish violet or deep purple parr marks

Spotting less diffuse and darker than sea-run form

Vivid red cutthroat mark

Body intense golden yellow below lateral line

Pectoral, pelvic, and anal fins deep orange-red with white tip on pelvic and anal fins

STREAM-RESIDENT FORM

with coastal cutthroat. In several lakes in British Columbia inhabited by both coastal rainbow trout and coastal cutthroat trout, the cutthroat are more predatory (piscivorous) in their feeding. The coexisting rainbow trout feed mainly on invertebrates and attain smaller sizes than the predatory cutthroat.

The lake-adapted coastal cutthroat trout attains the largest size known for the subspecies. The literature commonly cites a 17-pound (7.7-kg) coastal cutthroat trout from a lake in British Columbia; however, the name of the lake and documentation of this size are never given. The largest reliably documented coastal cutthroat is the angler-caught state record for Washington from Crescent Lake: 12 pounds (5.4 kg).

Given their predatory feeding habits and relatively long life span of seven to nine years, it seems unusual that no trophy size coastal cutthroat of 20 to 25 pounds (9–11 kg) or greater is known.

As with other subspecies of cutthroat trout and rainbow trout, coastal cutthroat trout spawn in the spring. In the moderate winter climate of the coastal rain forest zone of California, Oregon, and Washington, "spring" spawning typically occurs in late winter (February and March) when water temperatures are around 43 to 47 °F (6–8 °C).

In rivers where coastal cutthroat trout coevolved with steelhead (coastal rainbow trout), reproductive isolation is maintained by cutthroat trout spawning in the smallest tributaries and steelhead spawning in larger stream channels. However, reproductive isolation between coastal cutthroat trout and steelhead is tenuous; it depends on segregation during spawning and can be broken down by habitat disturbance and, especially, by the introduction of hatchery rainbow trout. Although hybridization can occasionally occur even under pristine conditions, the incidence of hybridization is greatly increased when hatchery rainbow trout are stocked.

DISTRIBUTION The natural range of the coastal cutthroat trout extends along the Pacific Coast for about 2,000 miles (3,200 km) from the Eel River of northern California to Prince William Sound, in southern Alaska, reaching westward limits near Gore Point on the southern side of the Kenai Peninsula. Coastal cutthroat trout are rarely found more than 100 miles (160 km) from the Pacific Coast.

The inland extent of distribution can be expressed either in "river miles" or straight-line (as the crow flies) miles. Coastal cutthroat trout in the upper North Umpqua occur up to 175 river miles (280 km) from the mouth of the Umpqua River proper, but due to twisting and turning in the sinuous Umpqua's course, this is only about 75 miles (120 km) on a straight line from the coast. Probably the farthest straight-line inland distribution occurs in the headwaters of the Stikine and Skeena River drainages in British Columbia, about 175 miles (280 km) from the coast. In Oregon, on the eastern side of the Cascade Range, coastal cutthroat trout are native to tributaries of the Columbia River; there the straight-line distance to the coast is about 140 miles (225 km).

EVOLUTION AND CLASSIFICATION
The coastal cutthroat trout is one of four major subspecies of cutthroat trout. Coastal cutthroat have been separated from all other subspecies for perhaps 1 million years. This amount of time should have provided opportunities for divergence and for derivative subspecies to arise, but this has not occurred. There is considerable diversity in morphological and genetic traits among individual

populations of the subspecies, but there is no geographical pattern to this diversity, either by river basin or by geographical region, that could logically divide the coastal cutthroat trout into derived "minor" subspecies as is the case with Yellowstone and Lahontan cutthroat trout. One explanation might be that considerable mixing or "homogenization" has likely occurred during and since the last glacial epoch. Thus there is a certain amount of unity in morphological and genetic characteristics throughout the range of the coastal cutthroat trout that maintains all populations as a single subspecies.

As discussed in the account of the full cutthroat trout species, some of the local diversity of coastal cutthroat trout prompted early investigators to describe several new species, such as *"Salmo crescentis"* and *"S. bathoecetor,"* from Crescent Lake, Washington, and *"Salmo jordani"* and *"S. declivifrons,"* from neighboring Lake Sutherland. Adhering to such extreme "splitting" in determining classifications would result in hundreds of new species or subspecies being described for the many local variations found in coastal cutthroat trout.

CONSERVATION Although there are still some pristine small watersheds in Alaska and British Columbia where coastal cutthroat trout have not been negatively affected by humans and by stocking of hatchery trout, the dependency of coastal cutthroat trout on small tributaries for spawning and the

The native range of the coastal cutthroat trout extends up the Pacific Coast for about 2,000 miles (3,200 km) from northern California to southern Alaska.

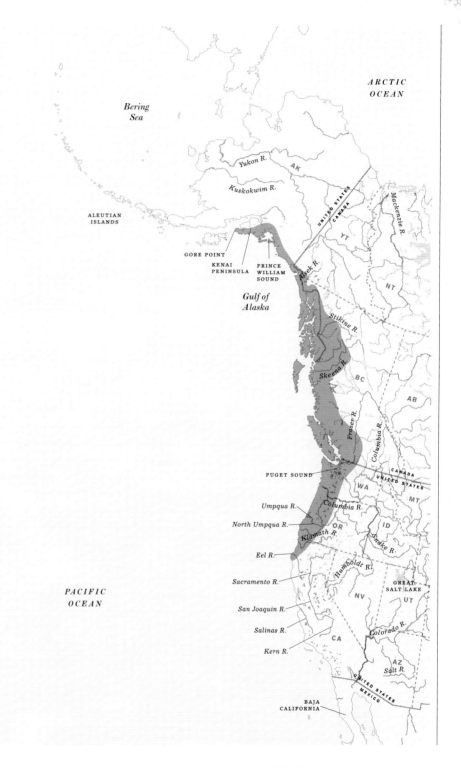

rearing of young makes them extremely susceptible to impacts of urbanization, logging, and associated road construction.

The size of the watersheds from which these small tributaries drain may be only from 50 to 100 acres (20–40 ha). Once urban sprawl or logging removes the forest, water temperatures rise, and erosion and sediment loads greatly increase. Studies have shown that in river drainages where the headwater watersheds were clear-cut, the coastal cutthroat trout is the first species affected and the last to come back. Coho salmon and steelhead, which have greater dependency on downstream sections of a drainage that suffer less thorough habitat degradation than the clear-cut headwaters, can return to former abundance within a few years. But it may take 20 years or more—until the headwater watershed is revegetated and stabilized and until trees grow to provide shade to cool the water—before cutthroat trout return to a semblance of their abundance before clear-cutting occurred.

There has been a long and consistent decline in populations of both sea-run and resident coastal cutthroat trout along the Pacific Coast in northern California, Oregon, and Washington. These trout are responding to increased human population and associated changes in land-use and to insensitive natural resource exploitation.

In addition to impacts from habitat degradation, the widespread stocking of millions of hatchery rainbow trout and steelhead and of hatchery sea-run coastal cutthroat trout over many years has resulted in great increases in the incidence of hybridization between rainbow trout (and steelhead) and coastal cutthroat trout. In 1999 the National Marine Fisheries Service (NMFS) of the U.S. Department of Commerce reported the results of genetic sampling from 97 populations of coastal cutthroat trout: 28 contained genes of rainbow trout.

The NMFS and the U.S. Fish and Wildlife Service share jurisdiction for Endangered Species Act (ESA) listing and enforcement actions concerning coastal cutthroat trout. All of the inland subspecies of cutthroat trout come under the jurisdiction of the U.S. Fish and Wildlife Service. In 1996, the coastal cutthroat trout of the North Umpqua River, Oregon, was listed as endangered by the NMFS. However, in 1999, the NMFS grouped all coastal cutthroat trout of California, Oregon, and Washington into six geographically based evolutionarily significant units (ESU), each of which could then be considered for determination as an endangered or threatened species for ESA protection.

The North Umpqua coastal cutthroat trout became part of the Oregon Coast ESU. Although the coastal cutthroat trout making up that ESU have suffered declines in abundance from habitat degradation and have an increased risk of hybridization from stocking of hatchery steelhead, the NMFS concluded that there was no threat of extinction of this ESU as a whole, and it was not proposed for listing and protection under the Endangered Species Act. Because of this decision, the North Umpqua coastal cutthroat trout, as part of the Oregon Coast ESU, was "de-listed" from ESA protection in April 2000.

In 1999 the NMFS proposed for ESA listing, as threatened, the coastal cutthroat trout making up the Southwestern Washington/Columbia River ESU. A final decision on this proposal is scheduled to be made by June 2002.

Westslope Cutthroat Trout
Oncorhynchus clarki lewisi

Westslope Cutthroat Trout
SPAWNING MALE

6–18"

Below the Great Falls of the Missouri River in present-day Montana, Captain Meriwether Lewis recorded in his journal entry of June 13, 1805:

> *"Goodrich had caught half a dozen very fine trout and a number of both species of the white fish. These trout (caught in the Falls) are from sixteen to twenty-three inches in length, precisely resemble our mountain or speckled trout in form and the position of their fins, but the specks on these are of a deep black instead of the red or gold color of those common to the U. States. These are furnished long sharp teeth on the palate and tongue, and have generally a small dash of red on each side behind the front ventral fins. The flesh is of a pale yellowish red or, when in good order, of a rose red."*

Lewis did not know it at the time, but he became the first European to describe what is known today as the westslope cutthroat trout. (Silas Goodrich was the angler of the Lewis and Clark expedition and is described by Clark as "remarkably fond of fishing.")

Clark's "mountain or speckled trout" was the brook trout, which he knew from the East. Although I do not doubt the veracity of his observations, lengths of 16 to 23 inches (41–58 cm) are extremely large for the westslope cutthroat as we know it today. No matter what its size, the westslope cutthroat trout was much appreciated by the corps of discovery, as is reflected in Lewis's journal which continues on this date:

> *"My fare is really sumptuous this evening: Buffalo's humps, tongues, and marrowbones, fine trout, parched meal, pepper and salt, and a good appetite."*

WESTSLOPE CUTTHROAT TROUT

SCIENTIFIC NAME
Oncorhynchus clarki lewisi

OTHER COMMON NAMES
Red-throated trout, mountain trout, black-spotted trout, common cutthroat trout

HABITAT
Small, cool streams and rivers; lakes

LENGTH AND WEIGHT
6–9" (15–23 cm) and 1–5 oz (28–142 g) in small streams. Typical maximum 16–18" (41–46 cm) and 1–3 lb (0.45–1.4 kg) in rivers and lakes; extreme maximum 24" (61 cm) and 5 lb (2.3 kg)

LIFE SPAN
3–4 years in small streams; 6–8 years in rivers and lakes

DIET
Primarily aquatic and terrestrial invertebrates in streams and rivers; insects and crustaceans in lakes; rarely piscivorous

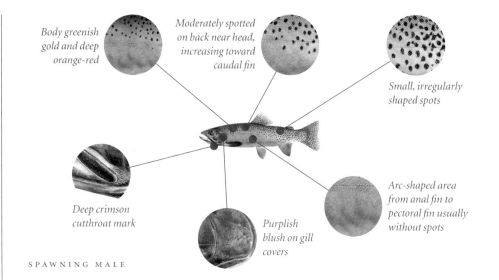

Body greenish
gold and deep
orange-red

Moderately spotted
on back near head,
increasing toward
caudal fin

Small, irregularly
shaped spots

Deep crimson
cutthroat mark

Purplish
blush on gill
covers

Arc-shaped area
from anal fin to
pectoral fin usually
without spots

SPAWNING MALE

The present subspecies name *(lewisi)* is based on specimens that George Suckley caught by fly-fishing in 1853 nearly 50 years after Silas Goodrich landed his trout; this form was officially named *"Salar lewisi"* in 1856. A surgeon-naturalist employed by the U.S. Army to participate in Pacific Railroad Surveys in the 1850s, Suckley was aware that Lewis and Clark had recorded trout below the Great Falls of the Missouri. In 1853, he took his fly rod and made a 30-mile (50-km) side trip from the route of the survey to reach the Great Falls of the Missouri, where he caught several trout about a mile below the falls. Suckley recorded that the fish he caught averaged about "three-quarters of a pound," which would have made them about 12 inches (30 cm) in length. What happened to the 16- to 23-inch (41–58 cm) fish caught by Goodrich nearly 50 years prior? It may be simply that Suckley, using dry flies, landed smaller fish near the surface and Goodrich, using bait, fished deep and landed larger fish. Whatever the reason, it supports the

common belief that fish were always larger in former times. Suckley may have been a pioneer "dry fly" angler many years before fishing flies on the surface of the water became formalized and enshrined as a distinct method of fly-fishing. He mentions that the trout were rising to and jumping at his flies.

Two of the trout specimens caught by Suckley were preserved and sent to the Smithsonian Museum to become the type specimens for *"Salar lewisi"* (now *Oncorhynchus clarki lewisi*). The Great Falls of the Missouri River became the type locality for the name *lewisi*. But how did the common name of Missouri River cutthroat trout become westslope cutthroat trout? In 1853, Suckley observed that the trout he caught in the upper Missouri River were identical to the trout he caught on the west side of the Continental Divide in the Flathead–Clark Fork River drainage of the upper Columbia River basin. In this observation, he would be in agreement with the present

classification that they are both of the same subspecies. However, later authors failed to note Suckley's remarks on the close identity between upper Missouri and upper Columbia basin cutthroat trout, and the common name westslope cutthroat trout, though erroneous, came into use.

DESCRIPTION Westslope cutthroat trout typically have small, irregularly shaped spots similar to those of coastal cutthroat trout, but the distribution of spots is distinctive on the westslope subspecies. Although not an infallible characteristic, if an arc is imagined from the anterior base of the anal fin forward to the pectoral fin, the area below the arc typically has no or very few spots.

Some populations of westslope cutthroat trout have spots much larger than those of typical westslope populations. The John Day River drainage of Oregon and some eastern-slope streams of the Cascade Range in Washington contain westslope cutthroat trout with larger spots that are comparable to the size and shape of spots on typical Yellowstone cutthroat trout.

Coloration of all cutthroat trout is variable. It is generally silver with yellowish tints, but more intense colors—such as bright yellow, orange, and especially red—can be expressed, especially in sexually mature males living in lakes.

Meristic counts for westslope cutthroat trout are as follows: vertebrae, 59 to 63, typically 60 to 61; scales in lateral series, 150 to 200 or more, mean values 165 to 180 (specimens from the Salmon and Clearwater drainages, and some British Columbia populations, have the highest lateral series

Westslope Cutthroat Trout
STREAM-RESIDENT FORM
John Day River Drainage

6–9"

counts, averaging more than 200); pyloric caeca, 25 to 50, mean values 30 to 40 (Missouri basin specimens generally have the lowest caecum counts); gill rakers, 17 to 21, mean values 18 to 19 (posterior gill rakers on the first gill arch absent or weakly developed).

There are no characteristics, such as the number of scales, vertebrae, fin rays, etc., that can distinguish westslope from Yellowstone cutthroat trout. Westslope cutthroat trout tend to have fewer meristic elements than Yellowstone cutthroat, but the variation in counts within each species and the overlap of counts between subspecies is considerable. The cutthroat trout native to Yellowstone Lake, which was widely stocked throughout the West from about 1905 to 1955 (up to 40 million or more eggs were taken annually at Yellowstone Lake), does have distinguishing diagnostic traits, such as the number of gill rakers on the anterior side (20–22 for Yellowstone cutthroat versus 18–19 for westslope cutthroat) and posterior side (5–15 versus 0–3) of the first gill arch and the number of basibranchial teeth (about 15–30 versus 5–10). These characters can be reliably used to identify Yellowstone Lake cutthroat trout that have become established within the range of the westslope cutthroat.

The number of chromosomes in the westslope cutthroat trout is unique. No other subspecies of cutthroat trout and no form of rainbow trout has 66 chromosomes.

BIOLOGY Three life history forms are found in westslope cutthroat trout: a resident (nonmigratory) form that occurs in small streams, a fluvial form that migrates between small streams for spawning and larger rivers for most of its life, and a lacustrine form that lives in lakes.

Maximum life span is typically six to eight years, but resident populations in small streams rarely live more than three or four years. Small-stream fish may grow to be no more than 6 to 9 inches (15–23 cm) in length and reach a weight of some 1 to 5 ounces (28–142 g). In larger rivers and some lakes, westslope cutthroat attain a moderately large size of 16 to 18 inches (41–46 cm) and 1 to 3 pounds (0.45–1.4 kg). A length of 24 inches (61 cm) and a weight of 5 pounds (2.3 kg) is an extreme size for this subspecies.

The relatively small maximum size of westslope cutthroat trout is a biological characteristic that appears to differ from other subspecies. The limitation on maximum size is attributed to their coevolution in the upper Columbia River basin with the predatory bull trout and the large northern pikeminnow. These two highly piscivorous (fish-eating) species actively prey on forage fishes, a diet that allows them to reach a

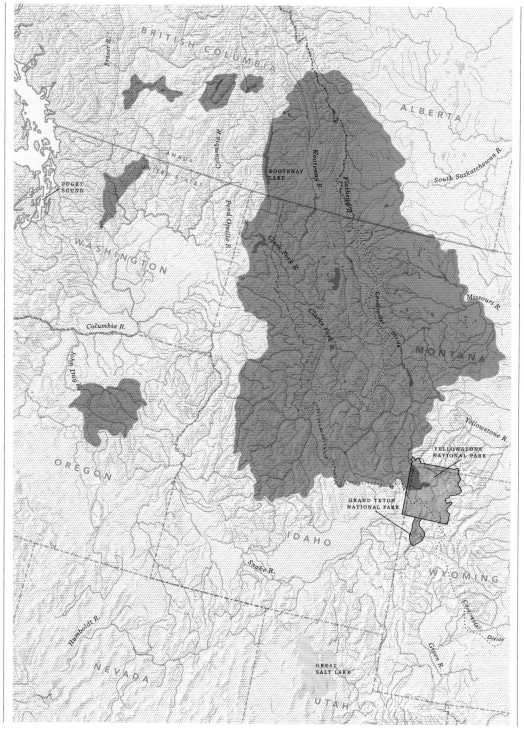

comparatively large size. The westslope subspecies rarely preys on fishes. Its diet consists almost entirely of aquatic and terrestrial insects in streams and insects and crustaceans in lakes.

Nothing in the subspecies' life history, ecology, or behavior clearly distinguishes the westslope cutthroat trout from other subspecies of cutthroat trout. They spawn on the same environmental cues as other cutthroat trout species, when water temperatures rise in the range of 43 to 48 °F (6–9 °C) from April into June.

DISTRIBUTION   The original area of distribution of the westslope cutthroat trout was the greatest of all the subspecies of cutthroat trout. The north–south distribution extended from the eastern slope of the Canadian Rockies draining to the South Saskatchewan River (a tributary to Hudson Bay) to the John Day River of Oregon, the Salmon and Clearwater Rivers of Idaho (the Columbia River basin), and the headwaters of the Madison and Jefferson River drainages of southwestern Montana (the Missouri River basin). The greatest north–south distance is roughly 1,000 miles (1,600 km). The coastal cutthroat trout has a greater north–south distribution—about 2,000 miles (3,200 km)— but rarely occurs more than 100 miles (160 km) inland.

As shown here, the westslope cutthroat trout once occupied a large area—the largest range of any subspecies of cutthroat. Although there are still areas of relative abundance, its present range is vastly reduced. In Montana, the westslope cutthroat now occupies less than 3 percent of its range from the mid-1800s.

The historical east–west distribution of the westslope cutthroat extended from the Judith River of central Montana (the Missouri River basin) to eastern-slope Cascade drainages to the Columbia River (the Yakima, Wenatchee, Entiat, Chelan, and Methow River drainages in Washington) and the John Day River drainage of Oregon. This distribution, although not continuous, also extended for about 1,000 miles (1,600 km).

Also, the westslope subspecies is native to several large lakes, such as Flathead, in Montana, Pend Oreille, Coeur d'Alene, and Priest Lakes, in Idaho, and Lake Chelan, in Washington. In addition to numerous smaller lakes, these large lakes provided about a half million surface acres (about 200,000 ha) of lacustrine habitat for westslope cutthroat trout. Considering the total lacustrine habitat and many thousands of miles of fluvial (stream) habitat within its original range, the westslope cutthroat would have been the most widely distributed and abundant of all the subspecies of cutthroat trout before environmental changes and the introduction of nonnative trout occurred.

In the major tributaries of the upper Columbia River basin, large falls believed to have formed about 60,000 years ago blocked the upstream migration of fishes, but cutthroat trout were established in upstream areas before the falls were formed. The barrier falls on the Kootenay River occurs between Troy and Libby, Montana. The barrier on the Pend Oreille River occurs below Lake Pend Oreille near the Washington–Idaho border. Spokane Falls at Spokane, Washington, blocked the Spokane–St. Joe River from upstream migration. Westslope cutthroat trout and bull trout are native above the barriers on the Kootenay, Pend Oreille, and Spokane River drainages.

The rainbow trout that are now common in these drainages above the barriers are not native; they are the result of introductions that began more than 100 years ago. The kokanee salmon that is now common in all of the large lakes above the barrier falls is also a nonnative species that is present as a result of introduction by humans.

Below the barriers, the westslope cutthroat occurs in the headwaters of tributaries draining the eastern side of the Cascade Range to the Columbia River and in the John Day River drainage, in Oregon. Isolated populations occur sporadically in small streams above waterfalls in the upper Columbia River basin (and a few in the Fraser River basin) of British Columbia. In 1931, these British Columbia populations were named as a new subspecies, "*Salmo clarki alpestris*"; these "mountain" cutthroat trout of British Columbia are disjunct populations of the westslope cutthroat trout (that is, populations occurring outside the continuous or common range). All of the present-day localities of westslope cutthroat in British Columbia were covered by glacial ice and were thus uninhabitable by fishes until after the glacial retreat about 10,000 years ago.

The distribution of disjunct populations of westslope cutthroat trout (formerly mountain cutthroat, "*O. c. alpestris*") in British Columbia include: Isaac, Frog and Canyon Creeks, tributaries to the Columbia River near Revelstoke; Crazy, Yard, and Frog Creeks, tributaries to the Eagle River and Marble Lake in the Fraser River basin; and Six Mile and Nine Mile Creeks, tributaries to the west arm of Kootenay Lake.

Considering the original distribution of the westslope cutthroat trout in several major river drainages on both sides of the Continental Divide, the close genetic similarity among all westslope cutthroat might seem surprising. The lack of clear-cut genetic differentiation associated with geographical regions indicates that the full extent of the historical distribution was achieved relatively recently, around the time the glaciers were retreating, or roughly 10,000 to 12,000 years ago—not sufficient time for populations isolated from each other in different regions to accumulate significant genetic differentiation.

The distribution of the westslope cutthroat trout in the eastern slope of the Cascade drainages and in the John Day River drainage is likely associated with the glacial-era Lake Missoula and the many failures of its ice dam that sent torrential floods of enormous magnitude across eastern Washington. Lake Missoula was created when a tongue of glacial ice dammed the Clark Fork River near present-day Lake Pend Oreille, in Idaho. At its maximum size, the lake covered about 3,100 square miles (8,000 sq km) and had a maximum depth of about 1,000 feet (300 m). During the last glacial period, Lake Missoula filled and burst through its ice dam some 40 times or more, scouring eastern Washington to create what is called the channeled scablands. It can be assumed that millions of westslope cutthroat trout would have flushed out from Lake Missoula with each failure of the ice dam.

EVOLUTION AND CLASSIFICATION

The oft-cited 1896–98 and 1902 publications of Jordan and Evermann were the authoritative works of their time on trout classification and distribution. Jordan and Evermann recognized that the type locality for *lewisi* was the Missouri River. However, they mistakenly believed that the ancestor that crossed the Continental Divide, from the Snake River drainage into the headwaters of the Yellowstone River, continued to disperse downstream in the Yellowstone River to its confluence with the Missouri River and then spread upstream in the Missouri River to its headwaters. This erroneous scenario led Jordan and Evermann to apply the name *lewisi* to the cutthroat trout of both the Missouri and the Yellowstone River drainages. Thus the name *lewisi,* until about 1975–80 was universally applied to Yellowstone cutthroat trout.

In the 1950s and 1960s the Yellowstone cutthroat trout was widely propagated and stocked in western states. Fish biologists and fish culturists in Montana and Idaho noticed distinct differences in spotting pattern and coloration between Yellowstone cutthroat trout and cutthroat trout native to the upper Columbia River basin (the Flathead–Clark Fork–Pend Oreille drainage of Montana and Idaho and the St. Joe–Spokane, Salmon, and Clearwater drainages of Idaho). They did not realize that the upper Columbia basin cutthroat trout with the brighter coloration and smaller, irregularly shaped spots also is native to the upper Missouri River (and to the South Saskatchewan River basin of Montana and Alberta, Canada) and that it had been

given the name *lewisi* in 1856. They thought instead that the so-called westslope cutthroat trout was an undescribed species or subspecies. Also, from 1966 to 1973 the U.S. Department of Interior issued an annual "redbook" of endangered fishes; the westslope cutthroat trout was included as an "undescribed species" in the first volumes and in later volumes was mentioned as of "uncertain" classification.

In reality, it was the Yellowstone cutthroat trout that was in need of a new subspecies name because the name *lewisi* is forever fixed to the type specimen and type locality of the Missouri River below the Great Falls and wherever else this same subspecies occurs. As recounted in the following chapter, the name *bouvieri* was applied to the Yellowstone subspecies by myself in 1979.

The westslope cutthroat trout is one of the four major subspecies of cutthroat trout, and as with the coastal cutthroat trout, it has not given rise to any minor subspecies. Genetic analyses have revealed a large amount of evolutionary divergence between westslope and Yellowstone cutthroat trout and between westslope cutthroat and all other cutthroat trout subspecies. Scientific comparisons of enzymes shows greater similarities between westslope cutthroat trout and rainbow trout than between westslope and Yellowstone cutthroat. Other genetic techniques, such as studies of mitochondrial DNA, more correctly group all subspecies of cutthroat trout together as quite distinct from the rainbow trout.

Different methods of molecular genetics can give contradictory results in terms of estimating the magnitude of genetic diver-

gence and the time since divergence from a common ancestor occurred. "Molecular clocks" are not reliable time pieces, except that there is agreement that the westslope cutthroat line of evolution has been separated from all other evolutionary divergences within the full cutthroat trout species for a long time.

CONSERVATION

As with cutthroat trout in general, the westslope cutthroat trout is highly susceptible to replacement by brook trout in small streams and by brown trout in larger rivers. Westslope cutthroat readily hybridize with nonnative rainbow trout. Westslope cutthroat trout coevolved and coexisted with native rainbow-redband trout (mainly with the steelhead life history) in the John Day River drainage, the eastern-slope Cascade drainages, and the Salmon and Clearwater River drainages. The introduction of hatchery rainbow trout into these locations tends to break down reproductive isolation between the coevolved cutthroat and rainbow trout populations.

Introduction of kokanee salmon, lake trout, and lake whitefish from the Great Lakes into most of the large lakes in the Columbia River basin has resulted in declines of 90 percent or more in westslope cutthroat trout from their historical abundance in these lakes. In Montana it is estimated that pure populations of westslope cutthroat trout occur in only 2.5 percent of the miles of stream in their original range. Moreover, this 2.5 percent of stream miles consists mainly of small, headwater tributaries. Because these headwater tributaries average 10 feet (3 m) in width compared to rivers averaging 100 feet (30 m) in width, where westslope cutthroat used to thrive, it is fair to say that the total abundance has declined by more than 97.5 percent.

Because of the large area of original distribution of westslope cutthroat trout, there are still pockets of abundance of these fish. In Glacier National Park, 20 lakes totaling about 7,000 surface acres (2,800 ha) in the Flathead River drainage of the upper Columbia River basin hold pure populations of westslope cutthroat trout and bull trout. The largest lake in Glacier National Park, Lake McDonald (whose surface area is equal to the sum of the 20 lakes containing pure native cutthroat trout), is now dominated by nonnative kokanee salmon, lake trout, and lake whitefish, and contains only a small remnant population of native cutthroat trout. The native westslope cutthroat trout is extinct in tributaries to the South Saskatchewan and Missouri River basins of Glacier National Park.

There are still some relatively abundant westslope cutthroat trout populations in rivers, where they are the basis for popular sport fisheries, such as Kelly Creek in the North Fork Clearwater River drainage and the upper St. Joe River, in Idaho. Most of the popular sport fisheries for westslope cutthroat trout are governed by restrictive fishing regulations whereby all or most of the fish caught must be released. Because cutthroat trout, in general, are highly vulnerable to anglers fishing with artificial flies and lures, these special-regulation fisheries maintain a high catch rate. In Kelly Creek, after restrictive regulations were instituted that resulted in release of almost all of the trout caught, the biomass (total

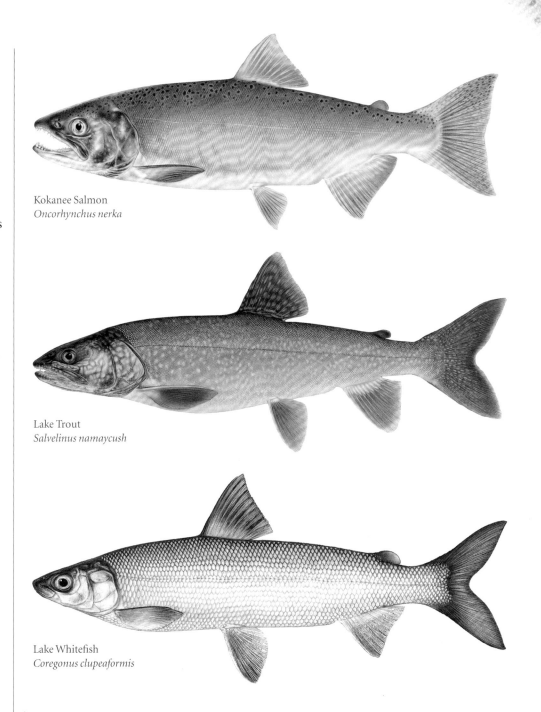

Kokanee Salmon
Oncorhynchus nerka

Lake Trout
Salvelinus namaycush

Lake Whitefish
Coregonus clupeaformis

The introduction of kokanee salmon, lake trout, and lake whitefish into native lake habitats of westslope cutthroat trout has reduced its population by 90 percent or more.

weight) of the westslope cutthroat population increased in the 1970s by thirteenfold within a few years. The state of Montana also maintains a propagation program for westslope cutthroat trout that stocks many mountain lakes for sportfishing.

Westslope cutthroat trout from Lake Chelan, Washington, have been propagated since 1903, but only in recent times has the westslope cutthroat been recognized as native to that state. A 1979 book on the fishes of Washington stated that the coastal cutthroat trout is the only subspecies native to the state. What was known as the "intermontane" or "Cascade" cutthroat trout (actually the westslope cutthroat trout) since 1903 was widely stocked in lakes of the Cascade Range. There was a common belief, however, that the "Cascade" cutthroat trout was not native to Washington; it was thought to have been introduced from other states.

As with other large lakes, Lake Chelan is now dominated by nonnative salmonid species, and the native cutthroat trout and bull trout maintain only small, remnant populations. The westslope cutthroat trout of Lake Chelan was first propagated in hatcheries in 1903. A brood stock from Lake Chelan was established in Twin Lakes, Washington, where propagation has been ongoing since 1915. Westslope cutthroat trout are also propagated in Washington from a brood stock in King's Lake. The origin of the King's Lake trout is Priest Lake, in Idaho. The westslope cutthroat trout propagated from both Twin Lakes and King's Lake and stocked into lakes in the Cascade Range are excellent representatives of the typical spotting pattern and coloration of westslope cutthroat.

In recent years, federal land management agencies (the U.S. Forest Service and the Bureau of Land Management) have become more sensitive to the need for habitat protection and restoration as they make decisions regarding logging, livestock grazing, and mining in watersheds where westslope cutthroat trout occur. Large watersheds often have a mix of federal, state, and private lands. Where this occurs, a successful protection and restoration program requires a cooperative agreement among all the government agencies and private landowners that is designed to protect or restore riparian vegetation, reduce sediment input, avoid input of toxic pollutants, and maintain flows.

Despite a great reduction in its historic range, the westslope cutthroat trout maintains some pure populations in all parts of its original range, including some areas with relatively high abundance. Overall, with ongoing programs for habitat restoration and enhancement and propagation programs, the outlook for the future of this subspecies is hopeful.

Yellowstone Cutthroat Trout
Oncorhynchus clarki bouvieri

Yellowstone Cutthroat Trout

14–24"

The best-known and most widely recognized form of cutthroat trout is the subspecies native to Yellowstone Lake and the Yellowstone River in Yellowstone National Park. Its fame stems from a long history of accounts in the popular and scientific literature that— since 1872, when Yellowstone became the country's first national park—have widely publicized the great abundance of the relatively large (14–18 inches/36–46 cm) cutthroat trout of Yellowstone Lake.

The lake—at 7,731 feet (2,356 m) elevation and with a surface area of about 88,000 acres (35,600 ha)—lies in a magnificent landscape that is a fitting home for the world's greatest population of pure cutthroat trout. Estimates of adult cutthroat of 14 inches

(36 cm) and larger in length in Yellowstone Lake range up to 1 million or more fish.

Because the lake is so large and it is difficult to obtain adequate samples, any estimate of the number of cutthroat trout that inhabit Yellowstone Lake must be regarded as more of an educated guess than a scientifically sound measurement. There is no doubt, however, that there are abundant cutthroat trout in Yellowstone Lake. In the 1950s and 1960s, before angling regulations greatly reduced the number of trout killed by anglers, more than 300,000 trout were taken by angling in some years, and fish-eating birds and bears consumed a roughly equal amount.

Early on, the abundance of cutthroat trout in Yellowstone Lake attracted the attention of fish culturists. From 1899 to 1955, some 818

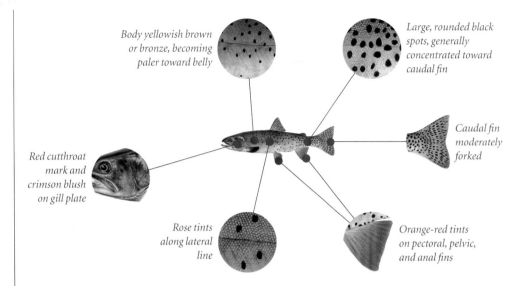

Body yellowish brown or bronze, becoming paler toward belly

Large, rounded black spots, generally concentrated toward caudal fin

Red cutthroat mark and crimson blush on gill plate

Caudal fin moderately forked

Rose tints along lateral line

Orange-red tints on pectoral, pelvic, and anal fins

BIOLOGY Most information on the life history and ecology of the Yellowstone cutthroat trout is based on studies of the cutthroat trout of Yellowstone Lake. As is typical for subspecies of cutthroat trout in general, distinctive life history traits are characteristic of individual populations, not the subspecies as a whole.

While no life history attributes distinguish Yellowstone cutthroat trout from other subspecies of cutthroat, there are differences associated with local populations within the subspecies. Populations living their whole life in small tributary streams rarely live more than three to five years or attain a length of more than 9 or 10 inches (23–25 cm). In Yellowstone Lake, cutthroat trout can reach eight or nine years of age and can grow to a length of about 21 inches (53 cm) and a weight of 4 pounds (1.8 kg). In Henrys Lake, the native cutthroat has a shorter life span (to six or seven years), but because of the rich food supply and longer annual growth period, Henrys Lake cutthroat grow more rapidly than the cutthroat trout of Yellowstone Lake, attaining a general maximum length of about 24 inches (61 cm) and a weight of 6 pounds (2.7 kg). Yellowstone cutthroat stocked in Utah's Strawberry Reservoir have been known to reach an extreme maximum weight of 27 pounds (12.2 kg).

As with all cutthroat and rainbow trout, Yellowstone cutthroat trout are spring spawners. Depending on temperature, spawning in different areas extends from April into July.

Besides cutthroat trout, the one other species of fish that is native to Yellowstone

million Yellowstone Lake cutthroat trout eggs (more than 40 million in some years) were taken, fertilized, and shipped to most U.S. states, Canada, and foreign countries.

DESCRIPTION The Yellowstone cutthroat trout typically differs from its cousin, the westslope cutthroat, in its less-intense coloration, in which yellowish brown or bronze predominates. Rose tints sometimes appear along the lateral line and on the lower fins. In both subspecies, spots are generally concentrated toward the posterior, but they tend to be more evenly distributed over the body in Yellowstone cutthroat trout. Variation in coloration and spotting in both the Yellowstone and the westslope subspecies is such that it can be difficult to distinguish between the two. For example, the Yellowstone cutthroat trout native to McBride Lake in Yellowstone National Park has a spotting pattern more similar to that of westslope cutthroat trout, and the

westslope cutthroat of the John Day River drainage, Oregon, has larger spots more typical of Yellowstone cutthroat.

Meristic (countable) characteristics—number of scales, gill rakers, vertebrae, fin rays, pyloric caeca, etc.—are not useful for distinguishing all Yellowstone cutthroat trout from other subspecies of cutthroat. However, the Yellowstone cutthroat trout native to Yellowstone Lake do have diagnostic traits that differ from other populations of Yellowstone cutthroat and from other subspecies. Yellowstone Lake cutthroat typically have more gill rakers on the anterior part of the first gill arch (20–22, versus 17–20 for other Yellowstone cutthroat and other subspecies) and 5 to 15 gill rakers on the posterior part of the first gill arch (versus 0–3). They also typically have more basibranchial teeth, averaging 20 or more in a sample of several specimens, versus 5 to 10 found in other cutthroat trout.

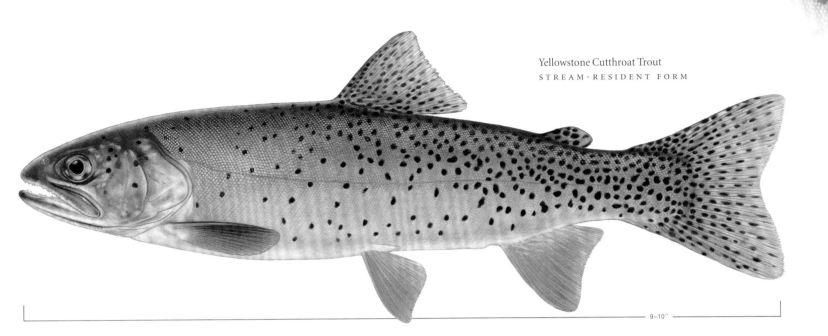

Yellowstone Cutthroat Trout
STREAM-RESIDENT FORM

9–10"

Lake and the Yellowstone River drainage above the two large falls in Yellowstone National Park is the longnose dace, which is rare. Essentially, for several thousand years the cutthroat trout in Yellowstone Lake evolved with no other species of fish, so there was no natural selection for coexistence with other fishes.

Unrecorded introductions established the redside shiner and the longnose sucker in Yellowstone Lake. These two species often have severe impacts on trout fisheries when introduced into lakes because they compete with trout for food. In Yellowstone Lake, however, no significant impacts on recruitment (number of fish reaching a certain age class), growth, or abundance of cutthroat trout were detected after the establishment of the redside shiner and the longnose sucker. Evidently the native cutthroat trout is

superbly adapted to the unique environment of Yellowstone Lake—its temperature regime, area and volume, and invertebrate food supply.

The expansive, deep, cold-water environment of Yellowstone Lake provides an ideal fit for the lake trout, which was illegally stocked some 25 years ago. It was hoped that the nonnative longnose sucker, which is relatively abundant in Yellowstone Lake, might act as a "buffer" species and control lake trout predation on cutthroat trout. This has not occurred. Studies show that nearly 99 percent of the fish consumed by lake trout are cutthroat trout. An intensive program is in place to remove lake trout from Yellowstone Lake; without it, the impact of lake trout on the native cutthroat trout would be devastating.

Except for in the Yellowstone River

Longnose Dace
Rhinichthys cataractae

The longnose dace and the Yellowstone cutthroat are the only fishes native to Yellowstone Lake and the Yellowstone River drainage above the two large waterfalls in Yellowstone National Park. These two fish have cohabitated for millenia.

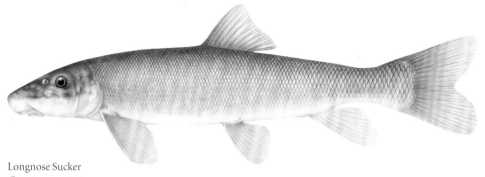

Longnose Sucker
Catostomus catostomus

Redside Shiner
Richardsonius balteatus

Along with the lake trout, two other species have been introduced into Yellowstone Lake, the redside shiner and the longnose sucker. In other western lakes these two introduced fishes compete with trout and other native fishes for food. However, in Yellowstone Lake they have had no detectable effect on the population of Yellowstone cutthroat trout.

drainage (including Yellowstone Lake) above the two major falls in Yellowstone National Park, the Yellowstone cutthroat trout has been mostly replaced by introduced brook, brown, and rainbow trout throughout its range; alternatively, it shows varying degrees of hybridization with rainbow trout.

Rainbow trout were first stocked in Henrys Lake in 1890 and 200,000 rainbow × cutthroat hybrids are still stocked annually. Also, brook trout have been established in Henrys Lake since the early 1900s. In some environments the native cutthroat trout appear to be well adapted and to have resisted replacement and hybridization. For example, the Yellowstone cutthroat trout native to Henrys Lake at the headwaters of the Henrys Fork of the Snake River is still the dominant trout of Henrys Lake despite the stocking of millions of rainbow trout and hatchery-created rainbow × cutthroat hybrids.

Henrys Lake is a shallow (mean depth 12 feet/3.6 m), nutrient-rich body of water of about 6,500 surface acres (2,600 ha). Although the cutthroat trout of Henrys Lake and Yellowstone Lake are regarded as virtually identical in genetic terms, the vastly different environments of the two lakes—their temperature regimes, area and volume, and food organisms—have exerted very different selective pressures for the cutthroat trout of the two lakes. The cutthroat trout of Yellowstone Lake and Henrys Lake have evolved life histories best adapted to survival in their respective environments.

As would be expected after a long history of stocking rainbow trout and rainbow × cutthroat hybrids, hybridization has occurred in Henrys Lake. Genetic testing of Henrys Lake cutthroat trout found that about 15 percent of the specimens contained genetic markers of rainbow trout, but most of the hybrids are predominantly cutthroat trout—that is, after many generations subjected to hybridization, the hybrids possess many more genes of cutthroat trout than they do of rainbow trout. This indicates that natural selection strongly favors the native cutthroat trout genotype over the rainbow trout genotype. It also appears obvious that the Yellowstone cutthroat trout native to Henrys Lake has superior adaptive qualities (which gives rise to a higher survival rate) to those of rainbow trout or hybrids in Henrys Lake; otherwise, the native cutthroat trout would have been lost and replaced by rainbow trout long ago.

In recent years, hybrid eggs in hatcheries have been heat-shocked to produce sterile triploid fish (fish with three sets of chromosomes rather than the normal diploid, or two, sets of chromosomes). These sterile fish are stocked for sportfishing with the hope that they will never reproduce and threaten native cutthroat. Rainbow trout are considered better game fish by most anglers. However, triploid sterility is produced in only about 97 percent of the heat-shocked embryos. This translates into about 6,000 normal diploid (fertile) hybrids for the 200,000 hybrids annually stocked. Many of these fertile first-generation hybrids are surviving and entering tributaries on spawning runs. More studies are necessary to determine if these fertile fish have influenced native stocks of cutthroat trout.

In the river environment of the Henrys

Fork from the Henrys Lake outlet downstream to its confluence with the Snake River, including Island Park Reservoir, the native cutthroat trout have been completely replaced by rainbow trout and brown trout. In the Yellowstone River, the native cutthroat trout are still relatively common, but the influence of hybridization appears to have increased in recent years. In autumn 2000, I fished the Yellowstone River between Gardiner and Livingston, Montana, a distance of about 50 miles (80 km). Downstream near Livingston, most of the trout I caught appeared to be typical rainbow trout, and hybrids appeared to be more rainbow than cutthroat. Upstream toward Gardiner, I caught trout resembling typical Yellowstone cutthroat, and hybrids appeared to be more cutthroat than rainbow.

After about 100 years of coexistence between introduced rainbow trout and native cutthroat trout in the Yellowstone River downstream from Yellowstone National Park, it appears that barriers to hybridization that allowed the two species to coexist without merging into a single hybrid population have broken down or have been compromised. Because rainbow trout are not native to the Snake River above Shoshone Falls, the native cutthroat trout had no evolutionary programming for coexistence with and reproductive isolation from rainbow trout, as occurred in the coastal cutthroat trout and some populations of the westslope cutthroat trout.

While the typical largespotted Yellowstone cutthroat occurs in the Snake River's larger tributaries, such as the Henrys Fork, Blackfoot, and Portneuf Rivers, the main

Snake River Finespotted
Cutthroat Trout
Oncorhynchus clarki behnkei

LARGESPOTTED VERSUS FINESPOTTED CUTTHROAT TROUT

A most unusual phenomenon is found in the upper Snake River drainage, where two forms of cutthroat trout occur that are sharply distinguished by the size of their spots. The typical largespotted Yellowstone cutthroat trout is found in Heart Lake, in the uppermost headwaters of the Snake River, and in all of the larger tributaries downstream to Spread Creek. The Gros Ventre River, the next drainage downstream from Spread Creek, has the largespotted Yellowstone cutthroat in headwater tributaries and a finespotted cutthroat trout in the rest of the drainage. Only the finespotted cutthroat is found in the main Snake River between Jackson Lake and Palisades Reservoir. The original distribution of the two forms is not known.

The finespotted cutthroat trout evolved from the Yellowstone cutthroat during the last glacial period, and the two forms can be distinguished only by the size of their spots. To date, all methods of genetic analysis have failed to find any consistent difference between the finespotted and largespotted forms. However, there obviously is a genetic basis for the spotting pattern and for the ecological differences that determine the different distributions of the two forms. The Snake River finespotted cutthroat is recognized as a separate subspecies, distinct from the Yellowstone cutthroat trout, and is treated in a separate account in this book.

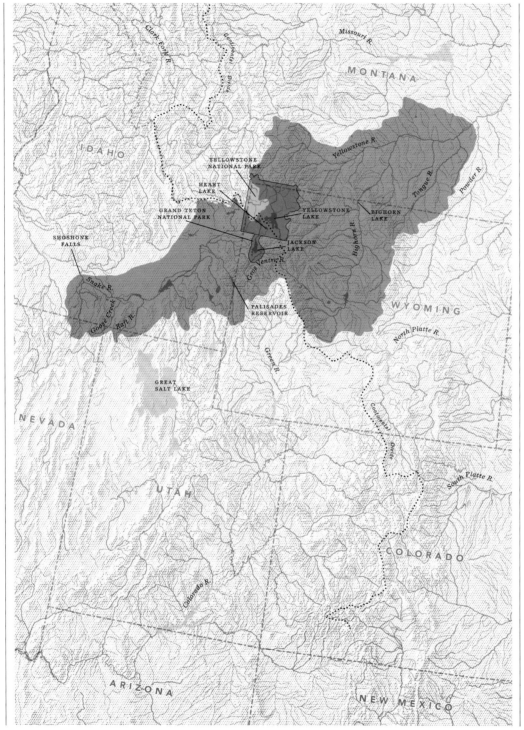

Snake River above Shoshone Falls in Idaho and Wyoming is home to a finespotted subspecies of cutthroat trout. How the two forms—the largespotted Yellowstone cutthroat trout and the Snake River finespotted cutthroat—maintain their separate distributions in the upper Snake River drainage is unknown, but they must have evolved differences in behavior and environmental preferences that reinforce their spatial separation.

DISTRIBUTION   The known historical distribution of the Yellowstone cutthroat trout is on both sides of the Continental Divide—in the upper Snake River drainage above Shoshone Falls on the western side and in the Yellowstone River drainage from its headwaters downstream to the Tongue River on the eastern side.

Before 1911, when a dam raised the level of Jackson Lake and blocked upstream movement of fish in the Snake River, trout could freely move upstream to Heart Lake in the headwaters of the Snake River. Another barrier to free movement of fish in the Snake River is Palisades Reservoir on the Idaho–Wyoming border. Below Palisades Reservoir, cutthroat trout are still the dominant trout caught by anglers in the Snake River (in Idaho, called the South Fork Snake River), but the size of their spots is distinctly larger than is typical of the finespotted cutthroat occurring in the Snake River above Palisades Reservoir (see

The native range of the Yellowstone cutthroat trout includes southern Montana, northwestern Wyoming, southern Idaho, and small portions of northern Nevada and Utah.

the box Largespotted versus Finespotted Cutthroat Trout, above).

The difference in spotting between the finespotted cutthroat trout upstream from Palisades Reservoir and the "medium-size" spotting characteristic of the cutthroat trout downstream from Palisades Reservoir probably reflects the influence of hybridization with nonnative rainbow trout that were stocked in large numbers in the South Fork Snake River in Idaho until the 1970s. Between Palisades Reservoir and Shoshone Falls, the larger tributary streams to the Snake River—the Henrys Fork, Teton Fork, Blackfoot, Portneuf, and Raft Rivers, and Goose Creek—all have the typical largespotted Yellowstone cutthroat as the native trout, although they have been replaced by nonnative trout and by hybridization with rainbow trout in most of this area of distribution.

The historic occurrence of the Yellowstone subspecies of cutthroat trout in Goose Creek makes the Yellowstone cutthroat trout native to a small area of the northeastern corner of Nevada that is drained by Goose Creek. Likewise, the Yellowstone cutthroat trout was native to a small section of northwestern Utah in the Raft River drainage, but it is now extinct there.

Pacific Creek, a tributary to the Snake River below Jackson Lake, has only the largespotted Yellowstone cutthroat trout. In postglacial times, an ancestor crossed the Continental Divide from Pacific Creek to Atlantic Creek to become established in the Yellowstone River drainage. It is still possible for fish to make this crossing of the Continental Divide. North Two Ocean Creek comes down the Continental Divide and branches. One section that drains to the west becomes Pacific Creek, while the other, draining to the east, becomes Atlantic Creek, a tributary to the Yellowstone River above Yellowstone Lake. There is no barrier to the movement and mixing of fish between Pacific Creek and Atlantic Creek. Cutthroat trout of Pacific Creek are non-migratory stream fish and the cutthroat of Atlantic Creek are migratory fish from Yellowstone Lake that run up to spawn in its headwaters and no farther. This difference in behavior has effectively isolated the two populations and they do not mix.

Large (typically 14–18 inches / 36–46 cm) adult cutthroat trout migrate from Yellowstone Lake and spawn in Atlantic Creek. After hatching, the young cutthroat migrate down Atlantic Creek to the Yellowstone River and to Yellowstone Lake. In North Two Ocean Creek and Pacific Creek, the cutthroat trout have a stream-resident life history. All ages from fry to adult are present, and adults attain only a modest size, typically 9 or 10 inches (23–25 cm). Thus, just as reproductive isolation between finespotted and largespotted cutthroat trout is maintained by behavioral and life history differences, the largespotted Yellowstone cutthroat trout exists in two life history forms that maintain isolation on each side of the Continental Divide in Pacific Creek and Atlantic Creek.

The downstream limits of natural distribution of cutthroat trout in the Yellowstone River system were documented in the diary of Captain John Bourke, an aide to General George Crook. In June 1876, General Crook's army was moving north in an attempt to join with other army groups. The strategy was to force thousands of Sioux and Northern Cheyenne warriors to return to their reservations. On June 16, Crook encountered a large number of well-armed and well-organized Native Americans on the Rosebud Creek, a drainage just to the east of the Little Bighorn River in southern Montana. Unlike the impetuous George Armstrong Custer, General Crook tried to avoid confrontations until the odds were decisively in his favor, and he judiciously withdrew his soldiers from the Rosebud battlefield and retreated to an encampment in the Tongue River drainage just west of present-day Sheridan, Wyoming. For the next couple of weeks, Crook's men enjoyed a leisurely life in camp while catching many thousands of cutthroat trout. On June 25, Custer's encounter with the Sioux and Northern Cheyenne warriors on the Little Bighorn River, about 50 miles (80 km) north of Crook's encampment, had a very different outcome.

EVOLUTION AND CLASSIFICATION

The common name cutthroat trout, which applies to the species as a whole, was first used for a population of Yellowstone cutthroat trout. In an 1884 issue of *American Angler* magazine, Charles Hallock, longtime editor of *Forest and Stream,* wrote of a memorable fishing experience he had had the previous year on Rosebud Creek, which drains from the Beartooth Mountains to the Yellowstone River in southern Montana, northeast of Yellowstone National Park. Hallock caught trout with "…a slash of intense carmine across each gill cover, as

MINOR SUBSPECIES DERIVED FROM YELLOWSTONE CUTTHROAT TROUT

During the past 100,000 years or so evolutionary differentiation from a Yellowstone cutthroat trout ancestor has given rise to six minor subspecies, all closely related to one another. This radiation has occurred in contiguous river basins across the range of this group of related fish. These subspecies of *Oncorhynchus clarki* include the cutthroat trout native to the Bonneville basin; the upper Colorado River basin; the headwaters of the South Platte and Arkansas River basins; Twin Lakes, Colorado (the yellowfin trout, now extinct); the Rio Grande basin; and the Snake River finespotted cutthroat trout found in certain parts of the upper Snake River drainage.

large as my little finger. It was most striking. For lack of a better description we call them 'Cut-throat' trout." Thus the type locality for the original description of the common name cutthroat trout is Rosebud Creek. Before 1884, cutthroat trout were most commonly referred to in the literature as "black-spotted trout," "speckled trout," or "Rocky Mountain trout." The term "black-spotted trout" continued to be used by fish culturists into the early 1900s.

The origin and evolutionary history of the Yellowstone cutthroat trout is associated with the Columbia River basin side of the Continental Divide—namely, the Snake River system and its former and present connections. The crossing of the Continental Divide and the establishment of cutthroat trout in the headwaters of the Yellowstone River drainage could not have occurred until about 6,000 to 8,000 years ago, after glacial ice left the Yellowstone Plateau and the waters became habitable to fishes and other aquatic life.

An ancient split from a 66-chromosome group (the westslope cutthroat trout) led to a 64-chromosome group that soon divided, with one ancestor isolated in the Lahontan basin (the Lahontan cutthroat) and one associated with the Snake River drainage (the Yellowstone cutthroat). The Lahontan cutthroat trout, a major subspecies, has given rise to four minor subspecies. The Yellowstone cutthroat trout, a major subspecies, has given rise to six minor subspecies (see box). The minor subspecies probably originated during the past 100,000 years.

The origin of the direct ancestor of the Yellowstone cutthroat trout—the separation of the 64-chromosome group from the 66-chromosome group—occurred perhaps in the mid-Pleistocene epoch, or about 1 million years ago. It seems likely that the subsequent evolution of the 66-chromosome group (the westslope cutthroat trout) was associated with the northern parts of the upper Columbia River basin: the headwaters of the Columbia, Kootenay, Pend Oreille, and Spokane River drainages. The evolutionary history of the Yellowstone cutthroat trout appears to be associated with the Snake River drainage.

In contrast to the distribution of the westslope cutthroat trout, which has many natural populations downstream of the major barrier falls on the Kootenay, Pend Oreille, and Spokane Rivers (in eastern-slope Cascade tributaries to the Columbia River, Washington, and in the John Day River drainage, Oregon), there are no known surviving populations of Yellowstone cutthroat trout downstream from Shoshone Falls on the Snake River. It would seem obvious that a Yellowstone cutthroat trout ancestor must have occurred in the Snake River drainage below the site of Shoshone Falls before the falls were created about 60,000 years ago. The disappearance of cutthroat trout below Shoshone Falls may be the result of later-invading rainbow trout that replaced Yellowstone cutthroat trout throughout the Snake River drainage up to Shoshone Falls. Yellowstone cutthroat trout persisted only where they occurred in isolation from rainbow trout.

The Salmon and Clearwater River drainages, major tributaries to the Snake River in Idaho, have westslope cutthroat trout as the native trout. Yellowstone cutthroat trout would be expected to have occurred in the Salmon and Clearwater drainages, but according to this scenario the original cutthroat trout were eliminated by the later-invading rainbow trout. Subsequently westslope cutthroat gained access to the Salmon and Clearwater Rivers via headwater stream transfers. This scenario of how the westslope cutthroat trout became established in the Salmon and Clearwater drainages assumes that Yellowstone cutthroat trout were there first and were eliminated by rainbow trout. It is based more on speculation than on hard evidence, but it is the basis for applying the subspecies name *bouvieri* to Yellowstone cutthroat trout.

In 1882 the name "*Salmo purpuratus bouvieri*" was used for a cutthroat trout with large, round spots from Waha Lake, near Lewiston, Idaho. Waha Lake is isolated from external connections, but during the last glacial period its outflow would have connected to the Clearwater River drainage. The indigenous occurrence of cutthroat trout in Waha Lake indicates that the connection between Waha Lake and the Clearwater drainage occurred before rainbow trout became established and eliminated the Yellowstone cutthroat from the Salmon and Clearwater drainages.

The large, round spots sparsely distributed on the body of the Waha Lake trout are typical of Yellowstone cutthroat trout and distinctly different from the westslope cutthroat now found in the Salmon and Clearwater drainages. Thus it has been assumed that the largespotted cutthroat trout of Waha Lake represented a relict population of Yellowstone cutthroat, and the subspecies name *bouvieri* was the first published describing Yellowstone cutthroat trout. It is, however, entirely possible that the Waha Lake cutthroat trout was a westslope cutthroat trout with a highly aberrant spotting pattern. If this were true, then the subspecies name *bouvieri* would be a synonym of the westslope cutthroat trout (*lewisi*), and a new subspecies name would have to be found for Yellowstone cutthroat trout.

The extinction of cutthroat trout in Waha Lake probably occurred 75 years ago or more after the stocking of many nonnative fishes, including rainbow trout and the common carp. A few museum specimens collected in about 1880 and 1881 are the only tangible remains of the Waha Lake cutthroat trout. Although it is sometimes possible to extract small amounts of DNA from long-preserved museum specimens for genetic testing, for the correct identification of the Waha Lake cutthroat trout we might best follow the old aphorism "Leave well enough alone" and continue to classify Yellowstone cutthroat as *Oncorhynchus clarki bouvieri*.

Another cutthroat trout with relatively large, round spots from Crab Creek, in eastern Washington, was described in 1909 as "*Salmo eremogenes*." Crab Creek drains to Moses Lake and is isolated from the Columbia River. Crab Creek flows through "scablands" scoured by the many great floods from ice-dam failures of glacial Lake Missoula. Any cutthroat trout transported in the floodwaters from glacial Lake Missoula would have been westslope cutthroat trout, but the spotting on specimens of Crab Creek cutthroat trout is more typical of Yellowstone cutthroat trout than of the westslope subspecies.

By the time the Crab Creek cutthroat trout was described in 1909, millions of cutthroat trout propagated from Yellowstone Lake had been widely stocked in many states. All descendants of Yellowstone Lake cutthroat trout can be recognized by their diagnostic characteristics of numbers of gill rakers and basibranchial teeth. The Crab Creek cutthroat trout were not the result of an introduction of Yellowstone Lake cutthroat trout, but whether they were truly Yellowstone cutthroat trout or instead westslope cutthroat trout with aberrant spots is not known. As with the Waha Lake trout, the Crab Creek cutthroat is long extinct.

Thus the historic distribution of the Yellowstone cutthroat trout downstream from Shoshone Falls is based on largespotted cutthroat trout described from Waha Lake, Idaho, in 1882 and from Crab Creek, Washington, in 1909. One or both of these records could, in reality, have been westslope cutthroat trout with highly unusual and deceptively large spots.

CONSERVATION   Nonnative trout (brook, brown, rainbow, and lake trout) began to be stocked in the waters of Yellowstone National Park in 1889. By the early 1900s, the westslope cutthroat trout (and the Arctic grayling) were eliminated from the headwaters of the Madison and Gallatin River drainages in the park (the upper Missouri River basin) and replaced by introduced brown trout and rainbow trout. There are records from the early 1900s of rainbow trout and Atlantic salmon being

Lake Trout
Salvelinus namaycush

The lake trout, stocked illegally in Yellowstone Lake over 25 years ago, would wipe out the native Yellowstone cutthroat were it not for a rigorous control program. In addition to netting by the Park Service, there is a "must kill" regulation for all lake trout caught by anglers in Yellowstone Lake.

stocked in Yellowstone Lake. Fortunately, these rainbow trout and Atlantic salmon were never seen again. If any rainbow trout survived to hybridize with the Yellowstone Lake cutthroat trout, no trace of hybridization has been detected.

Although Yellowstone Lake and the Yellowstone River drainage above the falls in Yellowstone National Park hold the world's greatest concentration of pure cutthroat trout, consisting of over 1 million adult fish, the Yellowstone cutthroat trout has been replaced by nonnative brook, brown, and rainbow trout throughout most of its original range in the upper Snake River drainage and the Yellowstone River drainage. For example, the largespotted cutthroat trout native to Waha Lake, Idaho, the type locality for the subspecies name *bouvieri,* are long extinct. The cutthroat trout of Rosebud Creek, Montana, the type locality for the name cutthroat trout, have been totally replaced by brook, brown, and rainbow trout. A similar fate has befallen the cutthroat trout of the Tongue River drainage, Wyoming, which were enjoyed by General Crook's troops in June 1876, and

the cutthroat trout that were in the Little Bighorn River in 1876—all long gone.

The gravest threat to the continued existence of the world's most abundant population and single greatest concentration of cutthroat trout, that of Yellowstone Lake, is predation from lake trout illegally introduced about 25 years ago. By the time lake trout were first documented in the lake in 1994, they had been there for many years; the population consisted of thousands of fish representing many generations. Since 1994, an intensive netting program has removed thousands of lake trout from Yellowstone Lake. Without this program, it is likely that the native cutthroat trout would be virtually eliminated from the lake.

The removal program uses nets set in areas where lake trout are known to congregate, such as spawning sites. Although it is unlikely that lake trout can be eliminated from Yellowstone Lake, the control program is designed to keep their numbers at sufficiently low levels so that the abundance of cutthroat trout is not significantly reduced by lake trout predation.

In 1998, another nonnative organism,

Myxobolus cerebralis, a microscopic parasite that causes whirling disease in trout, was found in some Yellowstone Lake cutthroat trout; these trout were from two to six years old, indicating that the whirling disease parasite had been in the Yellowstone drainage since at least 1992. *M. cerebralis* was first introduced into the United States from Europe, in shipments of frozen trout, in the late 1950s. It rapidly spread in cold-water habitat around the country. The impact of whirling disease on rainbow trout in the Madison River, in Montana, was first documented in 1994, but the parasite had been there for several years before 1994. From the Madison drainage, *M. cerebralis* might have been transported by American white pelicans that fed on infected trout in the Madison River and then flew the short distance from the Madison to the Yellowstone drainage, where they deposited feces containing *M. cerebralis* spores.

Brown trout coevolved with *M. cerebralis* in Europe and are highly resistant to the harmful effects of whirling disease. Rainbow trout and cutthroat trout are highly susceptible to whirling disease if exposed to high rates of infection (more than 100,000 parasites per fish) during the first year of life. Rates of whirling disease infection are related to water temperature and to the abundance of the intermediate host, a thread-like worm, *Tubifex tubifex*. Tubifex worms live in silty habitat. The cutthroat trout found to be infected by *M. cerebralis* to date have been lightly infected. It is hoped that in the spawning habitat in tributaries the infection rate will remain at low levels and whirling disease will not cause a significant decline in abundance of Yellowstone Lake cutthroat trout.

The state fishery agencies of Montana, Wyoming, and Idaho have programs to protect, enhance, and restore native cutthroat trout. The U.S. Forest Service and the Bureau of Land Management in these states also give special consideration to protecting cutthroat trout habitat from the effects of logging, road construction, mining, and livestock grazing.

Ideally no nonnative trout should be stocked where they might threaten native cutthroat trout by replacement (by brook trout and brown trout) or by hybridization (with rainbow trout). This policy may be difficult to implement, however, if it faces strong opposition. For example, in the 1980s biologists of the Idaho Department of Fish and Game developed a plan to protect and "purify" the Henrys Lake cutthroat trout by stopping the stocking of rainbow × cutthroat hybrids. Many anglers, who believed their right to fish for hybrid trout was threatened by an arbitrary action of a state agency, made vociferous protests to the news media, fish and game commissioners, and state legislators. The compromise solution was the continued stocking of hybrids, but sterile ones. This imperfect solution illustrates the fact that conservation issues and programs to protect native species are not always based on the best scientific evidence and can be unduly influenced by politics.

Snake River Finespotted Cutthroat Trout

Oncorhynchus clarki behnkei

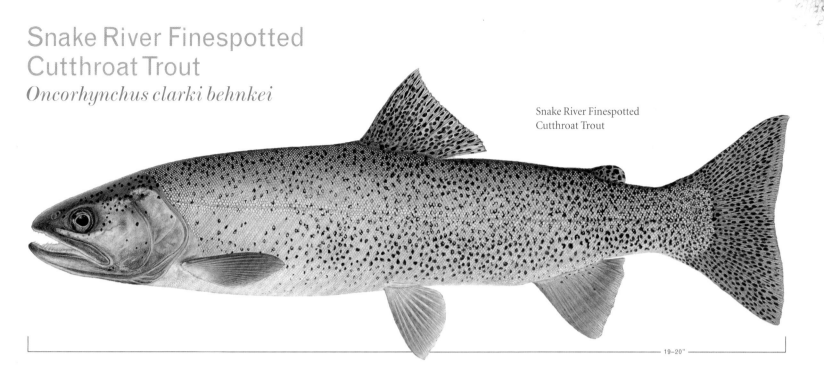

Snake River Finespotted
Cutthroat Trout

19–20"

In the Snake River, the finespotted cutthroat trout support a popular fishery and most anglers in the Jackson, Wyoming, area seek them out. There is a common belief that the Snake River finespotted cutthroat trout is the strongest fighter of all cutthroat trout, more like a rainbow trout in sporting quality. Because of its popularity among anglers and its adaptability to new environments, the Snake River finespotted cutthroat trout is the most widely propagated of all subspecies of cutthroat, and the one most widely stocked outside its native range.

The Snake River finespotted cutthroat trout got its subspecies name, *behnkei,* following the publication of my 1992 monograph *Native Trout of Western North America,* which included a morphological description and an illustration of the distinctive trout and noted that it had never been officially given a scientific name— it was considered an undescribed subspecies. In 1995 Simon and Schuster published *Many Rivers to Cross,* by M.R. Montgomery, a *Boston Globe* columnist; the book is about the author's search for native trout of the American West. In his chapter on the Snake River, Montgomery discusses the Snake River finespotted cutthroat trout and provides the descriptive information from my monograph under the name *Oncorhynchus clarki behnkei.*

DESCRIPTION The most diagnostic trait of the Snake River finespotted cutthroat trout is its unique spotting. This subspecies has the smallest spots of any trout native to

SNAKE RIVER FINESPOTTED CUTTHROAT TROUT

SCIENTIFIC NAME
Oncorhynchus clarki behnkei

OTHER COMMON NAMES
Jackson Hole cutthroat trout

HABITAT
Large rivers; widely adaptable to streams and lakes

LENGTH AND WEIGHT
Typical maximum 19–20" (48–51 cm) and 3 lb (1.4 kg); 27–28" (69–71 cm) and 9–10 lb (4.1–4.5 kg) under ideal conditions

LIFE SPAN
6–7 years

DIET
Aquatic and terrestrial invertebrates, fishes, amphibians, and crustaceans

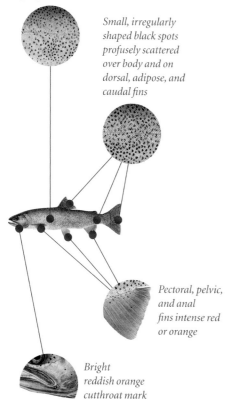

Body brownish yellow with dull silvery, greenish bronze, or sometimes purplish tints

Small, irregularly shaped black spots profusely scattered over body and on dorsal, adipose, and caudal fins

Pectoral, pelvic, and anal fins intense red or orange

Bright reddish orange cutthroat mark

western North America. The spots are profuse and generally resemble a heavy sprinkling of ground pepper on the sides of the fish. The size and shape of the spots typically found on the cutthroat trout in the Snake River downstream from Palisades Reservoir more closely resemble small, irregular flakes of dried chili pepper than they do coarsely ground peppercorns.

The finespotted's other characteristics are similar to those of Yellowstone cutthroat trout, except for some subtle trends of difference in coloration more commonly found in one subspecies or the other. The flanks of both typically are brownish yellow overlaid with dull silvery or greenish bronze colors. Purplish tints are more commonly found in finespotted cutthroat trout, and the pectoral, pelvic, and anal fins of finespotted cutthroat generally have more intense red or orange coloration.

Except for spot size and subtle color differences, the morphological traits of the Snake River finespotted cutthroat trout overlap with the largespotted Yellowstone cutthroat trout.

Different populations of finespotted trout from different tributaries of the Snake River exhibit differences in the numbers of scales, vertebrae, pyloric caeca, and basibranchial teeth. These differences demonstrate that the Snake River finespotted cutthroat trout population found above Palisades Reservoir is not a single homogeneous entity but consists of several subpopulations associated with different tributary streams and different life histories (migratory and nonmigratory) that maintain a high degree of reproductive isolation.

BIOLOGY   The finespotted cutthroat trout evolved with many species of minnows, suckers, and sculpins in a big-river environment in the upper Snake River. This type of evolutionary programming evidently has made the finespotted cutthroat trout the most adaptable and successful of any cutthroat trout subspecies when introduced into new environments outside its native range. When stocked in lakes representing a range of different environments, the finespotted cutthroat trout opportunistically feeds on the most seasonally available forage organisms, readily adapting to feeding on the bottom, in open water, and on the surface.

A typical maximum age is six or seven years, and maximum size is about 19 or 20 inches (48–51 cm) and 3 pounds (1.4 kg). With ideal feeding conditions, finespotted cutthroat trout can attain sizes of 27 or 28 inches (69–71 cm) and 9 or 10 pounds (4.1– 4.5 kg).

Scientists in Colorado discovered an interesting phenomenon concerning the finespotted cutthroat trout and whirling disease. Tests of the survival of different races and subspecies of cutthroat trout and rainbow trout after exposure to the parasite causing whirling disease found that the finespotted cutthroat has the greatest resistance to whirling disease, but the reason is not known.

DISTRIBUTION   The stocking of rainbow trout was underway by 1890 in the upper Snake River drainage, and there is a long history of propagation and widespread stocking of both the largespotted Yellowstone and the Snake River finespotted cutthroat. Both factors have contributed to the problem of clearly determining the original distribution of the largespotted and finespotted cutthroat in the entire Snake River system above Shoshone Falls.

The known present distribution of the Snake River finespotted cutthroat trout is from Palisades Reservoir to Jackson Lake in the main Snake River and in tributary streams from the Gros Ventre River downstream to Palisades Reservoir. In the first three tributary streams below Jackson Lake—Pacific Creek, Buffalo Fork, and Spread Creek—the largespotted Yellowstone cutthroat trout is the native trout. The largespotted cutthroat occurs in headwater tributaries to the Gros Ventre, and the finespotted cutthroat occurs in the rest of the drainages. How can two distinct forms (subspecies in this case) of cutthroat trout, so closely related that they cannot be distinguished by the most sensitive genetic techniques, so neatly partition their distributions in a continuous environment? There are no physical barriers that isolate the finespotted and largespotted forms from each other. So why is there is no overlap? How are distributional boundaries separating the two forms maintained?

These questions currently cannot be answered with any basis in fact. There is no doubt, however, that the finespotted and largespotted cutthroat trout maintain distinct and nonoverlapping distributions. The two forms are "sympatric" (both occur in the continuous environment of the upper Snake River drainage without physical isolation), but they are not "syntopic" (they do not occur together at the same site at the same time).

Before a dam was constructed to raise the level of Jackson Lake in 1911 and before the dam creating Palisades Reservoir was completed in the 1950s, there were no barriers

The known present native range of the Snake River finespotted cutthroat trout is from Palisades Reservoir to Jackson Lake in the main Snake River and in tributary streams from the Gros Ventre River downstream to Palisades Reservoir.

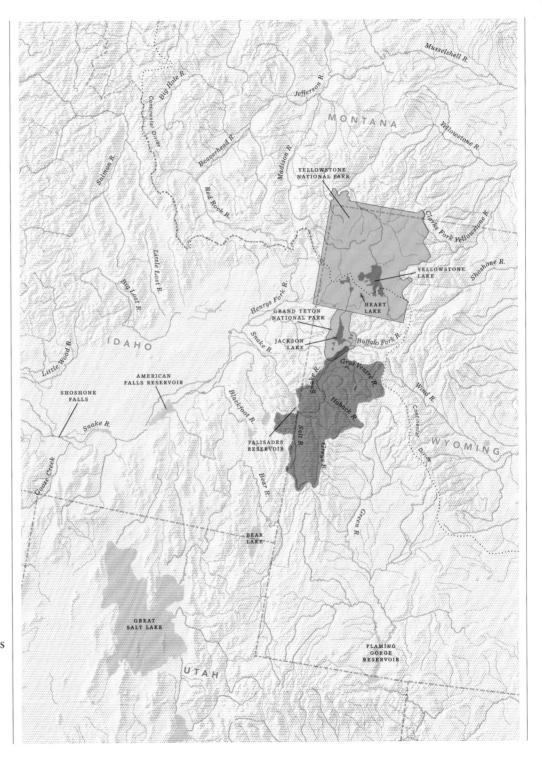

SUBSPECIES OR FULL SPECIES?

In the Colorado River basin, three full species of the minnow genus *Gila*—the roundtail, bonytail, and humpback chubs—can be identified only by a morphological distinction, their distinctively different body shapes. And in the Mississippi–Missouri River basin the full species called the pallid sturgeon and the shovelnose sturgeon are indistinguishable by genetic analysis but have obvious morphological differences. Based on these examples, it could be argued that the Snake River finespotted cutthroat trout should also be classified as a full species, because it maintains its identity by reproductive isolation from the largespotted Yellowstone cutthroat in the upper Snake River system. However, such a classification would reflect an incongruous and unnatural evolutionary branching sequence: a subspecies, the Yellowstone cutthroat, giving rise to a full species. Also, the precise original distributions of finespotted and largespotted cutthroat trout in the Snake River drainage above Shoshone Falls, before intervention and widespread stocking of nonnative trout, is not known. There may have been areas of natural intergradation between the two forms. Taxonomy is often "messy" and controversial. Yet there is no doubt that the Snake River finespotted cutthroat trout represents a biological entity and an evolutionary reality. Its recognition as a subspecies is a practical compromise.

to movement in the channel of the Snake River from Shoshone Falls to the uppermost headwaters coming from Heart Lake. It is known that the cutthroat trout native to Heart Lake is a typical Yellowstone cutthroat trout with large, rounded spots. Also, in all of the larger streams tributary to the Snake River from Palisades Reservoir to Shoshone Falls, from the Henrys Fork to Goose Creek, the native trout is the largespotted Yellowstone cutthroat trout.

Hybridization between native cutthroat trout and introduced rainbow trout downstream from Palisades Reservoir is well documented, and genetic monitoring has shown that the rate of hybridization has increased in recent years. It is unlikely that before rainbow trout were stocked and before Palisades Dam blocked movement of fish in the Snake River, the size of the spots on the finespotted cutthroat trout became larger at the Wyoming–Idaho border.

EVOLUTION AND CLASSIFICATION

The origin of the Snake River finespotted cutthroat trout probably occurred during the later stages of the last glacial period, about 20,000 years ago. During this period, ice-dam and/or landslide lakes in the upper Snake River system created opportunities for the isolation of a population of largespotted cutthroat trout and their evolutionary change into finespotted cutthroat trout. Breeding experiments in Norway with brown trout found that the genetic basis for large spots or very small spots, comparable in size to the spots of Snake River finespotted cutthroat trout, is due to different forms of a gene (called alleles) at a single gene locus.

There has been a relatively short geological time of divergence and probable occasional hybridization and genetic interchange between finespotted and largespotted cutthroat trout, and no diagnostic genetic marker has yet been found that can identify one subspecies from the other. But an observer can distinguish the two subspecies by looking at specimens and observing the striking distinction between finespotted and largespotted trout.

It is unusual that such a distinctive trout was not commonly recognized historically. In the late nineteenth century the U.S. Fish Commission conducted two surveys and collected fish in the upper Snake River system, but all localities studied—Heart Lake, Henrys Lake, Pacific Creek, and the Portneuf River—had only the largespotted Yellowstone subspecies. The first published reference to the finespotted cutthroat of which I am aware is in a 1970 revised edition of the *Wyoming Game and Fish Bulletin: Wyoming Fishes,* which has photographs of both the Yellowstone cutthroat and the Snake River finespotted cutthroat. It is mentioned that the distinctive finespotted cutthroat is "worthy of recognition."

If it weren't for the distinction in the size of spots of the finespotted and largespotted cutthroat trout in the upper Snake River system, the reality of the coexistence of the two forms would not be known. As mentioned, no genetic distinctions have been found that can identify one form from the other. The lack of a known genetic distinction can easily lead to a wrong conclusion: If no differences can be found by modern methods of genetic analysis, then there are no genetic (hereditary) differences.

That such a conclusion is obviously wrong can be seen in the size of the spots that clearly differentiate between largespotted and finespotted cutthroat trout, and the consistent and stable pattern of nonoverlapping distributions of the two forms. The genetic or hereditary basis for the size of spots can be observed in hatchery propagation: Largespotted cutthroat trout give rise to largespotted offspring, and finespotted cutthroat produce finespotted offspring.

Extremely slight genetic differences are often not detectable by the most modern techniques of molecular genetics, yet they can result in large differences in life history. This fact is well illustrated by comparing steelhead and resident rainbow trout and sockeye salmon and kokanee: One life history form is anadromous and roams thousands of miles in the open ocean, whereas the other spends its whole life confined to a river or a lake. Where the anadromous and resident life history forms coexist in the same area with occasional genetic interchange, it is likely that no genetic distinctions will be found between the two forms. Nevertheless, it would be wrong to conclude that there is no hereditary basis for anadromous versus resident life histories.

It must be accepted that there is a heredity basis for the difference between the finespotted and the largespotted cutthroat trout. This hereditary difference extends to subtle biological differences in life history, behavior, and habitat preference that maintain the separate, nonoverlapping distributions of the two subspecies in the upper Snake River system.

In modern taxonomy, it is unusual to name a taxon (a taxonomic category, such as a species or subspecies) in "popular" literature, such as Montgomery's book. Although Montgomery's description of a new taxon does not strictly follow standard taxonomic procedure, it conforms to the standards of the International Code of Zoological Nomenclature. According to the Code, in the case of a subspecies a valid name must include a diagnostic description that differentiates the subspecies for which the new name is proposed from all other subspecies within its species—in this case, the cutthroat trout. The diagnostic characteristic of Snake River finespotted cutthroat trout is extremely small spots. The description must be published and the publication must be available according to definitions given in the Code, and Montgomery's book meets both criteria. Also, no other subspecies or species name had been previously published for the same taxon, accompanied by a valid description.

Since no species or subspecies name meeting the criteria for validity according to the Code was published before the 1995 publication of *Many Rivers to Cross, Oncorhynchus clarki behnkei* is a valid name—that is, it is available for use as the name for the finespotted cutthroat trout. However, the actual recognition of the finespotted cutthroat trout as a subspecies distinct from the Yellowstone cutthroat trout is a matter of individual preference.

CONSERVATION   If the area of the Snake River between Palisades Reservoir and Jackson Lake is considered, the Snake River finespotted cutthroat trout is the only subspecies of cutthroat trout that still completely dominates in its native range. It has not been replaced by nonnative trout, nor has it hybridized with rainbow trout. Downstream from Palisades Reservoir in Idaho, hybridization with rainbow trout has occurred, and a trout with somewhat larger spots but still overwhelmingly of cutthroat trout ancestry dominates in the angler's catch.

Efforts to reduce and reverse the effects of hybridization in Idaho consist of placing weirs across spawning tributaries and removing rainbow trout and obvious hybrids before they can reproduce. Restrictive angling regulations have virtually eliminated angling mortality of cutthroat trout in the Snake River of Idaho. At the same time, these regulations encourage anglers to remove rainbow trout and obvious hybrids. In Wyoming, important spawning tributaries used by the finespotted cutthroat trout have been restored.

All in all, comparing present distribution and abundance with known historical distribution, the Snake River finespotted cutthroat trout has fared better than any other subspecies of cutthroat trout. ◆

Bonneville Cutthroat Trout
Oncorhynchus clarki utah

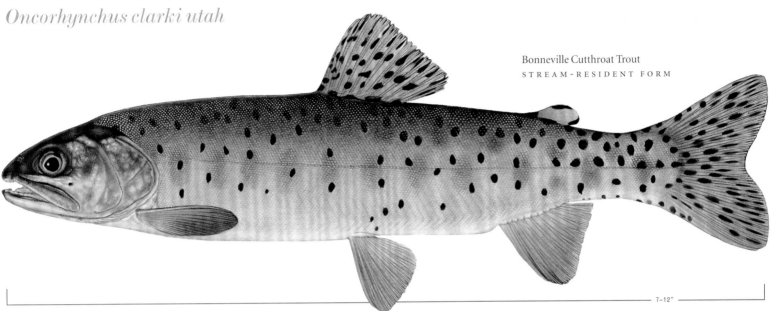

Bonneville Cutthroat Trout
STREAM-RESIDENT FORM

7–12"

Lake Bonneville was the largest of the Great Basin lakes that formed during the last glacial period, which ended about 11,000 years ago. Today, the Bonneville basin, the area once occupied by the glacial lake and its drainages, covers most of Utah and small parts of Nevada, Idaho, and Wyoming. At its maximum extent about 15,000 years ago, Lake Bonneville covered an enormous area—20,000 square miles (51,800 sq km), equal to roughly a quarter of the size of Utah or nearly the size of Lake Michigan.

Today, Interstate-80 drops below the level of the old lake as it descends the Wasatch Front from the east toward Salt Lake City. About 15,000 years ago the site of the city was under 1,100 feet (335 m) of water. West from Salt Lake City, I-80 crosses the ancient lake bottom, the Great Salt Lake Desert; its Bonneville Salt Flats were created by salts deposited during the final desiccation of Lake Bonneville about 8,000 years ago.

Cutthroat trout are thought to have originated in the Bonneville basin between 50,000 and 100,000 years ago, a relatively short period of time compared to some other subspecies of cutthroat. An ancestral cutthroat trout entered the Lahontan basin of present-day Nevada perhaps 1 million years ago. Most likely, at least two northern invasions of ancestral Yellowstone cutthroat trout from the Snake River drainage gave rise to the Bonneville cutthroat trout. Thus the Bonneville cutthroat is considered a minor subspecies

---

BONNEVILLE CUTTHROAT TROUT

SCIENTIFIC NAME
Oncorhynchus clarki utah

OTHER COMMON NAMES
Utah cutthroat trout

HABITAT
Clear, cool streams and rivers; lakes

LENGTH AND WEIGHT
7–12" (18–30 cm) and 2.1–8 oz (60–227 g) in small streams. 14–18" (36–46 cm) and 1–3 lb (0.45–1.4 kg) in larger streams, rivers, and lakes

LIFE SPAN
3–4 years in small streams; longer in river and lakes

DIET
Aquatic and terrestrial invertebrates; large fish in lakes become piscivorous

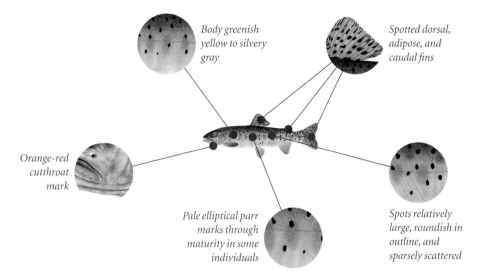

Body greenish yellow to silvery gray

Spotted dorsal, adipose, and caudal fins

Orange-red cutthroat mark

Pale elliptical parr marks through maturity in some individuals

Spots relatively large, roundish in outline, and sparsely scattered

STREAM-RESIDENT FORM

of the major subspecies Yellowstone cutthroat trout.

The first entry of cutthroat trout into the Bonneville basin probably occurred via an interbasin transfer from the Snake River drainage into the Bonneville basin. Until about 30,000 years ago, the Bear River (the largest river drainage in the Bonneville basin) was a tributary to the Snake River. Volcanic activity and lava flows blocked the north-ward-flowing Bear River and diverted it to the south to become part of the Bonneville basin. The additional flow from the Bear River raised the level of Lake Bonneville and cut an outlet at Red Rock Pass, Idaho, about 14,500 years ago. This event, called the Bonneville flood, released an enormous volume of water (and fishes) into the upper Snake River and rapidly reduced the depth of the lake by some 350 feet (100 m).

The level of Lake Bonneville subsided and over a period of about 7,000 years the lake vanished, leaving its vestiges, the Great Salt Lake and the adjacent Utah Lake. Great Salt Lake, the fourth largest terminal lake (no outlets) in the world is completely devoid of fish. Fed by the Provo River, Utah Lake (presently 32 miles/51 km away from Great Salt Lake) maintained a continuous freshwater lacustrine environment after Lake Bonneville desiccated.

After the disappearance of Lake Bonneville, Utah Lake became the sole site where the most ancient fish species of the basin persisted—a highly specialized species of sucker of the genus *Chasmistes*. After surviving for many millions of years, since Miocene times, *Chasmistes* species have become threatened with extinction during the past 100 years. This threat is mainly a result of depleted flows in spawning rivers caused by human development. Living species of *Chasmistes* today are found only in Utah Lake (the June sucker, now partially hybridized with the Utah sucker), Upper Klamath Lake, Oregon (the shortnose sucker),

and Pyramid Lake, Nevada, of the Lahontan basin (the cui-ui sucker). All three sucker species are listed as endangered under the Endangered Species Act.

The Bonneville cutthroat trout did not fare much better. The subspecies was thought to be extinct by the 1950s, but fortunately because of protection and enlightened stocking programs, the Bonneville cutthroat has persisted.

There are three differentiated geographical groupings of Bonneville cutthroat trout (four, if you separate the Bear Lake cutthroat trout). These populations are found in the main Bonneville basin, in the Snake Valley of the Bonneville basin along the Nevada–Utah border, and in the Bear River drainage.

DESCRIPTION   The Bonneville cutthroat trout and its older cousin the Yellowstone cutthroat trout share somewhat similar coloration, but Bonneville cutthroat have a tendency for silvery gray versus yellowish brown background colors. As with the Yellowstone subspecies, Bonneville cutthroat trout do not develop brilliant crimson colors, but sexually mature males living in a lake environment can exhibit distinctive rose and orange colors. The azure blue color of the entire dorsal surface of Bear Lake cutthroat gave rise to the local common name "bluenose trout."

Spots are relatively large, roundish in outline, and sparsely and somewhat evenly scattered over the sides of the body. This spotting pattern is most typically expressed on the trout native to the Bear River drainage.

There is a distinctive trend for the cutthroat trout native to the Bear River

Bear Lake Cutthroat Trout

22–24"

drainage to have more scales along the sides (165–180 versus 150–165) and more pyloric caeca (40–45 versus 30–40, but 50 or more in Bear Lake cutthroat) compared with other populations of Bonneville cutthroat trout.

The cutthroat trout of Bear Lake live in a large lacustrine environment and, as is typical of trout living in lakes or in the sea, have silvery coloration on the sides of the body that obliterates large spots or greatly modifies them into small speckles.

The Snake Valley section of the Bonneville basin was connected to Lake Bonneville only during the period of the highest lake level. Long isolation of the trout in the Snake Valley area resulted in differences in the numbers of gill rakers (20–22 versus 17–20) and basibranchial teeth (about 20 or more versus 5–15) compared to other Bonneville basin cutthroat trout.

BIOLOGY   As with all other cutthroat trout subspecies, there are no biological or life history traits that are unique to Bonneville cutthroat trout. However, evolutionary adaptive distinctions are associated with populations of Bonneville subspecies, such as the specializations for life in Bear Lake.

Another aspect of the diversity within the Bonneville basin cutthroat trout is the persistence of the native cutthroat trout in the Bear River drainages of Wyoming, a harsh, highly fluctuating environment.

That the life histories of the Bear Lake and Bear River cutthroat trout are indeed highly adapted to their specific environments can be perceived by their persistence despite a long history of nonnative trout introductions. Without superior survival capabilities, they would have been displaced long ago by nonnative trout, as has occurred with

BEAR LAKE CUTTHROAT TROUT

SCIENTIFIC NAME
Oncorhynchus clarki utah

OTHER COMMON NAMES
Bluenose trout

HABITAT
Bear Lake, Idaho and Utah

LENGTH AND WEIGHT
22–24" (56–61 cm) and 3–5 lb (1.4–2.3 kg); historical maximum 23–26 lb (10.4–11.8 kg)

LIFE SPAN
10–11 years

DIET
Primarily terrestrial invertebrates; become piscivorous at 16" (41 cm), after which feed almost exclusively on sculpins and whitefishes

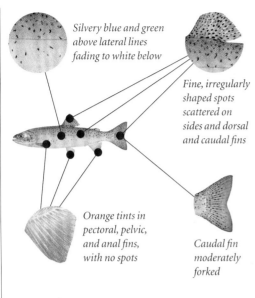

Silvery blue and green above lateral lines fading to white below

Fine, irregularly shaped spots scattered on sides and dorsal and caudal fins

Orange tints in pectoral, pelvic, and anal fins, with no spots

Caudal fin moderately forked

BEAR LAKE CUTTHROAT TROUT

Bonneville cutthroat trout in most of the Bonneville basin.

The major hereditary distinctions of the Bear Lake cutthroat trout are reflected in its specialized lacustrine life history: older age at maturity, longer life span, and highly predatory feeding habits. Bear Lake lies at an elevation of almost 6,000 feet (1,830 m) and was never submerged under Lake Bonneville. The lake is also semi-isolated from the Bear River; only during prolonged periods of high precipitation does Bear Lake overflow to the north and connect to the Bear River. When full, Bear Lake covers about 109 square miles (282 sq km) in Utah and Idaho and has a depth of 207 feet (63 m); its mean depth is 92 feet (28 m). Bear Lake is low in nutrients. In the 1950s two reports on the lake said that the native cutthroat trout must be extinct there as a pure population, a conclusion that seemed logical because

of a long history of stocking the lake with millions of nonnative trout (rainbow trout, nonnative cutthroat trout, rainbow × cutthroat hybrids, and lake trout) combined with the degradation of two spawning tributaries, St. Charles Creek and Swan Creek. However, in the 1970s some of the few remaining cutthroat trout in Bear Lake were critically examined and found to be identical to museum specimens of Bear Lake cutthroat from the early 1900s. Genetic tests verified their purity. Obviously, the native cutthroat trout is highly adapted to the Bear Lake environment. An artificial propagation and restoration program begun in the 1970s has led to several studies on the life history and ecology of the Bear Lake cutthroat.

Because of the scarcity of aquatic invertebrates in Bear Lake, during their first few years of life the cutthroat there rely heavily on terrestrial insects that blow onto the lake surface; these insects constitute at least 50 percent of the trout's total food supply, supplemented with zooplankton, chironomid (midge) larvae, and, as the trout grow larger, sculpins. At lengths of 16 inches (41 cm) and larger, Bear Lake cutthroat trout feed mainly on fishes: Sculpins and whitefishes (mainly the Bear Lake cisco) make up 90 to 95 percent of their diet.

In Bear Lake, the native cutthroat trout has a maximum life span of 10 or 11 years. Typically, sexual maturity and first spawning is attained at six to nine years of age, when the trout are 22 to 24 inches (56–61 cm) long and weigh 3 to 5 pounds (1.4–2.3 kg). Age at sexual maturity is determined by both hereditary (genetic) and environmental factors. For example, when Bear Lake

cutthroat trout are stocked into more productive waters, such as Strawberry Reservoir, Utah, and experience rapid growth during their first few years, sexual maturation occurs sooner (generally in four years) than in Bear Lake.

Bear Lake cutthroat trout are the only trout, except for Arctic char, known to increase in weight during winter months when water temperatures are below 39 °F (4 °C). All experiments with brook trout, brown trout, rainbow trout, and other forms of cutthroat have demonstrated that when water temperature falls to 39 °F and lower (as occurs in most natural environments where trout live), the fish stop growing and eventually lose weight, even with unlimited food. The reason Bear Lake cutthroat trout can continue to gain weight during winter is not known, but it may be the result of evolutionary programming. The major food source, especially in winter, of large (16 inches/41 cm or larger) cutthroat trout in Bear Lake is the Bear Lake cisco, which spawns in winter, mainly in January. Since the cutthroat trout most likely prey on spawning aggregations of the cisco, it appears that a life history of active feeding and growth in winter allows the cutthroat to capitalize on this opportunity.

Another interesting aspect of Bear Lake cutthroat trout is their ability to coexist with lake trout. Popular among anglers, lake trout were first stocked in Bear Lake in 1911 and have continued to be stocked on a regular basis. Elsewhere, the introduction of lake trout into large lakes has been a major factor in reducing cutthroat populations to small remnants of their former abundance.

In Bear Lake, however, lake trout have not produced large numbers of surviving offspring compared to those in lakes such as Yellowstone, perhaps because of limited spawning habitat and/or predation on lake trout eggs and young by sculpins and white-fishes. Bear Lake is low in nutrients, and the number of invertebrate fish prey is a small fraction of that found in more fertile lakes. The three species of endemic Bear Lake whitefishes and the Bear Lake sculpin are highly adapted to utilize the small invertebrate organisms in Bear Lake. Even if millions of lake trout hatch from eggs, very few baby lake trout are likely to obtain sufficient food to survive and grow to a size (12–14 inches/30–36 cm) at which they can effectively prey on fishes. Once lake trout begin to feed on fishes in Bear Lake, their annual survival greatly increases. From about ages four or five, taking into account fish caught by anglers, annual survival of lake trout averages about 60 percent until they are 20 years old or older, at which point they are about 33 to 36 inches (84–91 cm) long and weigh 15 to 18 pounds (7–8 kg). Thus, the major negative impact of lake trout on cutthroat trout in Bear Lake is not due to predation; cutthroat trout comprise less than 10 percent of the lake trout diet.

The main negative interaction between lake trout and cutthroat trout in Bear Lake is competition for a common food supply. The forage fishes in the diet of both species are sculpins and whitefishes, especially the Bear Lake cisco. Competition is most severe during periods of low abundance of forage fishes. In the early 1990s, drought conditions lowered lake levels, exposing much of the shallow

Bear Lake Cisco
Prosopium gemmifer

The Bear Lake cisco, native to no other lake in the world, makes up a large portion of the diet of adult Bear Lake cutthroat trout.

littoral zone, the lake's most productive habitat in terms of providing food for the prey species. With loss of much of the littoral zone, the abundance of sculpins and whitefishes declined, and the intensity of competition between lake trout and cutthroat trout increased, resulting in the reduced growth and survival of cutthroat trout.

If lake trout stocking in Bear Lake ceased, lake trout would eventually become extinct in the lake or their natural abundance would be maintained at a very low level. The native fishes would revert to their original balance with the Bear Lake cutthroat trout as the sole top level predator.

Because the lake trout is a popular sport fish in Bear Lake, there is substantial angler demand for continued stocking. It might be hoped, however, that in an era of more enlightened fishery management with an emphasis on native species, the fishery agencies of Utah and Idaho can agree on a management program to phase out lake trout stocking and return the fishery to its original condition. This would reinstate the native Bear Lake cutthroat as the only large preda-tory species and the dominant sport fish.

Although Bear Lake is in the Bonneville basin and its native cutthroat trout is classified as the Bonneville cutthroat trout, the biological distinctions of the

Bear Lake population apply only to it and not to the subspecies or the species as a whole. In the rest of the Bonneville basin outside the Bear River drainage, the native cutthroat trout, adapted for many thousands of years for life in an enormous lake, were forced to survive in streams after the desiccation of Lake Bonneville. As a result, they do not grow as large as the Bear Lake form, at sexual maturity ranging in size from 7 inches (18 cm) in tiny streams up to an extreme maximum of 18 inches (46 cm) in large streams and rivers. Besides Bear Lake, which was never submerged by Lake Bonneville, only two relatively large lakes in the basin—Utah Lake and Panguitch Lake—had native cutthroat trout, and the cutthroat trout of both became extinct by the 1930s.

Except for those in the Bear River drainage, Bonneville cutthroat trout evidently were not well adapted for life in streams. In the twentieth century, they were rapidly replaced by nonnative brook, brown, and rainbow trout. This replacement was so rapid that by the 1950s it was believed that pure populations of the Bonneville cutthroat trout were extinct. Fortunately, a few pure populations persisted in small headwater habitats where they were isolated from nonnative trout.

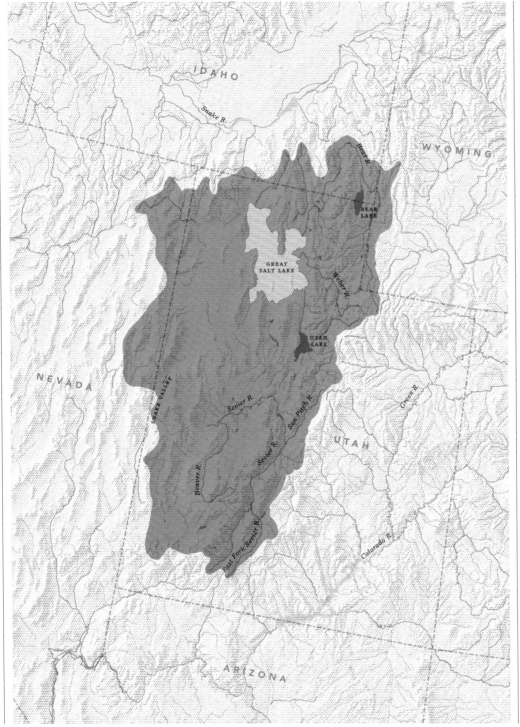

In some sections of the Bear River drainage, such as the Thomas Fork and Smith Fork tributaries in Wyoming, a form of the Bonneville cutthroat trout persisted and was not replaced by nonnative trout. A long evolutionary history of existence in semi-arid watersheds subjected to great environmental extremes of floods, droughts, and high sediment loads endowed the Bear River fluvial form of cutthroat trout with superior survival capabilities. Nonnative trout are rare in this area of the Bear River drainage, found only in the "best" trout habitat—cold, clean streams. In what would be judged to be submarginal trout habitat—warmer, silty streams with late summer flows reduced to a trickle—only the native Bear River cutthroat trout is found, another example of a distinctive biological specialization that characterizes local populations but not the subspecies as a whole.

Among the native fish fauna of the Bonneville basin, the cutthroat trout was the only large predatory species. Only in Bear Lake, however, has the naturally evolved predator-prey relationship between cutthroat trout and native prey species persisted, but this coevolved relationship has been distorted by competition with introduced lake trout. In the late nineteenth and early twentieth centuries Bear Lake sustained a commercial fishery for whitefishes and cutthroat trout. Old accounts and photographs of cutthroat trout that weighed from 23 to 26 pounds (10.4–11.8 kg) testify to the

The native range of the Bonneville cutthroat trout includes much of western Utah and some areas of Nevada, southeastern Idaho, and southwestern Wyoming.

large size the cutthroat attained before lake trout were introduced. In more recent times, which have included periods of severe competition for a common food supply, few cutthroat trout exceed 24 inches (61 cm) and 5 pounds (2.3 kg).

DISTRIBUTION   This subspecies occurs in the Bonneville basin of Utah, Wyoming, Idaho, and Nevada. A typical Bonneville basin cutthroat trout is also found in the headwaters of the Santa Clara River in the Pine Valley area of the lower Colorado River basin in southwestern Utah. This trout still occurs in two small streams in Reservoir Canyon and Water Canyon near Pine Valley, in southern Utah. Reliable local testimony reports that trout were there in 1864 when the Mormon settlers arrived.

The topography and geology of the present contiguous boundary between the Bonneville basin and the headwaters of the Santa Clara River in the Pine Valley area suggest that a natural headwater transfer occurred that brought cutthroat trout from the Bonneville basin into the Santa Clara drainage. If this is true, a natural transfer must have occurred in relatively recent geological times, within the past few thousand years. The cutthroat trout in Reservoir Canyon and Water Canyon appear to be identical to the cutthroat trout native to the southern part of the Bonneville basin.

EVOLUTION AND CLASSIFICATION
All genetic evidence agrees that Bonneville basin cutthroat trout are derived from and closely related to the Yellowstone subspecies. Bear River cutthroat trout are essentially genetically identical to Yellowstone cutthroat trout of the Yellowstone and upper Snake River drainages. The degrees of genetic relatedness are indicative of an earlier invasion of an ancestral cutthroat trout from the Snake River drainage into the Bonneville basin, perhaps some 50,000 to 100,000 years ago, and of a later transfer of Snake River cutthroat when the Bear River changed its course as a tributary to the Snake River to become a tributary to Lake Bonneville about 30,000 years ago.

From the point of view of a classification system based on degrees of differentiation, the cutthroat trout native to the Bear River drainage could be classified as Yellowstone cutthroat trout. From a more practical point of view, subspecies classification historically has not adhered to strict evolutionary interpretation, but to some commonalities within geographical boundaries, such as drainage basins. It is more practical to include all cutthroat trout native to the Bonneville basin as one subspecies, the Bonneville cutthroat trout. Also, during the many thousands of years when the Bear River flowed into Lake Bonneville, some mixing and intergradation almost certainly occurred between the "original" Bonneville cutthroat trout and the Bear River cutthroat trout.

In the late 1800s and early 1900s, Bonneville basin cutthroat trout were variously classified as "*Salmo virginalis*," "*S. mykiss virginalis*," and "*S. clarki virginalis*." "*Salmo virginalis*" was the name given in 1856 to Rio Grande cutthroat trout collected from Ute Creek in the San Luis Valley of southern Colorado. Somehow Ute Creek became "Utah Creek" in the early literature and was assumed to be a stream in the Bonneville basin of Utah.

George Suckley, a surgeon-naturalist with the Pacific Railroad Survey during the 1850s, compiled a manuscript, called *On the North American Species of Salmon and Trout* (sometimes referred to as Suckley's monograph of the genus *Salmo*), that he completed in 1861 and published in 1874. In this work, Suckley mentions a "variety" of "*Salmo virginalis*" that occurs in Utah Lake. When he compared the Utah Lake specimens with other cutthroat specimens from the Bonneville basin, Suckley saw that lake specimens were "less spotted." He wrote: "For this variety or kind we will, for the present, apply the provisional name of *Salmo utah*." Existence in a large lake environment results in a silvery coloration with large, round spots modified into small, irregularly shaped, speckle-like spotting. Although Suckley intended the name *utah* only to distinguish the cutthroat trout of Utah Lake from other Bonneville basin cutthroat trout, which he classified as "*Salmo virginalis*," the name *utah* is the first name published for any Bonneville basin cutthroat trout, and *Oncorhynchus clarki utah* is now the subspecies name for all cutthroat trout native to the basin.

CONSERVATION   The unique adaptations of the Bear Lake and the Bear River cutthroat trout fortify the argument that a conservation program to preserve and restore a subspecies should have the goal of preserving diversity within the subspecies. Conservation and management programs for the Bonneville basin cutthroat trout in Utah, Wyoming,

Idaho, and Nevada now seek to maintain all of the remaining diverse populations of Bonneville basin cutthroat trout. When pure populations are documented, a common practice is to transplant some of the native trout into other streams in the area after the elimination of all nonnative trout by chemical treatment. These treatments use a chemical that suffocates and kills fishes when they are exposed to it in sufficient quantities. A proper program for the conservation of biodiversity (versus the conservation of species or subspecies as a whole) includes the notion that "minor variation" is important.

About 50 pure populations of Bonneville cutthroat trout now occur in the Bonneville basin. State fish and wildlife agencies have cooperative programs to protect, enhance, and restore Bonneville cutthroat, and the U.S. Forest Service and the U.S. Bureau of Land Management have revised their management programs, especially for livestock grazing, to protect and restore habitat in watersheds with Bonneville cutthroat trout.

Representatives of state and federal resource agencies involved with natural resource management in the basin participate in the development and implementation of the Bonneville Cutthroat Trout Management Plan. A large artificial propagation program for Bonneville basin cutthroat trout exists in Utah, mainly targeting Bear Lake cutthroat but also including other forms of the subspecies. These hatchery-reared cutthroat are widely stocked in lakes and reservoirs for sportfishing, and the propagation and stocking program helps gain popular support for restoration programs. The Bonneville cutthroat trout is the official state fish of Utah.

The outlook for the continued existence of the cutthroat trout of the Bonneville basin, once considered extinct, and all of its remnant diversity is optimistic, based on many successful restoration projects, improved habitat protection and restoration in cutthroat trout watersheds, and large-scale propagation and stocking to make the Bonneville cutthroat a popular sport fish. In October 2001 the U.S. Fish and Wildlife Service rejected a petition to list the subspecies for protection under the Endangered Species Act. 🐟

Colorado River Cutthroat Trout
Oncorhynchus clarki pleuriticus

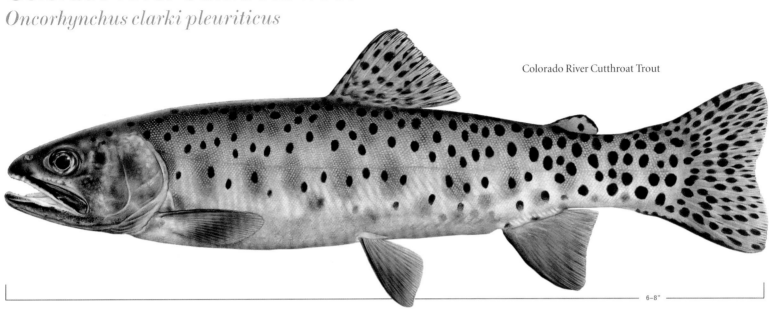

Colorado River Cutthroat Trout

6–8"

The Colorado River cutthroat trout is a descendant of the Yellowstone cutthroat trout and is one of the minor subspecies of the cutthroat trout. This status as minor merely denotes its lineage and in no way diminishes its importance as a native fish in its range. The Colorado River cutthroat and its descendants, the Rio Grande and the greenback cutthroat trout, differ from their Yellowstone ancestor in their potential to develop brilliant coloration. The rather subdued rose, yellow, and orange colors in the Yellowstone and the Bonneville cutthroat trout can transform into intense crimson and bright golden yellow in Colorado River cutthroat trout and its two descendant subspecies. The intense coloration of the Colorado cutthroat trout is why the first writer to mention the golden trout of the Kern River drainage in the nineteenth-century literature mistakenly believed it to be a form of *"Salmo pleuriticus."* The Colorado River cutthroat is now classified as *Oncorhynchus clarki pleuriticus.*

DESCRIPTION   The hereditary basis to develop intense coloration is the characteristic that most clearly differentiates the Colorado River cutthroat trout from Yellowstone and Bonneville cutthroat trout. In addition, the Colorado River cutthroat typically has more scales along the sides of the body than Yellowstone and Bonneville cutthroat trout; in the Colorado River subspecies scales average 180 to 200 versus 160 to 175 for the Yellowstone and Bonneville forms.

There is considerable diversity, especially in the size and pattern of spots on the body,

COLORADO RIVER CUTTHROAT TROUT

SCIENTIFIC NAME
Oncorhynchus clarki pleuriticus

OTHER COMMON NAMES
Native trout

HABITAT
Small, clear streams and rivers; small to medium-size lakes

LENGTH AND WEIGHT
6–8" (15–20 cm) and 1–5 oz (28–142 g) in headwater streams. 16–20" (41–51 cm) and 2–5 lb (0.9–2.3 kg) in larger streams, rivers, and lakes

LIFE SPAN
Probably 4–5 years in headwater streams; 5–8 years in rivers and lakes

DIET
Primarily aquatic and terrestrial invertebrates; occasionally fishes and amphibians

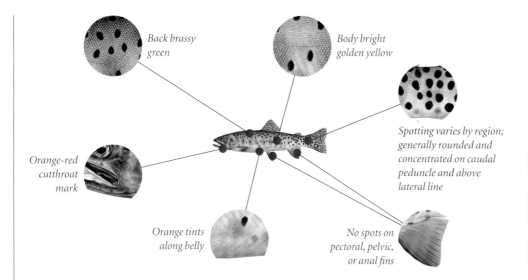

Back brassy green

Body bright golden yellow

Orange-red cutthroat mark

Spotting varies by region; generally rounded and concentrated on caudal peduncle and above lateral line

Orange tints along belly

No spots on pectoral, pelvic, or anal fins

among Colorado River cutthroat trout. This difference in appearance is associated with different areas of distribution and is likely due to more than one ancestor making a headwater transfer from the upper Snake River drainage into the upper Green River drainage of the Colorado River basin (see Evolution and Classification, below).

The spots of the Colorado River cutthroat trout are rounded in outline and their size and pattern vary. In trout native to the headwaters of the Green River, the spots are relatively small (about the diameter of the pupil of the trout's eye or smaller) and are distributed mainly on the caudal peduncle and above the lateral line on the anterior part of the body. In Colorado River cutthroat native to the Little Snake River drainage in Wyoming (a tributary to the Yampa River, in turn a major tributary to the Green River) the spots are large (almost equal to the diameter of the full eye) and are distributed more or less evenly over the sides of the body.

BIOLOGY The life history and ecology of the Colorado River subspecies is typical of cutthroat trout in general. After the period of the last glaciation, approximately 11,000 years ago, there were no large natural lakes formed in the upper Colorado River basin comparable to Bear Lake, in the Bonneville basin. Thus no population of Colorado River cutthroat trout acquired special adaptations to a large lake environment. The subspecies was native to a few lakes of moderate size (smaller than 500 surface acres, or 200 ha)—including Grand Lake, Trappers Lake, and some lakes on the Grand Mesa in Colorado—but, as in stream populations, these lake populations were rapidly replaced by nonnative trout, except for the Trappers Lake cutthroat, which persisted as a relatively pure population until the 1970s, when rainbow trout gained access to the lake and hybridization began.

In small headwater streams, Colorado River cutthroat usually grow no larger than 8 inches (20 cm). In larger rivers and lakes,

these cutthroat can grow to a maximum of approximately 20 inches (51 cm).

Similar to other inland subspecies that evolved in isolation from rainbow trout, the Colorado River cutthroat is highly susceptible to replacement by brook trout and brown trout and to hybridization with rainbow trout. In one small area of their range, however, Colorado River cutthroat trout have persisted after introductions of nonnative trout. In some small foothill tributaries to the upper Green River, in Wyoming, a cutthroat trout with a slightly hybrid influence from rainbow trout, but still bearing the appearance of a typical native cutthroat trout, persists. The environment of these foothill streams is comparable to that of the Bear River drainage of the Bonneville basin—highly fluctuating and unstable.

During the past 100 years these watersheds have been further degraded by livestock grazing that has increased erosion and siltation, also called sediment loads. Evidently these small populations in their limited habitat—like the Bear River cutthroat form of the Bonneville basin—have evolved a life history that allows them to cope with unstable and fluctuating environments, a hereditary legacy that has also allowed them to successfully resist replacement by nonnative trout.

DISTRIBUTION The original range of the Colorado River cutthroat trout is the upper Colorado River basin of Colorado, Wyoming, Utah, and New Mexico. The northernmost distribution was in the headwaters of the Green River in Wyoming and the southernmost distribution was the San

Juan River drainage in northern New Mexico. Only nonnative trout are now known from the San Juan drainage of New Mexico. Although there is no documentation that the Colorado River cutthroat trout or any cutthroat trout is native to Arizona, streams of the Chuska Mountains, near the New Mexico border, now inhabited by nonnative trout, almost certainly held Colorado River cutthroat trout before nonnative trout were introduced.

Specific areas—including the main stems of the Green River (near the town of Green River, Wyoming) and the Colorado River (near Rifle, Colorado) and the lower-elevation sections (below about 5,000 feet / 1,500 m) of tributary rivers that make up most of the area within the original range of the Colorado River cutthroat trout—lacked suitable temperatures and water quality to maintain trout. Many tributaries to the main stems at higher elevations held thriving native trout populations, but it was not until the intervention of modern water management that suitable habitats were formed in the larger rivers. Some of today's notable tailwater fisheries for nonnative trout in the Green River downstream from Flaming Gorge Dam, in the Colorado River below Glen Canyon Dam, and in the San Juan River below Navajo Dam were not hospitable to native or nonnative trout before dams and

The original native range of Colorado River cutthroat trout was large but most likely discontinuous. Just as today, warmer silt-laden waters at lower elevations would not have been suitable habitat. The present native range is restricted to the upper Colorado River basin above the Grand Canyon; to the west, it is restricted by the Escalante River of Utah and to the south by the San Juan River drainage of Colorado, New Mexico, and Arizona.

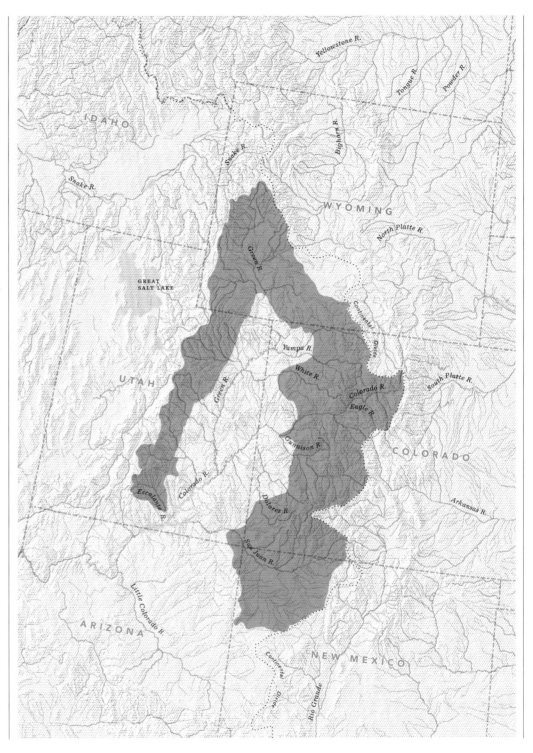

reservoirs were constructed. Reservoirs settle out sediment and dams control the release of clear, cold water in a regulated flow, creating the present tailwater environments in which trout flourish.

After nonnative trout began to be introduced into the upper Colorado River basin, the native cutthroat trout was rapidly replaced. For example, the upper Gunnison River in Colorado was first stocked with rainbow trout (10,000 newly hatched fry) in 1883. By 1897 the Gunnison was famous for its rainbow trout fishery. A photo in the *Rocky Mountain News* that year shows two anglers displaying eleven rainbow trout weighing 5½ to 9 pounds (2.5–4 kg) from the Gunnison River. Around the same time another news item told of an angler catching a 12-pound (5.4-kg) native cutthroat trout from the Gunnison, perhaps the last of the natives.

A 1905 article in *Outdoor Life* magazine made a plea not to introduce rainbow trout in the Yampa River (called the Bear River at that time), in Colorado; the author claimed that the upper Yampa was the last place in Colorado he could find native cutthroat trout. The plea was not heeded.

In 1963, the Colorado Division of Wildlife estimated that cutthroat trout made up only 2 percent of all trout caught in the state. Only a tiny fraction of this 2 percent would have consisted of truly native cutthroat trout (Colorado River, Rio Grande, and greenback cutthroat). Almost all the cutthroat trout caught in Colorado in 1963 would have been from hatchery stocks of mixed ancestry that were regularly stocked in mountain lakes. Most high-elevation lakes in the Rocky

Mountains were originally devoid of fish because of barrier falls that blocked natural access. In the twentieth century, cutthroat trout were most commonly encountered in high-elevation lakes, and anglers and angling writers shared the belief that these lakes were the original home of the cutthroat. In fact, almost all of these lakes originally had no fish; the cutthroat trout they now hold are the result of the stocking of hatchery fish.

By the mid-twentieth century, Colorado River cutthroat trout occupied only a tiny fraction of their original distribution, mainly in small headwater streams isolated by barrier falls from contact with nonnative trout.

EVOLUTION AND CLASSIFICATION

More than one ancestor of the Colorado River cutthroat trout made a headwater transfer from the upper Snake River drainage into the upper Green River drainage of the Colorado River basin. The fact that other species native to the upper Colorado basin— the mountain whitefish, speckled dace, mountain sucker, mottled sculpin, and Paiute sculpin—are derived from the upper Snake River indicates that several opportunities existed for small streams in the Snake River drainage to be diverted or temporarily connected to the Green River drainage, probably during the last glacial period. It is also possible that natural transfers of cutthroat into the Green River drainage occurred from the Bonneville basin.

After establishment in the Green River drainage, cutthroat trout spread throughout most of the upper Colorado River basin, but the warm, turbid waters in most of the main stem habitat of the Green and Colorado

Rivers, as well as in lower-elevation segments of their larger tributaries, would have greatly limited further dispersal. These environmental barriers resulted in effective isolation of cutthroat trout in different regions of the upper Colorado River basin.

The spotting pattern of the Little Snake River drainage cutthroat is very similar to that of the greenback cutthroat. It is likely that this form of the Colorado River cutthroat trout gained access to the South Platte River basin and gave rise to the greenback cutthroat trout.

Like most subspecies names now used to classify cutthroat trout, the subspecies name *pleuriticus* for Colorado River cutthroat trout requires interpretation. "*Salmo pleuriticus*" was described in 1872 based on preserved specimens of cutthroat trout collected by a U.S. Geographical Survey headed by Ferdinand Hayden and commonly known as Hayden's Survey. "*Salmo pleuriticus*" was described from several cutthroat trout specimens from different river basins. Among them were specimens from the upper Green River near Fort Bridger, Wyoming. The specimens on which the name is based also included fish from the South Platte River (greenback cutthroat) and the Yellowstone River (Yellowstone cutthroat).

The diagnostic characteristic for all specimens named *pleuriticus* was a ridge on the midline of the skull, but the ridge evidently was an artifact of improper preservation; the specimens probably had become dehydrated, causing the frontal bones and the overlying skin to form a ridge. Although the diagnostic trait for the name *pleuriticus* is an invalid characteristic, it was the first name proposed for the cutthroat trout of the upper Colorado River basin.

Because many of the nineteenth-century names of species or subspecies of trout and other fishes are questionable due to inadequate or erroneous descriptions and wrong localities (as with the greenback cutthroat trout, see next account), their present usage as subspecies names is based on redescriptions by a "first reviser." In an 1891 publication, David Starr Jordan redescribed *pleuriticus* and acted as the "first reviser" to fix the name *pleuriticus* with the cutthroat trout native to the upper Colorado River basin.

CONSERVATION   As with other cutthroat trout subspecies, modern conservation approaches emphasize the preservation of native species. This approach has made the Colorado River cutthroat trout a high priority for protection and restoration among state and federal resource agencies in the trout's native range in Colorado, Wyoming, and Utah. Enhancement activities include transplants to establish new populations, stream improvements, and better management of livestock to restore riparian vegetation for stream-bank stability and reduced siltation levels. The restoration and enhancement programs for the Colorado River cutthroat trout have been formalized in a conservation agreement among the resource agencies.

Presently there are about 100 pure populations of the Colorado River cutthroat trout. Most exist in small, isolated streams, most of which have only about 1 or 2 miles (2–3 km) of suitable habitat, so the populations are not large. However, in the headwaters of the Little Snake River, in Wyoming, Colorado River cutthroat trout occur in 36 miles (58 km) of continuous stream habitat above a barrier constructed to protect against invasion by nonnative trout.

For about 100 years, Trappers Lake was the source of most Colorado River cutthroat trout that were artificially propagated and stocked in the mountain lakes of Colorado. After hybridization with hatchery rainbow trout was detected in Trappers Lake, a new source for the propagation of pure Colorado River cutthroat trout was found in a lake in Rocky Mountain National Park. However, the pure form of the original Trappers Lake cutthroat trout is not extinct. In 1931, an exchange of fish was made between the fish and game agencies of Colorado and California in which Trappers Lake cutthroat trout were sent to California. These trout were stocked in the Williamson Lakes in a remote area on Mount Williamson in the southern Sierra Nevada; the lakes had no fish at the time. These Trappers Lake cutthroat reproduced and still exist in the Williamson Lakes. In 1987, about 300 pure Colorado cutthroat trout from Williamson Lakes were returned to Colorado and stocked in Bench Lake in the Colorado River drainage of Rocky Mountain National Park, where they have maintained a healthy population.

Greenback Cutthroat Trout
Oncorhynchus clarki stomias

Greenback Cutthroat Trout
BEAR LAKE SPAWNING MALE

17–18"

The greenback cutthroat was the trout caught and consumed in great quantities by the first European American settlers in the Denver area and along the Front Range of Colorado. It rapidly disappeared due to pollution from mines, irrigation diversions, overfishing, and, especially, the introduction of nonnative trout. A 1937 publication on the trout of Colorado declared that the greenback cutthroat trout was extinct. Since 1969 a few pure populations have been discovered, and many transplants by the U.S. Fish and Wildlife Service and Colorado state hatcheries have established new populations.

The early descriptions of greenback cutthroat were inadequate or erroneous and not useful for identification of specimens as to subspecies. Thus, during the time that the greenback cutthroat trout was believed to be extinct, there was no description that could properly identify pure greenback trout if they were found. Fortunately, several specimens of cutthroat trout from the South Platte and Arkansas drainages were collected in the nineteenth century and preserved in museums. These ancient specimens provided the basis to better characterize the greenback cutthroat trout for comparisons with contemporary specimens from extant populations. This set the stage for the "rediscovery" of the greenback cutthroat trout.

DESCRIPTION Neither the scientific name *stomias* (implying a large mouth) nor the common name are useful to identify

GREENBACK CUTTHROAT TROUT

SCIENTIFIC NAME
Oncorhynchus clarki stomias

OTHER COMMON NAMES
Cutthroat

HABITAT
Mountain and foothill headwater streams and rivers; ponds and lakes

LENGTH AND WEIGHT
10–12" (25–30 cm) and 6–11 oz (170–312 g) in small streams. 17–18" (43–46 cm) and 2 lb (0.9 kg) in larger streams, rivers, and lakes; historical maximum 5 lb (2.3 kg)

LIFE SPAN
Probably 5–8 years

DIET
Primarily aquatic and terrestrial invertebrates

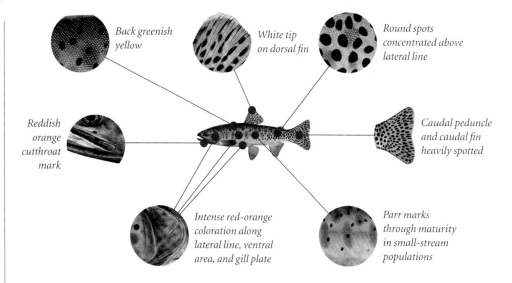

Back greenish yellow

White tip on dorsal fin

Round spots concentrated above lateral line

Reddish orange cutthroat mark

Caudal peduncle and caudal fin heavily spotted

Intense red-orange coloration along lateral line, ventral area, and gill plate

Parr marks through maturity in small-stream populations

STREAM-RESIDENT FORM

the greenback subspecies. The mouth of the greenback cutthroat is no larger than that of any other subspecies, and the back is no greener.

The greenback cutthroat trout derived from the Colorado River cutthroat trout, probably during the last glacial period. No diagnostic characteristics, either morphological or genetic, can clearly separate the greenback from the Colorado River cutthroat trout. Both subspecies can develop intense coloration under the proper conditions of age, sex, and diet.

There are tendencies for the greenback cutthroat to have larger spots that are more sparsely and evenly distributed over the sides of the body, and to have more scales along the body (190–215) than the "typical" Colorado River cutthroat trout (180–200). However, Colorado River cutthroat native to the headwaters of the Little Snake River drainage, in Wyoming, more resemble greenback cutthroat in their spotting pattern

and scale counts than they do "typical" Colorado River cutthroat trout. It was probably this form of Colorado River cutthroat trout that crossed the Continental Divide into the South Platte River basin to give rise to the greenback cutthroat.

Greenback cutthroat trout were never noted for large size. Nineteenth-century accounts cite a maximum size of about 5 pounds (2.3 kg). Yearling (one-year-old) greenbacks stocked into a small pond with abundant food on the Fort Carson Military Reservation in Colorado have grown to 4 or 5 pounds (about 2 kg) in three or four years after stocking.

BIOLOGY In respect to life history and ecology, the greenback cutthroat trout is wholly typical of other cutthroat trout subspecies. In fact, it might be said that the greenback cutthroat trout is the "most typical" cutthroat trout because of its susceptibility to extinction: By the 1960s only

a few pure populations existed. Two of those populations became extinct soon after being exposed to introduced brook trout. All the remaining pure greenbacks were fortunately isolated by barriers from contact with nonnative trout.

Greenback cutthroat trout were native to only one relatively large lake area, Twin Lakes, in the headwaters of the Arkansas River drainage near Leadville, Colorado. Twin Lakes consists of two connected lakes that total about 1,000 surface acres (400 ha). According to nineteenth-century accounts, the greenback trout of Twin Lakes was abundant and readily caught but was small in size (to 10–12 inches, or 25–30 cm). Twin Lakes also held a distinct form of a larger lacustrine-specialized cutthroat trout, the yellowfin cutthroat.

Beginning in the 1890s, nonnative brook, rainbow, and lake trout and Atlantic salmon were introduced into Twin Lakes, and both the yellowfin and greenback populations were soon gone. Sampling of Twin Lakes in 1902 and 1903 failed to find any yellowfin trout, and the rainbow trout was the dominant species. About half of the greenback trout (or what appeared to be greenbacks) collected in 1902 and 1903 showed signs of hybridization with rainbow trout; within a few years, pure greenbacks were gone from Twin Lakes.

A distinctive life history trait is associated with one of the original pure greenback populations found in the uppermost head-waters of the Little South Poudre River of the South Platte basin. This population occurs at elevations exceeding 10,500 feet (3,200 m) in a cold environment in which the maximum

Greenback Cutthroat Trout
STREAM-RESIDENT FORM

10–12"

temperature rarely exceeds 54 °F (12 °C). In similar streams with an extremely cold temperature regime, transplanted greenback cutthroat have not successfully reproduced. Spawning does not occur until mid-July, and young do not emerge until mid- to late September. By that time, winter conditions have begun, and the juvenile trout do not have sufficient time to feed and store the energy needed to survive the long winter. The Little South Poudre greenback population evidently acquired an adaptation that allows their eggs to develop at a more rapid rate and to hatch sooner than is typical for other greenback populations and other species of trout, and so they persist in this harsh environment.

This distinctive trait was observed during artificial propagation of greenback cutthroat trout. At the Saratoga National Fish Hatchery in Wyoming (a U.S. Fish and Wildlife Service hatchery), eggs from Little South Poudre greenbacks were incubated alongside eggs of a greenback population from Cascade Creek, in the Arkansas River drainage. The eggs of the Cascade Creek greenbacks hatched after the accumulation of 312 centigrade temperature units. An average incubation temperature of 46 °F (8 °C) equals the accumulation of 8 temperature units per day and requires 39 days to accumulate 312 units. This amount of time and number of accumulated temperature units is typical for the hatching of cutthroat and rainbow trout eggs. In comparison, the eggs for the Little South Poudre greenback trout hatched after accumulating only 256 temperature units. Thus they hatched sooner than the Cascade Creek greenbacks, a trait that would allow the greenback fry in the higher elevations of

the Little South Poudre the necessary time to feed and overwinter to reach sexual maturity.

DISTRIBUTION   The original range of the greenback cutthroat trout is almost entirely within the state of Colorado. The headwaters of tributaries, such as Dale Creek, southeast of Laramie, extended the original distribution of the greenback cutthroat into a small area of Wyoming, just north of the Colorado border.

The greenback cutthroat's original distribution—restricted to the mountain and foothill sections of the South Platte and Arkansas River drainages, mainly above 5,000 feet (1,500 m) elevation—was reduced to "almost extinction." By 1969, when the first pure greenback population was discovered, populations of the greenback cutthroat trout with no hybrid influence from rainbow trout or other subspecies

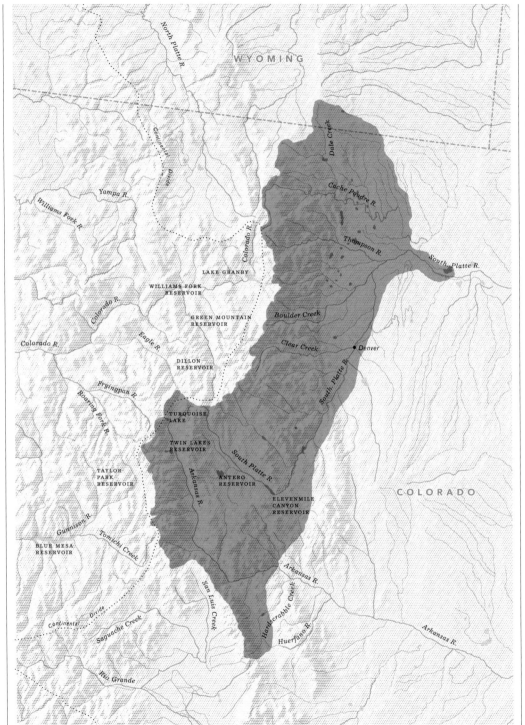

of cutthroat trout existed in only a few miles of a few very small streams isolated from contact with nonnative trout.

EVOLUTION AND CLASSIFICATION

It is likely that all greenback cutthroat trout of the South Platte and Arkansas River drainages came from a single transfer across the Continental Divide from the headwaters of the Colorado River basin into the South Platte basin. In contrast to the transfer of fishes from the upper Snake River drainage into the Green River drainage of the Colorado River basin—which includes five species in addition to cutthroat trout and indicates that there were many opportunities for interbasin transfers—the cutthroat trout is the only fish species that crossed the Continental Divide from the Colorado River basin to the South Platte drainage of the Missouri–Mississippi basin. From the South Platte drainage a connection to the Arkansas River drainage, allowing transfer of greenback cutthroat, probably occurred in the vicinity of Trout Creek Pass, where only a gentle divide now separates the two drainages.

The same 1872 publication proposing the name *pleuriticus* for the Colorado River cutthroat trout also contains a description of "*Salmo stomias.*" As with the taxon *pleuriticus*, the name *stomias* is associated with doubt and confusion as to which cutthroat trout from which river drainage it refers to.

The original native distribution of the greenback cutthroat trout was restricted to mountain foothill sections of the South Platte and Arkansas River drainages.

Two specimens of cutthroat trout were collected during an 1856 round-trip U.S. Army expedition from Fort Riley, Kansas, to Fort Bridger, Wyoming. All natural history specimens collected on the expedition were labeled "Fort Riley, Kansas" and shipped to the Philadelphia Academy of Natural Science. The 1872 description of *stomias* lists the "type locality" for the name as "South Platte River, Kansas." After it was realized that the South Platte River drainage does not enter Kansas, later references to *stomias* gave the type locality as the "Kansas River at Fort Riley." No trout are native to the Kansas River or to any waters anywhere near the state of Kansas.

The route of the 1856 expedition would have encountered cutthroat trout in two river basins. The Green River at Fort Bridger, Wyoming, the "type locality" for the name *pleuriticus,* had Colorado River cutthroat trout, and the upper parts of the South Platte River basin in Colorado had what we now call greenback cutthroat trout. Thus it is not known with certainty if the name *stomias* was actually based on cutthroat trout specimens from the South Platte basin. In an 1891 publication, David Starr Jordan fixed the name *pleuriticus* to the Colorado River cutthroat trout and revised the 1872 description of *stomias* to fix that name with the cutthroat trout native to the South Platte River basin of Colorado. Jordan also first used the common name greenback.

CONSERVATION   The greenback cutthroat trout was classified as endangered under the 1973 Endangered Species Act. The early restoration of the greenback cutthroat trout was accomplished by transplanting greenback cutthroat from pure populations to small isolated streams that were naturally fishless or that had been chemically treated to eliminate nonnative trout. Because of several successful transplants, in 1978 the greenback cutthroat trout was downlisted from endangered to threatened.

About 60 transplants of greenbacks have been made in both the South Platte and Arkansas drainages. In recent years introductions have been from stocks artificially propagated in federal (U.S. Fish and Wildlife Service) and Colorado state hatcheries. The most abundant greenback populations are found in several lakes and some streams of Rocky Mountain National Park. After a transplant is made, a few years of monitoring is necessary to be certain that no nonnative trout remain and that the greenbacks are successfully reproducing.

Several restoration projects that attempted to restore greenback cutthroat trout in small streams, after chemical treatment to remove brook trout, have failed because not all the brook trout were eliminated. If even a few brook trout survive the chemical treatment (probably no more than one male and one female), within a few years the brook trout rapidly repopulate the stream and eliminate the newly established greenback population. It is puzzling why the offspring of the few surviving nonnative trout fail to show any negative effects of "inbreeding depression"— that is, an extreme low level of genetic diversity, which is expected when a population is founded on very few individuals. Inbreeding depression generally results in loss of vigor and fertility, posing a serious disadvantage to survival. It is not known why these "inbred" brook trout continue to thrive in these circumstances.

If the restoration is deemed a success, most of the waters are open to angling with catch-and-release regulations (all fish must be released). There is a popular catch-and-release sport fishery for large greenback trout (18–19 inches, or 46–48 cm) at Lily Lake, along a state highway on the border of Rocky Mountain National Park. Lily Lake lacks an inlet stream, so natural reproduction does not occur. Hatchery-reared fingerling greenbacks are regularly stocked there in numbers that optimize growth.

In lakes with inlet streams where natural reproduction occurs, reproduction is often "too successful," and within a few generations the lake is overpopulated by a dense population of small (9–10 inches, or 23–25 cm), slow-growing greenbacks. When existing greenbacks are counted, these overpopulated lakes produce impressive statistics.

During the past 30 years, the numbers of greenback cutthroat have increased by about a thousandfold or more. The greenback cutthroat trout is often cited as a success story that shows how the Endangered Species Act can work with proper hatchery management and stocking programs. Although greatly diminished in their original range, greenbacks are "back" and like other minor subspecies came very close to extinction. 🐟

Yellowfin Cutthroat Trout
Oncorhynchus clarki macdonaldi

Yellowfin Cutthroat Trout

28"

The yellowfin cutthroat trout formerly of Twin Lakes, Colorado, has been extinct for about 100 years and the only hard evidence that this trout really existed comes from preserved specimens collected in 1889 and now held in museums. The mysterious appearance of the yellowfin and its subsequent eradication from Twin Lakes may be the result of many factors, and speculation persists to this day. However, it is most likely that introduction of nonnative rainbow trout caused its extinction. From the time it was first discovered by anglers only 17 years elapsed before it was declared extinct from Twin Lakes. It may be one of the most rapid eliminations of a subspecies known in America's history.

DESCRIPTION   In 1889, David Starr Jordan was leading a fisheries survey of the West for the U.S. Fish Commission. He collected from Twin Lakes several specimens of greenback cutthroat trout and seven specimens of a silvery trout he called "yellowfin trout." These specimens were preserved and became part of the fish collections at Stanford University and the National Museum of Natural History, Smithsonian Institute.

After more than 100 years preserved in alcohol, the seven specimens of yellowfin cutthroat trout are perfectly distinct from the 21 greenback specimens in background coloration and spotting. More important is the significant difference in the number of gill rakers: 20 to 22 (mean 21) in yellowfin specimens and 18 to 21 (mean 19) in greenback specimens. All the specimens of both

YELLOWFIN CUTTHROAT TROUT

SCIENTIFIC NAME
Oncorhynchus clarki macdonaldi

OTHER COMMON NAMES
None known

HABITAT
Known only from Twin Lakes, Colorado, where reportedly inhabited deepest portions of lake

LENGTH AND WEIGHT
Maximum 28" (71 cm) and 10 lb (4.5 kg), based on historical accounts

LIFE SPAN
Unknown

DIET
Most likely aquatic and terrestrial invertebrates; larger fish piscivorous

THREE HISTORICAL YELLOWFIN CUTTHROAT

The June 16, 1891, issue of *Sports Afield* magazine ran a photo of three cutthroat trout weighing 6 pounds, 12 ounces (3 kg), 4 pounds, 12 ounces (2.2 kg), and 3 pounds, 8 ounces (1.6 kg), caught from "Thompson's Ranch Pond, near Buena Vista," about 15 miles (24 km) south of Twin Lakes. The photo clearly shows the spotting pattern. The very small, irregularly shaped spots concentrated on the caudal peduncle would be expected for westslope cutthroat, Snake River finespotted cutthroat, and yellowfin cutthroat trout. At that time, there were no westslope or Snake River finespotted cutthroat trout in Colorado. Most probably some yellowfin cutthroat were obtained from the hatchery operation of the Colorado Fish Commission at Twin Lakes in 1885 and/or 1886 and stocked in the nearby pond. The fish in the photo are almost certainly yellowfin cutthroat trout. No other photo of yellowfin cutthroat trout is known to exist. Additional historical mention of the three large trout from Thompson's Ranch Pond is found in the *Rocky Mountain News* of May 12, 1891. They were presented to President Benjamin Harrison when his train made a stop at Buena Vista.

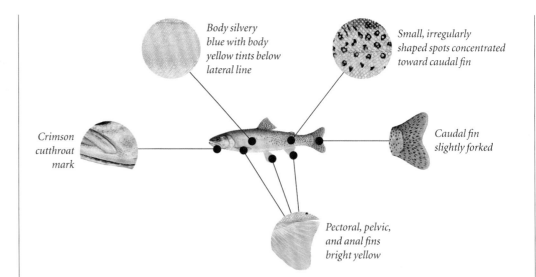

Body silvery blue with body yellow tints below lateral line

Small, irregularly shaped spots concentrated toward caudal fin

Crimson cutthroat mark

Caudal fin slightly forked

Pectoral, pelvic, and anal fins bright yellow

greenback and yellowfin cutthroat were 6 to 12 inches (15–30 cm) long.

The yellowfin specimens have fewer scales along the body: 159 to 185 (mean 175) in the yellowfins versus 170 to 202 (mean 189) in the greenback specimens. The yellowfin specimens average 42 scales above the lateral line (counted from beginning of the dorsal fin downward to the lateral line), and the greenback specimens average 48. There is no doubt that two distinct populations of cutthroat trout were living together in Twin Lakes in 1889 without hybridizing.

Angler accounts from the 1870s relate that Twin Lakes was noted for an abundant population of small greenback cutthroat trout. Large numbers of greenback trout, rarely more than 12 inches (30 cm) long, were caught by anglers, but there was no mention of large, silvery trout with very small spots until 1885. At that time, the Colorado Fish Commission began artificial propagation of the silvery trout, which were claimed to attain weights of 10 pounds (4.5 kg) or more. The

maximum length of the yellowfin at 28 inches (71 cm) is estimated from this extreme weight. The existence of a large trout in Twin Lakes was publicized, and it influenced a decision to build a federal fish hatchery at nearby Leadville in 1890.

Introductions of brook trout, rainbow trout, lake trout, and even Atlantic salmon were made in Twin Lakes in the 1890s. Collections made in 1902 and 1903 from Twin Lakes failed to find the yellowfin cutthroat trout. The rainbow trout had already become the dominant trout species, and hybridization between greenback cutthroat trout and rainbow trout was well underway. Within a few years, the Twin Lakes population of greenback cutthroat trout followed the yellowfin cutthroat trout into extinction.

BIOLOGY   All that is known about the life history of the yellowfin cutthroat trout is in the realm of speculation and hearsay. Jordan believed reproductive isolation between yellowfin and greenback cutthroat in Twin

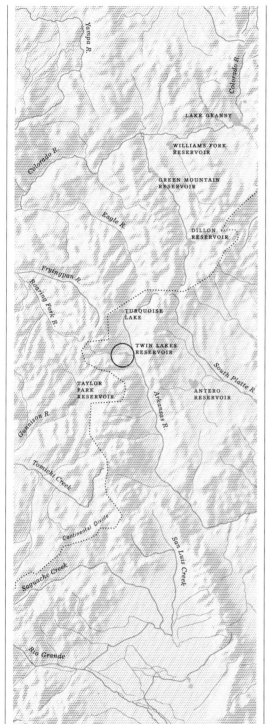

The yellowfin cutthroat trout was known from only Twin Lakes, Colorado, in the headwaters of the Arkansas River.

Lakes was maintained because the yellowfin cutthroat trout spawned earlier in the lake, while the greenback spawned later in the inlet stream, but his views were not based on first-hand observation.

He also believed that the diet of the yellowfin cutthroat trout consisted mainly of fish, while the greenback cutthroat fed on insects and crustaceans. This belief was mainly based on the larger size attained by the yellowfin cutthroat and the observation that the flesh of yellowfin was pale in contrast to the red flesh of the greenback.

DISTRIBUTION   The yellowfin cutthroat trout was known from only Twin Lakes, Colorado, in the headwaters of the Arkansas River. David Starr Jordan wrote in his autobiography, published in 1922, that he had visited Twin Lakes in 1889 and obtained specimens of yellowfin cutthroat trout.

Jordan wrote that although by 1922 the yellowfin cutthroat was extinct in Twin Lakes, eggs from the Leadville hatchery had been shipped to France, where they were "now established." While Jordan did not note why he believed the yellowfin cutthroat was established in France, in 1902 Siegfried Jaffe, who operated a hatchery at Sandfort, Germany, recounted in an article in a French fish-culturist journal that he had received 10,000 eggs of yellowfin cutthroat trout *(truite à nageoires jaunes)* from the Grand Mesa in May 1899 and an additional 20,000 eggs in July 1902 (eggs shipped from the

ENGLISHMAN OF THE GRAND MESA

From 1899 to 1910, the U.S. Fish Commission leased land for fish culture in the Grand Mesa from William Radcliff. Radcliff, a graduate of Oxford University, was a wealthy English sportsman who owned property ideal for raising trout. The abundant populations of native Colorado cutthroat trout on the Grand Mesa had long attracted poachers from local communities. Radcliff freely gave permits to anglers who agreed to abide by state laws in regard to season and catch limits, and he hired guards to protect the trout from poachers. The local people bore strong resentment against the wealthy Englishman who would dare to take away their "rights" to poach. In 1901, one of Radcliff's guards confronted a poacher. An argument ensued, and the poacher was shot dead. When word spread, a lynch mob formed and stormed onto Radcliff's estate. Radcliff had the good fortune to be in England at the time, but the angry mob torched his buildings. Radcliff never returned to the Grand Mesa. He did firmly establish his reputation in the literature of fishing with his 1921 book *Fishing from Earliest Times,* an erudite and widely acclaimed work on ancient fishing methods. As far as is known, Radcliff never mentioned and may have been unaware of the belief that yellowfin cutthroat trout occurred on his Grand Mesa estate.

THE YELLOWFIN CUTTHROAT TROUT'S MYSTERIOUS FATE

Mystery swirls around the fate of the yellowfin cutthroat trout. Enough unknowns remain to stimulate an active imagination to consider the possibility that, somewhere, a population of yellowfin cutthroat trout still exists.

The slight possibility that the yellowfin cutthroat trout is not extinct rests on the hatchery propagation and distribution of yellowfin cutthroat trout by the Colorado Fish Commission beginning in 1885 and continuing to some unknown date, and by the Leadville federal hatchery from 1892 to 1897. For many years, there was a belief that yellowfin cutthroat trout occurred somewhere on the Grand Mesa and that they were propagated at least until 1929 and distributed in large numbers, though there is no hard evidence or documentation explaining the origin and persistence of this belief.

Colorado River cutthroat trout commonly have yellow-gold colors, and early fish culturists on the Grand Mesa may have mistaken the native Colorado River cutthroat trout for the yellowfin cutthroat trout of Twin Lakes. Despite belief that the yellowfin cutthroat trout (or, more probably, Colorado River cutthroat trout mistaken for yellowfin cutthroat trout) would become established in Europe, there is no record of yellowfin cutthroat trout in Europe beyond their brief moment of fame at the Paris Fish Cultural Exposition at the beginning of the 20th century.

During the past 20 years or so, an occasional flurry of excitement has erupted when someone in Colorado has thought they may have found the extinct yellowfin cutthroat trout. All such reports have turned out to be based on the Snake River finespotted cutthroat trout that has been widely propagated and stocked in Colorado for the past 25 years. Yet the mysteries surrounding the yellowfin cutthroat trout have a certain appeal, and since its extinction cannot be proved with certainty, a tiny glimmer of hope can always remain that some day, somewhere, a population of these fish will be found.

Leadville hatchery). Jaffe displayed some of his "yellowfin" trout at a fish-culture exposition in Paris, where they were awarded first prize. Jaffe had distributed some of his "yellowfin" trout to other hatcheries, and he believed that they "were almost certain to become established."

The U.S. Fish Commission reports for 1899 and 1902 verify shipments of 10,000 and 20,000 eggs to Jaffe's hatchery, but they are identified only as "black-spotted trout." This was a common all-inclusive term used for every form of cutthroat trout at the time. During those years and until 1905, the U.S. Fish Commission reported that yellowfin cutthroat trout were being held in a pond at the Leadville hatchery, but no mention is made of their propagation, nor of yellowfin cutthroat trout on the Grand Mesa. The U.S. Fish Commission reports that 10,000 eggs of "black-spotted trout" were shipped to France in 1908 and another 10,000 were shipped in 1910. The origin of these black-spotted trout eggs was not given, but it is likely they were of Yellowstone cutthroat trout from Yellowstone Lake.

In 1910, the superintendent of the Leadville hatchery wrote that the yellowfin cutthroat trout, "had gone the way of the buffalo"; the yellowfin, however, had most likely gone all the way to extinction.

EVOLUTION AND CLASSIFICATION

One of the mysteries surrounding the yellow-fin cutthroat trout concerns its origins. This trout's high number of gill rakers and its large size and silvery coloration suggest that it was a lake-specialized trout that had had several thousand years of evolution in Twin Lakes.

The yellowfin form may have arisen from an ancestor that crossed the Continental Divide from the Colorado River basin

In 1899, the Leadville hatchery began the propagation of cutthroat trout from lakes on the Grand Mesa of Colorado. The Grand Mesa is in the Colorado River basin, and its native trout would have been the Colorado River cutthroat trout. All of the cutthroat trout shipped from the Leadville hatchery were listed as "black-spotted trout." There was a prevalent assumption that yellowfin cutthroat trout also occurred on the Grand Mesa. There is no record of yellowfin cutthroat trout from Twin Lakes ever being stocked on the Grand Mesa, but an unrecorded transplant could have occurred.

The notion of yellowfin cutthroat trout on the Grand Mesa persisted for some time. A report of the U.S. Bureau of Fisheries mentions fish propagation by the U.S. Forest Service on the Grand Mesa in 1929, when "over 3,000,000 eggs of rainbow trout, yellowfin trout, and black-spotted trout" were taken for hatching and stocking.

The extinct yellowfin cutthroat trout was initially named in 1891 as *"Salmo mykiss macdonaldi"* after the U.S. Fish Commissioner Marshall MacDonald and is now classified as the subspecies *Oncorhynchus clarki macdonaldi*.

Most of the historical research pertinent to the yellowfin cutthroat trout and fish propagation on the Grand Mesa was done by William J. Wiltzius and is found in his 1985 publication *Fish Culture and Stocking in Colorado, 1872–1978* (Colorado Division of Wildlife Report Number 12).

ARTIST'S NOTE Susan Jewett of the National Museum of Natural History, Smithsonian Institution, Washington, D.C., loaned a specimen of yellowfin cutthroat trout for me to create the illustration in this account. It was shipped to Andrew Bentley at the University of Kansas Ichthyology Laboratory in Lawrence, Kansas. Collected and preserved in 1889 by David Starr Jordan, the fish is in remarkable shape. After nearly 115 years, the fins are mostly intact and the spotting is distinct. The tail fin is shortened from breakage, as is common with older specimens, so I recreated a portion of it for the illustration. The coloration of the fish relies on David Starr Jordan's original notes and on my personal experience with lake-dwelling cutthroat trout, including the Snake River finespotted cutthroat from south-central Colorado. I have given this long-extinct cutthroat the silvery blue sheen that is characteristic of so many trout from clear lakes. ◄━

Rio Grande Cutthroat Trout
Oncorhynchus clarki virginalis

Rio Grande Cutthroat Trout

6–10"

The range of the cutthroat trout native to the Rio Grande basin represents the southernmost distribution of the cutthroat trout species. The Rio Grande subspecies also was the first trout in North America to be encountered by Europeans. In 1541, Francisco de Coronado's expedition in search of mythical cities of gold failed to find gold but did find the beautiful Rio Grande cutthroat trout in the upper Pecos River in New Mexico.

DESCRIPTION   Like the Colorado River and the greenback cutthroat trout, the Rio Grande cutthroat possesses the potential to develop bright red, orange, and golden yellow colors. Its spots are relatively large, rounded in outline, and concentrated on the caudal peduncle and, anteriorly, above the lateral line. There is a tendency in the Rio

Grande cutthroat trout for some spots on the caudal peduncle to coalesce into large, club-shaped spots. Rio Grande cutthroat typically have fewer scales (150–180) along the lateral line than the Colorado River cutthroat trout or the greenback cutthroat (180–215).

The headwaters of the Pecos River drainage, in New Mexico, has a form of Rio Grande cutthroat with larger spots and generally higher scale counts (170–180). The Pecos form of the Rio Grande cutthroat trout resembles the greenback cutthroat.

BIOLOGY   There are no distinctions of life history and ecology unique to Rio Grande cutthroat trout. No large natural lakes occurred in the Rio Grande basin, so no populations of the Rio Grande cutthroat trout evolved with a lacustrine specialization.

It is believed that Rio Grande cutthroat

RIO GRANDE CUTTHROAT TROUT

SCIENTIFIC NAME
Oncorhynchus clarki virginalis

OTHER COMMON NAMES
Red-bellied trout

HABITAT
Mountain and foothill headwater streams and rivers

LENGTH AND WEIGHT
6–10" (15–25 cm) and 1–6 oz (28–170 g) in small streams; 12–15" (30–38 cm) and 8–16 oz (227–454 g) in larger pools and beaver ponds. 14–15" (36–38 cm) and 1 lb (0.45 kg) in larger streams and rivers

LIFE SPAN
Probably 5–8 years

DIET
Primarily aquatic and terrestrial invertebrates

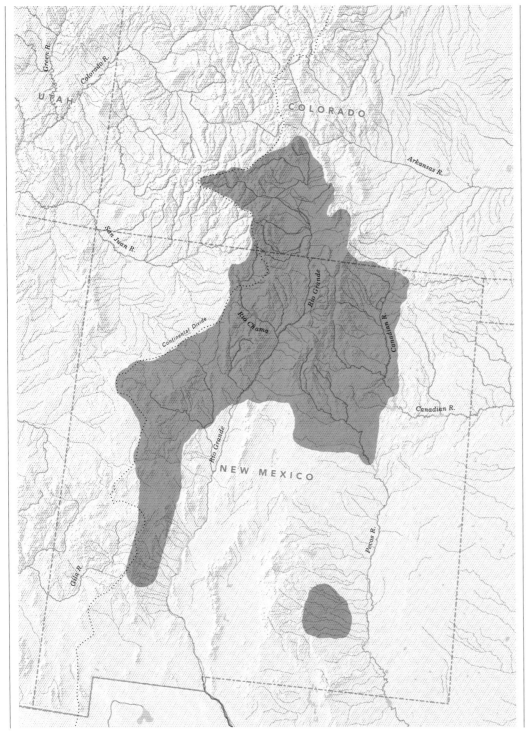

trout live five to eight years. These stream- and river-dwelling trout range in size from 6 to 10 inches (15–25 cm) and 1 to 6 ounces (28–170 g) in small streams to 14 to 15 inches (36–38 cm) in larger streams and rivers. Fish stocked in lakes can grow up to 5 pounds (2.3 kg).

As with other interior subspecies, the Rio Grande cutthroat trout is vulnerable to replacement by nonnative trout. In New Mexico, the brown trout is the most common nonnative species threatening the remnant populations of Rio Grande cutthroat trout in small streams.

However, some populations of Rio Grande cutthroat trout have continued to coexist with brown trout in some drainages. Rio Grande cutthroat typically occupy colder headwaters and brown trout occur in warmer, lower elevations.

DISTRIBUTION Rio Grande cutthroat trout are found today in the Rio Grande basin of Colorado and New Mexico, including the upper Pecos River drainage of New Mexico (the Pecos connects to the Rio Grande in Texas). Although no nineteenth-century museum specimens exist to document its occurrence, the Rio Grande cutthroat trout is almost certainly native to the uppermost headwaters of the Canadian River (of the Mississippi basin) in New Mexico and a tiny portion of Colorado.

There are credible reports from Civil War

The historic range of the Rio Grande cutthroat is not known with certainty, but most likely included much of the Rio Grande drainage including the Rio Chama, Jemez, and Rio San Jose drainages along with areas of suitable habitat in the headwaters of the Pecos and Canadian Rivers.

Rio Grande Cutthroat Trout
PECOS STRAIN

6–10"

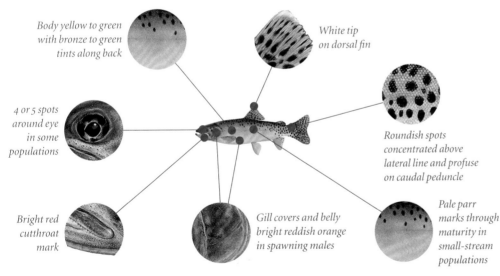

Body yellow to green with bronze to green tints along back

White tip on dorsal fin

4 or 5 spots around eye in some populations

Roundish spots concentrated above lateral line and profuse on caudal peduncle

Bright red cutthroat mark

Gill covers and belly bright reddish orange in spawning males

Pale parr marks through maturity in small-stream populations

PECOS STRAIN

times that the Rio Grande cutthroat trout occurred in the Davis Mountains of western Texas in tributaries to both the Rio Grande and the Pecos River. Cutthroat trout are long gone from Texas, but a few populations of the Rio Grande cutthroat trout are still found in a few small headwater streams in the Pecos and Canadian River drainages. And an 1877 story on "Rio Grande trout" in *Forest and Stream* magazine claimed that the finest fishing was found in the headwaters of the Vermejo River, a tributary to the Canadian River that begins in Colorado just north of the New Mexico border.

In the nineteenth century, the American scientist E. D. Cope reported on finding cutthroat trout from an unknown drainage of southern Chihuahua, Mexico, at an elevation of "7,000 to 8,000 feet." He based his assessment on the presence of basibranchial teeth in the specimens, which are absent in the Mexican golden trout and a rainbow-like trout found in a similar range and elevation. Cope's preserved specimens are lost and cannot be examined to verify his findings. It is unlikely that these fish were cutthroat trout; they were most likely Mexican golden trout. If these Mexican specimens were cutthroat trout, they would have been from the Río Conchos, in the Rio Grande basin of Mexico. The Río Conchos, however, is not known to have native trout. That is not to say that at one time, hundreds, or likely thousands of years ago, cutthroat were not native to tributaries entering the Rio Grande, such as the Río Conchos.

EVOLUTION AND CLASSIFICATION

The Rio Grande cutthroat derived from the Colorado River cutthroat. The Rio Grande subspecies is more differentiated from the Colorado River cutthroat trout than is the greenback cutthroat trout. The transfer of an ancestor from the Colorado River basin into the Rio Grande basin probably occurred at an earlier time than the transfer to the South Platte drainage that gave rise to the greenback cutthroat.

The name *virginalis* (meaning "like a virgin") is based on specimens collected by a Pacific Railroad Survey in 1853 from Ute Creek in the San Luis Valley of Colorado. In 1856, "*Salar virginalis*" was described from these specimens, but the locality was given as "Utah Creek," mistakenly assumed to be in the Bonneville basin by later authors. In the literature of the late nineteenth and early twentieth centuries, *virginalis* was the name used for the Bonneville cutthroat trout. During that time the Rio Grande cutthroat was classified as "*Salmo spilurus*."

When the correct type locality for Ute Creek in the Rio Grande basin was straightened out, *virginalis* was recognized as the valid name for the Rio Grande cutthroat trout. The name *spilurus* was described for Rio Grande cutthroat trout in 1872, 16 years after the 1856 description of *virginalis*. Thus *virginalis* is the valid name, either as a species or subspecies name for Rio Grande cutthroat, by the rule of priority.

CONSERVATION

Rio Grande cutthroat trout have been replaced by nonnative trout throughout 90 to 95 percent of their historic range, but many pure populations have persisted in about 75 small headwater streams of the Rio Grande basin in Colorado and New Mexico, and in a few tributaries to the Pecos and Canadian River drainages of New Mexico. From these pure populations, several transplants of this subspecies have increased the distribution and abundance of the Rio Grande cutthroat trout.

State and federal agencies in Colorado and New Mexico have cooperated to protect and enhance populations of the Rio Grande cutthroat trout through habitat-improvement projects, fencing to exclude livestock, and construction of barriers to protect upstream populations against invasion by nonnative trout.

Large holdings of private lands in the Rio Grande basin, such as the Forbes Trinchera Ranch and a ranch owned by Ted Turner, comprise hundreds of thousands of acres. The managers of these ranches have the protection and restoration of the Rio Grande cutthroat trout as a high priority.

In 1916, the pioneer ecologist-conservationist Aldo Leopold criticized prevailing attitudes and government policies and programs that were causing the loss of native cutthroat trout (at that time Leopold was employed by the U.S. Forest Service in New Mexico). He lamented the fact that although the streams in New Mexico once teemed with a beautiful native trout (the Rio Grande cutthroat), state and federal agencies seemed determined to eradicate it with their policy of stocking great numbers of nonnative trout.

Eventually, because of dedicated people such as Aldo Leopold, public policies and natural resource programs have changed for the better, and during the past 25 years, the long historical decline of the Rio Grande cutthroat has been reversed. Unfortunately, there is often a considerable lag time before enlightenment takes hold.

Lahontan Cutthroat Trout
Oncorhynchus clarki henshawi

Lahontan Cutthroat Trout
LAKE FORM

8–22"

The largest of the cutthroat, the Lahontan is one of the four major subspecies of cutthroat trout together with the coastal, westslope, and Yellowstone cutthroat trout. Fossil-dated remains of its progenitor thought to be more than 600,000 years old have been found in the Lahontan basin, an area inclusive of northwestern Nevada, eastern California, and a small section of southeastern Oregon. In more recent geological times, probably during and since the last glacial period (from about 10,000 to 60,000 years ago), the Lahontan cutthroat trout gave rise to four closely related, minor subspecies: the Alvord, the Humboldt, the Whitehorse basin, and the Paiute cutthroat trout. Two of these minor subspecies, the Humboldt and the Whitehorse basin, have not been formally named, and the Alvord is extinct. The Paiute is designated *Oncorhynchus clarki seleniris* and the Lahontan carries the name *Oncorhynchus clarki henshawi,* named by the scientists Gill and Jordan in 1878 as *"Salmo henshawi"* after the naturalist H.W. Henshaw.

DESCRIPTION Typically, the Lahontan cutthroat has greenish bronze colors over the dorsal region, and the sides of the body have a light yellowish copper coloration, with faint rose colors around the lateral line. Although the Lahontan cutthroat trout does not develop intense crimson or gold colors, mature males can develop red coloration on the sides and the ventral region.

The long period of isolation in the Lahontan basin and specializations for a large lake environment (see below) make the

LAHONTAN CUTTHROAT TROUT

SCIENTIFIC NAME
Oncorhynchus clarki henshawi

OTHER COMMON NAMES
Cutthroat

HABITAT
Streams and rivers, ponds and lakes; tolerant of alkaline lakes

LENGTH AND WEIGHT
8–9" (20–23 cm) and 4–6 oz (113–170 g) in streams. 8–22" (20–56 cm) and 4 oz–8 lb (113 g–3.6 kg) in rivers and lakes (average varies by population and habitat); angler record 39" (99 cm) and 41 lb (18.6 kg)

LIFE SPAN
Probably 8–10 years

DIET
Primarily aquatic and terrestrial invertebrates in stream and river populations; larger fish in lakes become piscivorous

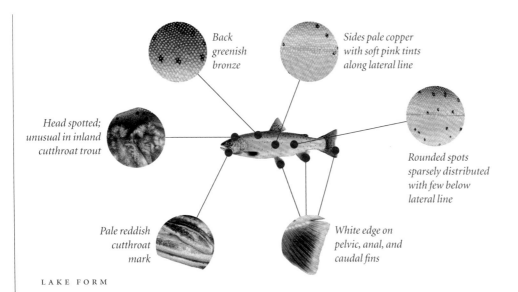

Back greenish bronze

Sides pale copper with soft pink tints along lateral line

Head spotted; unusual in inland cutthroat trout

Rounded spots sparsely distributed with few below lateral line

Pale reddish cutthroat mark

White edge on pelvic, anal, and caudal fins

LAKE FORM

Lahontan cutthroat trout the most sharply differentiated subspecies of cutthroat trout.

Besides several genetic markers, three diagnostic morphological traits distinguish the Lahontan cutthroat trout from other subspecies. Relatively large, rounded spots are evenly distributed on the sides of the body. Sometimes spots extend over the ventral region, and in contrast to other inland subspecies of cutthroat trout, spots may occur on top of the head. Gill raker numbers are higher in the Lahontan cutthroat trout than in any other subspecies of cutthroat or any form of rainbow trout. Typical counts range from 21 to 28, with an average count in different populations of 23 to 25 (versus 17–20 in other subspecies).

A higher number of gill rakers is a lacustrine adaptation for feeding on small planktonic organisms. Pyloric caeca numbers are also higher in the Lahontan cutthroat than in any other subspecies, typically 50 to 60 versus 25 to 40. In salmonid fishes, there is

a trend for higher numbers of pyloric caeca to be associated with predatory feeding.

The Lahontan cutthroat trout is the largest of any cutthroat subspecies. The official angler-caught record of 41 pounds (18.6 kg) was caught in 1925. A person who sold cutthroat trout caught by the Paiute tribe claimed to have handled a fish of 62 pounds (28.1 kg) in 1916.

BIOLOGY A distinctive biological trait of Lahontan cutthroat trout is their tolerance for high levels of alkalinity, basic as opposed to acidic, or neutral pH levels of the water in which they live. This trait was probably acquired during the subspecies' long evolution in the Lahontan basin and resulting exposure to high salinity-alkalinity levels—more precisely, to high concentrations of total dissolved solids (TDS) when large lakes were drying up and ion concentrations increased. It is not fully known what ions become toxic to most fishes and at what concentrations, but

carbonate, bicarbonate, and sulfate ions play a major role, often exacerbated by ammonia.

Lahontan cutthroat trout and other fishes native to the Lahontan basin can thrive in lakes with TDS concentrations lethal to other fishes—to 10,000 parts per million (ppm) and higher (but note that the ratios of the ions that make up TDS are more important than the total concentration of dissolved solids for determining toxic levels for various fish species). From 1906 to the 1970s, Pyramid Lake, Nevada, dropped by 80 feet (24 m) due to diversion of flow from the Truckee River. Pyramid Lake's surface area, which included connecting Lake Winnemucca, shrank from about 200,000 acres (81,000 ha) to about 110,000 acres (45,000 ha), and TDS levels increased to 5,500 ppm. The level of Walker Lake dropped by about 130 feet (40 m) during this period. Walker Lake lost about two-thirds of its volume, and its TDS levels more than doubled, reaching 12,500 ppm and higher.

All spawning ceased in the Walker River in the 1940s, but the Lahontan cutthroat trout native to Walker Lake has been maintained at the Verdi, Nevada, state fish hatchery since 1949. During the past 50 years they have had no opportunity for natural selection to work to evolve higher TDS tolerance, generation by generation, during the period of increasing TDS concentrations in Walker Lake. High TDS levels combined with reduced oxygen levels in the deeper, colder water of Walker Lake have greatly impacted the cutthroat trout fishery in Walker Lake. When the trout propagated from the Walker Lake brood stock are stocked into Walker Lake during periods of low lake level, high TDS concentrations, and low

Lahontan Cutthroat Trout
STREAM-RESIDENT FORM

8–9"

oxygen, they suffer high mortality and reduced growth rates.

As noted, Lahontan cutthroat trout have been known for their large size. The largest of the large (somewhere between the 41-pound world record and the reported 62-pound fish) are associated with the original population of Pyramid Lake. The largest Lahontan cutthroat trout known from Lake Tahoe was caught in 1911 and weighed 31 pounds, 8 ounces (14.3 kg). Walker Lake was famed for its large and abundant cutthroat trout before the Walker River, the only spawning stream, was dammed and diverted. As with Pyramid Lake, Walker Lake supported a commercial fishery in the late nineteenth and early twentieth centuries. The maximum size of Walker Lake trout is not known, but in 1949 the Nevada Fish and Game Department netted 39 cutthroat trout weighing 16 to 22 pounds (7.3–10 kg) to establish the Walker Lake brood stock

at the Verdi hatchery. Some Lahontan cutthroat spend their entire lives in rivers and small streams and may grow no larger than 8 or 9 inches (20–23 cm), depending on habitat conditions and the availability of food.

The weak link in the life history of the Lahontan cutthroat trout of Walker and Pyramid Lakes (and of all cutthroat and rainbow trout) is that they are obligatory stream spawners. After the Walker River and the Truckee River were dammed and diverted, spawning habitat was lost, and self-sustaining populations were extirpated.

DISTRIBUTION   The native distribution of the Lahontan cutthroat trout is restricted to the Lahontan basin of Nevada and California, and a small section of Oregon where the headwaters of the Quinn River drainage originate. The persistence of a few introductions outside of the Lahontan

basin have proved to be important. Unique populations have been preserved after extinction in their native waters, such as the existence of the Pyramid Lake cutthroat trout in a tiny, isolated stream on Pilot Peak of the Bonneville basin. It is likely that this stream was fishless at the time of the introduction.

Similarly, the Lahontan cutthroat trout native to Lake Tahoe has been extinct since the 1940s. The California Department of Fish and Game propagated and distributed Lahontan cutthroat trout from Lake Tahoe from 1882 to 1938. Many of these introductions of Lake Tahoe trout were made outside of the Lahontan basin. In the 1890s, Lahontan cutthroat trout from Lake Tahoe were stocked above a barrier falls in the headwaters of the Santa Ana River in southern California (no fish occurred above the falls before the stocking), and a new population was established. When this transplanted population was later

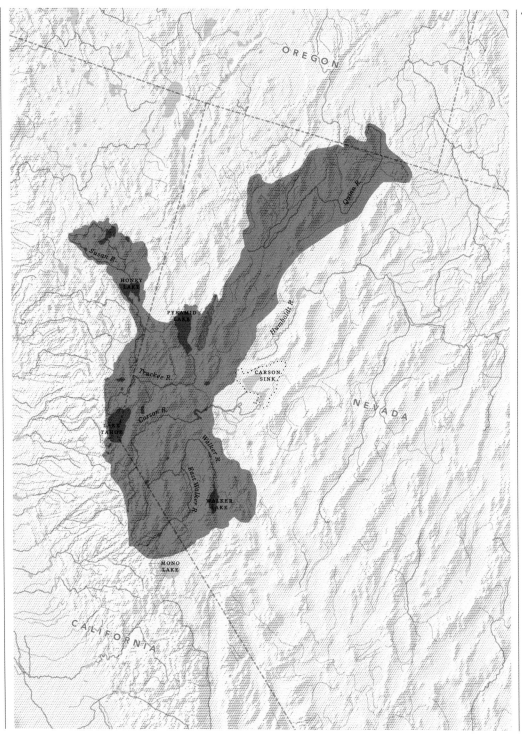

"discovered" in 1908, it was described as a new species, *"Salmo evermanni."* After rainbow trout were stocked, *"evermanni"* became extinct. Like the Santa Ana River population, most of the Lahontan cutthroat trout stocked outside the Lahontan basin in California soon disappeared after the stocking of rainbow, brown, and brook trout, but a few populations have persisted in small, isolated streams of the Sacramento–San Joaquin basin.

Lahontan cutthroat trout may have been the first trout artificially propagated in North America after the propagation of brook trout began in 1853. A private hatchery began operation on the Truckee River in 1867 or 1868. The California Acclimatization Society obtained some of these Lahontan cutthroat trout eggs in the 1870s and made a shipment to New Zealand in 1875 (eight years before the first rainbow trout eggs were shipped to New Zealand). The fate of the Lahontan cutthroat trout in New Zealand is not known. Because of their tolerance for high levels of alkalinity, Lahontan cutthroat are regularly stocked in alkaline lakes such as Lenore, Omak, and Grimes Lakes in the coulee country of Washington, where they support popular sport fisheries.

EVOLUTION AND CLASSIFICATION

The Lahontan basin of Nevada, California, and a small part of Oregon is the second-largest basin of the Great Basin, after the Bonneville basin. During the last glacial

The original native range of the Lahontan cutthroat trout was restricted to western Nevada in the Lahontan basin including small areas in southeastern Oregon and eastern California.

period, Lake Lahontan was the second-largest lake in the Great Basin; at its maximum size, the lake had a surface area of 8,665 square miles (22,450 sq km), or roughly the present size of Lake Erie. The largest of the Great Basin lakes, Lake Bonneville had a maximum surface area of about 20,000 square miles (51,800 sq km), slightly smaller than the present Lake Huron, but the cutthroat trout native to the Lahontan basin had a considerably longer period of time to evolve in a large lake environment than did the Bonneville cutthroat.

The origin of cutthroat trout in the Lahontan basin extends back to about mid-Pleistocene times, perhaps about 1 million years. During this long period, more than one Lake Lahontan existed, and probably several smaller but still sizable lakes occurred during cooler, wetter periods of interglacial times.

The cutthroat trout was the only large, predatory species among the fishes of the Lahontan basin. This long history of evolutionary programming as the top predator is reflected in the large size attained by the Lahontan cutthroat trout. The largest Lahontan cutthroat existed in Pyramid Lake, the sump of ancient Lake Lahontan—that is, the lowest elevation in the Lahontan basin. It is the only water in the basin that maintained the full array of the Lahontan fish fauna and where the native cutthroat trout could continue the evolutionary predator-prey relationships established in Lake Lahontan.

John Charles Fremont, during his western explorations in search of the mythical Buenaventura River (believed to flow from the Rocky Mountains to the Pacific Ocean), was the first European American to see Pyramid Lake, in January 1844. At the mouth of the Truckee River, members of the Pyramid Lake Paiute tribe presented Fremont and his men with several large cutthroat trout. Fremont wrote that these "salmon trout" were of "extraordinary size," were "two to four feet in length," and were comparable to Columbia River salmon (Chinook salmon). He also was impressed by their excellent flavor, "superior to that of any fish I have known."

CONSERVATION   The first project of the newly created U.S. Bureau of Reclamation in 1905 was the Newlands Project, named for Nevada senator Francis G. Newlands. Key to the Newlands Project was a diversion dam on the Truckee River, the only spawning tributary to Pyramid Lake. Derby Dam was sited about 30 miles (50 km) above Pyramid Lake (about 50 years later, after Pyramid Lake had considerably shrunk in size, Derby Dam was about 40 miles, or 65 km, above the lake). After 1906 more and more of the Truckee River flow was diverted at the dam for irrigation.

The prevailing paradigm of the first decade of the twentieth century concerning environmental conservation, which was in conflict with water development, was succinctly put by Frederick Newell, the first commissioner of the Bureau of Reclamation, who stated, "Fish have no rights in water law." Senator Newlands added his opinion that "Pyramid Lake exists solely to satisfy the thirsting sun." He neglected to recognize that the existence of Pyramid Lake and a free-flowing Truckee River was of great importance to the Pyramid Lake Paiutes for their food supply, economy, and culture. The cui-ui sucker, found only in Pyramid Lake, was more abundant than the cutthroat trout (the sucker's niche occupied a lower position in the food web) and was of great importance to the tribe. The Native American name of the Pyramid Lake Paiute people was *kuyui dokado,* the cui-ui eaters, not the trout eaters.

As more and more water was diverted from the Truckee River, successful spawning of Pyramid Lake cutthroat trout became more infrequent. The last spawning run occurred in 1938 and consisted of large trout seven to ten years of age or older. Federal fish biologists were on hand to document the demise of the Pyramid Lake population as the flow in the Truckee River was shut off, stranding the fish attempting to spawn. Observers measured 195 of the dying trout, which averaged about 36 inches (91 cm) long and 20 pounds (9 kg).

Since the 1950s, millions of Lahontan cutthroat trout, mainly from Summit Lake, in Nevada, and Heenan Lake, in California, have been stocked into Pyramid Lake, but none have attained the average size of the 1938 spawning run of the native Pyramid Lake population. The Heenan Lake stock is originally derived from an 1864 transplant of Lahontan cutthroat trout from the Carson River to Blue Lakes in the Sacramento River basin; over many years of propagation, it became slightly hybridized with rainbow trout. Summit Lake was formed by a landslide about 25,000 years ago, isolating a population of Lahontan cutthroat trout, but with no other fish species to maintain their predator-prey evolutionary heritage. Obviously the original Pyramid Lake cutthroat trout have a hereditary basis for great size, one that is not possessed by other populations of the Lahontan cutthroat trout, which lack the continuous evolutionary programming to be an efficient predator in Pyramid Lake.

In 1938, biologists observing the demise of the last spawning run from Pyramid Lake knew that this population would soon be extinct, and although they found this unfortunate, no one noted that a unique, irreplaceable resource—the largest cutthroat trout in the world—was being lost. The prevailing biological thinking of the time did not comprehend the significance of special adaptations at the population level. Biologists assumed that since the full cutthroat trout species was not extinct and other populations of the Lahontan cutthroat subspecies still existed, any population of the species, and particularly of the same subspecies, could be stocked into Pyramid Lake and grow to sizes comparable to the original Pyramid Lake cutthroat trout.

For those who have doubts about the hereditary basis for great size of the original Pyramid Lake cutthroat trout, the July 1932 issue of *Sierra Sportsman* magazine contains a story of two anglers fishing in Pyramid Lake in 1928, accompanied by a photo of the anglers with their catch of 11 cutthroat trout, which weighed a total of 238 pounds (108 kg; an average of 21 pounds, 10 ounces, or 9.8 kg). The largest trout weighed 39 pounds (17.7 kg). During the past 50 years, with the Pyramid Lake fishery dependent on the stocking of Pyramid Lake with millions of Lahontan cutthroat trout from non–Pyramid Lake parental sources, trophy trout caught

from the lake would weigh in the range of 5 to 8 pounds (2.3–3.6 kg).

The final episode of the original Pyramid Lake trout has a surprising and happy ending. In 1979 I coauthored a publication on a population of Lahontan cutthroat trout found in a tiny stream on Pilot Peak on the Nevada–Utah border. Pilot Peak is in the Bonneville basin, so the Lahontan cutthroat trout had to be introduced. The Lahontan cutthroat had been in this tiny stream for a long time; the oldest residents of the area believed they had always been there. Before the 1950s, the only propagation and distribution of Lahontan cutthroat in Nevada came from Pyramid Lake. Subsequent investigations into the history of fish stocking in the Pilot Peak area support the story's circumstantial evidence that a small part of the original Pyramid Lake population of Lahontan cutthroat trout persisted in this small stream on Pilot Peak, where they were introduced perhaps 100 years ago or earlier. Discoveries such as this create a spark of hope that someday, somewhere, an introduced population of the yellowfin cutthroat trout might be found. Native only to Twin Lakes, Colorado, the yellowfin has been extinct for 100 years.

The nineteenth-century abundance of Lahontan cutthroat trout in Pyramid Lake, Walker Lake, and Lake Tahoe would have totaled in the millions of pounds. When these lake populations were lost or reduced to a small fraction of historical abundance, the total abundance, in both weight and number, of the Lahontan cutthroat trout became minuscule in comparison.

The introductions of rainbow, brown,

and brook trout virtually eliminated the Lahontan cutthroat trout from river drainages of the Lahontan basin except for the Humboldt drainage. However, the Humboldt form of Lahontan cutthroat trout is considered to be a separate subspecies from the Lahontan cutthroat trout. The Lahontan cutthroat trout in the Truckee, Walker, and Carson River drainages persisted in only a few small headwater streams isolated from nonnative trout. Two native, self-sustaining populations persisted in two lakes— Independence Lake, in California, and Summit Lake, in Nevada.

The first listing of species under the 1973 Endangered Species Act included the Lahontan cutthroat trout, which was given a status of endangered; in 1975, it was down-listed to threatened, a change in status mainly due to the fee-based sport fishery for hatchery-reared Lahontan cutthroat trout stocked in Pyramid Lake, which became an important part of the Paiute tribal recreational enterprise. Angling is prohibited for an endangered species, but regulated angling is allowed for a threatened species or subspecies.

Several transplants have been made to establish new populations in small, isolated streams. The main abundance of the Lahontan cutthroat trout depends on artificial propagation. Millions of Lahontan cutthroat trout are annually stocked in lakes and reservoirs for angling, both within and outside the Lahontan basin. These populations are artificially maintained and are not self-sustaining.

Paiute Cutthroat Trout
Oncorhynchus clarki seleniris

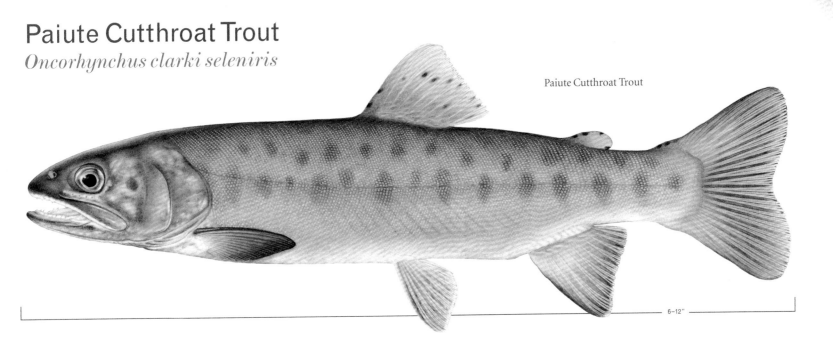

Paiute Cutthroat Trout

6–12"

The Paiute cutthroat trout is one of the four minor subspecies that derived from the Lahontan cutthroat trout, which is considered a major subspecies. The Alvord, Whitehorse basin, and Humboldt cutthroat trout comprise the other three minor subspecies. The Paiute cutthroat trout is the "most minor" of the minor subspecies in terms of the area of its original and present distribution and in its genetic relatedness within the Lahontan group of subspecies. As the basis for its recognition as a subspecies, it possesses a unique characteristic shared by no other subspecies of cutthroat or rainbow trout—it has no spots on its body. However, it may retain its juvenile parr marks into maturity, as do many small-stream populations of rainbow and cutthroat trout.

The common name of this cutthroat trout derives from the Northern Paiute tribe of Native Americans, although it is unlikely that this small subspecies of cutthroat made up even a portion of their diet. However, one group of Northern Paiute is named in their own language *agai-ticutta*, meaning trout eaters. This name is associated with the Walker River Paiutes, who fished extensively for the large Lahontan cutthroat trout, which was a significant part of their culture.

DESCRIPTION The Paiute cutthroat trout's unique characteristic, the absence of spots on the body, differentiates it from all other trout, especially from its closest relative, the Lahontan cutthroat trout, which typically has numerous, relatively large spots all over the body. The tail, or caudal fin, also lacks spots. A few small, elliptical dark areas may appear on the dorsal fin, but a heavily spotted dorsal (and caudal) fin,

PAIUTE CUTTHROAT TROUT

SCIENTIFIC NAME
Oncorhynchus clarki seleniris

OTHER COMMON NAMES
Cutthroat

HABITAT
Small headwater streams; thrives when stocked in lakes

LENGTH AND WEIGHT
6–12" (15–30 cm) and 1–11 oz (28–312 g) in streams. Maximum 18" (46 cm) and 2½ lb (1.1 kg) in lakes

LIFE SPAN
4 years

DIET
Aquatic and terrestrial invertebrates

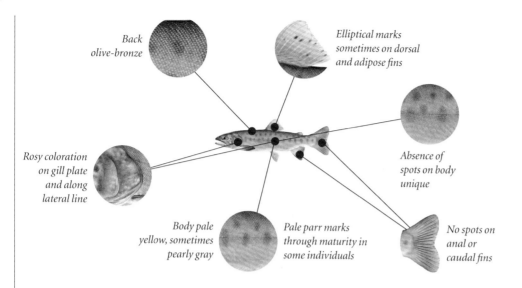

Back
olive-bronze

Elliptical marks
sometimes on dorsal
and adipose fins

Rosy coloration
on gill plate
and along
lateral line

Absence of
spots on body
unique

Body pale
yellow, sometimes
pearly gray

Pale parr marks
through maturity in
some individuals

No spots on
anal or
caudal fins

typical in most cutthroat and rainbow trout, is absent in the Paiute cutthroat.

The coloration of the Paiute cutthroat is typical of Lahontan cutthroat trout living in small-stream habitat: olive-bronze dorsally, shading to light yellow below. A faint rose band may occur around the lateral line. Some specimens, influenced by age and sex, can be quite pale: almost colorless or with pearly gray body colors.

Apart from its lack of spots, the Paiute cutthroat trout is wholly typical of the Lahontan cutthroat trout in all characteristics: Its gill rakers number 21 to 27 (average 24), the scales along the sides of the body number 150 to 180, and pyloric caeca number 50 to 70, identical to a typical population of Lahontan cutthroat trout.

BIOLOGY   Similar to populations of Lahontan cutthroat trout living in small streams, the Paiute cutthroat trout is extremely susceptible to extinction after nonnative trout are introduced. The original

and present range of the Paiute cutthroat is at elevations of more than 8,000 feet (2,450 m). With water temperatures influenced by runoff from snowmelt, spawning can begin in May when water temperatures reach 42 to 48 °F (6–9 °C) and extend into July. In small, headwater habitat, maturity is reached at two or three years of age, when the trout are 6 to 10 inches (15–25 cm) long. Few Paiute trout live more than four years, attaining a length of 12 inches (30 cm) and a weight of 11 ounces (312 g). Paiute trout stocked in lakes have reached a length of up to 18 inches (46 cm) and a weight of 2 pounds, 8 ounces (1.1 kg)

DISTRIBUTION   The original distribution of the Paiute cutthroat trout was limited to no more than 10 miles (16 km) of Silver King Creek, in Alpine County, California, from a canyon area upstream to a barrier (Llewellyn Falls). The original distribution included the lower sections of two tributary streams, Corral Valley and Coyote Valley Creeks. In

1912, a sheepherder transplanted some trout above Llewellyn Falls, starting a new population with access to a few additional miles of stream. Transplants were also made above barrier falls in Corral Valley and Coyote Valley Creeks at an unknown time and new populations also became established above the falls in these small streams.

By 1933, only the transplanted populations of Paiute trout above the barrier falls remained. Below the falls, the original parental stock had become thoroughly hybridized with introduced, nonnative rainbow trout. In 1949, the California Department of Fish and Game was still engaged in what, for native trout, was an anachronistic, useless, and often devastating practice—namely, "seeding" headwater streams with baby rainbow trout carried by pack trains of horses and mules. This "Johnny Appleseed" era of fish stocking extended for many years beyond any useful purpose it may have had, such as the introductions of trout in areas above barriers that were originally fishless.

It was known that Silver King Creek above Llewellyn Falls and the headwaters of Corral Valley and Coyote Valley Creeks were the home of the Paiute cutthroat trout, and that the rainbow trout fry carried by the pack train should not have been stocked in these streams. The pack train took a wrong turn on the trail, and the route traversed upper Silver King, Corral Valley, and Coyote Valley Creeks, resulting in the stocking of rainbow trout into the populations of Paiute cutthroat trout. Predictably, hybridization was soon underway.

About ten years later, during an aerial stocking of Lahontan cutthroat trout, a plane inadvertently stocked Lahontan cutthroat trout in a lake tributary to Silver King Creek. Some of the Lahontan cutthroat worked their way down the outlet stream to Silver King Creek. By 1964, the trout of Silver King, Corral Valley, and Coyote Valley Creeks were thoroughly hybridized. The distribution of pure Paiute cutthroat trout was reduced almost to the vanishing point. Again, previous transplants of Paiute trout saved it from extinction the second time.

In 1964, some Paiute cutthroat from Corral Valley Creek were transplanted into a tiny, fishless stream in southern California, where they became established. In 1947, Paiute cutthroat from Silver King Creek were transplanted above a falls into Fly Valley Creek, a small tributary to Silver King Creek. The restoration of Paiute cutthroat in Silver King Creek came from transplanted pure populations from Fly Valley Creek and Four Mile Canyon Creek.

EVOLUTION AND CLASSIFICATION

Genetically the Paiute cutthroat is closely related (and essentially identical) to the Lahontan cutthroat native to the Carson River drainage. In fact, the Carson River Lahontan is more closely related to the Paiute than it is to other Lahontan cutthroat native to the Truckee or Walker River drainages. The Paiute cutthroat population originated when a small population of Lahontan cutthroat were isolated in a tributary to the East Carson River, which explains the close genetic relationship between the two. However, long before the isolation of the Paiute population occurred, the Carson, Truckee, and Walker Rivers had been isolated from one another

as a result of the desiccation of Lake Lahontan (about 8,000 to 10,000 years ago). Thus the Paiute trout has been isolated from Carson drainage Lahontan cutthroat for only a few thousand years, not sufficient time for the trout to evolve genetic distinctions that are detectable by modern techniques of molecular genetics. Obviously there is a genetic basis for spots versus no spots on the body, but this is likely governed by the occurrence of different forms of genes (alleles) at a single gene locus. Such differences represent a tiny fraction of the total genome of the fish, but are responsible for considerable variation in appearance.

The Paiute cutthroat trout was first described in 1933 by John Otterbein Snyder. Its almost colorless or pearly gray body suggested the name "*Salmo seleniris*" because of the "fanciful resemblance of its evanescent tints to the lunar rainbow." Selene is the lovely goddess of the moon from ancient Greek mythology.

In 1933, the 1912 transplant above the falls was not known, and it was assumed that the headwaters of Silver King Creek above Llewellyn Falls were the native or original distribution. If transplants above the barrier falls had not been made before rainbow trout were stocked in Silver King Creek, this peculiar spotless trout would have become extinct before it was known to exist.

CONSERVATION

The Paiute cutthroat trout, like the Lahontan cutthroat, was included in the first list of the 1973 Endangered Species Act, with a status of endangered. In 1975, again as with the Lahontan cutthroat, the Paiute cutthroat's endangered status was downlisted to

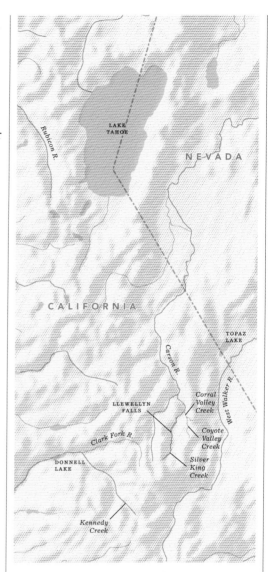

The original range of the Paiute cutthroat trout was limited to no more than 10 miles (16 km) of Silver King Creek and the lower sections of two tributary streams, Coyote Valley Creek and Corral Valley Creek. This is the smallest original range of any subspecies of cutthroat trout.

Nearly hybridized out of existence by the introduction of hatchery rainbow trout, Paiute cutthroat trout persist because of careful stream management.

threatened, mainly to facilitate restoration projects using chemical treatments. Since 1964, Silver King Creek above Llewellyn Falls has been chemically treated many times to eliminate hybrids. Consistently, a few hybrids survived the treatment, and within a few years hybrids (trout with spots on the body) had reappeared. It is hoped that intensive chemical treatments have finally eliminated all hybrid influence.

In addition to the 1946 transplant of Paiute trout to southern California, a few other populations have been established in small, isolated streams outside of the Silver King Creek drainage.

Silver King Creek is in a wilderness area of the Toiyabe National Forest. Despite this, and despite the subspecies' protection under the Endangered Species Act, the habitat of the Paiute cutthroat trout in Silver King Creek has a long history of severe impacts from livestock grazing. In the late 1980s, the U.S. Forest Service finally revised their livestock allotment plans to remove livestock from the upper Silver King watershed.

If hybrid trout do not reappear in Silver King Creek above Llewellyn Falls, there is hope that with improved habitat and further transplants of populations, the Paiute trout will become more abundant and more widely distributed than they were in 1933, when the Paiute cutthroat trout was first described.

Alvord Cutthroat Trout
Oncorhynchus clarki alvordensis

Alvord Cutthroat Trout

8–20"

The Alvord cutthroat trout became extinct in the mid- to late 1980s due to hybridization with stocked rainbow trout. Rainbow trout were first introduced into the Trout Creek and Virgin–Thousand Creek drainages 70 years ago. Most of what is known about this subspecies prior to hybridization is based on collections made by scientist Carl Hubbs in 1934 from Trout Creek and the head-waters of Virgin Creek. These specimens are now preserved in the University of Michigan's Museum of Zoology.

Amazingly, a population of pure or only slightly hybridized Alvord cutthroat was found in the headwaters of Virgin Creek in 1984. They were discovered among a rapidly hybridizing population; evidently a few of the older trout were born before the influence of introduced rainbow trout had completely spread throughout the population. These older fish, the eldest being seven years old, were the last remnants of Alvord cutthroat trout that had evolved in the Alvord desert basin for tens of thousands of years.

Rainbow trout were stocked in Trout Creek in 1929 and in Virgin Creek in 1933. Carl Hubbs's collections made in 1934 revealed that the fish in Trout Creek were hybrids of rainbow trout and the native cutthroat trout. The 1933 stocking of rainbow trout in Virgin Creek resulted in hybridi-zation except in a small headwater section of the creek above a rockslide. The rockslide had created a barrier, isolating the native fish from the invading rainbow trout.

It was in these headwaters of Virgin Creek that Alvord cutthroat trout persisted, and where they were rediscovered in

ALVORD CUTTHROAT TROUT

SCIENTIFIC NAME
Oncorhynchus clarki alvordensis

OTHER COMMON NAMES
None known

HABITAT
Small headwater streams of Alvord basin, Oregon and Nevada

LENGTH AND WEIGHT
8–20" (20–51 cm) and 3.2 oz–3 lb (91 g–1.4 kg)

LIFE SPAN
Probably 7 years

DIET
Aquatic and terrestrial invertebrates

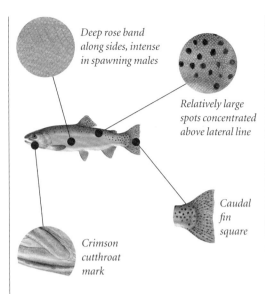

Deep rose band along sides, intense in spawning males

Relatively large spots concentrated above lateral line

Caudal fin square

Crimson cutthroat mark

the 1980s. However, in the 1940s, rainbow trout had been stocked in a reservoir above the headwaters of the Virgin Creek drainage. Apparently, during a high-water year, the reservoir spilled into Virgin Creek and introduced rainbow trout. This was the *coup de grâce* to the Alvord cutthroat trout. The fish found in the 1980s were the very last of the relatively pure Alvord cutthroat trout. Attempts to transplant these fish failed and the Alvord cutthroat is no more, a victim of circumstance and early misguided stocking practices.

DESCRIPTION   Although extinct, the Alvord cutthroat trout is here formally described as a new subspecies *Oncorhynchus clarki alvordensis* in recognition of the late Carl L. Hubbs, discoverer of the Alvord cutthroat trout and one of America's foremost ichthyologists of the twentieth century.

Hubbs's field notes of August 2, 1934, give a manuscript name (unpublished name) of *Salmo clarki alvordensis* to the cutthroat trout he collected that day from Virgin Creek. By publishing Hubbs's description of *alvordensis* with a designation of the type specimens, the name *alvordensis* becomes a valid published name for the Alvord cutthroat trout. Authorship for the name is Carl L. Hubbs, in this book, *Trout and Salmon of North America*, Behnke 2002.

The description of *alvordensis* as given in Hubbs's field notes is as follows:

"*Locality, Nevada, Virgin Creek, Humboldt Co., T44N; R25E, just below mouth of box canyon. Method of capture, 6 ft. and 10 ft. minnow seines. Collected by: Hubbs and family. Date: Aug. 2, 1934. University of Michigan Museum of Zoology Collection No. 130532; 82 specimens designated as paratopotypes. One specimen, UMMZZ12693 designated as holotype.*

"*Similar to Trout Crk 'native' but much brighter. Above olive with blue and gold reflections. Sides more or less bright brassy yellow with a deep rose band; opercles also rosy in larger ones. Spots large with trace of pale ring about them. Lower sides with brassy color on a gray background. Cutthroat mark intense red. Lower fins deep but rather bright purplish rosy without pale border.*"

Also in Hubbs's field notes he mentions that 11 rainbow trout were collected along with the 83 cutthroat trout. The ranch owners, on whose property the collections were made, "insisted that no trout were introduced until last fall (1933) when 6,000 rainbow fingerlings were planted." The fate of the native cutthroat can be surmised by Hubbs's comment that, "The rainbow trout had

grown very well. The largest trout we caught and by far the best in condition were a few rainbows." By publishing Hubbs's original description in this book, his manuscript name *alvordensis* becomes the subspecies name for an extinct cutthroat trout and makes a small contribution to the enormous volume of publications that made Carl L. Hubbs a recognized authority on fishes.

Hubbs was part of an American dynasty of ichthyology. About 1870, Louis Agassiz of Harvard University sought the brightest student, who he envisioned would become America's leading authority on fishes. Agassiz chose David Starr Jordan. About 1915, while President of Stanford University, Jordan searched for his successor to carry on as America's leading ichthyologist. He chose Carl Hubbs, who was then an undergraduate student at Stanford. The dynasty continues to the present. Carl Hubbs's son, Clark, now retired from the University of Texas, has had a distinguished career in ichthyology and conservation. Carl Hubbs's son-in-law, Robert Rush Miller, now retired from the University of Michigan, has long been recognized as an authority on southwestern fishes and on the fishes of Mexico. Robert Rush Miller named both the Gila trout and the Apache trout.

Color photographs of the 1984 Virgin Creek Alvords show intense rose coloration over much of the body, indicating that the Alvord was considerably more colorful than its closely related neighbor, the Lahontan cutthroat trout.

The following supplemental description is based on my examination of Hubbs's 1934 collection, University of Michigan Museum of Zoology no. 130532. The Alvord cutthroat was distinguished from the typical Lahontan cutthroat trout by having few (25–50) moderate-size spots on the body; almost all spots occurred above the lateral line. The number of scales along the body was fewer than in the Lahontan cutthroat trout, ranging from 125 to 150 (an average of 137), versus 150 to 180 in the Lahontan.

Likewise, Alvord cutthroat trout had 35 to 50 (an average of 42) pyloric caeca, versus a typical range of 40 to 75 in the Lahontan cutthroat. The number of gill rakers in the Alvord was similar to the Lahontan cutthroat trout: 20 to 26 (an average of 23).

BIOLOGY   No life history studies were made of the Alvord cutthroat trout, but it most likely shared the same feeding and spawning behaviors of other cutthroat trout of adjacent areas, especially the Lahontan cutthroat trout.

After the desiccation of Lake Lahontan and Alvord Lake (about 9,000–10,000 years ago), the life history of the native cutthroat trout was not finely attuned for existence in small streams. The trout were highly susceptible to replacement and hybridization by introduced fish.

Although most Alvord cutthroat in small stream habitats did not attain a great size— Hubbs's 1934 collections were mostly 4 to 7 inches (10–18 cm) in length—some specimens found in deeper pools in the headwaters of Virgin Creek in the 1980s were large. One

Two stream drainages once maintained populations of Alvord cutthroat trout: Virgin Creek (and its tributary, Thousand Creek) and Trout Creek (and its tributary, Little Trout Creek).

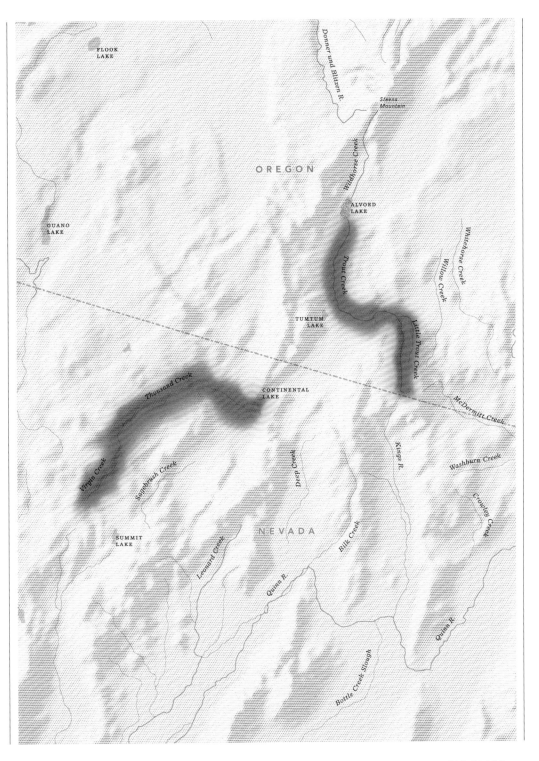

measured almost 20 inches (51 cm) in length and weighed 3 pounds (1.4 kg). This larger than average size for trout in such a small stream is an indication of the subspecies' former life in Alvord Lake, which at its peak some 13,000 years ago stretched over 100 miles (160 km) across the basin. In these formerly vast waters, the Alvord cutthroat could grow large, feeding on smaller Gila chub in the lake.

DISTRIBUTION
The Alvord basin extends from northern Nevada, where its southern rim borders the Lahontan basin, into Oregon, where it is contiguous with the Whitehorse basin in the east and separated from the Malheur and Catlow basins in the west by Steens Mountain. At its maximum extent, about 13,000 to 14,000 years ago, Alvord Lake filled much of the basin; it had a surface area of 4,927 square miles (12,761 sq km) and extended slightly more than 100 miles (160 km) in a north–south axis. A series of lakes existed in the Alvord basin over a period of many millions of years, going back to Miocene times.

After the desiccation of Alvord Lake, two stream drainages maintained the Alvord cutthroat: Virgin Creek (and its major tributary, Thousand Creek) and Trout Creek.

EVOLUTION AND CLASSIFICATION
The headwaters of Virgin Creek in the Alvord basin begin in northwestern Nevada and are closely associated with the headwaters of Mahogany Creek of the adjacent Lahontan basin. The Alvord cutthroat was a member of the group of minor subspecies that derived from the major subspecies, the Lahontan cutthroat trout.

The topography of alluvial deposits between the Mahogany Creek and Virgin Creek drainages suggests that the origin of the Alvord cutthroat trout occurred when Mahogany Creek temporarily changed course to connect to Virgin Creek, transferring cutthroat trout from the Lahontan basin into the Alvord basin. The now desiccated Alvord Lake provided further opportunity for lake-adapted specializations and for the extension of the subspecies' distribution to the adjacent Trout Creek drainage.

CONSERVATION
Efforts to preserve the Alvord cutthroat were too little and too late. One such attempt in 1986 involved transplanting fish from upper Virgin Creek that most resembled the native cutthroat trout. About 25 of these trout were transplanted into a small fishless stream in the Lahontan basin, Jackson Creek in the Jackson Mountains of Nevada. Subsequent genetic analysis indicated that about 50 percent of the genes of these cutthroat-like trout were from rainbow trout parents. Nevertheless, this last attempt to preserve a small part of the Alvord cutthroat evolutionary line failed. The transplanted fish, or any offspring they may have produced, were never seen again. Flows in the previously fishless stream may not have been sufficient to maintain a population, or seepage from abandoned mines in the drainage might have created lethal toxicity. This stream remains fishless, and the Alvord cutthroat trout remains extinct.

ARTIST'S NOTE
Dennis Shiozawa at Brigham Young University in Utah loaned three adult specimens of Alvord cutthroat trout to me to create the illustration for this account. All three exhibit tiny white tips on the pelvic and anal fins, and suggest an orange-tipped dorsal fin in life, indicating that they may possibly have been influenced by stocked rainbow trout. However, they strongly resemble cutthroat trout in nearly all of their physical characteristics. The three trout were caught in the summer of 1985 in Virgin Creek by Bob Smith, who spent his later years catching almost every subspecies of trout in North America. Fortunately, Smith also photographed the specimens and his color prints were also used for the drawing. I chose the largest of the specimens to create the illustration—a female fish, 19 inches (48 cm) in length with high scale counts, a long upper jaw, red coloration, and exhibiting the spotting pattern described by Carl Hubbs in his notes from the 1930s. According to Bob Smith, and Jim French of the Nevada Division of Wildlife, male Alvord cutthroat trout were even more strikingly red than the females.

Whitehorse Basin Cutthroat Trout

Oncorhynchus clarki subspecies

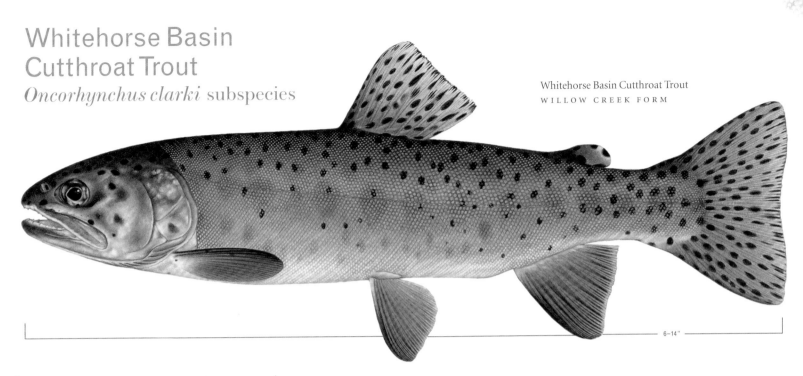

Whitehorse Basin Cutthroat Trout
WILLOW CREEK FORM

6–14"

The Whitehorse basin, also known as the Coyote basin, receives its drainage from the Trout Creek Mountains, in Oregon just north of the Nevada border, on the northern rim of the Lahontan basin. The Whitehorse basin is contiguous to the west with the Alvord basin, and to the north and east with the Columbia River basin. Two streams in the basin, Willow Creek and Whitehorse Creek, are home to an "undescribed" subspecies of trout commonly named the Whitehorse basin cutthroat trout or Willow–Whitehorse Creek cutthroat trout.

DESCRIPTION The Whitehorse basin cutthroat trout is essentially similar to the Humboldt cutthroat trout, and both are considered minor subspecies derived from the major subspecies, the Lahontan cutthroat trout. In the populations of Whitehorse and Willow Creeks, gill raker numbers average 21 or 22, and scale counts along the body range from 131 to 164, averaging 147 to 150. The main distinction of the Whitehorse basin cutthroat from the Humboldt cutthroat is the Whitehorse's lesser number of pyloric caeca, which range from 35 to 50 and average 40 to 43, about 15 fewer than is typical of Humboldt cutthroat trout. The coloration and spotting of the Whitehorse basin cutthroat is similar to that of the Humboldt: brassy, yellowish colors and relatively large, round spots sparsely distributed on the body, mainly above the lateral line.

BIOLOGY Most of the stream habitat of Willow and Whitehorse Creeks that is inhabited by trout occurs in a desert-like environment. Stream flows depend on

WHITEHORSE BASIN CUTTHROAT TROUT

SCIENTIFIC NAME
Oncorhynchus clarki subspecies

OTHER COMMON NAMES
Willow–Whitehorse Creek cutthroat trout

HABITAT
Small, unstable streams

LENGTH AND WEIGHT
6–14" (15–36 cm) and 1–16 oz (28–454 g)

LIFE SPAN
Probably 4–5 years

DIET
Aquatic and terrestrial invertebrates

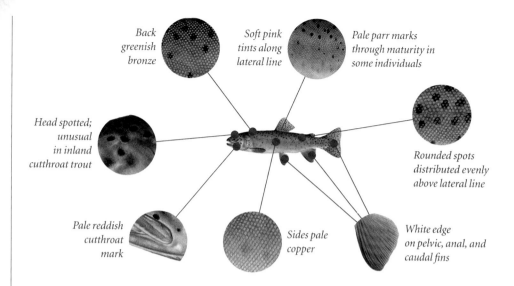

Back greenish bronze

Soft pink tints along lateral line

Pale parr marks through maturity in some individuals

Head spotted; unusual in inland cutthroat trout

Rounded spots distributed evenly above lateral line

Pale reddish cutthroat mark

Sides pale copper

White edge on pelvic, anal, and caudal fins

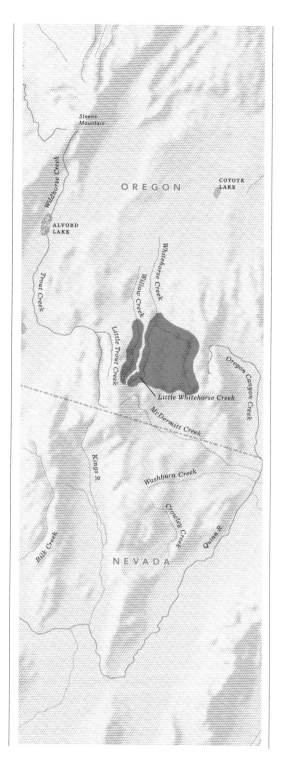

precipitation, mainly snow, in the Trout Creek Mountains, which rise to 10,000 feet (3,000 m). In the lower gradient, lower-elevation sections of the streams, flow is reduced and the water warms in the summer. Water temperatures in July often reach and exceed 80 °F (26 °C) but cool overnight in this cold, high-desert climate to 55 to 60 °F (13–15 °C). The evolutionary programming of Whitehorse basin cutthroat trout for survival in a harsh, fluctuating environment is similar to—or, in view of their origin, a continuation of—the evolutionary programming of the Humboldt cutthroat.

As in the Humboldt and Quinn River drainages, habitat degradation from a long history of livestock grazing has compounded and exacerbated problems associated with survival in an unstable environment, but the Whitehorse basin cutthroat have persisted. Although their growth potential is limited by the degraded small-stream habitat in which they live, Whitehorse basin cutthroat trout attain a general maximum length of about 14 inches (36 cm) and a weight of 1 pound (450 g).

DISTRIBUTION   Two streams, Willow Creek and Whitehorse Creek (and its main tributary, Little Whitehorse Creek), are the only waters in the Whitehorse basin that have maintained trout since Coyote Lake desiccated about 9,000 to 10,000 years ago. Willow and Whitehorse Creeks drain to a desert and are isolated from each other. Slight differences in the number of scales, gill rakers, and pyloric caeca between the populations in the two creeks reflect this isolation.

EVOLUTION AND CLASSIFICATION
The cutthroat trout native to the Whitehorse basin was derived from the Quinn River drainage of the Lahontan basin, and it is only slightly differentiated from the Quinn and Humboldt form of Lahontan cutthroat trout.

Whitehorse basin cutthroat trout are native to two streams in the Whitehorse basin, Whitehorse Creek and Willow Creek.

Recognition of the Whitehorse basin cutthroat trout as a subspecies is based mainly on its occurrence in a now-isolated internal basin of the Great Basin. Another option would be to combine the Whitehorse basin (and Quinn drainage) cutthroat trout with the Humboldt cutthroat as a single subspecies that is, as yet, undescribed.

The cutthroat trout is the only fish species native to the Whitehorse basin. This denotes that the transfer from the Quinn River drainage into the Whitehorse basin involved an uppermost headwater occupied only by cutthroat trout. Evidently no nonnative trout were ever stocked in Willow or Whitehorse Creeks. No nonnative trout occur in the basin, and the native cutthroat trout show no sign of a hybrid influence.

CONSERVATION   Because of its origin and close relationship to the Lahontan cutthroat trout, particularly to the Humboldt cutthroat, the Whitehorse basin cutthroat trout has been protected since 1973 under the Endangered Species Act (ESA) as a form of Lahontan cutthroat trout. Despite this legal protection, livestock grazing on U.S. Bureau of Land Management (BLM) lands, which include virtually the entire distribution of the Whitehorse basin cutthroat, continued to degrade the watershed and the stream habitat for many years. The denuded watershed and the destabilized and silted stream channels caused by livestock obviously were a violation of the ESA by a federal agency.

Overgrazing, which causes loss of fish and wildlife habitat, is characteristic of the Great Basin and is particularly acute in arid lands. By mid-summer, all palatable vegetation preferred by livestock is essentially gone from upland acres, and the only green vegetation occurs in a narrow riparian zone along streams. Even with a low livestock density of less than one cow per 100 acres (40 ha), all of the cattle on the grazing allotment concentrate along streams, virtually eliminating the vegetation, caving in stream banks, and greatly increasing the sediment load and siltation of streams.

In the 1970s, the BLM undertook some token projects on behalf of the Whitehorse basin cutthroat. A livestock exclosure area (that is, an area from which livestock are excluded) was constructed on a section of Whitehorse Creek. Inside the exclosure, lush vegetation grew—its root system stabilizing stream banks and its leaves shading and cooling the water—and provided a food supply for the trout: terrestrial insects attracted to vegetation and dropping on the water. Outside the exclosure, continued livestock grazing maintained a barren, lunar-like landscape. The exclosure dramatically demonstrated what Whitehorse and Willow Creeks could be if the BLM had obeyed the directives of the Endangered Species Act, which mandated that any action of a federal agency should not further jeopardize the continued existence of a listed species.

By the early 1990s, the BLM had revised their grazing management program to exclude livestock from the area of the Willow and Whitehorse drainages inhabited by the Whitehorse basin cutthroat trout. A fish census of Willow and Whitehorse Creeks in 1994 and in 1999 yielded hopeful figures for the numbers of Whitehorse basin cutthroat trout. Despite 1994 being one of the driest years on record, the Oregon Department of Fish and Wildlife estimated a population of 40,000 fish after a low in 1989 of only 8,000 fish. The 1999 census confirmed that the population was stable, and in January of 2001 the area was opened to catch-and-release angling.

With proper protection of the watershed, the continued existence of this subspecies should be ensured. ◄━━

Humboldt Cutthroat Trout
Oncorhynchus clarki subspecies

Humboldt Cutthroat Trout

6–14"

The Lahontan cutthroat trout native to the Humboldt River drainage—the largest drainage of the Lahontan basin—differs from the Lahontan cutthroat subspecies of the Truckee, Carson, and Walker River drainages. One major difference concerns its life history and ecology. The evolutionary adaptation of the Humboldt cutthroat trout is for life in streams, particularly survival under a harsh, wildly fluctuating environment of floods, droughts, and the high siltation levels characteristic of arid watersheds. The Humboldt cutthroat trout has not been officially described with its own subspecies name. Referred to as the Humboldt form of Lahontan cutthroat trout, it is considered an "undescribed," or unnamed, subspecies.

DESCRIPTION The coloration of the Humboldt cutthroat trout is typical of the Lahontan cutthroat: rather somber bronze or copper tones with yellowish or often dull red background colors. The spotting pattern is variable among populations, but there is a trend for Humboldt cutthroat trout to have fewer spots on the body than Lahontan cutthroat.

The Humboldt subspecies differs from the Lahontan cutthroat trout in having fewer gill rakers, typically 20 to 22 (Humboldt) versus 23 to 25 (Lahontan), and fewer scales, typically 130 to 160 (Humboldt) versus 150 to 180 (Lahontan).

Almost all existing Humboldt cutthroat exist as small populations in small headwater streams, isolated from one another. This isolation allows for considerable variation

HUMBOLDT CUTTHROAT TROUT

SCIENTIFIC NAME
Oncorhynchus clarki subspecies

OTHER COMMON NAMES
Cutthroat

HABITAT
Small, unstable streams; adaptable to rivers, lakes, and reservoirs

LENGTH AND WEIGHT
6–14" (15–36 cm) and 1–16 oz (28–454 g) in small streams. Bigger in larger bodies of water: typically 14–18" (36–46 cm) in reservoirs; maximum 5–10 lb (2.3–4.5 kg)

LIFE SPAN
Probably 4–5 years in headwater streams; 5–8 years in larger bodies of water

DIET
Primarily aquatic and terrestrial invertebrates

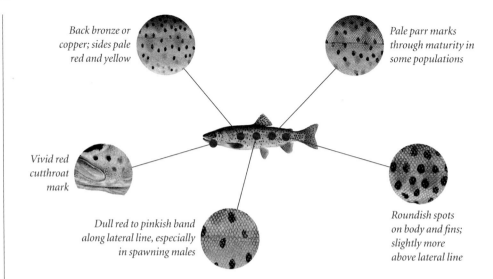

Back bronze or copper; sides pale red and yellow

Pale parr marks through maturity in some populations

Vivid red cutthroat mark

Dull red to pinkish band along lateral line, especially in spawning males

Roundish spots on body and fins; slightly more above lateral line

among populations. For example, the trout of Gance Creek, a small tributary to the North Fork Humboldt River, average only 126 scales along the lateral line, as is typical of coastal rainbow trout. The number of pyloric caeca is typical of the Lahontan cutthroat (50–60), but the trout native to Hanks Creek, a tributary to the Marys River, average 66 pyloric caeca, the maximum known for any form of cutthroat or rainbow trout.

BIOLOGY   The outstanding feature of the life history and ecology of Humboldt cutthroat trout is their amazing ability to persist under the harsh and highly unstable environments of small streams in arid watersheds. These fish are thought to live for four or five years in headwater streams (5–8 years in larger bodies of water) and reach an average length anywhere between 6 to 12 inches (15–30 cm) depending on availability of food and stream habitat. By late summer, many of these home streams become intermittent, and trout persist in

pools and beaver ponds fed by groundwater. Such habitat is also critical for survival over the winter. Lahontan trout that inhabit larger pools and beaver ponds can grow to a length of 14 inches (36 cm) or larger.

Since the 1870s, most small streams and their watersheds in the Humboldt drainage have been further stressed and degraded by livestock grazing, which destabilizes stream banks and channels and increases erosion and sediment loads. It is in such badly degraded streams that Humboldt cutthroat trout still persist and where all introductions of nonnative trout have failed. Only in some of the "best" trout streams in the Humboldt drainage—ones with clear, cold, perennial flow, such as those in the Ruby Mountains—have nonnative brook, brown, and rainbow trout become established.

The Humboldt cutthroat trout's adaptation to life in unstable streams parallels that of the Bear River form of the Bonneville cutthroat trout. Like the Bear River cutthroat, the Humboldt cutthroat is highly resistant

to replacement by nonnative trout, especially in what would normally be considered submarginal habitat.

The toughness of the Humboldt cutthroat is well illustrated by its persistence in Willow Creek Reservoir in the Rock Creek drainage southwest of Tuscarora, Nevada. Willow Creek Reservoir was constructed for the storage of irrigation water in the early 1900s. During the early years and into the 1920s, the reservoir was noted for large cutthroat trout that weighed 5 to 10 pounds (2.3–4.5 kg). Degradation of the Willow Creek watershed by livestock greatly increased sediment loads and eventually eliminated the native cutthroat trout and any possible spawning habitat except in two small headwater tributaries. The volume of Willow Creek Reservoir is now reduced by half from sediment input and is "enriched" by high levels of nutrients; during summer, intense blooms of blue-green algae make the reservoir resemble green pea soup. Water temperatures in the inlet and on the surface of the reservoir can reach 80 °F (27 °C) and higher. The present fish fauna of Willow Creek Reservoir consists mainly of nonnative warm-water species, such as sunfishes and catfishes (among anglers, the reservoir is noted for its crappie fishing).

Despite the very untrout-like environment, some juvenile cutthroat trout from the upstream tributaries still migrate downstream to live and grow (now only to 14–18 inches, or 36–46 cm, in length) in the reservoir for a year or two before returning to the tributaries for spawning. Each year many anglers, mainly fishing for crappie, are pleasantly surprised with an occasional catch of a native Humboldt cutthroat trout. More surprising is how any trout can survive and grow in such an environment.

DISTRIBUTION   The range of the Humboldt cutthroat trout is in the Humboldt River drainage in Nevada, and probably also the Quinn River drainage of the Lahontan basin. Presently the Quinn River watershed is mostly desert country. The Quinn River drains to the Black Rock Desert, while its headwaters are in the Trout Creek Mountains of southeastern Oregon. (This area is adjacent to the Whitehorse basin, making the Quinn River the likely source of the Whitehorse basin cutthroat trout from an interbasin transfer.)

Except for a few small mountain and spring-fed tributaries, there is little habitat for trout in the Quinn drainage, and Lahontan cutthroat trout native to the Quinn drainage are rare; only a few small populations remain. Like the Humboldt cutthroat trout, the remnant cutthroat populations in the Quinn drainage differ from the Lahontan cutthroat in their number of gill rakers (average 20–21). It is not known, however, whether the similarities between Humboldt and Quinn cutthroat trout are the result of common ancestry from a previous connection of the Humboldt and Quinn drainages, or if they are the result of independent, parallel evolution.

A geomorphic study by J.O. Davis of the University of Nevada, Reno, led him to the conclusion that up to the time of the

The historic range of the Humboldt cutthroat trout included the Humboldt River drainage in Nevada and most likely the Quinn River drainage of the Lahontan basin.

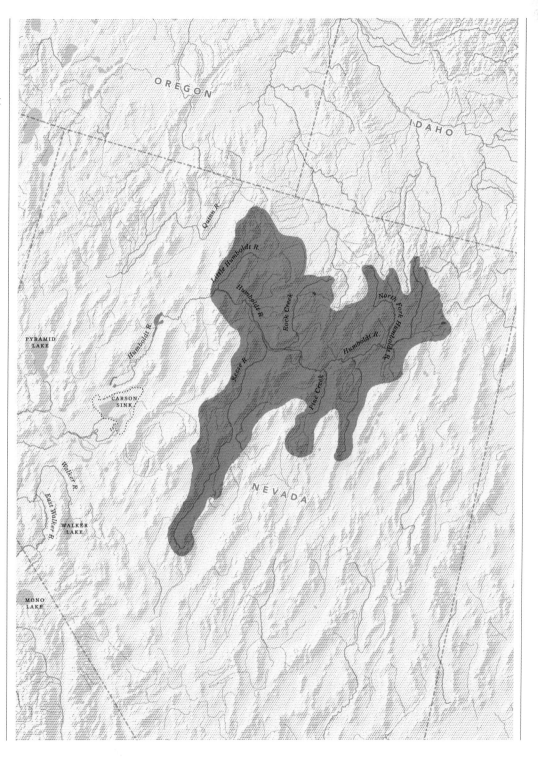

BEAVER OF THE HUMBOLDT DRAINAGE

The natural distribution of beaver is of interest for estimating times of connections of Lahontan basin drainages adjacent to the Humboldt drainages. In 1828, Peter Skene Ogden, fur trader and early western explorer, was the first European American to see the Humboldt River. His journal recounts that beaver and beaver ponds were common in the Humboldt drainage, but no beaver occurred in the Quinn River drainage or any other drainage of the Lahontan basin.

Among early western explorers, a well-known sign that one had crossed the divide between the Lahontan and Sacramento River basins was the presence of beaver dams in streams on the Sacramento side of the divide. In the Lahontan basin, beaver are native only to the Humboldt drainage, though they are now established in the other drainages through introductions.

The entry of beaver into the Humboldt drainage most probably occurred in post-glacial times. Presently, southwest of Tuscarora, Nevada, only a slight gradient and a few miles separate water in the Jack Creek drainage (tributary to the Owyhee River of the Columbia River basin) and water in the Willow Creek drainage of the Lahontan basin. The landscape suggests a likely site where beaver gained entry into the Humboldt drainage. Beaver, like the cutthroat, are native to the Humboldt drainage and beaver ponds allow cutthroat trout to persist, especially over winter, in many small headwater streams in the drainage. Coexistence with beaver for the past few thousand years has been beneficial for the Humboldt cutthroat trout.

dessication of Lake Lahontan (about 9,000–10,000 years ago) an alluvial barrier had diverted the course of the Humboldt River through Provo Gap, near Rye Patch, Nevada, to connect with the Quinn River. With the dessication of Lake Lahontan, the alluvial barrier was breached and the Humboldt River established its present drainage route to the Humboldt sink. Professor Davis presented his findings at the 1990 annual meeting of the Geological Society of America. Unfortuantely, Davis died before his complete paper could be published.

EVOLUTION AND CLASSIFICATION

The parallel between the Humboldt cutthroat trout and the Bear River form of the Bonneville cutthroat is noted under Biology, above. However, the Humboldt cutthroat trout has been evolving separately from other Lahontan cutthroat trout of the subspecies *henshawi* for a longer period of time than the Bear River cutthroat trout of the Bonneville basin. This longer period of evolutionary separation is reflected in the morphological distinctions between the Lahontan cutthroat and Humboldt cutthroat that are the basis for recognizing the Humboldt cutthroat as a subspecies, although it has not been formally described.

How else can we deduce that the Humboldt cutthroat has evolved separately from Lahontan cutthroat for such a long time? It is necessary to look back in geological time and examine the life of ancient Lake Lahontan.

Lake Lahontan was a pluvial lake that

formed during a long period of great precipitation from the early to late Pleistocene epoch (about 1.8 million–8,000 years ago). During the maximum extent of Lake Lahontan, about 14,000 years ago, the lower half of the present Humboldt River was below the highest lake level. It would be assumed that large Lahontan cutthroat from Lake Lahontan utilized the Humboldt River, the largest tributary to the lake, for spawning. If so, how did the stream-adapted Humboldt cutthroat maintain reproductive isolation from the lake-adapted Lahontan cutthroat?

The fact that all of the many populations of existing Humboldt cutthroat trout consistently differ from all populations of Lahontan cutthroat trout native to the Truckee, Carson, and Walker River drainages signifies that the distinctions of the Humboldt cutthroat were already evolved, and that they were maintained by avoiding hybridization with other Lahontan cutthroat trout during the existence of Lake Lahontan.

The chronology of isolation of the rivers of the Lahontan basin as the level of Lake Lahontan declined toward desiccation (except for its sump, Pyramid Lake) also supports the assumption that the origin and isolation of Humboldt cutthroat dates to a pre–Lake Lahontan time period. The sequence of isolation of individual rivers during the decline of Lake Lahontan is: Walker, Truckee, Quinn, Humboldt, and Carson. The present Carson River drainage terminates in the Carson sink, while the Humboldt River terminates in the Humboldt sink, and during prolonged periods of above-normal precipitation, the waters of the Carson and Humboldt sinks connect. Thus,

based on the length of time that the Lahontan cutthroat trout native to the different river drainages have been isolated, the Humboldt cutthroat should be most identical to the Lahontan cutthroat of the Carson drainage.

In fact, this is not the case. The Lahontan cutthroat of the Carson, Walker, and Truckee drainages are virtually identical, and they all are clearly differentiated from Humboldt cutthroat. This indicates that the differentiation of Humboldt cutthroat trout began before Lake Lahontan formed and that their differentiation was maintained during the existence of Lake Lahontan. When the Humboldt cutthroat originated is not known, but its emergence may be associated with the previous interglacial period, about 100,000 years ago.

CONSERVATION   The Humboldt cutthroat is protected under the Endangered Species Act as the Humboldt form of Lahontan cutthroat trout; that is, it is included with the subspecies *henshawi* and is covered by the protection and restoration program for Lahontan cutthroat. As noted above, because of life history adaptations to survive under harsh environmental regimes, the Humboldt cutthroat has fared much better than other Lahontan cutthroat trout exposed to environmental degradation, and especially the introduction of nonnative trout.

Pure or essentially pure Humboldt cutthroat exist in about 90 streams with about 250 miles (400 km) of stream habitat. (Quantification of the length of stream habitat is elusive and variable; a stream with 8 to 10 miles, or 13–16 km, of flowing water habitat during spring run-off might

be reduced to a dry stream channel with intermittent pools in summer, fall, and winter.) The present distribution and abundance of Humboldt cutthroat trout is only a small fraction of their historic distribution, especially in relation to the volume of habitat. Now virtually all populations are restricted to small headwater tributaries; the upper Marys River now has the largest population in the largest area of continuous stream habitat.

Before impacts from irrigation diversions, livestock grazing, mining, introductions of nonnative fishes, and other human interference, the Humboldt cutthroat occupied about 2,220 miles (3,500 km) of stream. Its habitat included the main channel of the Humboldt River downstream to about the town of Battle Mountain, Nevada, and all of the major tributaries, such as the Marys River, North Fork Humboldt River, Little Humboldt River, Rock Creek, and Reese River. Diversion of water out of stream channels and the pervasive impact of overgrazing on arid watersheds eliminated trout habitat in all of the larger streams, eventually restricting the native cutthroat to small headwater tributaries.

The decline of the Humboldt cutthroat trout can be understood from observations of Maggie and Susie Creeks and their watersheds. These two creeks enter the Humboldt River at Carlin, Nevada. In the 1870s, the *Elko* newspaper reported large catches of trout from Maggie and Susie Creeks and from the Humboldt River near Carlin. The abundance of trout stimulated a "commercial" fishery, with boys selling their catch for about twenty-five cents per trout or per pound. A dining stop on the transcontinental railroad was located at Carlin, and the restaurant often featured Humboldt cutthroat trout. After many years of impact from livestock grazing, Susie Creek lost all of its trout and trout habitat; no trout now exist anywhere in the entire drainage. In the Maggie Creek drainage the main stream is heavily silted and turbid; the native cutthroat trout persists in three small headwater tributaries where steep canyon areas limited livestock access and a few miles of suitable habitat were maintained.

The attitudes, programs, and policies of the U.S. Forest Service and U.S. Bureau of Land Management (almost all of the existing populations of Humboldt cutthroat trout occur within federal lands) have gradually changed during the past 20 to 30 years in regard to multiple-use management of their lands. In reality, "multiple use" became the use of federal lands for dominant commodities—livestock grazing, timber, water development, and mining—with little consideration of other environmental values. A growing public awareness of environmental values and of long-term, often irreversible losses from environmental degradation resulted in Congress passing new laws, such as the Endangered Species Act and the National Environmental Policy Act, that provided a strong legal basis to force needed changes in multiple-use management.

However, there can often be considerable lag time before environmental laws are implemented in their full intent. For example, the Multiple Use and Sustained Yield Act of 1957 directed the U.S. Forest Service to give equal rank to all environmental values, such as protection of fish and wildlife habitat, not just to the dominant commodity in their multiple-use management programs. Despite this direction, in 1964 the U.S. Department of Agriculture (Forest Service and Soil Conservation Service) published a plan for phreatophyte control in the Humboldt River drainage. (A phreatophyte is a plant whose roots generally extend downward to the water table; the term literally means water-loving plants.)

All vegetation was divided into "beneficial" vegetation (plants consumed by livestock) and "non-beneficial" vegetation (riparian vegetation that transpired large amounts of water). The plan called for application of a herbicide to eradicate large areas of willow, aspen, and cottonwood trees that annually transpire a volume of 2 to 4 acre feet of water (1 acre of water 1 foot deep equals 1 acre foot).

To the proponents of phreatophyte control, the elimination of riparian trees and conversion of the water "wasted" by transpiration in order to provide more water for irrigated agriculture was true conservation in that it was a "wise and beneficial" use of natural resources. The loss of fish and wildlife habitat was deemed insignificant, of no important consequence. This program designed to increase flows in the Humboldt was halted before it was widely implemented.

It was such federal policies and programs—influenced by the contemporary paradigm of the times, which emphasized strictly "anthropocentric" rather than more "ecocentric" values—that have resulted in the decline of Humboldt cutthroat trout and of all other native trout in the West.

Genus *Salmo*

Two species of the genus

Salmo occur in North America: the Atlantic salmon and the brown trout. The Atlantic salmon is native to both northeastern North America and western Europe, and the brown trout, although not native to North America, has been successfully established in most cold-water habitats of the 48 contiguous states and southern Canada. Since its introduction into American waters in the eighteenth century, the brown trout has become a major sport fish.

In terms of distribution, abundance, familiarity, and economic importance, brown trout and Atlantic salmon comprise the sum of the genus *Salmo.* Other species, and even genera that could be construed as subgenera of *Salmo* are localized in single lakes in Europe, an area of spring-fed streams along the Adriatic coast of former Yugoslavia, and a few small headwater streams in south-central Turkey.

Morphologically and anatomically the Atlantic salmon and brown trout are highly similar. However, looks can be deceiving. The evolutionary legacies of the two species that determine their range of life history types, the types of environmental niches they fill, and their tolerance for new and changing environments, are very different. This evolutionary legacy explains how the two species have fared in North America. Atlantic salmon can be characterized as a "narrow-niche" species more susceptible to extirpation. Its distribution and abundance depends on anadromous populations that utilize the resources of the North Atlantic Ocean, but that are entirely dependent on access to clean rivers for reproduction and rearing of juveniles. A dam blocking access to a spawning river eliminates native Atlantic salmon from that location. In New England, despite determined and costly efforts to prevent extinction of Atlantic salmon, the species has all but vanished as wild, native populations.

In contrast, the brown trout is a more "broad-niche" species. Brought to North America from Europe, its adaptive diversity has allowed it to go forth and multiply in new environments in the land and waters of opportunity. As wild, self-sustaining populations, the brown trout is the most widely distributed and most abundant trout species in the 48 contiguous states. It's an immigrant success story. However, its success has come at a price in the form of ecological impacts on native populations of brook trout and cutthroat trout.

The name "salmo" has ancient European roots tracing back to Latin, Middle English *(samoun),* and Old French *(saumon).* It is the original or archetypal salmon, now identified as the Atlantic salmon, *Salmo salar.* When the common name "salmo" was transformed into the genus *Salmo,* it become the "type species" of the family, the nucleus of the family Salmonidae. The brown trout, *S. trutta,* is the archetypal trout known as *trutta* or *truite* of ancient Europe.

The genus *Salmo,* as presently conceived, has a tortuous and confusing history, reflecting changing opinions of classification for more than 200 years. The composition of the genus *Salmo* has varied greatly since 1758, when the tenth edition of Linnaeus's work, *The System of Nature,* was published. This work introduced binomial nomenclature, a naming system by which all species of plants and animals could be designated with two words: a genus name, followed by a species name. In Linnaeus's classification, all species of the present family Salmonidae—the trout, salmon, char, whitefishes, and grayling—were included in the genus *Salmo*.

Beginning in the late eighteenth century and continuing into the twentieth century, various classification schemes split *Salmo* into several genera, such as *Salar, Fario,* and *Trutta.* In 1930, David Starr Jordan's last classification of North American salmonid fishes was presented in the *U.S. Fish Commission Report* 1928, *Part 2.* Jordan divided the genus *Salmo* into two subgenera. The subgenus *Salmo* included the Atlantic salmon (*S. salar*), "*S. mykiss*" of Kamchatka (then mistakenly believed to be derived from Atlantic salmon), and "*S. regalis*," the royal silver trout of Lake Tahoe, based on Lahontan cutthroat trout × rainbow trout hybrids that were stocked in the lake. The subgenus *Trutta* included brown trout as well as 15 species now classified in the species *O. mykiss* and 16 species of cutthroat trout.

Until 1989, the genus *Oncorhynchus* consisted only of Pacific salmon species that clearly differed in life history from species classified as *Salmo* (all Pacific salmon die after spawning) and in the number of anal fin rays. Under these criteria, all of the rainbow and cutthroat trout and their derivative species were classified in the genus *Salmo*.

In more recent times, taxonomists have emphasized classification that best reflects true evolutionary relationships rather than morphological and life history similarities. One result is that rainbow and cutthroat trout have been transferred from *Salmo* to *Oncorhynchus* because they are more closely related to Pacific salmon than they are to brown trout and Atlantic salmon.

In the Miocene epoch, perhaps about 20 million years ago, a common ancestor to both *Salmo* and *Oncorhynchus* divided. One branch became isolated in the North Pacific Ocean basin, giving rise to species now classified in the genus *Oncorhynchus,* and one branch became isolated in the North Atlantic Ocean basin, giving rise to species now classified in the genus *Salmo*.

Aside from the highly restricted distribution of species in western Europe, Yugoslavia, and Turkey, the diversity that occurs in *Salmo*—as represented by the brown trout and the Atlantic salmon as the end products of evolution in the North Atlantic basin— is only a fraction of the diversity produced by the evolution of *Oncorhynchus* species in the North Pacific basin. It might be assumed that during the past 15 to 20 million years, evolutionary divergences and radiations of new evolutionary lines occurred in the genus *Salmo* comparable to the lines of Pacific salmon and trout of the genus *Oncorhynchus.* If this is true, then extinction of ancestral divergences of *Salmo* was more prevalent than that in *Oncorhynchus,* resulting in the survival of only two widely distributed species, the brown trout and Atlantic salmon, and the highly localized distribution of a few other related species.

Atlantic Salmon
Salmo salar

Atlantic Salmon
Salmo salar

Atlantic Salmon
SPAWNING MALE

30–36"

The highly esteemed and awe-inspiring Atlantic salmon is often called the "king of fishes." Wild native populations of Atlantic salmon once returned in large numbers to their natal rivers in North America to spawn. Long, sleek, and silvery, they swam up raging rivers from bays, estuaries, and the open ocean, leaping above barriers to reach spawning streams. After spawning, some fish returned to the sea, and some survived to spawn again. Their wondrous perseverance, combined with their strength, speed, and beauty— and their reputation as sport fish— has created an enduring mystique about Atlantic salmon.

While in some years large runs of wild Atlantic salmon take place in Canadian waters, the varied and abundant races of wild fish in the United States are long gone. When Europeans first colonized North

America in the seventeenth century, salmon were plentiful, and fishermen netted, clubbed, and speared them in streams and rivers all along the northeastern seaboard to as far south as the Housatonic River.

There is considerable debate about the importance of Atlantic salmon to Native American culture; not enough evidence exists to determine if these fish were a significant food source. Nevertheless, Atlantic salmon quickly became important to European immigrants, who fished these stocks extensively throughout New England. An oft-repeated myth concerns servants who contracted with their employers not to be fed Atlantic salmon more than once or twice a week. The implication was that the salmon were so abundant they were a glut on the market and the cheapest source of food. This story is often associated with the Connecticut River, which lost its runs of salmon after a

ATLANTIC SALMON

SCIENTIFIC NAME
Salmo salar

OTHER COMMON NAMES
None known

HABITAT
Streams and rivers; intertidal areas and open ocean

LENGTH
Smolt 5–7" (13–18 cm) and 2–4 oz (57–113 g); grilse 18–28" (46–71 cm); after 2–3 years at sea 30–36" (76–91 cm) and 10–20 lb (4.5–9.1 kg); typical maximum 30 lb (13.6 kg)

LIFE SPAN
Typically 5–6 years; maximum 11 years

DIET
At sea a variety of shrimp and fishes, such as herrings, sand lances, and capelin

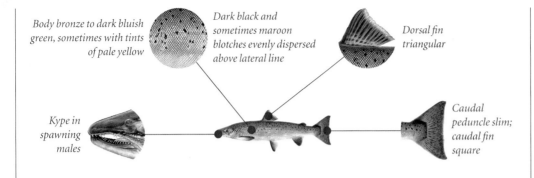

Body bronze to dark bluish green, sometimes with tints of pale yellow

Dark black and sometimes maroon blotches evenly dispersed above lateral line

Dorsal fin triangular

Kype in spawning males

Caudal peduncle slim; caudal fin square

SPAWNING MALE

dam was constructed in 1798, but it has no basis in fact and can be traced back to ancient folklore of Scotland and England.

By the early 1950s, however, in the United States, runs of Atlantic salmon were reduced to a few hundred fish in only five rivers in Maine, and fresh wild Atlantic salmon became an expensive delicacy. Restoration efforts increased and escalated in the 1980s, but at the beginning of the twenty-first century, still only a few hundred wild fish are making the journey from the Atlantic Ocean up rivers in New England. What happened? Over the past two hundred years the combination of dams, pollution, and, more recently, decreased ocean productivity devastated these wild runs. They have never recovered and it is highly unlikely the species will ever reach its former abundance in the wild. However, and it is amazing to contemplate, the Atlantic salmon has never been as abundant as it is today. Off the shores of Maine, over 10 million hatchery-bred Atlantic salmon swim in pens. Over 95 percent of Atlantic salmon abundance consists of domesticated fish that are selectively bred as a commodity—cultured salmon raised in

cages in bays and fjords and fattened for market like cattle in a feedlot. Atlantic salmon now sells in the market for less than flounder or catfish.

The United States' cultured salmon industry is relatively new and much smaller than similar operations around the world. Norway, Scotland, and Chile produce more than 1 billion pounds (454,000 metric tons) of ocean-farmed (cage-cultured) Atlantic salmon each year. Maine's salmon aquaculture industry produced a little more than 36 million pounds (16,329 metric tons) in 2000. Current worldwide annual production exceeds the maximum commercial catches of the nineteenth and early twentieth centuries by at least twentyfold, and in recent years, the annual production of Atlantic salmon in ocean-farming operations has exceeded the commercial catch of wild Atlantic salmon by about a hundredfold.

Although cultured salmon is the same species as wild salmon and has the same fine flavor, the massive production of aquacultured salmon has caused intense controversy because of its environmental impacts, especially on wild Atlantic salmon

and sea-run brown trout. Cultured salmon can carry pathogens and parasites. When thousands of them escape from their pens and run up rivers to spawn, they threaten to replace or compromise the genetic integrity of wild populations.

To the average person, the controversy might seem to be much ado about nothing. Surely many consumers have a favorable view on how modern technology and marketing have transformed a source of food that at one time was costly and in limited supply into an abundant, reasonably priced commodity.

Many Atlantic salmon anglers, who have an emotional, almost mystical attachment to a species they regard as a magnificent creation of nature, take a different view of ocean-farmed Atlantic salmon. To them the distinction between wild and cultured salmon is comparable to the difference between an original van Gogh and a mass-produced copy. The distinction between wild and cultured Atlantic salmon is very apparent to an angler who might spend $10,000 for a trip to Iceland, Norway, or northern Russia for a week of fishing for wild Atlantic salmon and then release all the catch. How much would such an angler pay for the opportunity to cast a line into a pen swarming with cultured Atlantic salmon, even if allowed to take the catch home for dinner? Fish for fish and pound per pound, the Atlantic salmon has an enormously greater economic value as a sport fish than as a commercial product. The value placed on wild Atlantic salmon by salmon anglers is the basis for the determined efforts to preserve wild populations, even though angling for sea-run Atlantic salmon is prohibited by law in the United States and is strictly controlled in Canadian waters. No other species of fish could attract such committed advocacy.

The production of cultured Atlantic salmon has become a cause for concern among fishing and marketing organizations dealing with Pacific salmon. Atlantic salmon aquaculture now approximates the total world commercial catch of all Pacific salmon and therefore depresses the price paid for Pacific salmon species. Atlantic salmon aquaculture supplies 90 percent or more of the ocean-farmed salmon on the market.

DESCRIPTION The characteristics of Atlantic salmon broadly overlap those of brown trout and rainbow trout. In Europe, where anglers may catch both Atlantic salmon and silvery sea-run brown trout, the Atlantic salmon is identified by its proportionally slimmer, more streamlined caudal peduncle; the absence of red or orange spots and of a border on the adipose fin; and its typical spotting patterns. The black and red spots of Atlantic salmon are highly irregular in outline—more like blotches than spots—and tend to be more concentrated toward the front of the body. The lake form or "landlocked" Atlantic salmon shares similar characteristics to sea-run Atlantic salmon.

As spawning time approaches and the salmon return from the sea to fresh water, coloration darkens as the silvery appearance changes to bronze, dark bluish green, and sometimes combined with pale yellow. By the time of spawning, males have developed pronounced kype. Darkening coloration reaches its extreme in kelts (post-spawning

salmon), which are also commonly called black salmon.

BIOLOGY The main life history distinction in the Atlantic salmon is between sea-run and lake-form salmon. The life history of sea-run Atlantic salmon is similar to that of the steelhead form of coastal rainbow trout: Both species depend on fresh water for the first two or three years of life. This dependence on fresh water limits adult abundance compared to species of Pacific salmon. In a small river, chum and pink salmon can produce hundreds of thousands of newly hatched fry that migrate to the ocean. A comparable eastern North American river with spawning runs of Atlantic salmon would probably produce only a thousand or so two- or three-year-old smolts. In their worldwide range, the maximum abundance of Atlantic salmon, even in ancient times, would have been only a small fraction (about 5 percent) of the total abundance of the five species of Pacific salmon. Despite this, some of the most enduring legends of salmon abundance center on Atlantic salmon. Tales endure of spawning runs so numerous that horses and wagons were knocked over while trying to ford streams choked with fish.

Sea-run Atlantic salmon spawn in the fall, typically in October and November. Larger adult salmon weighing from 10 to 20 pounds (4.5–9.1 kg) that have spent two or three years (winters) in the ocean return to rivers first, usually in April, May, or June. Grilse, Atlantic salmon that spend only one year (winter) in the ocean, return later, generally in June and July. The timing of spawning runs can vary greatly. In some populations in

DWARF ATLANTIC SALMON

Isolated above a waterfall on the Namsen River of Norway is a population of Atlantic salmon that live their entire lives in a stream. This Norwegian population was the only known exclusively stream-resident Atlantic salmon until, in the 1990s, dwarf populations were discovered living with brook trout in some acidic, nutrient-poor rivers in Newfoundland. These populations of dwarf salmon live their entire lives in rivers, spawning when they are only 5 or 6 inches (13–15 cm) long and attaining a maximum length of about 8 inches (20 cm). It appears that in these dwarf stream salmon—one of the most unusual and extreme life histories known for the species—both male and female parr mature sexually and reproduce, omitting the smolt and migrating segments of the species' normal life history.

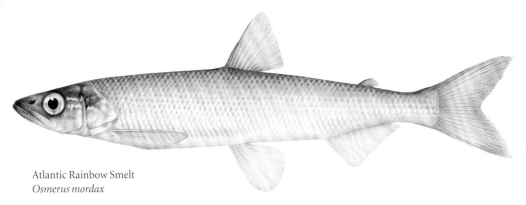

An abundance of forage fishes, such as the Atlantic rainbow smelt, is necessary for lake salmon to reach a large size.

Atlantic Rainbow Smelt
Osmerus mordax

the northern parts of the range, returning adults enter rivers as late as September through November, and they remain in the river, without feeding, for 12 or 13 months before they spawn the following autumn.

Grilse typically weigh from 3 to 6 pounds (1.4–2.7 kg). From area to area and year to year, spawning runs have grilse and older adults in different proportions. In some Irish rivers, virtually all the salmon spawning for the first time are grilse. Atlantic salmon native to Maine rivers had virtually no grilse in their spawning runs. There are both males and females among Atlantic salmon grilse, unlike the steelhead and coho salmon "jacks," fish that return to spawn before spending a winter in the ocean, which are almost all males.

Not all Atlantic salmon die after spawning—each year spawned-out kelts survive and return to the sea the following spring. In their weakened condition, few kelts survive in the ocean, but those that do can grow to a large size. In most populations repeat spawning fish are rare, typically less than 10 percent of a spawning run. Some of the largest salmon—those about

30 pounds (13.6 kg) or more—are likely to be repeat spawners.

The new-generation young hatch and emerge from the redds of the spawning streams in the spring; depending on the water temperature, hatching can be as early as March and April and as late as June in different parts of the range. Most spend one to four years in the juvenile or parr stage before smolting, at lengths of about 5 to 7 inches (13–18 cm), and then migrate to the ocean. In most of the range, smolt age is commonly from two to four years, but this varies among populations, depending on the length of time required for a parr to attain the required size to transform into a smolt. In southern areas of the range, which provide a longer growing season and abundant food (mainly aquatic insects), smolting may occur predominantly at one year of age. In tributaries to Ungava Bay, Canada, the northernmost part of the range, smolts are more commonly five and six, or even eight years old, before they migrate seaward. A common phenomenon in Atlantic salmon, in contrast to Pacific salmon, is for male parr to mature sexually before they become smolts.

Atlantic salmon from both Europe and North America feed in the North Atlantic Ocean; the feeding grounds of the two groups overlap in the area of Greenland. Ocean migration patterns differ for salmon populations that spawn in different areas. For example, Baltic Sea salmon feed in the Baltic and do not roam the North Atlantic Ocean.

In the ocean, Atlantic salmon, like Pacific salmon, feed opportunistically on fishes and large crustaceans. The world-record angler-caught sea-run Atlantic salmon was taken in 1928 from the Tana River, Norway, and weighed slightly over 79 pounds (36 kg). The Baltic Sea is noted for large salmon. In 1996, an Atlantic salmon taken commercially weighed 79 pounds, 13 ounces (36 kg) and measured 51 inches (1.3 m).

Landlocked populations of Atlantic salmon are typically 13 to 21 inches (33–53 cm) long and weigh up to 3 pounds, 8 ounces (1.6 kg); they require abundant forage fishes to attain a size of more than 5 pounds (2.3 kg). Predation on smelt (a small, slender fish of the family *Osmeridae*) is typically associated with large size in landlocked salmon. However, perhaps the

Atlantic Salmon
LAKE FORM

13–21"

largest landlocked or lake salmon population once occurred in Lake Ontario, where the native fish fauna did not include smelt; whitefishes of the genus *Coregonus* probably were the main forage fish. Individual fish weighing up to 45 pounds (20.4 kg) were known from Lake Ontario, but this population is now extinct.

Lake Vänern, in Sweden, has two races of lake salmon. One race that spawns in the Klar River reaches sexual maturity and spawns at four or five years of age, weighing about 6 to 8 pounds (2.7–3.6 kg). The race that spawns in the Gullspång River typically does not spawn until the age of six, and in some years the average weight of Gullspång spawning males can be up to 19 pounds (8.6 kg). In 1975, some offspring of the Gullspång salmon were stocked in Lake Michigan, and in 1981 two of these were caught weighing 32 and 34 pounds (14.5 and 15.4 kg). In the

1990s, Gullspång salmon were stocked in Lake Vättern, Sweden, where they fed on an abundant population of the European cisco, and in 1997 an angler caught a Gullspång salmon of 43 inches (1.1 m) weighing 45 pounds (20.4 kg). This is the greatest documented weight for landlocked Atlantic salmon.

DISTRIBUTION   North American distribution extends from New England northward to Newfoundland and reaches its northern limits in tributaries to Ungava Bay. The Atlantic coast of Canada has suffered much less human impact than areas farther south, and, although some important Atlantic salmon populations in Canada were lost to dams, most of the distribution and diversity of Atlantic salmon in Canada has persisted. A landlocked population of salmon occurs above falls in a drainage tributary to

LAKE FORM ATLANTIC SALMON

SCIENTIFIC NAME
Salmo salar

OTHER COMMON NAMES
Landlocked salmon, lake salmon, Ounaniche salmon, Sebago salmon

HABITAT
Cold, deep lakes; spawn in tributaries

LENGTH AND WEIGHT
13–21" (33–53 cm) and 1–3½ lb (0.45–1.6 kg); typical maximum 5 lb (2.3 kg); historical North American maximum 45 lb (20.4 kg) from Lake Ontario; current angler world record 43" (1.1 m) and 45 lb (20.4 kg) from Lake Vättern, Sweden

LIFE SPAN
Maximum 13 years

DIET
Aquatic invertebrates and other fishes, especially smelt

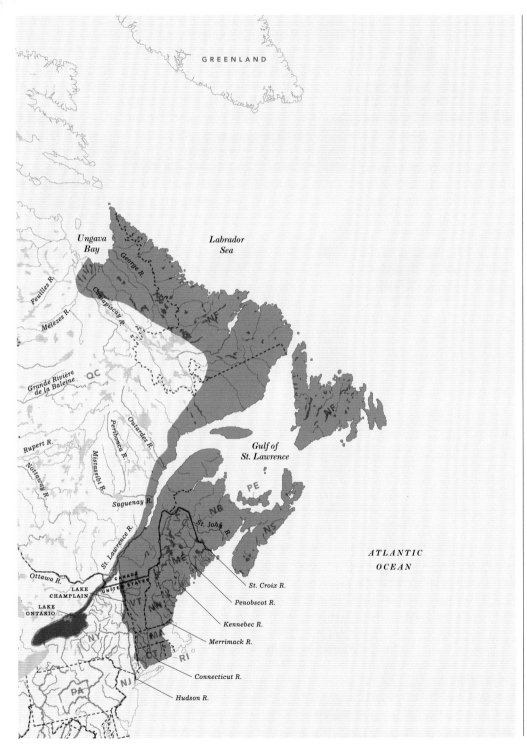

GREENLAND

Ungava
Bay

Labrador
Sea

Feuilles R.

George R.

Mélezes R.

Caniapiscau R.

NF

*Grande Rivière
de la Baleine*

QC

Rupert R.

Perihonca R.

Outardes R.

NF

Nottaway R.

Mistassibi R.

Gulf of
St. Lawrence

Saguenay R.

PE

St. Lawrence R.

NB

St. John R.

NS

Ottawa R.

LAKE
CHAMPLAIN

CANADA
UNITED STATES

ME

ATLANTIC
OCEAN

LAKE
ONTARIO

VT

NH

St. Croix R.

NY

MA

CT

Penobscot R.

RI

Kennebec R.

MI

Merrimack R.

PA

NJ

Connecticut R.

Hudson R.

northeastern Hudson Bay. Most likely this
population is derived from a headwater
transfer from the east, not from an ancestor
migrating from Hudson Bay.

Documented historic distribution of
sea-run Atlantic salmon in the United
States includes 28 New England rivers, the
southernmost being the Housatonic. Today,
the southernmost river with returning fish
(all hatchery stocked fish) is the Connecticut
River, which is heavily stocked. In 2000,
over 9 million salmon fry were released in
the Connecticut, and in the year 2001,
41 returning fish were counted.

Nearly 70 percent of all Atlantic salmon
returning to United States rivers, including
escapees from pens, returning hatchery-bred
fish, and wild salmon, occur in the Penobscot
River basin in Maine. Of the total number
of 803 returning salmon of all types to
New England's rivers in 2000, 225 fish were
considered wild, but most likely came from
hatchery parents that had spawned naturally.

Historic reports of Atlantic salmon in
the Hudson River are based on misidentification, strays, or introduced hatchery fish,
as falls blocked access to the upper parts
of the Hudson River basin, where potential
spawning and juvenile rearing habitat existed.

In Europe, the original distribution
extended from the Douro River of Portugal,
northward around Norway and eastward
in tributaries to the White and Barent Seas
of the Arctic Ocean basin of northwestern

*Historically, the sea-run Atlantic salmon spawned in
North American rivers tributary to Ungava Bay, Canada,
inland up the St. Lawrence River perhaps to Lake Ontario,
and south along the Atlantic Ocean to the Housatonic
River, which feeds into Long Island Sound.*

Russia. The large Pechora River basin (about 52° to 60 °E longitude), in Russia, is the easternmost river that maintains relatively large runs of Atlantic salmon, but sporadic reports extend the species' occurrence to the Kara River at about 65 °E longitude.

Landlocked or resident freshwater populations of Atlantic salmon are much more prevalent in North America than in Europe. In Europe, lake populations of salmon are native to four lakes in Norway, one each in Sweden and Finland, and six in northwestern Russia. Three of the largest lakes in Europe have native populations of landlocked salmon: Lake Vänern in Sweden, and Lakes Ladoga and Onega in Russia, which have a total surface area of some 7.5 million acres (3 million ha).

In eastern Canada, landlocked salmon—or ouananiche, as they are called locally—are common in lakes of Quebec, on the island of Newfoundland, and in Labrador. No precise count is available of how many Canadian lakes hold ouananiche, because many are in remote areas and these populations are yet to be surveyed, but lake salmon are a common element in the fish fauna of the lakes of eastern Canada.

In North America, the natural occurrence of lake salmon populations in the southern part of the range was sparse and restricted to

On November 13, 2000, the U.S. Fish and Wildlife Service and the National Marine Fisheries Service listed the Atlantic salmon as endangered under the Endangered Species Act. The listing covers the wild populations of Atlantic salmon found in rivers and streams in Maine from the lower Kennebec River north to the U.S.-Canada border. These waters include the Dennys, East Machias, Machias, Pleasant, Narraguagus, Ducktrap, and Sheepscot Rivers and Cove Brook.

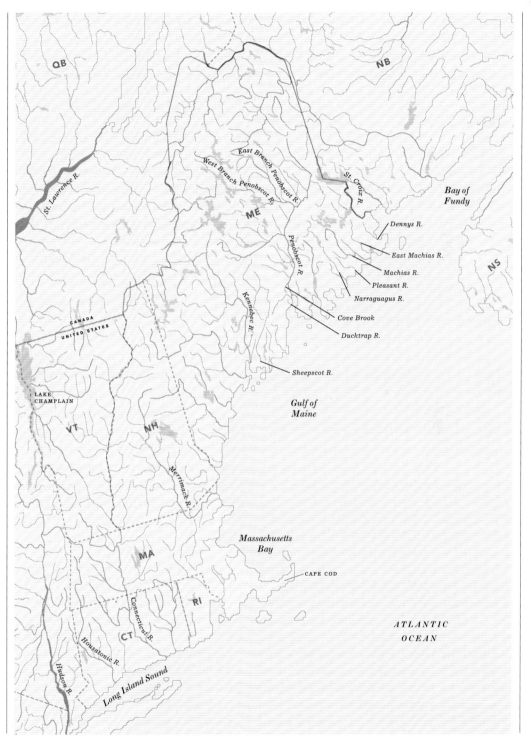

REMNANTS OF THE PAST

Brown trout (Salmo trutta) have resident populations in tributaries to the Mediterranean and Adriatic Seas. Because of this, biologists assume that sea-run brown trout were distributed around the Mediterranean and Adriatic Seas during glacial periods, and that during postglacial warming the sea-run populations disappeared, leaving only freshwater populations. Atlantic salmon are similar to Pacific salmon in that they left no glacial or preglacial "relict" populations outside of the range of sea-run populations. But it is logical to assume that, like brown trout, Atlantic salmon also had sea-run populations south of their known historical distribution and could have left freshwater populations. Such an assumption led to a theory that a peculiar small-mouth trout found in a few spring-fed streams tributary to the eastern Adriatic Sea is derived from the Atlantic salmon. This peculiar trout is classified as Salmothymus obtusirostris. Under the assumption that this fish represented a glacial relict of the Atlantic salmon, the older European literature classified it as "Salmo salar obtusirostris." In fact, Salmothymus obtusirostris is more closely related to the brown trout than to the Atlantic salmon. In a more evolutionarily based classification, it could be placed in the genus Salmo.

Maine. Four river basins in Maine had native lake salmon: St. Croix (Grand Lakes), Union (Green Lake), Penobscot (Sebec Lake), and Presumpscot (Sebago Lake). Presently about 300 lakes in Maine are stocked with hatchery-reared landlocked salmon. A few lakes in New Hampshire, Vermont, and New York also have sport fisheries for landlocked Atlantic salmon based on stocking hatchery-reared fish.

Although lake populations of Atlantic salmon are numerous in North America, the once most abundant population, that of Lake Ontario, has been extinct since about 1900. Lake Ontario has a surface area of about 7,600 square miles (19,750 sq km), a considerably greater area of habitat than all other North American salmon lakes combined. Lake Ontario has many tributary rivers that served as spawning and juvenile rearing habitat. Much of the folklore of great abundance of salmon from colonial times is associated with Lake Ontario spawning rivers. Mill dams, pollution, and commercial fishing are cited as the major causes of the extinction of this stock of fish. Agencies and organizations have been trying to restore salmon to Lake Ontario for 100 years without much success.

Lake Champlain, extending over 600 square miles (1,560 sq km) once had sea-run Atlantic salmon that migrated from the St. Lawrence River to spawn, but it is not known if it also contained a landlocked population. Because smelt, the important Atlantic salmon forage fish, are native to Lake Champlain, it is likely that a nonmigratory population of salmon also occurred there.

Atlantic salmon have been widely stocked outside their native range. In 1903, land-locked salmon from Maine were stocked in Lake Nahuel Huapi, Argentina. They became established and attained large sizes, from 25 to 35 pounds (11–16 kg). Atlantic salmon populations were established in several lakes of Argentina and Chile, but after brown trout and rainbow trout were introduced and became the dominant species, Atlantic salmon declined. Presently, Atlantic salmon are relatively common in Chilean rivers as escapees from large-scale cage-culture operations. They migrate up rivers on spawning runs, but it is questionable whether they could maintain themselves on a long-term, self-sustaining basis if cage culture were to cease. Farm-cultured Atlantic salmon sites are established in the Pacific Northwest, and cage-escaped adult salmon are commonly found in rivers at Vancouver Island. Two-year classes of Atlantic salmon parr from natural reproduction of escaped cultured fish have also been found in a river on Vancouver Island, British Columbia.

EVOLUTION AND CLASSIFICATION

In Latin, Salmo salar means "leaping salmon." Since 1758, when the Atlantic salmon was first described with a genus and species name, several additional species names have been proposed, but because of its relatively limited diversity of life history forms and stable morphology throughout its range, the Atlantic salmon has many fewer invalid species names than the brown trout.

Although brown trout and Atlantic salmon are not sharply differentiated from each other in their overall appearance or in their distinguishing characteristics, genetic evidence indicates that their evolutionary lines have been separated from each other for a long time, probably since the Pliocene epoch (2–5 million years ago). Their relationships are sufficiently close that hybrids between the two species have been documented (generally by genetic analysis), and the hybrids have some degree of fertility. Hybrids are more prevalent where brown trout have been introduced, such as in some rivers of Newfoundland. In North America, Atlantic salmon did not coexist and coevolve with brown trout and are more susceptible to hybridization than in Europe, where coevolved life history distinctions act to separate the two species during spawning. In a highly altered river in Sweden, with introductions of hatchery stocks of Atlantic salmon and brown trout, reproductive isolation has broken down, and hybrids have become common.

In the scientific and angling literature of the nineteenth century, bitter debates and opinionated theories surrounded the two major Atlantic salmon life history forms: sea-run and landlocked salmon. Did the completely freshwater life history represent a separate species, or was it only an alternative life history form of the Atlantic salmon? There is no longer any reasonable doubt that throughout much of its range sea-run Atlantic salmon gave rise to landlocked populations, but this was not so evident in the nineteenth century, and the debate raged on into the twentieth century.

In 1935, William C. Kendall published a scientific paper on New England salmon in which, after many pages of reasoned arguments and detailed analysis of their characteristics, he concluded that the landlocked populations of salmon represented a separate species. He was mistaken. The similarities of body proportions of all lake salmon is due to their spending their entire life in fresh water, rather than to a common ancestor.

Although all Atlantic salmon, including landlocked salmon, share a common ancestor from perhaps 2 million years ago, the landlocked salmon arose in lakes independently in their range over the past 10,000 years, or so. The species as a whole, *Salmo salar*, is monophyletic, but landlocked salmon are polyphyletic—they do not have a single common ancestor that gave rise to all landlocked salmon. All completely freshwater populations of Atlantic salmon in their native range occur in areas that were covered by glacial ice up to about 10,000 years ago and are all of postglacial origin.

"*Salmo sebago*" was described for the landlocked salmon of Maine in 1853, under the assumption that a completely freshwater life history must represent a species different from sea-run *S. salar*. In 1894, the landlocked salmon of Quebec was described as a subspecies, "*S. salar ouananiche*." Because, as with rainbow trout, sockeye salmon, and brown trout, all landlocked populations of Atlantic salmon have derived independently from sea-run populations, "*S. salar sebago*" denotes a freshwater life history form, not a single evolutionary line that gave rise to all lake salmon. It is an ecological rather than an evolutionary subspecies.

"*S. salar sebago*" is commonly used in the literature in reference to lake populations of Atlantic salmon, just as lake populations of brown trout are called "*S. trutta lacustris*." A problem with such a classification would arise if North American and European Atlantic salmon were to be recognized as separate subspecies. (North American *salar* differ from European *salar* by having 56, versus 58, chromosomes.) Because all landlocked and all sea-run Atlantic salmon are now classified as *S. salar*, and "*sebago*" is the first name proposed for any form of North American Atlantic salmon, both landlocked and sea-run Atlantic salmon of North America would become "*S. salar sebago*" and European salmon would be "*S. salar salar*."

CONSERVATION   In North America and Europe the Atlantic salmon long ago became extinct in many of the largest river basins. An obvious inverse relationship exists between the distribution and abundance of Atlantic salmon and the concentrations of human populations and degree of industrial development. In colonial New England, transportation and commerce depended on ships and seaports, and new towns rose near the mouths of rivers. These rivers were soon dammed up to power mills, blocking runs of sea-run fishes.

The largest river basin in New England with runs of Atlantic salmon, the Connecticut River, was dammed in its lower reaches in 1798, and soon thereafter the salmon native to this river system became extinct. Many smaller rivers had lost Atlantic salmon long before that time. From the Housatonic to the St. Croix, a total of 28 New England rivers were known to have had runs of Atlantic salmon, and it is likely that a few additional small rivers had lost their runs before records were kept. By the 1900s, only a few rivers in Maine still had runs of native Atlantic salmon.

Dams and pollution are the banes of Atlantic salmon. The original Atlantic salmon of the Connecticut River has been extinct for 200 years. In the southern parts of the range, New England and southern Europe, Atlantic salmon have been reduced to only a tiny trace of their original distribution and abundance. In the densely populated and industrialized parts of Europe, Atlantic salmon were eliminated long ago from the larger rivers: the Rhine, which drains waste from the industrial heartland of central Europe; the Seine, which runs through Paris; and the Thames, which runs through London.

By the 1940s and 1950s, only a small remnant of the original diversity of New England salmon remained in a few hundred spawners returning to a few rivers in Maine. By 1958, pollution of Penobscot Bay had caused a depletion of oxygen that effectively blocked access to the Penobscot River to salmon returning to spawn. The Penobscot strain of hatchery Atlantic salmon, the major source for hatchery propagation and stocking in New England rivers since 1872, had to be reconstructed from remnant runs that occurred in the Narraguagus and Machias Rivers. It is obvious that the present Penobscot salmon is not the same as the original salmon that spawned in the Penobscot basin; according to commercial catch records, the original spawning run in the Penobscot occurred mainly in April and May, and now the run occurs mostly in June and July. The Atlantic salmon of seven rivers and one brook in Maine that continually maintained

runs of at least a few wild salmon have been designated for protection under the Endangered Species Act. Because of widespread stocking of hatchery fish over a long period of time, none of these populations are "pure" descendants of the native salmon, but they are all that is left to work with in restoring New England salmon.

Efforts to increase the abundance of sea-run Atlantic salmon have included increased hatchery production, improvement and restoration of habitats and environmental quality of rivers, and elimination of commercial fishing in marine waters. Despite these efforts, the total number of returning fish in the United States declined to a low of about 2,000 fish annually in the late 1980s, with decreasing numbers almost every year. A cycle of deteriorating ocean conditions depressed the abundance of wild Atlantic salmon: Lower ocean temperatures caused reduced levels of nutrients and low productivity in the North Atlantic. During a strong and persistent downward trend, ocean productivity cycles can override the most determined efforts to increase Atlantic salmon abundance.

A few pockets of destructive commercial fisheries for Atlantic salmon remain, especially legal and illegal European fisheries that indiscriminately take salmon destined for other countries. The traditions and culture imbued in commercial fishing communities are deep-rooted and not easily changed. When commercial fishermen discovered feeding areas of Atlantic salmon off Greenland that contained North American and European salmon, they rapidly exploited

this opportunity. In 1971, almost 6 million pounds (2.7 million kg) of salmon were taken in the Greenland fishery. Greenland has only one river with native Atlantic salmon. Thus this fishery was taking fish that would have returned in the following year (at a larger size) to North American and European rivers. International cooperation would be necessary to resolve problems such as this, but it would be a long, difficult, and imperfect process.

The North Atlantic Salmon Conservation Organization (NASCO), founded in 1984, is an international body designed to arbitrate controversial issues and set commercial catch quotas. Through negotiations and buyouts of commercial fishing rights, the Greenland catch of Atlantic salmon was greatly reduced. In 1976, all foreign-registered boats were barred from the Greenland fishery, and in 1998 Greenland agreed to an annual commercial take of no more than 44,000 pounds (20,000 kg).

The "long-line" ocean commercial fishery of the Faeroe Islands (a self-governing part of Denmark north of the British Isles) presented another problem of open-seas interception of salmon originating in other countries. No Atlantic salmon are native to streams in the Faeroe Islands, but hatchery-reared salmon are stocked in a "home stream" to establish an ocean-ranching fishery. A long-line consists of miles of floating line with up to 4,000 hooks baited with fish dangling near the surface. In the 1960s, long-line fisheries began taking salmon in coastal waters of the Faeroe Islands, mainly salmon native to Scotland and Ireland. Later, moving the fishery farther north, the long-lines caught older, larger salmon mainly destined for Norwegian rivers. NASCO negotiations set catch quotas for the long-line fishery, and buyouts of quotas from private funds reduced the long-line catch. In 1998, the annual quota was set at about 725,000 pounds (330,000 kg), but such a fishery is difficult to monitor to verify catch quotas.

At the beginning of the twenty-first century, the total annual legal and illegal commercial catch of Atlantic salmon in European waters of the North Atlantic may be around 5 million pounds (2.3 million kg). There is still a way to go before 100 percent of the market for Atlantic salmon is entirely supplied from aquaculture (it's now about 99.5 percent if the Baltic Sea fishery—a special situation—is omitted) and wild Atlantic salmon become exclusively a sport fish to maximize their economic potential.

The Baltic Sea fishery for Atlantic salmon is likely to remain a predominantly commercial fishery. All major Baltic spawning rivers have been dammed to produce hydropower. A few highly valuable sport fisheries remain in some of the smaller, undammed rivers, but most (90–95 percent) of the Baltic salmon are from sea-ranching hatcheries. The Baltic Sea is a highly productive body of water, maintaining high abundance of herring and other fishes the salmon feed on; however, continued pollution has become apparent in zones of oxygen depletion and massive fish die-offs, and in fish diseases. The highest known survival of hatchery salmon—from smolts to adults caught in fisheries and returning to their home hatchery rivers—has been

with Baltic salmon and has ranged from 10 to 20 percent in fish released from Swedish hatcheries. In 1990, the total commercial salmon catch from the Baltic Sea was 12.4 million pounds (5.64 million kg). However, since 1990, the Baltic Sea salmon catch has consistently declined and in 2000 the total catch was 5 million pounds (2.28 million kg).

The Atlantic salmon native to the Baltic Sea represent a separate category in regard to conservation of the species. They are still relatively abundant, but 90 to 95 percent of this abundance is maintained by artificial propagation.

In the Baltic Sea, Atlantic salmon hatcheries are "river-specific." Each large river has a hatchery below the lowermost hydroelectric dam, and because of homing of the hatchery fish, river-specific populations are maintained and much of the original natural diversity of Baltic salmon has been preserved—in contrast to New England salmon, which are also 90 to 95 percent dependent on hatcheries, but where almost none of the original native population diversity remains.

Norway, Scotland, and Chile have most of the world's Atlantic salmon farms. The great increases in the production of pen-reared, aquaculture Atlantic salmon in the 1990s have depressed the value of wild salmon taken in commercial fisheries. This has facilitated the buyouts of commercial fishing rights and allowed for higher survival of wild salmon. Salmon culture, however, has negative aspects that create opposition. In areas of intensive culture there are complaints about pollution from excessive nutrients

EIGHTEENTH-CENTURY FLY-FISHING FOR SALMON

One of the first accounts of fly-fishing for salmon in America dates to 1786, when a British officer, Lt. John Enys, amazed the local populace by catching Lake Ontario salmon on a fly in the Saranac River; he also caught salmon on a fly in the Chazy River, tributary to Lake Champlain. At that time, most Americans considered Atlantic salmon as a source of food to be taken by any means possible, including nets, spears, clubs, and pitchforks.

and chemicals used to control both disease and parasites.

For example, in Norway, pen-reared salmon from the Baltic Sea region brought with them a parasitic fluke, *Gyrodactylus salaries*. This parasite is native to the Baltic Sea, and Baltic salmon coevolved with and have a high resistance to the debilitating effects of the parasite. But Atlantic salmon native to Norway, where this parasite did not occur before it was introduced by escaped cultured salmon, have no resistance to the parasite and have suffered great losses in rivers infested by the fluke. Massive numbers of escaped cultured salmon have overwhelmed spawning runs of wild salmon in several Norwegian rivers, threatening the genetic integrity of the wild populations.

In Scotland, in bays with intensive culture of pen-reared salmon, salmon and native wild sea-run brown trout smolts migrating from rivers are exposed to abnormally high concentrations of a parasitic copepod, the sea louse *(Lepeophtheirus salmonis)*. This parasite burrows through the skin of its host and can cause lesions, which may lead to infection and death of its host. Evidently the young sea trout spend a longer period in these bays than the young salmon, and sea-run brown trout are more severely impacted. In recent years, runs of adult sea trout to rivers tributary to bays with intensive salmon culture have significantly declined. Sea trout runs in rivers tributary to bays in Scotland where no salmon culture occurs have had stable or increasing populations.

Acid rain can be a problem in watersheds that lack the buffering capacity to neutralize acidity. Salmon and resident trout populations have been lost in some streams of eastern Canada and Scandinavia after their pH dropped below 5 on the scale of acidity.

Because of the importance and prestige of Atlantic salmon, determined efforts are underway in both North America and Europe to restore salmon to rivers where extinction has occurred and to increase the abundance of wild populations where they exist. The project to restore Atlantic salmon to the Connecticut River, the most intensive and expensive of the restoration projects, has been ongoing for more than 30 years but has met with only limited success.

In addition to passage up rivers and environmental degradation, a major problem confronting salmon restoration concerns the origin of the parental populations used in propagation and stocking. The Connecticut and Penobscot Rivers of New England must once have had several races or groups of populations with different life histories that spawned and reared in different parts of these large basins. The different timings of the spawning runs and times of seaward migration of smolts were evolutionarily programmed to maximize the abundance of each race and, in total, the abundance of salmon returning to each river. This diversity of populations or races was lost with the extermination of the original salmon runs in New England.

Throughout the native range of the Atlantic salmon, it is generally recognized that sport fisheries have an enormously greater economic value compared to commercial fisheries, especially in recent times as the ever-increasing production of aquaculture salmon has depressed the value of wild salmon taken in commercial fisheries.

Despite all of the problems facing the continued existence of wild Atlantic salmon, members of this species are not only leapers, but also survivors. And a hard-core group of dedicated advocates are committed to ensuring that the noble Atlantic salmon will endure.

Brown Trout

Salmo trutta

Brown Trout
Salmo trutta

Brown Trout

10–30"

The story of how the European brown trout was introduced to North America begins in 1880. At that time, the fish culturist Fred Mather was appointed as a representative of the U.S. Fish Commission to the Berlin Fish Cultural Exposition in Germany. Mather befriended the Baron Friedrich Felix von Behr, a wealthy sportsman and president of the German Fish Culturists Association. Mather and von Behr fished together in the beautiful streams of the Black Forest, and Mather was so impressed by the species of trout he caught there, he made plans to import it to America.

Transoceanic shipments of trout had become a reality in the late nineteenth century; it was discovered that converting a room on a ship into an ice house, with temperatures just above freezing, prolonged the incubation period of developing trout eggs. Three years after his visit to Berlin in February 1883, Mather received 80,000 brown trout eggs from aboard the German steamship *Werra*, which he delivered to a New York State hatchery at Cold Spring Harbor, Long Island. There the eggs were divided: Some remained at Cold Spring Harbor, some were sent to a hatchery in Caledonia, New York, and the rest went to the U.S. Fish Commission hatchery in Northville, Michigan. The 1883 shipment consisted of 60,000 eggs from a large lake form of brown trout (the "lake trout" of Europe, called *Seeforelle* in Germany), and 20,000 eggs came from brown trout inhabiting small brooks (the "brook trout" of Europe, called *Bachforelle* in Germany).

The 1883 shipment and many subsequent shipments of brown trout eggs from Germany, England, and Scotland (the latter called Loch

BROWN TROUT

SCIENTIFIC NAME
Salmo trutta

OTHER COMMON NAMES
German brown trout, von Behr trout, Loch Leven trout; salters, sea trout (sea-run form)

HABITAT
Streams and rivers; lakes; intertidal areas

LENGTH AND WEIGHT
10–12" (25–30 cm) and 8–12 oz (227–340 g) in small streams; 14–30" (35–76 cm) and 1–12 lb (0.45–5.4 kg) in rivers and lakes; angler record 40 lb, 4 oz (18.3 kg)

LIFE SPAN
Typical maximum 4 years in small streams; 5–12 years in rivers; 15 years or more in lakes

DIET
Aquatic and terrestrial invertebrates; become piscivorous at 12" (30 cm)

Leven trout) represented a large proportion of the diversity of life history forms found in the brown trout of western Europe. The mixing of these forms in American waters provided a broad basis of genetic diversity and promoted the rapid naturalization of self-sustaining populations of brown trout across the continent. This mixing of diverse parental populations also explains the great range of coloration and spotting patterns now exhibited by American brown trout.

The surviving offspring of the 1883 shipment from Germany were retained at the American hatcheries to establish brood stocks. The first actual stocking of brown trout in public waters occurred a year later in 1884, from a shipment of eggs sent by Baron von Behr. At the Northville, Michigan, hatchery, 4,900 of the newly hatched fry were loaded on the U.S. Fish Commission's railroad car and, on April 11, 1884, were planted from a railroad trestle into the Baldwin River, a tributary to the Pere Marquette River, which flows into Lake Michigan.

Through many subsequent stockings from hatcheries around the nation, brown trout rapidly became established in most of the larger trout streams of North America. Around the Great Lakes and in the East, brown trout quickly replaced the native brook trout, and in the West they replaced native cutthroat trout from the larger rivers. For example, the only salmonid species native to the Pere Marquette River, in Michigan, was the Arctic grayling, which became extinct in all Michigan waters by the early twentieth century, after the introductions of nonnative trout.

Much more difficult for anglers to catch

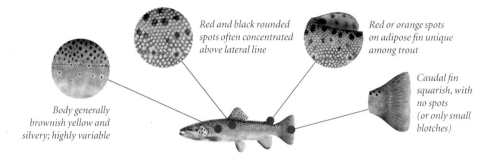

Body generally brownish yellow and silvery; highly variable

Red and black rounded spots often concentrated above lateral line

Red or orange spots on adipose fin unique among trout

Caudal fin squarish, with no spots (or only small blotches)

than native trout, brown trout had become less popular as a sport fish in North America by the early 1900s. In addition, brown trout had earned a reputation as voracious predators that eliminated native fish. Many states stopped propagating and stocking brown trout, but by then the alien species was widely established.

The selective feeding habits of brown trout, their wariness, and the difficulties they present to anglers gave birth to a new genre of American angling literature. The consistent taking of brown trout by fly-fishing called for refined techniques and new patterns of artificial flies. The challenge that brown trout posed to anglers became the basis for much of the literary lore and many of the legendary authors associated with American trout fishing.

DESCRIPTION   Brown trout have both red and black spots on the body, as opposed to rainbow and cutthroat trout species, which have only black spots. However, at some stage of their lives some brown trout—such as silvery specimens from marine waters or large lakes—may lack red spots. The brown trout is the only species of trout with a red or orange border or red or orange spots on

the adipose fin, but some individuals may lack red on the adipose fin during their life. Spotting in brown trout can range from a profusion of irregularly shaped spots all over the body, like the coastal cutthroat trout, to large, rounded spots that are sparsely distributed, like some inland subspecies of cutthroat trout. Brown trout can be most readily distinguished from rainbow and cutthroat trout by the absence of spots or only a few blotches on the caudal fin.

Coloration in brown trout extends over such a broad spectrum that it is difficult to describe a typical appearance. The common brownish yellow background color of the body of the fish is the basis for its common name, but coloration varies among individuals from pale, silvery gray tinted with shades of greenish blue, to deep golden yellow, dark red, or orange that suffuses the lower half of the body. Because of the mixed and diverse ancestry of brown trout introduced into North America, nearly the complete spectrum of spotting and coloration in brown trout worldwide can be found among American brown trout populations.

In European rivers where both Atlantic salmon and sea-run brown trout occur, anglers distinguish the two species by the

Brown Trout
SPAWNING MALE

10–30"

depth of the caudal peduncle, the narrowest part of the body behind the adipose fin. Brown trout have a thicker peduncle, similar to rainbow and cutthroat trout, as opposed to that of the Atlantic salmon, which is narrower and makes for a more streamlined appearance. Some anglers call the caudal peduncle area the "wrist," especially on Atlantic salmon.

Characteristics such as the number of scales, gill rakers, and pyloric caeca broadly overlap among brown trout, Atlantic salmon, and rainbow trout. However, despite morphological similarities, brown trout, Atlantic salmon, and rainbow trout exhibit large differences in genetic composition that reflect long periods of separation. Brown trout have 80 chromosomes, while Atlantic salmon have 56 to 58 and rainbow trout 58 to 64.

BIOLOGY   Like rainbow and cutthroat trout, brown trout have three basic life history forms: stream-resident, lake-adapted, and anadromous (sea-run). Some anadromous populations of brown trout are similar to steelhead in that they spend more than a year in the ocean before returning to spawn. Most anadromous populations are similar to coastal cutthroat trout in that they feed in bays and estuaries for only a few months before returning to fresh water.

In small streams with a limited food supply, brown trout may rarely live more than four years and rarely reach more than 10 inches (25 cm) in length. In rivers and lakes, adult fish may range in size from 14 inches to a typical maximum of 30 inches (35–76 cm) long and weigh up to 12 pounds (5.4 kg). In lakes, predatory brown trout may live 15 years or more. The life span of brown trout is

greatly extended if they become piscivorous; such fish can have rapid growth at a later stage of their normal life span. A study of brown trout inhabiting lakes of Scotland found that the average brown trout rarely grew longer than about 16 inches (41 cm) or lived more than six to eight years. A few large trout occurring in these lakes attain weights of 15 to 20 pounds (6.8–9.1 kg) and life spans of 15 to 16 years. They are called ferox trout and were once considered a separate species, *"Salmo ferox."* All lakes containing ferox trout also have populations of Arctic char. When a few trout, toward the end of their normal life span, move into deeper water and feed on the char, their growth rate dramatically increases and their life span is effectively doubled.

A similar phenomenon can be found in brown trout inhabiting North American waters. A stream where brown trout rarely

THE WILY BROWN TROUT

Generally the rank for anglers from easiest to hardest to catch is: cutthroat trout, brook trout, rainbow trout, brown trout. Why are brown trout the most difficult to catch? In rivers where both rainbow and brown trout occur in about equal numbers, typically three rainbow trout are caught to every brown trout. In Wyoming, along a section of the North Platte River known as the Miracle Mile—actually 6 miles long (10 km)— the brown trout population is entirely self-sustaining, while the rainbow trout population is supplemented by stocking. A study estimated that the Miracle Mile section contained 21,000 brown trout of "catchable" size, averaging 16 inches (41 cm) in length, and 5,800 rainbow trout averaging 17 inches (43 cm), for a ratio of brown to rainbow trout of 78:22. During a single year anglers caught 24,500 brown trout and 45,300 rainbow trout, for a catch ratio of rainbow to brown trout of 65:35. On average, during the year, each brown trout was caught 1.2 times and each rainbow trout was caught almost 8 times. Part of this more than sixfold difference is explained by the greater susceptibility to angler catch of hatchery rainbow trout compared to wild rainbow, but it is obvious that brown trout are much more resistant to deception by anglers. It is not likely that brown trout have greater intelligence; they have a typical simple trout brain that lacks a cerebrum, or "gray matter," for cognitive thinking. The brown trout's preference for cover and dim light might be part of the explanation, but whatever the reason, brown trout have a well-deserved reputation as the most wary of trout.

exceed 12 inches (30 cm) or five or six years of age may contain a deep pool inhabited by a single large brown trout. At about four or five years of age, such trout begin to prey on smaller fish, often small brook trout or rainbow trout, and grow rapidly for the next several years, attaining a weight of 10 to 15 pounds (4.5–6.8 kg) before succumbing to old age when they are 10 to 12 years old.

When brown trout and rainbow trout occur in the same river, the diet and growth rate of the brown trout broadly overlap that of the rainbow trout of similar size. Both feed mainly on invertebrates—mostly aquatic and terrestrial insects and crustaceans. The oldest and largest trout in rivers where brown and rainbow trout coexist tend to be brown trout that became predatory fish-eaters.

Because of the broad niche overlap between rainbow trout and the nonnative brown trout, it is difficult to delineate the habitat characteristics that favor one species or the other. Why do some rivers have solely or predominantly rainbow trout or brown trout, while in other rivers the two species coexist at about a 50:50 ratio? One possible explanation is that brown trout tend to prefer bank areas with abundant cover, while rainbow trout are more oriented to stream channels. Generally the two species coexist only in relatively large rivers that provide sufficient habitat complexity for each species to find its niche.

The eye of the brown trout is better adapted for vision in dim light than the eye of the rainbow, cutthroat, or brook trout, because the retina of the brown trout contains more rod cells. Rod cells allow an animal to see in dim light, while cone cells are

responsible for color vision and precise discrimination. Brown trout have enough cone cells to discriminate potential food items—as is frustratingly obvious to fly-fishers attempting to deceive a selectively feeding brown trout—but the rod-to-cone ratio in brown trout is greater than in other trout species.

Brown trout typically breed in the fall when water temperatures decline and the length of the days begins to shorten. Depending on the location, when water temperatures begin to lower from the 50s to the 45 °F (7 °C) range, brown trout spawn. The female constructs a redd in a shallow, gravelly area by swimming on her side and stirring up the bottom with her tail fin to remove larger stones. This activity may take place over several days and draws the attention of male suitors. Males compete to fertilize the eggs released by females and sometimes many males will swarm around a female at the redd awaiting the moment of spawning. The number of eggs depends on the size of the female and can range from a few hundred in a small female to many thousands in larger fish. Successfully fertilized by males, the eggs develop over winter in the gravel and hatch in the spring.

The diversity of parental forms of brown trout introduced into North America likely provided the genetic diversity that promoted the rapid and successful establishment of the species in so many American waters. The greatest success of the brown trout is in the range of the brook trout and the cutthroat trout. In Pacific Coast rivers—where native coastal cutthroat trout and resident rainbow trout occupy smaller streams, and steelhead

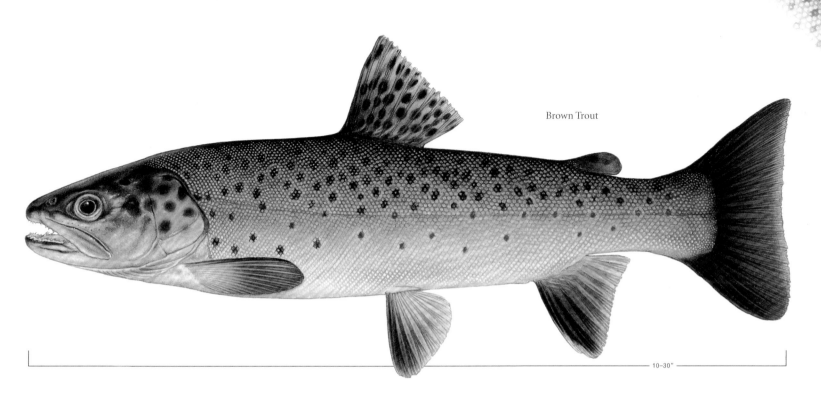

Brown Trout

10–30"

and Pacific salmon species occur in larger rivers—the available salmonid habitat is more saturated with native species than in waters where the cutthroat or brook trout are the only native trout species. The saturation of habitat by native species likely explains why brown trout abundance and distribution in rivers flowing to the North Pacific Ocean is sporadic. For example, in the Columbia River basin, brown trout are more common in areas where steelhead and Chinook salmon do not occur.

In North America, brown trout frequently feed in marine waters in the estuarine parts of rivers and in bays, but no steelhead-like anadromous population of brown trout, in which fish forage in the ocean for more than a year, has been documented. The exception is observed in the Avalon Peninsula of Newfoundland. Large brown trout ranging up to 25 to 30 pounds (11–14 kg) have been caught in bays of the peninsula, where they obviously have had a long period of feeding in marine waters.

The large brown trout of the Avalon Peninsula is the only North American population that consistently attains a large size after an extended period of foraging in marine waters. Its European ancestry is unknown. The first introduction of brown trout in Newfoundland came from Loch Leven, Scotland, in 1884, and several transfers of brown trout of mixed ancestry were made from hatcheries in the United States to Canada beginning in 1890. A shipment of brown trout eggs of unknown ancestry was made from Germany to Newfoundland in 1892 and may have contained eggs from a sea trout, a sea-going form of brown trout (*Meeresforelle* in German). It is doubtful, although possible, that Avalon Peninsula brown trout are the direct descendants of the 1884 shipment of trout from Loch Leven.

Brown trout in their native and introduced range are known for large size. The "official" world-record rod-and-reel, angler-caught brown trout of 40 pounds, 4 ounces (18.3 kg) was taken in the Little Red River, in Arkansas, in 1992; tailwater fisheries (fisheries below dams) in the Ozark region of the south-central United States are famed for large brown trout. The official world-record size is less than the 42-pound (19.1-kg) record for rainbow trout, but in their native range, there are recorded weights of non-rod-and-reel commercial catches of brown trout greater than 50 pounds (23 kg).

In alpine lakes of central Europe, where large predatory brown trout feed on Arctic char and whitefishes, catches of brown trout

The great morphological and life history variations found in brown trout have given rise to the naming of about 50 species, now all regarded as *Salmo trutta.* However, this classification is misleading in relation to the structure of the species—that is, how many distinct evolutionary lines have developed since the origin of all brown trout from a common ancestor. The range of genetic variation among brown trout is large, reflecting the species' broad distribution and indicating an ancient origin, probably several million years ago during the Pliocene era. The genetic variation, however, is not clearly partitioned by geographical regions, as is the case with the four major subspecies of cutthroat trout.

For modern taxonomy—which emphasizes relationships based on sequences of evolutionary branches in denoting species and subspecies—the taxon *S. trutta* presents problems. "*S. ishchan*" of Lake Sevan, in the Armenian Republic, and "*S. letnica*" of Lake Ohrid, in the former Yugoslavia and Albania, are valid or "good" morphological species by older taxonomic standards, because of their high degree of differentiation from all other forms of *S. trutta.* By modern evolutionary standards, however, they are not valid evolutionary or phylogenetic species because their evolutionary branching sequence most probably occurred after the origin of *S. trutta*—that is, they evolved within and not before the origin of *S. trutta.*

A more perplexing problem concerns the marble trout. This fish is native to large rivers tributary to the Adriatic Sea, from the Po River of northern Italy southward into the former Yugoslavia. The marble trout is completely distinct from all forms of brown trout in having only light-colored marbled marking on the body and no black or red spots. With this trait, it resembles species of char of the genus *Salvelinus.* The marble trout is also a valid biological species because it historically occurred together with brown trout without hybridization.

The marble trout evolved as a large predator; in rivers where it coexisted with brown trout, the marble trout attained the larger maximum size, reputedly about 50 pounds (22.7 kg). The marble trout was described as a separate species, *Salmo marmoratus,* and despite morphological and biological evidence making *marmoratus* a good species, genetic analysis shows that its evolutionary line evolved within *S. trutta,* not before the origin of *trutta.* Based on genetic data, *marmoratus* is virtually indistinguishable from some forms of *S. trutta.*

Some brown trout are more distantly related to other, geographically distant, brown trout than they are to *marmoratus.* Some contemporary European classifications treat the marble trout as a subspecies, "*S. trutta marmoratus.*" Such a classification is in agreement with modern evolutionary classification, but it is unsatisfactory because it ignores the fact that *marmoratus* and *trutta* coexisted over a broad area and both maintained their separate identities. The marble trout is an example of one evolutionary line within *S. trutta* evolving morphological and life history differences at a more rapid rate than other evolutionary lines.

Another classification problem concerns the brown trout of Lough Melvin, Ireland, where three distinct populations—a large predatory trout known as "*ferox,*" a moderate-size invertebrate feeder known as "*sonaghen,*" and a smaller trout specializing on benthic food, snails, and crustaceans, known as "*gillaroo*"—coexist and maintain their identity. They are valid biological species but not valid evolutionary species because they are all derived from branches within *S. trutta.* In the past, the large predatory ferox trout of Great Britain and Ireland were classified as "*S. ferox.*" (The large predatory trout on the European mainland were classified as "*S. lacustris.*")

Genetic studies have demonstrated that "*ferox*" and "*lacustris*" populations share no genetic distinctions that would differentiate them from other forms of brown trout. All have evolved in each lake independently. They share no common ancestor; no distinct evolutionary line gave rise to all large predatory brown trout found in European lakes. Thus "*ferox*" and "*lacustris*" cannot be evolutionary species.

It is common to find literature references to "*S. trutta trutta*" (sea trout), "*S. trutta fario*" (stream-resident trout), and "*S. trutta lacustris*" (lake trout). Such a classification reflects three life history types that have been evolved many times, independently, not three separate evolutionary lines.

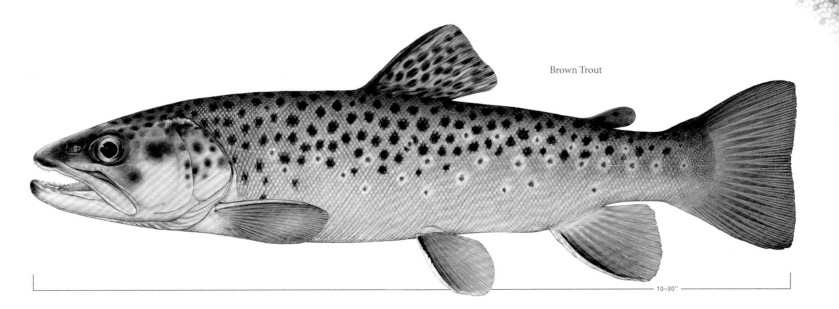

Brown Trout

10–30"

from 50 to 68 pounds (23–31 kg) were recorded in the early 1900s and into the 1930s. Pollution of these lakes resulted in the loss of oxygen in the deeper waters, eliminating or greatly reducing the char and whitefish populations, which are the food supply of large trout. Brown trout of these lakes no longer attain such a great size.

The Caspian Sea once had many populations of brown trout represented by numerous life history distinctions. The largest of the Caspian brown trout was the winter-run race in the Kura River. In the Russian literature, an 1897 report based on personal observation mentions a trout from the Kura River weighing more than 72 pounds (33 kg). Another reported weight given is of a 112-pound (51-kg) fish. The average size of Kura trout in the commercial catch of 1916 was 33 pounds (15 kg). The Kura River winter-run race of Caspian brown trout probably attained the maximum size of any

form of brown trout. This race is now likely extinct. The Kura River and most other tributaries to the Caspian Sea have been polluted, and dams now block most Caspian trout from their former spawning grounds.

DISTRIBUTION   In North America, there are now self-sustaining brown trout populations in 40 of the 48 contiguous states of the United States, and in southern Canada and Newfoundland, the northernmost distribution of brown trout in the continent.

As "naturalized citizens," brown trout are found in most cold-water habitat throughout the world: New Zealand, Australia, South America, and mountain streams of Africa in the Southern Hemisphere. Brown trout have been imported to Japan, but self-sustaining populations are rare.

In the northern part of its range, the natural distribution of the brown trout extends from Iceland, eastward to the Kola

and Kanin Peninsulas of Russia, in the Barents Sea basin. The species occurs throughout Europe southward to the Mediterranean Sea basin, including the Atlas Mountains of North Africa. Eastward, the natural distribution includes the headwaters of the Tigris and Euphrates Rivers in Turkey and two internal basins of Iran; the eastern limit is the Aral Sea basin (Amu Darya River drainage). In the headwaters of rivers draining from the Himalayas to the Indian Ocean, brown trout as nonnative populations occur in India, Bhutan, and Nepal, and even in Tibet, in the headwaters of the Brahmaputra River.

EVOLUTION AND CLASSIFICATION
The great range of variation in the appearance of brown trout resulted in about 50 species being described originally for what is now regarded as a single species. The name *Salmo trutta,* which appeared in the tenth edition of Linnaeus's *System of Nature* in 1758, was

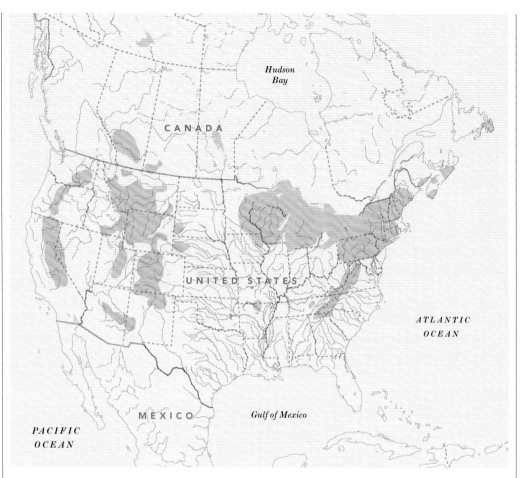

The brown trout is now established over much of North America. Most populations are self-sustaining—their abundance is not dependent on stocking.

intended for the brown trout of large rivers and likely included sea-run brown trout. Linnaeus described the brown trout of small streams (the European "brook trout") as "*Salmo fario,*" the sea-run brown trout (the "sea trout" of Europe) as "*Salmo eriox,*" and the lake form of brown trout as "*Salmo lacustris.*"

In 1883, when the shipment of brown trout eggs was received in North America by Fred Mather, a portion went to a Caledonia, New York, hatchery operated by Seth Green. Mather used the common name brown trout, but Green named the new import German trout. (Green and Mather were great rivals for recognition as America's leading fish culturist.) The early American literature compromised with the name German brown trout.

Eggs of brown trout native to Loch Leven, Scotland, were received and propagated at the U.S. Fish Commission's hatchery at Northville, Michigan, in 1885. At the time, Loch Leven trout were classified as "*Salmo levenensis.*" For the next several years, the U.S. Fish Commission kept the brood stocks of Loch Leven and German brown trout separate in their propagation and distribution program. The German brown trout was designated as the von Behr trout to distinguish it from Loch Leven trout. In practice, the diverse sources of *S. trutta* imported from Germany, England, and Scotland during the period from 1883 to about 1890 were inextricably mixed in American hatcheries.

In 1890, both von Behr and Loch Leven trout were shipped to Yellowstone National Park. Loch Leven trout (and native North American lake trout from Lake Michigan) were stocked in Lewis Lake. The upper Lewis River, a tributary to the Snake River above a large falls, had no fish in 1890. There are no further records of the stocking of brown trout in the upper Lewis River or its source in Lewis Lake and Shoshone Lake. Thus the most likely place in North America to find a pure population of Loch Leven trout is these two lakes in Yellowstone National Park.

CONSERVATION Nonnative brown trout have replaced brook trout and cutthroat trout in large parts of the range of these native species. From the viewpoint of the conservation of native North American trout species, the brown trout is a harmful alien. Brown trout were propagated throughout North America so successfully that many populations of native fish never had a chance—they were dominated quickly in many areas and their original numbers never recovered. Programs to restore native brook trout and cutthroat trout have eradicated brown trout and nonnative rainbow trout. These programs, however, have met with varying degrees of success. Stocked throughout North America for nearly 120 years, brown trout are here to stay.

Some popular sport fisheries are managed by agencies in order to recycle the brown trout that are caught to "conserve" them for other anglers to catch. These "catch-and-release" areas are designated for recreational angling, and some prohibit the killing of fish for any reason. These "no-kill" areas are created to allow increased use by anglers. Other areas allow fish to be taken above a certain size during a particular time of year, or year-round, depending on the fishery.

Most waters across North America are no longer stocked with brown trout. These once-stocked areas now hold abundant and self-sustaining populations that anglers refer to as "wild" brown trout. They are wild in the sense that they were not raised in hatcheries, but they are not native to the waters where they live. Many of these fisheries exist in locations, such as tailwaters below dams, where trout, either native or nonnative, never existed but now draw anglers in large numbers. ◂━

Char of the Genus *Salvelinus*

The members of this genus are by far the most active and handsome of the trout, and live in the coldest, cleanest, and most secluded waters. No higher praise can be given to a Salmonid than to say, it is a charr.

—JORDAN AND EVERMANN
The Fishes of North and Middle America, VOL. 1, 1896

North America is home to

five species in the genus *Salvelinus:* the brook trout, the lake trout, the bull trout, the Arctic char, and the Dolly Varden. All members of this genus are also known as char. Three are exclusively native to North America: the brook trout, the lake trout, and the bull trout. Lake trout and especially brook trout have been introduced into European and South American countries and New Zealand, but they have never become as widely established as transplanted rainbow trout and brown trout.

Hybrid populations of char occur in some North American habitats, such as the splake (brook trout × lake trout), the brook trout × bull trout hybrid, and the tiger trout, a cross between brook trout and nonnative brown trout. The tiger trout is created in hatcheries and is an exceedingly rare cross in reproducing populations of brook trout and brown trout in natural habitats.

Members of the species of the genus *Salvelinus* are some of the most beautiful fishes of the family Salmonidae, especially in their spawning colors, and they are also the most controversial in their classification and in their common names. As the scientist Dr. Albert Günther wrote in 1866, "There is no other group of fishes which offer so many difficulties to the ichthyologist with regard to the distinction of species as well as to certain points in their life history as this genus."

DESCRIPTION All members of the genus *Salvelinus* are distinguished from all species in the genera *Salmo* and *Oncorhynchus* by a lack of black spots on the body. *Salvelinus* trout have red, pinkish, orange, or light cream-colored spots that are lighter than the body's background hues. Also, *Salvelinus* species have teeth only on the anterior part of the vomer (the narrow bone in the roof of the mouth), whereas *Salmo* and *Oncorhynchus* have teeth on both the head and shaft of the vomer.

Salvelinus species have the smallest scales of any salmonid fish—so small that scales occur in 220 to 300 rows along the side of the body. Species of *Salmo* and *Oncorhynchus* typically have about 120 to 180 such scale rows. Except for char, only some inland subspecies of cutthroat trout have 200 or more scale rows along the body. The scales of char are so tiny that to the casual observer they appear to be fish without scales.

BIOLOGY The biological trait that distinguishes species of the genus *Salvelinus* from species of *Salmo* and *Oncorhynchus,* and from just about all freshwater fishes, is their degree of adaptation to and their preference for cold water. In general, the optimum range for char is about 50 to 57 °F (10–14 °C), as compared with about 57 to 65 °F (14–18 °C) for trout and salmon. Brook trout are the most tolerant of warm temperatures; in this regard, they are more comparable to rainbow trout and brown trout than to other char.

Arctic char and lake trout have the most extreme adaptations for cold water. Actively feeding Arctic char have been recorded in marine waters at temperatures below the freezing point of fresh water (32 °F/0 °C). Perhaps they have an antifreeze-like substance in their blood, as is found in some Arctic-dwelling marine fishes that exist at below-freezing temperatures.

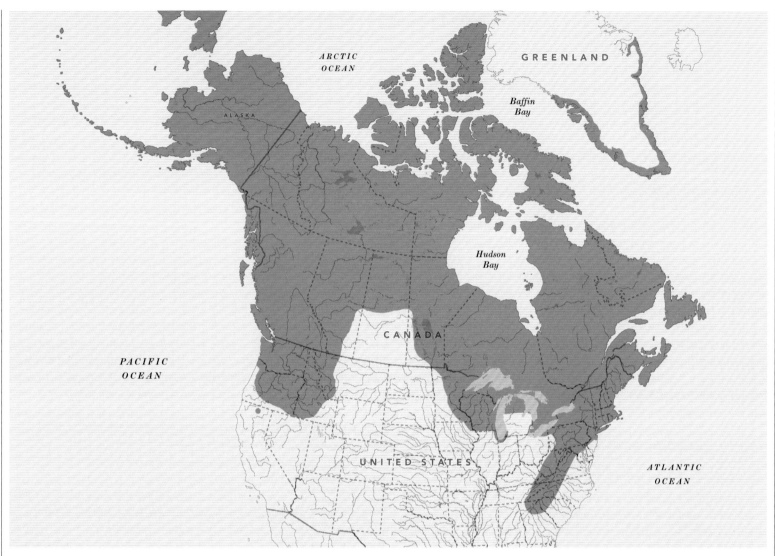

ARCTIC OCEAN

GREENLAND

Baffin Bay

ALASKA

Hudson Bay

PACIFIC OCEAN

CANADA

UNITED STATES

ATLANTIC OCEAN

Char of the genus Salvelinus *are the most broadly distributed native salmonid in North America.*

Arctic char and, particularly, lake trout are almost obligatorily lacustrine, or lake-adapted. Many populations of Arctic char live their entire lives in lakes, as do most populations of lake trout. Some populations of anadromous Arctic char feed in marine waters of the Arctic for about 30 to 60 days and return to fresh water to live the rest of the year in lakes or, in some instances, in deep, slow sections of rivers that provide a lake-like environment.

The most extreme form of deep-water lacustrine specialization is found in a distinctive form of lake trout, the siscowet, in the depths of Lake Superior. The siscowet typically occurs from below 300 feet (100 m) to the greatest depths of Lake Superior at 1,333 feet (406 m), where the external pressure is 40 atmospheres. One atmosphere of pressure equals 14.7 pounds per square inch; a tire with 30 pounds per square inch of pressure would be at slightly more than two atmospheres. Thus the air bladder of siscowet living at the great depths in Lake Superior would be inflated to about 20 times the pressure of a typical automobile tire.

The main difference between "normal"

lake trout and the siscowet of Lake Superior is that siscowet have a much higher fat content. Siscowet are an "oily" fish; about 40 percent or more of their total weight consists of fat.

The brook trout, Dolly Varden, and bull trout are more generalists in their range of habitats. These three species have lake (lacustrine), stream (fluvial), and sea-run (anadromous) populations. Sea-run populations of these three species, as well as of Arctic char, spend a relatively brief period of the year—some 40 to 90 days in summer—feeding in marine waters.

Char feed on a broad range of organisms. The lake trout has the most specialized diet. After reaching a length of about 18 inches (46 cm), almost all of a lake trout's diet consists of forage fishes, if they are available. Without fish in its diet, the lake trout grows slowly, and its life span is shortened. Bull trout and large Arctic char also eat fish. The diets of brook trout and Dolly Varden are typically dominated by invertebrates, but they will prey on other fish if the opportunity arises.

Char are fall spawners, generally spawning during periods of declining temperatures and shortening days. Some populations may spawn over a broad period of time. For example, in populations of Arctic char and lake trout spawning deep in lakes under a relatively uniform annual temperature regime, spawning may occur from June through February.

With very few exceptions, lake trout spawn on lake bottoms. The other *Salvelinus* species can spawn in streams or in lakes, in sites with clean gravel and with water that

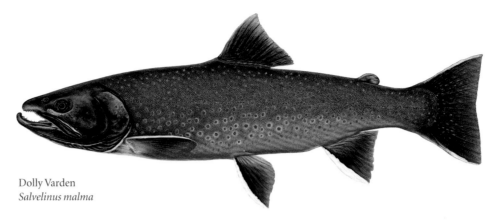

Dolly Varden
Salvelinus malma

Whether one spells it "charr" or "char," it is no wonder the name for these brilliantly colored fishes derives from the word "blood" in Celtic. The vivid spawning hues of many species in the genus Salvelinus *make them some of the most beautiful of all fishes.*

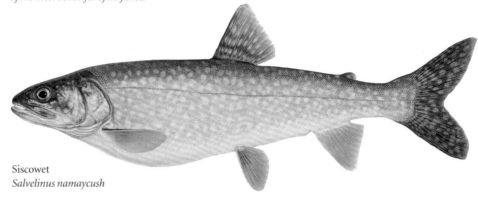

Siscowet
Salvelinus namaycush

The siscowet occurs only in the deep, cold waters of Lake Superior at depths down to 1,333 feet (406 m).

Arctic Char
Salvelinus alpinus

The Arctic char is the northernmost species of any freshwater fish.

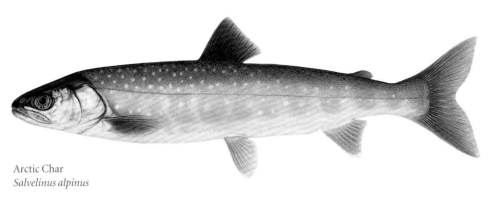

Arctic Char
Salvelinus alpinus

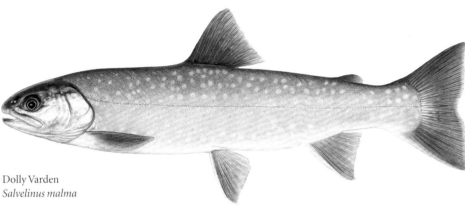

Dolly Varden
Salvelinus malma

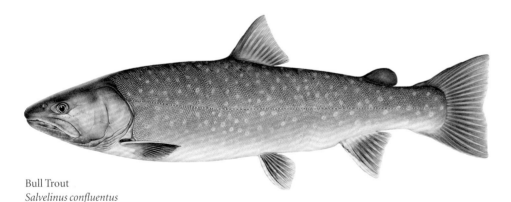

Bull Trout
Salvelinus confluentus

These three species were once commonly confused with one another by anglers and naturalists. Each is now classified as its own distinct species.

has a high oxygen content. In areas where species' ranges overlap—as is the case with brook trout, lake trout, and Arctic char in northeastern North America, and with bull trout and Dolly Varden on the western coast of Canada—hybridization among species is minimized by their segregating to different habitats and/or spawning at different times.

Natural hybridization has been recorded between lake trout and Arctic char and between Arctic char and brook trout in Labrador, and between bull trout and Dolly Varden in the Skagit River of British Columbia.

Brook trout have been widely introduced in the western United States, and hybridization between brook trout and bull trout is common. Although brook trout and lake trout are not known to hybridize in nature, hybrids between these species, known as splake, are produced in hatcheries and stocked for sportfishing.

DISTRIBUTION Worldwide, char of the genus *Salvelinus* occur in the Holarctic: Eurasia and North America, including Iceland and Greenland.

The Arctic char is the northernmost species of any fish found in fresh water. This char occurs in a lake on Ellesmere Island in the high Arctic at 82° N latitude. The bull trout, a threatened species, was once found in the McCloud River, in California, the southernmost historical limit of the genus in Pacific Coast drainages. Extirpated in the McCloud, the bull trout now has its southern limit in the Upper Klamath Lake basin, in Oregon. The Dolly Varden occurs from the Mackenzie River, in Canada, westward

Brook Trout
Salvelinus fontinalis

Hatchery brook trout have been stocked into many rivers and lakes throughout western North America as a sport fish. They pose a serious threat to many native trout including their own cousin, the western bull trout.

through Alaska and southward to Puget Sound, in Washington.

On the East Coast, the brook trout occurs in the southern Appalachian Mountains to northern Georgia and western South Carolina, the southernmost natural distribution of the genus in the world.

Lake trout are restricted to cold, deep lakes from northeastern North America to the Great Lakes, and northward and westward to the upper Yukon River basin and Brooks Range, in Alaska. Their distribution is almost completely encompassed by the maximum extent of the most recent glaciation.

EVOLUTION AND CLASSIFICATION

Jordan and Evermann, in their landmark work *Fishes of North and Middle America* (1896–98), spelled the common name as "charr." The word, spelled "charre" in the sixteenth century, is of Celtic origin and denotes a blood red color. "Charr" would be the favored spelling by precedent and for its lack of ambiguity—charr are red, not charcoal black—but the American

Fisheries Society (AFS) committee on names of fishes has chosen "char," which this guide uses. Both "char" and "charr" can be considered correct.

The first European settlers in North America knew trout from their experience with the European brown trout, but they were not familiar with char, secretive fishes occurring in deep waters of northern European lakes (from the Alps northwest to the Arctic, the British Isles, and Iceland; see the Arctic char account for more discussion). Because char look so much like trout the new Americans called *Salvelinus* species "trout," as in brook trout and lake trout. The North American tradition of using the common name "trout" for species of *Salvelinus* has been perpetuated and standardized in the AFS *Common and Scientific Names of Fishes, Fifth Edition.* That volume lists the species of the genus *Salvelinus* that occur in North America as brook trout, lake trout, bull trout, Dolly Varden, and Arctic char. As with the variant spellings of "char," both "trout" and "char" can be considered

acceptable common names for species of *Salvelinus*. In recent years, the terms "brook char" and "lake char" have become more common in the scientific literature.

Whether called trout or char, the species of the genus *Salvelinus* can be clustered into three main evolutionary lines within the genus. Two of these lines lead to single species that are native only to North America—the lake trout and the brook trout, the best-known species of North American char.

Trying to unravel the cluster of species associated with the third evolutionary line, which includes Arctic char, Dolly Varden, and bull trout, is enormously difficult and complex. Only an educated guess can be made as to how many phylogenetically valid —or, at least, reasonable—species are included among the char currently lumped as Arctic char in Europe, Asia, and North America.

For many years, the Arctic char, the Dolly Varden, and the bull trout were commonly confused with one another based on their morphological similarities. Although the bull trout was described as a new species in 1858, it was not recognized as a separate species until 1978. And even the fish-eating behavior of the Arctic char and the bull trout has been mistakenly associated with the Dolly Varden. One consequence of this mistaken association was that, in the 1920s and 1930s, a bounty ranging from two to five cents was paid in Alaska for each Dolly Varden killed, after tails were turned in for payment. This ill-founded predator-control program was intended to increase the survival of juvenile salmon, based on the naive belief that for each Dolly Varden killed, a thousand young salmon would be saved. Ironically, close examination of the tails that had been turned in for the bounty payment determined that less than half were from Dolly Varden. Most of the tails were from rainbow trout and coho salmon. Dolly Varden will indeed eat as many salmon fry as they can, but the Dolly Varden is far less piscivorous than bull trout or Arctic char, feeding primarily on aquatic invertebrates.

The Sunapee trout, Quebec red trout, and blueback trout are very similar and often classified as a subspecies (*S. alpinus oquassa*) of the Arctic char. But a footnote to the entry for Arctic char in the AFS list states: "Sunapee trout, blueback trout, and Quebec red trout are regarded by some authors as species distinct from the Arctic char." This note hints at the long-standing controversies surrounding the classification of *Salvelinus* species and clarifies that some forms or subspecies of Arctic char in the AFS list are called "trout." The disagreements concern interpretation of the evidence of relationships, as well as differing philosophies about classification systems. For more discussion, see the accounts on the Arctic char, the Dolly Varden, and the bull trout.

CONSERVATION   In the United States, the bull trout is protected as a threatened species under the Endangered Species Act. Bull trout have been extirpated in the McCloud River, in California, their historical southernmost distribution. Their distribution and abundance in the Columbia River and Puget Sound basins have been greatly reduced.

Lake trout abundance was greatly reduced in the Great Lakes after the sea lamprey gained access to the upper lakes. In Lake Michigan, where the lake trout had been most abundant and supported a large commercial fishery, it became extirpated. Lamprey control and restocking have restored lake trout to the Great Lakes, but at a lower level of abundance.

Populations of Arctic char are particularly sensitive to extirpation. The remaining population of Sunapee trout in Maine is now intensively managed and monitored, and artificial spawning beds have been built to help preserve it. A few natural populations of blueback trout remain in Maine, and several introductions have been made to ensure their continued existence.

A peculiar form of brook trout, called the "silver trout," became extinct in the early twentieth century. And while the range of the southern Appalachian brook trout has been greatly reduced by nonnative trout, protection programs have improved the prospects of southern Appalachian brook trout.

The widespread stocking of brook trout and lake trout in the western United States has had serious impacts on native trout. Brook trout have replaced native subspecies of cutthroat trout over large areas of the West and have commonly hybridized with and replaced bull trout in the Columbia River basin. Lake trout eliminated the native Lahontan cutthroat trout from Lake Tahoe and greatly reduced the abundance of both native cutthroat trout and bull trout in lakes of the Columbia River basin.

Currently a large-scale control program is underway in Yellowstone Lake, in northwestern Wyoming, to remove illegally stocked lake trout. Many thousands of lake trout have been netted from their spawning grounds during the past few years. Yellowstone Lake holds the greatest concentration of cutthroat trout in the world. Without the intensive lake trout removal program, the cutthroat trout would be lost or reduced to a small remnant population as a result of lake trout predation.

Brook Trout
Salvelinus fontinalis

Brook Trout
Salvelinus fontinalis

Brook Trout
FEMALE

5–12"

The brook trout is the most "trout-like" of all the species of char. Its life history, ecology, and habitat are more similar to rainbow trout and brown trout than to any species of *Salvelinus*. Although its water temperature preference is lower than that of brown trout and rainbow trout, the brook trout is the most warm-adapted, thermally tolerant and generalist (least specialized) species of char.

DESCRIPTION Brook trout differ from all other species of *Salvelinus* (also species of *Oncorhynchus* and *Salmo*) by wavy, pale yellow markings called vermiculations on the dorsal surface and on the dorsal fin. Small red spots, surrounded by light blue halos, are scattered among larger light yellow spots. The ventral region in sexually mature fish,

especially males during spawning, can range from yellow-orange to intense crimson. Lower fins (pectoral, pelvic, and anal fins) display various shades and intensities of red with black and white borders. Older, larger males typically develop hooked jaws (kype). Brook trout living in lakes or spending time in marine waters are typically more silvery in color.

Adult length in dense, slow-growing populations is attained at 5 to 7 inches (13–18 cm). The maximum, world-record weight is 14 pounds, 8 ounces (6.6 kg).

BIOLOGY Brook trout spawn in the fall, typically in October or November. Most spawning occurs in streams, similar to rainbow and brown trout. In lakes, brook trout may spawn on lake bottoms,

BROOK TROUT

SCIENTIFIC NAME
Salvelinus fontinalis

OTHER COMMON NAMES
Eastern brook trout, brook char, speckled trout, square tail

HABITAT
Clear, cool streams and rivers; cold ponds and lakes; intertidal areas

LENGTH AND WEIGHT
Typically 5–7" (13–18 cm) and 1.5–3 oz (43–85 g) in small streams; 12" (30 cm) and 8 oz (227 g) and larger in rivers and lakes; extreme maximum 28" (70 cm) and 14½ lb (6.6 kg)

LIFE SPAN
2–3 years in small streams; 9–10 years in larger rivers and lakes; maximum known 24 years

DIET
Aquatic and terrestrial invertebrates, smaller fishes, and amphibians

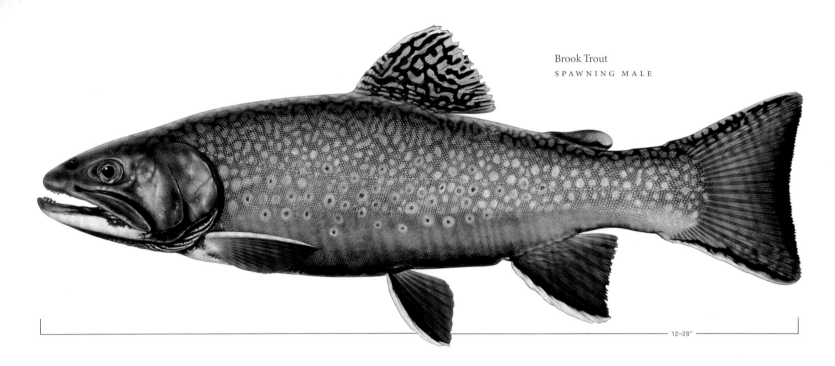

Brook Trout
SPAWNING MALE

12–28"

successfully reproducing where other species of trout cannot. In a typical small-stream population, brook trout will sexually mature and spawn at a young age of two years. In dense, small-stream populations, few live beyond three years. However, in large rivers and lakes of northern Canada, brook trout may reach nine or ten years of age and 9 to 10 pounds (4–4.5 kg) in size. There are both hereditary and environmental factors that influence age at maturity and maximum life span. The greatest age recorded in brook trout concerns fish of a hatchery strain that generally would not live more than three years. When these fish were stocked in a very cold, high-elevation lake in the Sierra Nevada of California, where the food supply was sparse, their life was greatly prolonged. The extreme conditions in the lake reduced their

metabolic rates to very low levels and greatly extended their life span. The last surviving brook trout recorded from this lake was 24 years old; about a six- or sevenfold increase over its normal maximum life span.

Brook trout, as with brown and rainbow trout, feed opportunistically. Under similar conditions brook trout feed on the same organisms (mainly aquatic insect larvae) as brown and rainbow trout. When two or more of these species occur together in a stream, the brook trout tend to feed more on bottom-dwelling organisms while the rainbow and brown trout feed more on organisms drifting in the water column and on the surface.

The brook trout shares parts of its native range with two other char species, the lake trout and the Arctic char. Brook trout rarely

hybridize with Arctic char. Likewise, no known natural hybridization occurs between brook trout and lake trout, although hybrids of brook trout and lake trout, called splake, are readily produced in hatcheries. Outside its native range, in the Columbia River basin, brook trout hybridize with native bull trout. Hybrids between brook trout and brown trout are called tiger trout, named for their striped pattern.

DISTRIBUTION   The native range of the brook trout covers much of northeastern North America. Northward, brook trout are native to the Atlantic drainages of Newfoundland, Labrador, and Quebec, and to tributaries of James Bay and Ungava Bay. Distribution in the Hudson Bay drainage on the eastern side extends southward

Brook Trout

12–28"

from the Ungava Peninsula, Quebec. On the western side of Hudson Bay, brook trout occur northward to the Seal River of northeastern Manitoba.

Southward, brook trout are native to the Great Lakes basin and in headwater tributaries of the Mississippi River of Minnesota, Wisconsin, and northeastern Iowa. In the northeastern United States brook trout are native to all Atlantic coastal drainages southward to Virginia and in parts of the Ohio River system of the Mississippi basin. In the southern Appalachian Mountains brook trout are native to higher-elevation streams draining both to the Atlantic Ocean and to the Mississippi (headwaters of the Tennessee River drainage). The southernmost natural distribution of brook trout (and of any species of the genus *Salvelinus*) is the

headwaters of the Chattahoochee River, in northern Georgia.

There are some mysteries surrounding the natural distribution of brook trout, especially in the Great Lakes basin. Brook trout are native only to the uppermost part of Michigan's Lower Peninsula (Jordan River, northward). But in other Michigan tributaries to both Lake Michigan and Lake Huron, brook trout did not naturally occur below this northern boundary. This area includes some of Michigan's most famous trout streams— the Manistee, Muskegon, and Au Sable Rivers—where all species of trout are introduced, not native. The Arctic grayling, the only salmonid species native to the rivers of Michigan's Lower Peninsula, became extinct soon after brook trout, brown trout, and rainbow trout were introduced.

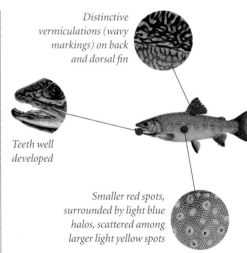

Distinctive vermiculations (wavy markings) on back and dorsal fin

Teeth well developed

Smaller red spots, surrounded by light blue halos, scattered among larger light yellow spots

Given several thousands of years to move along the shorelines of Lake Michigan and Lake Huron, why didn't brook trout naturally extend their range southward into drainages of the Lower Peninsula? Similarly, brook

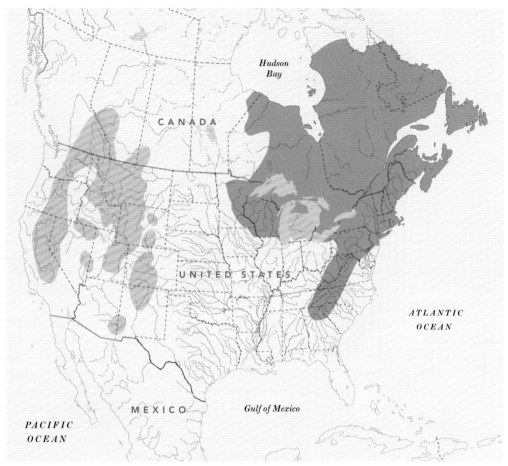

The native range (red) of the brook trout includes much of northeastern North America and extends south as far as northern Georgia and west as far as the Mississippi headwaters. The introduced range of the brook trout (yellow) includes a variety of streams in the Great Plains and Rocky Mountains, where its presence is a threat to native trout, such as the bull trout.

trout did not occur in Lake Erie drainages of Ohio except for the Chagrin River near the eastern border of the state, even though Ohio has several spring-fed streams with excellent habitat for trout. Brook trout flourished in these streams after they were stocked, but why did they never make it on their own? It is possible that these populations of ancestral brook trout were "homebodies" and found no need to populate other areas.

Brook trout have been widely introduced outside their native range in North America and in many foreign countries primarily for sportfishing.

EVOLUTION AND CLASSIFICATION

Compared to other species of char, there is little controversy associated with the classification of brook trout and lake trout. Some distinctive life history types occur that were regarded as separate species in the nineteenth century. Along the Atlantic Coast from Cape Cod northward and around Hudson Bay, some brook trout migrate into bays and estuaries to feed. Such fish are known as "salters" or "sea trout." In salt water, brook trout take on a silvery appearance and look quite different from a brook trout in fresh water. This pronounced difference in coloration between brook trout in fresh water and in salt water led to an erroneous classification recognizing a separate species for the "sea trout" or "salter."

In Lakes Nipigon and Superior brook trout of some populations migrate along the lake shores to feed. Such brook trout are known as "coasters." Coaster brook trout are noted for their size—the world-record brook trout caught by an angler was a "coaster" weighing 14 pounds, 8 ounces (6.6 kg).

In the mid-nineteenth century a peculiar char was discovered in Dublin Pond, New Hampshire. Called the "silver trout" and described as a new species, *"Salvelinus agassizi,"* it was thought to be derived from Arctic char rather than brook trout. Later studies left no doubt that the "silver trout" of Dublin Pond was a highly specialized form of brook trout, although it lacked the diagnostic vermiculations (wavy markings) on its dorsal surface. Unfortunately, the "silver trout" of Dublin Pond disappeared before more was learned about it.

A similarly peculiar silvery char without vermiculated markings was discovered in White Pine Lake and Whirligig Lake in northeastern Ontario, Canada. This char was called the "aurora trout" and described as a new species "*S. timagamiensis.*" The "aurora

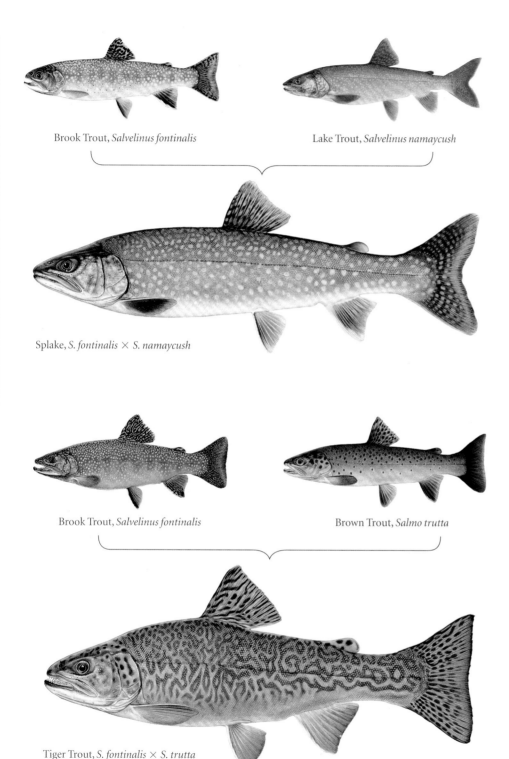

Brook Trout, *Salvelinus fontinalis*

Lake Trout, *Salvelinus namaycush*

Splake, *S. fontinalis* × *S. namaycush*

Brook Trout, *Salvelinus fontinalis*

Brown Trout, *Salmo trutta*

Tiger Trout, *S. fontinalis* × *S. trutta*

Hatcheries produce hybrids of char for stocking purposes. One such cross is the brook trout and the lake trout, which are called splake. These fish are fertile and may reproduce in nature.

trout" was almost lost in its native lakes due to acidification of the waters, but was saved from extinction by artificial propagation and stocking in protected areas. Modern genetic analysis leaves no doubt that the "aurora trout" is, in reality, a brook trout, albeit a highly peculiar brook trout that lacks the characteristic markings of *S. fontinalis*.

The most genetically divergent group within *S. fontinalis* is the southern Appalachian brook trout that is native to parts of Virginia, Tennessee, North Carolina, South Carolina, and Georgia. The southern Appalachian brook trout is similar to other brook trout in appearance, but genetic markers clearly differentiate southern Appalachian brook trout from all other brook trout.

CONSERVATION In the United States, the brook trout has been largely replaced in its native range by nonnative brown and rainbow trout. This is particularly true for the southern Appalachian form and has led to several restoration projects to remove nonnative trout and restore native brook trout.

North American hatcheries create the rather ferocious-looking tiger trout by crossing brook trout with the nonnative brown trout. This hybrid is a rare occurrence in nature where the two species cohabitate. Tiger trout are infertile, so there are no successive generations of tiger trout or backcrosses to either of the parent species.

While brook trout have greatly declined in distribution and abundance in their native range in the United States, they have vastly increased their distribution and abundance as a nonnative species in the western United States, where they pose a threat to rare forms of cutthroat trout and to bull trout.

In the Rocky Mountain region, brook trout are the most common species in small mountain streams where they have replaced various subspecies of cutthroat trout. Restoration projects for preserving rare forms of cutthroat trout involve chemical treatment of streams to eradicate nonnative brook trout.

In the Columbia River basin, nonnative brook trout are a serious threat to bull trout, a species now protected under the Endangered Species Act. The bull trout is the larger species and can behaviorally dominate smaller brook trout. Hybridization often occurs when larger bull trout males drive off smaller brook trout males to fertilize the eggs of brook trout females.

Lake Trout
Salvelinus namaycush

Lake Trout
Salvelinus namaycush

Lake Trout

16–40"

The lake trout has an almost fanatical following among anglers across North America. Known to attain large sizes, these fish-eaters will greedily strike lures and bait and, especially in colder months of the year in shallow water, will fight hard when hooked. They are by far the largest species of char and the third-largest species of the family Salmonidae—a 102-pound (46.3-kg) lake trout was caught in 1961. Individuals of this species have lived 62 years, longer than any other salmonid.

Given its widespread distribution and its popularity as a sport fish, the lake trout has accumulated a variety of common names, including the gray trout, the mackinaw, and the lake char; in New England it is called the togue, and in Quebec the Touladi, after Lake Touladi.

A voracious predator on fishes in lakes, the lake trout is one of the most specialized species of the subfamily Salmoninae. The species represents an ancient evolutionary line that has been restricted to fresh water for so long that it has lost the ability to live in the sea and cannot survive more than about one-third the salinity of the ocean. Lake trout are limited to salinities of less than 10 to 12 percent or parts per thousand of salts. This lack of salinity tolerance—the lake trout cannot travel through seawater—has restricted its distribution to North America.

Lake trout in search of food can descend to great depths. They have been recorded at more than 1,400 feet (430 m) down, where their air bladders, to be in equilibrium with external pressure, would be pressurized to more than 40 times atmospheric pressure at sea level.

LAKE TROUT

SCIENTIFIC NAME
Salvelinus namaycush

OTHER COMMON NAMES
Laker, gray trout, mackinaw, lake char, togue, Touladi

HABITAT
Cold lakes and ponds; some populations in deep, slow-moving rivers; rarely in brackish water

LENGTH AND WEIGHT
Typically 16–24" (41–61 cm) and 2–5 lb (1–2.3 kg); typical maximum 40" (1.2 m) and 25 lb (11.3 kg)

LIFE SPAN
20–25 years; maximum known 62 years

DIET
Aquatic and terrestrial invertebrates, become piscivorous at 14–18" (36–46 cm)

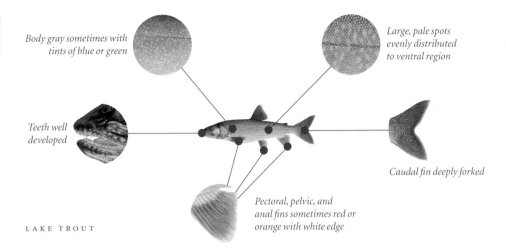

Body gray sometimes with tints of blue or green

Large, pale spots evenly distributed to ventral region

Teeth well developed

Caudal fin deeply forked

Pectoral, pelvic, and anal fins sometimes red or orange with white edge

LAKE TROUT

DESCRIPTION   The lake trout is not easily confused with any other species, but a hatchery-created hybrid with brook trout, called splake, can be confused with brook trout.

Lake trout look like the lake-adapted predators that they are. Highly piscivorous, they have a large head and large jaws with well-developed teeth for taking prey fish that are up to one-half their own body length. They have a deeply forked tail, unlike brook trout, which have a straight-edged tail and are often called "square tails."

The lake trout is the least colorful char. The body's background color is typically gray and is sometimes infused with bluish or greenish colors. Large, pale spots cover the whole body down to the ventral region; there are no red spots—only white or pale yellowish ones. The pectoral, pelvic, and anal fins can develop red or orange tints, and they have a white anterior border (brook trout have black and white borders on the lower fins). Lake trout never develop bright red colors on the body's ventral region, as is common in brook trout and other char species.

Despite their reputation for attaining great size, most lake trout in most populations are slow-growing and rarely weigh more than 10 pounds (4.5 kg) even at age 20 or older. However, some exceptional individuals can grow very large; there are many records of lake trout weighing more than 60 pounds (27 kg). The largest known lake trout, which weighed 102 pounds (46.3 kg), was taken by a commercial fisherman from Lake Athabasca, in Saskatchewan, in 1961. This was truly an exceptional lake trout: Estimated to be between 20 and 25 years old, it was a male whose testes had failed to develop. With no energy diverted to sexual development, all of the energy the trout derived from its food— except that spent as the metabolic energy required for daily activity—went into body growth. This 102-pound monster was 49½ inches (126 cm) long. A "normal" lake trout at that length would weigh about 50 pounds (22.7 kg).

The "official" world-record rod-and-reel, angler-caught lake trout—weighing 72 pounds (32.7 kg) and caught in 1995 in Great Bear Lake, in the Northwest Territo-ries, Canada—was an exception to the average growth rate of lake trout in Great Bear Lake. Although lake trout can reach old ages (the maximum recorded in Great Bear Lake is 53 years), they typically exhibit a slow growth rate. It takes 20 years for the "average" Great Bear Lake individual to reach 25 inches (63 cm) and a weight of about 6 pounds (2.7 kg).

Compared to other species of char, lake trout have many more pyloric caeca, from about 90 to 200. Brook trout have 25 to 50 pyloric caeca. The hybrid splake is intermediate between the parent species in numbers of caeca (typically 60–85).

Lake trout have well-developed basi-branchial teeth, located on the floor of the pharynx between the gill arches. Brook trout lack these teeth except for the rare occurrence of vestigial teeth. Splake have basibranchial teeth that are not as fully developed as in lake trout.

BIOLOGY   As with all species of char, the lake trout spawns in the fall, typically during October and November; however, in deep water, where temperatures are relatively stable throughout the year, some populations spawn as early as August and as late as December. The tendency for spawning in lakes, charac-teristic of the genus *Salvelinus,* reaches its extreme specialization in lake trout. Nearly all lake trout spawn in lakes, though some populations reproduce in rivers.

The spawning of lake trout is unique among species of trout and salmon. Female lake trout do not construct a redd or nest. Instead they deposit their eggs on a rocky area on the lake bottom. During the

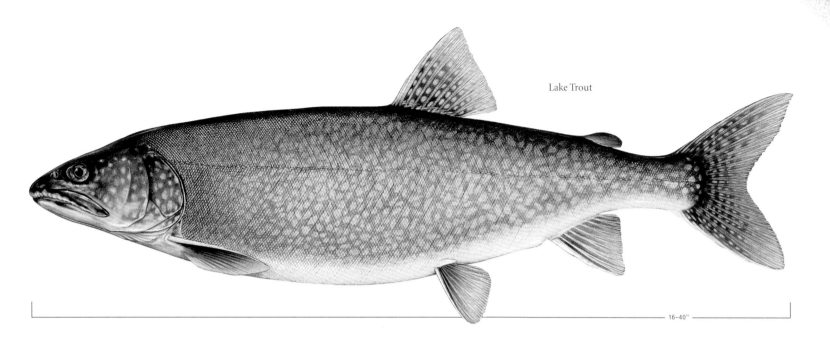

Lake Trout

16–40"

spawning season males and females congregate over such areas. In contrast to other trout, salmon, and char species, in which a female constructs a redd and aggressively protects it, spawning in lake trout is more of a group activity. When a female is ready to release her eggs, a male comes to her side and fertilizes the eggs as they drop into the rocky substrate. Survival to hatching depends on the fertilized eggs dropping into protected crevices among the rocks, as fishes and invertebrates will eat any exposed eggs. Lake trout fry hatch and emerge in the spring, four to six months after spawning, depending on the lake and the region.

Lake trout are introduced as a sport fish in many lakes. But if a lake lacks suitable rocky areas, spawning is not successful, and such lakes need continual stocking to maintain a lake trout fishery. Wildlife managers have created artificial spawning grounds by placing rock clusters in some lakes to enhance natural reproduction.

In the northern part of the species' range, in Hudson Bay and Arctic Canada, some lake trout populations live their entire lives in deep, slow-moving rivers with a lake-like environment. When feeding, these river populations often descend into brackish water with salinities up to about 8 parts per thousand. Also, toward the northern limits of the range, lake trout live in small ponds of no more than 1 surface acre (0.4 ha)— a sharp contrast to their image as a species that is restricted to large, deep lakes.

The fact that we associate lake trout with large, deep lakes has to do with the species' temperature and oxygen tolerances and its food supply. Like most char, lake trout are cold-adapted, preferring temperatures lower than those preferred by species of *Oncorhynchus* and *Salmo*: about 50°F (10°C).

And they avoid water with less than about 4 parts per million (ppm) of oxygen. In most of the temperate parts of the lake trout's range, suitable temperature and oxygen conditions can be best maintained throughout the year in large, deep lakes.

Oxygen concentrations of more than 4 ppm in deeper, colder water (the deepest water layer) are consistently maintained throughout the summer only in lakes of low productivity (those low in nutrients). High-productivity lakes create high levels of organic matter (from dead plants and animals) and high rates of decomposition (breakdown of organic matter by bacteria and fungi) that consume oxygen and deplete oxygen levels, and lake trout cannot exist under these conditions. During the summer, the upper layers of water in high-productivity lakes contain adequate oxygen concentrations but are too warm for lake trout.

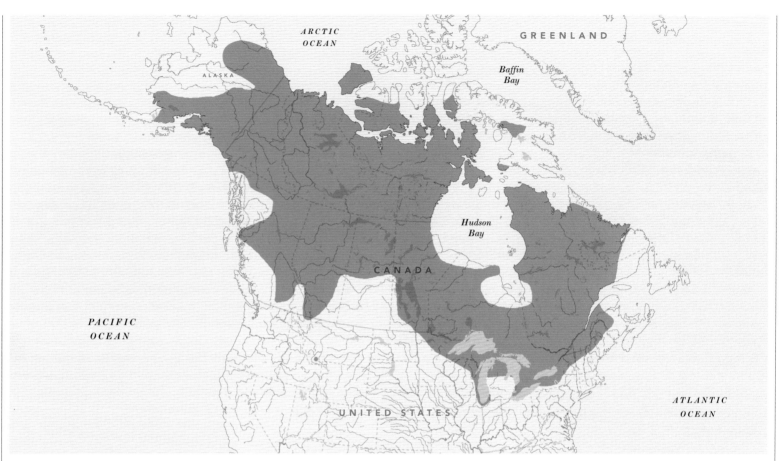

ARCTIC OCEAN · GREENLAND · ALASKA · Baffin Bay · Hudson Bay · CANADA · PACIFIC OCEAN · UNITED STATES · ATLANTIC OCEAN

Lake trout are the most widely distributed native salmonid in North America, inhabiting cold-water lakes and ponds from New York to Alaska. This map shows the native range of the lake trout; they are widely stocked as a sport fish outside of their native range.

Low-productivity lakes have low levels of fishes and invertebrates. Thus it takes a relatively large lake (on the order of more than 500 surface acres, or 200 ha) to provide sufficient food to sustain a relatively abundant population of lake trout.

Within their range of temperature and oxygen tolerances, lake trout follow their food. In Lake Tahoe, in California and Nevada (where the lake trout and its favored prey species, the opossum shrimp, are nonnative species), and in Great Bear Lake, Canada, lake trout feeding on shrimp have been recorded to depths of more than 1,400 feet (430 m). In early spring in southern parts of the range, when the surface-water temperature is around 50°F (10°C), lake trout feed on or near the surface. In northern parts of the range, in lakes where surface temperatures remain cold through the summer, lake trout may feed mainly in shallow water.

Anglers who catch lake trout near the surface find them to be worthy sport fish. However, when hauled up too rapidly from deeper, colder water into warmer surface water, a lake trout generally puts up a sluggish fight. Individuals caught in water about 100 feet (30 m) deep, where the air bladder becomes pressurized to 4 atmospheres, will suffer from an overinflated air bladder if hauled up too rapidly. Adjustment of air-bladder pressure is a slow process. It may take 15 to 20 minutes for a lake trout to gradually equalize an internal pressure of 4 atmospheres at 100 feet to 1 atmosphere at the surface.

During the first year of life, when young lake trout have grown to a length of about 4 or 5 inches (10–13 cm), they feed on zooplankton and small benthic invertebrates,

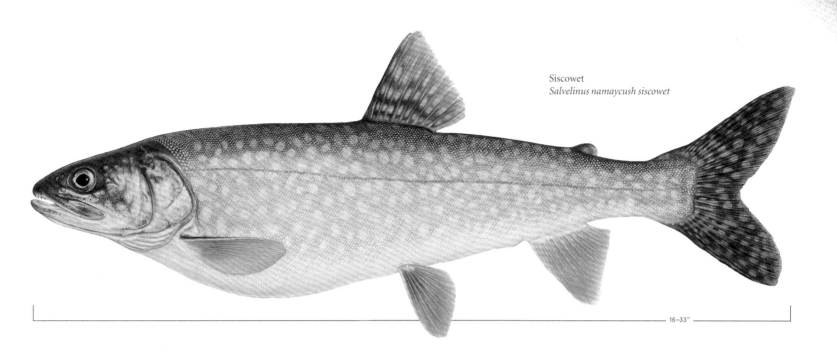

Siscowet
Salvelinus namaycush siscowet

16–33"

such as chironomid larvae ("midge" larvae).
A key to abundance in lake trout populations
is a food supply adequate for the fish to attain
lengths of about 14 to 18 inches (36–46 cm),
the point at which they are capable of preying
on a variety of fishes. Most lakes in the species'
native range contain opossum shrimp, which
can grow to almost 1 inch (25 mm) long.
This shrimp, which occurs to the greatest
depths in lakes and is a favorite food of lake
trout, is especially important in a lake trout's
diet until it is large enough to become an
effective predator on other fishes. The slimy
sculpin and the deep-water sculpin, which
occur in most lakes in the native range of lake
trout, are another important food, especially
for smaller lake trout, those about 10 to
18 inches (25–46 cm) long.

Lake trout can consume fishes that are
half their own body length, but most of the
fishes they prey upon are less than one-third
their length. The larger the lake trout, the
larger their prey and the greater range of fish
species they can exploit. Lake trout are
opportunistic, preying on any available fishes
of an appropriate size.

In the native range of the lake trout,
sculpins and whitefishes are the most ubiquitous associates of lake trout and the major
food of the species in many lakes. Lake trout
also eat several species of minnows and
suckers. In the upper Great Lakes (Huron,
Michigan, and Superior), once smelts and
alewives became established and abundant
they became important food sources for
lake trout.

Lake trout can attain great ages. The
standard method of determining fish age—
evaluating annual marks on the scales—
is not reliable for lake trout, since after about

*The distended belly of the siscowet, pictured above,
is most likely the result of an overinflated air bladder
when it was landed. Native to Lake Superior, these
fish typically live at depths of at least 300 feet (90 m)
beneath the surface.*

age seven, annual marks on lake trout scales
are generally not decipherable. Examination
of tiny bony elements in the inner ear
(otoliths) is the most accurate method for
determining age. Based on otoliths, the
oldest lake trout known to date came from
Kaminuriak Lake, in the Northwest Territories of Canada, and was 62 years old.
The next oldest, from Great Bear Lake, in
the same region, was 53.

The coldest waters with the shortest
growing seasons produce the oldest lake
trout. In more temperate regions with longer
growing seasons, lake trout older than ten
years are rare in many populations. In these

relatively short-lived populations, sexual maturity and first spawning can occur in four- and five-year-old lake trout. In the northern parts of the range, first spawning may not occur until lake trout are ten years old or older, while lake trout of Kaminuriak Lake do not spawn for the first time until they are 19 years old.

Lake trout and brook trout coexist in the same river basins in northeastern North America, but their niches are distinct, and interactions between the two species are minimized. Although lake trout × brook trout hybrids (splake) are easily produced in hatcheries, the natural spawning habitat of the two species is very different; brook trout spawn in streams or shallow areas of lakes. No natural hybrids between the two species have ever been found, though lake trout × Arctic char hybrids have been documented in Labrador, Northwest Territories, and in a lake in Sweden. The Swedish hybrid, before its true identity was verified, was believed to be the largest Arctic char ever caught in Sweden; it weighed about 29 pounds (13 kg).

The Arctic char is a lake-specialized species whose niche overlaps that of the lake trout, and the ranges of the two species overlap in Arctic regions. Where the species occur together, the Arctic char have life histories and habitat preferences, such as anadromy, that reduce direct contact with lake trout. In northern New England, relict populations of Arctic char (the Sunapee trout of New Hampshire, Vermont, and Maine, and the blueback trout of Maine) were found only in lakes without lake trout. After lake trout were stocked into three of the four lakes with native Sunapee trout, the native char became

extinct in all three lakes. When introduced outside of its range, the highly carnivorous lake trout can exterminate native species.

DISTRIBUTION   Lake trout have a broad northern and southern distribution in Alaska, but they are absent from the Yukon River basin of central Alaska. In Canada, they occur in lakes (and some rivers) tributary to the Arctic Ocean and Hudson Bay eastward to Labrador and Nova Scotia and southward to the Great Lakes basin, but are absent from the island of Newfoundland (postglacial dispersal was blocked by the salinity barrier). In the United States, lake trout are native to inland areas of northern New England westward and including the Great Lakes basin.

Two native lake trout populations exist in the upper Missouri River basin in Montana in the headwaters of the Jefferson River drainage. Virtually the entire native range of the lake trout lies within the maximum extent of the last glaciation. Lake trout must have survived the last glacial epoch in unglaciated refugia: one or more in the north in Alaska, and one or more to the south in the upper Mississippi–Missouri basin. The occurrence of lake trout in two lakes in Montana, Elk Lake and Twin Lakes, indicates that around 10,000 years ago, as the glacial ice receded and the present Great Lakes came into existence, there was a continual area of suitable habitat that allowed lake trout to disperse from a glacial refugium into the Great Lakes and westward to the present upper Missouri River basin, where only two lakes provided a suitable environment for the species to persist.

Lake trout have been introduced into

many lakes outside their native range, especially in western areas. Introduced populations of lake trout have become established outside North America in a few lakes of northern Europe, South America, and New Zealand.

EVOLUTION AND CLASSIFICATION
Lake trout and brook trout represent the end products of an ancient branch of *Salvelinus* that evolved in North America, separate from other branches in the genus, probably since Pliocene times (2–5 million years ago).

The lake trout is the most differentiated species of char. In older literature, this degree of differentiation was emphasized by classifying lake trout in a separate genus, *Cristivomer,* that current taxonomy does not recognize. However, it can be argued that subgeneric ranking is justified; such a classification would be genus *Salvelinus,* subgenus *Cristivomer,* species *namaycush.*

The scientific name *namaycush* is an English language rendering of a Native American word for the fish, meaning "dweller in the deep." It is often cited as a word of Cree origin for lake trout, *namekos.* In 1792, Johann Walbaum named *Salmo namaycush* in the same publication in which he described the species of Pacific salmon, rainbow trout, and Dolly Varden char. The name *namaycush* can be traced to journals and writings of employees of the Hudson Bay Company of the 1770s, who described some fishes of the Hudson Bay region.

The lake trout generally has the same appearance throughout its range, but between 1817 and 1865 various authors offered no less than seven additional species

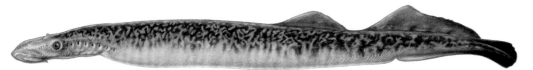

Sea Lamprey
Petromyzon marinus

names for local variations. Each was more poetic than accurate.

The most distinctive form of lake trout is the siscowet, found only in the deep waters of Lake Superior, typically at least 300 feet (90 m) down. Although virtually identical genetically to other lake trout of the Great Lakes, the siscowet is distinguished by its much higher fat content. Other lake trout are esteemed as fine food fish, but siscowet are considered to be inedible when fresh and are smoked to make them palatable. The siscowet, named *Salmo siscowet* in 1850 by Louis Agassiz, is still commonly recognized as a subspecies, *Salvelinus namaycush siscowet*.

Despite the stable morphological characteristics of the lake trout throughout its range, ecological differentiation and specializations have evolved in populations during roughly the past 10,000 years. A stocking program illustrates that this is so. The New York Conservation Department propagates lake trout from two parental sources and stocks them into lakes for sportfishing. One source is Seneca Lake, one of the Finger Lakes, in upstate New York. Seneca Lake is more than 600 feet (180 m) deep, has a relatively alkaline pH, and contains opossum shrimp. The other source is the lake trout of Upper Saranac Lake, in northeastern New York. This lake is shallower (100 feet, or 30 m, deep), has a more acidic pH, and lacks opossum shrimp.

When equal numbers of similar-size fish from the Seneca Lake and Upper Saranac Lake populations were stocked into eight Adirondack lakes that were environmentally similar to Upper Saranac Lake (but very different from Seneca Lake), the evolutionary heritages and specializations of the two populations became apparent. Over the next several years, 495 of the stocked lake trout were caught by anglers from the eight lakes. Of these, 467 (94 percent) were of Upper Saranac Lake origin and 28 (6 percent) were of Seneca Lake origin. Obviously ecological specializations among lake trout populations had evolved under different influences of natural selection. In attempts to restore lake trout to Lake Ontario, a deep lake with native opossum shrimp, the lake trout from Seneca Lake have by far the greatest survival and most successful reproduction of any of the many "strains" of lake trout used.

CONSERVATION   Lake trout abundance can be quantified in terms of pounds of fish per surface acre. Because of the long life span of lake trout, most of the biomass of a population will consist of fish five to 15 years of age and older. If these larger fish are removed in a commercial or sport fishery, it will take several years to replace them and restore the biomass to its original abundance. Production rates are low in lake

trout populations, making them vulnerable to overfishing.

Because lake trout feed at the top of the food chain in nutrient-poor lakes, lake trout abundance will be low compared to other species such as rainbow trout that feed at many different levels of a food chain, tolerate a broader range of temperatures, and have shorter life spans and therefore higher production rates. High-abundance lake trout populations have biomasses of only about 2 to 4 pounds per surface acre (about 2–4.5 kg per ha), while the most productive trout streams with rainbow or brown trout can sustain an abundance of 500 pounds per acre or more (560 kg per ha).

Before the sea lamprey invaded the upper Great Lakes and became abundant in the 1940s, the greatest conservation problem for lake trout concerned their vulnerability to overfishing or overexploitation by commercial fisheries. Because of the enormous area covered by Lakes Superior, Huron, and Michigan, these upper Great Lakes maintained the largest commercial catches of lake trout: in the early 1900s, total combined annual catches up to 20 million pounds (9 million kg). This maximum catch amounted to only about one-half pound per surface acre (560 g per ha) of the three lakes. At that catch rate, lake trout populations were overexploited;

that is, their removal exceeded their ability to replace themselves.

The lamprey is one of the most primitive vertebrate animals; a cartilaginous rod functions as a "backbone" but lacks vertebrae. The mouth, which lacks the supporting elements of a true jaw structure, is armed with circular rows of teeth that the lamprey uses to attach to a fish, rasp through the outer body surface, and suck out body fluids. The relatively large size of lake trout and their occurrence in deep water near the lake bottom make them an ideal target species for lampreys.

The impact of lamprey predation, exacerbated by continued commercial exploitation of the lake trout, was devastating to the lake trout populations of the Great Lakes. By the early 1950s, lake trout became extinct in Lake Michigan and were reduced to sparse, remnant populations in Lake Huron. Lake Superior lake trout also suffered severe losses, but some "offshore" populations were less affected because in their habitat they encountered fewer lampreys. Lakes Erie and Ontario also lost their lake trout. The lake trout of Lake Erie, the shallowest of the Great Lakes (maximum depth 208 feet, or 63 m), were not historically abundant and were lost when pollution caused oxygen depletion in the deeper, colder water.

The sea lamprey is native to Lake Ontario, which is located below Niagara Falls. Niagara Falls was a barrier to lamprey dispersal before the Welland Canal was constructed around the falls in 1829. Lampreys were first recorded in Lake Erie in 1921, in Lake Huron in 1932, and in Lake Michigan in 1936. Lampreys were never as abundant in Lake Ontario as they became in the upper Great Lakes, but their abundance increased as land-use changes increased sediment loads in streams and created silt beds, the required spawning habitat of lampreys.

Besides the increased abundance of lampreys, the extirpation of lake trout in Lake Ontario can be attributed to multiple factors, such as continued overexploitation and the stocking of millions of coho and Chinook salmon to fill the lake trout's niche as the top predator. And some lake trout populations were seriously affected by the insecticide DDT, which contaminated lakes where tributary streams drained agricultural watersheds. Because of the lake trout's long life span and relatively old age at maturity (typically seven or eight years), trout in DDT–contaminated lakes suffered from many years of accumulated DDT. To make matters worse, DDT and its derivatives, which have a high affinity for fat molecules, concentrated in the fatty yolk of eggs within the bodies of female lake trout. When newly hatched fry absorbed the yolk, the toxic effect of DDT was rapid and lethal. The banning of DDT has resolved this problem.

In recent years, government agencies have attempted to restore lake trout to the Great Lakes. However, restoration to historical abundance cannot be achieved. The abundance of lampreys has been greatly reduced by trapping them in streams during their spawning migrations and by killing larval lamprey with a chemical, called TFM, but lampreys cannot be completely eliminated.

The top predator niche in all the Great Lakes is now mainly occupied by nonnative Chinook and coho salmon and brown and rainbow trout (steelhead), and most of the original diversity of the lake trout of the Great Lakes has been lost. Originally the lake trout of each lake consisted of several discrete "subpopulations" with different life histories, each spawning and feeding in different areas of the lake. Attaining maximum total abundance depends on maintaining all "the parts of the whole," and this is no longer possible.

Bull Trout
Salvelinus confluentus

Bull Trout

Salvelinus confluentus

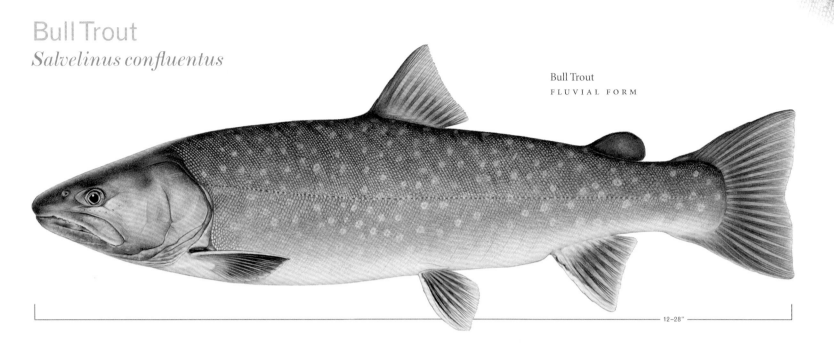

Bull Trout
FLUVIAL FORM

12–28"

Native to western North America, the bull trout is widely known as a voracious predator of other fishes. This char may reach a large size, especially in deep lakes in its range, and will feed opportunistically on any smaller fishes available. Bull trout are probably named for the stocky, flat head of larger fish and for their aggressive feeding habits.

Two other members of the genus *Salvelinus*, the lake trout and the brook trout, exemplify valid, or noncontroversial, classifications of species of char—a lake trout is a lake trout no matter where it is found, and a brook trout is a brook trout wherever it happens to be. This is the fact despite the transgression of species boundaries in hatchery-produced splake (lake trout × brook trout hybrids) and despite occasional hybridization between lake trout and Arctic

char. Species boundaries are not so clear-cut with the other three species of North American char: the bull trout, the Dolly Varden, and the Arctic char. Complexity and confusion have often reigned as changing classifications "lumped" or "split" species and as different philosophies of classification went in and out of favor. Diverse taxonomic schemes have resulted in some classifications with a myriad of species and others that group all the forms of bull trout, Dolly Varden, and Arctic char into a single, highly variable species, *Salvelinus alpinus*.

The bull trout and the Dolly Varden were long confused with one another because they are generally similar in overall appearance and in number of gill rakers, vertebrae, and pyloric caeca. In 1978, Ted Cavender of Ohio State University published a comprehensive and detailed account of the skeletal

BULL TROUT

SCIENTIFIC NAME
Salvelinus confluentus

OTHER COMMON NAMES
None known

HABITAT
Coastal and mountain streams; deep pools of large, cold rivers; deep, cold lakes; rarely brackish and salt water

LENGTH AND WEIGHT
8–10" (20–25 cm) and 4–6 oz (91–170 g) in small streams; typically 12–18" (30–46 cm) and up to 2½ lb (1.1 kg) in rivers and lakes; typical maximum 28–36" (71–91 cm) and 5–20 lb (2.3–9 kg); world record 32 lb (14.5 kg)

LIFE SPAN
4–10 years or more

DIET
Aquatic and terrestrial invertebrates in small streams; become piscivorous in larger rivers and lakes

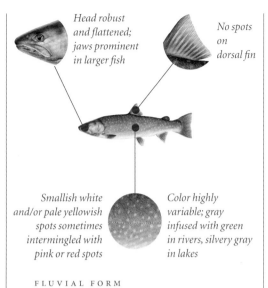

Head robust and flattened; jaws prominent in larger fish

No spots on dorsal fin

Smallish white and/or pale yellowish spots sometimes intermingled with pink or red spots

Color highly variable; gray infused with green in rivers, silvery gray in lakes

FLUVIAL FORM

characteristics of char, demonstrating that the bull trout is a valid species. After Cavender's publication, the world-record "Dolly Varden" of 32 pounds (14.5 kg) from Lake Pend Oreille, Idaho, became the world-record bull trout.

Subsequent genetic analyses and chromosome counts have shown that, despite the similarities between the bull trout and the Dolly Varden, the bull trout is distinct from both the Dolly Varden and the Arctic char. Genetic analysis also indicates that the closest relationships of bull trout are not with North American char, but more probably with char of the Far East and Kamchatka.

DESCRIPTION The bull trout's coloration is highly variable. Generally the body's background color is gray infused with green, though bull trout in lakes may be silvery gray. The body is covered with relatively small white and/or pale yellowish spots with intermingling pink or red spots that may not be apparent on all individuals. The ventral region can change from white to orange, and the lower fins can develop orange and red colors. As with most salmonid fishes, mature males are more colorful than females with increasing age and size.

The ranges of the bull trout and the Dolly Varden overlap from Puget Sound drainages northward in rivers of British Columbia that drain to the Pacific Ocean. Where the two species occur together and are of similar size, they look so alike that genetic analysis may be required for positive identification. This is especially true where hybridization occurs between the two species.

The bull trout's typical number of gill rakers (15–19), vertebrae (63–66), and pyloric caeca (22–35) are similar to those found in the southern subspecies of Dolly Varden.

Where bull trout have the opportunity to attain a large size of about 5 pounds (2.3 kg) and larger, their appearance becomes more clearly differentiated from Dolly Varden. The head and jaws are larger in bull trout, and the top of the head is flattened. Their eyes are positioned more toward the top of the head for better perception of prey swimming above them. Overall, large bull trout definitely look like the predatory fish they are.

In the Columbia River and Upper Klamath Lake basins, introduced brook trout have frequently hybridized with bull trout, producing trout that have an appearance intermediate between the two species. Bull trout have spotless fins. (The spotless fins of the bull trout have led to a saying, "Fin black, put it back," which is promoted by agencies and organizations to help anglers distinguish this protected native char from other fishes.)

The dorsal and caudal fins of bull trout × brook trout hybrids have spotting that is not as pronounced as in brook trout, in which those fins have a mottled appearance. The bull trout's lower fins have only white anterior borders, while those of hybrids have anterior borders that are black and white, with the black border of hybrids less distinct than in brook trout.

BIOLOGY The bull trout is represented by different life history forms, including river-resident populations, lacustrine populations, and sea-run populations. The latter appear to be relatively rare, although the name *confluentus* (meaning confluence, or where two waters meet) is based on a silvery specimen that foraged in Puget Sound.

The stream-resident form is subdivided into two basic types: One lives its entire life in small headwater streams, often isolated above waterfalls; the other typically spawns in smaller tributary streams but spends most of its time foraging in larger rivers. This second form, often called fluvial, occurs only in relatively larger river basins that contain a network of headwater spawning tributaries connected to larger riverine habitat, allowing bull trout to undertake movements of more than 100 miles (160 km) as they search for prey.

The bull trout has a well-deserved reputation as a predator. Populations resident in small headwaters typically feed on invertebrates and may be only 8 to 10 inches (20–25 cm) long at ages of 8 to 10 years. Bull trout of fluvial and lacustrine populations feed predominantly on other fishes when they are available. Bull trout in areas where

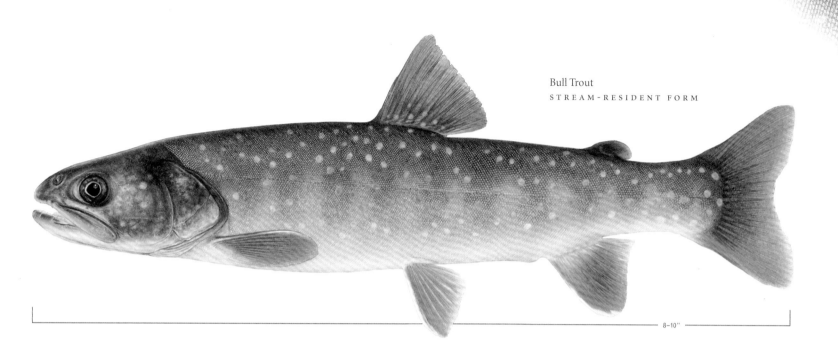

Bull Trout
STREAM-RESIDENT FORM

8–10"

prey fishes are abundant can attain a large size, typically 28–36 inches (71–91 cm) and 10 to 20 pounds (4.5–9 kg) or more. The largest bull trout, which weigh 20 pounds (9 kg) or more, are associated with lakes that have an abundance of kokanee salmon as the major prey species. Kokanee salmon are not native to Lake Pend Oreille, Idaho, but after kokanee were introduced and became abundant there by the 1930s, the growth and maximum size of Pend Oreille bull trout increased. The official angler-caught record of 32 pounds (14.5 kg) was taken there in 1949. Unverified weights to 40 pounds (18 kg) are claimed for bull trout in Kootenay Lake, British Columbia, where kokanee salmon are native.

Many lacustrine populations of bull trout have declined and some are extinct. In several western lakes introductions of lake trout—

especially when combined with the introduction of the lake trout's favored prey species, the opossum shrimp—have had depressing effects on the growth and abundance of bull trout and cutthroat trout. The opossum shrimp (crustaceans of the order Mysidacea) actually compete with kokanee salmon for zooplankton, depressing kokanee abundance, and at the same time provide an additional source of food for lake trout. This allows more lake trout to survive to a length of 18 inches (46 cm), at which size they further impact the kokanee population and increase predation pressure on other fishes.

Where the nonnative brook trout has been introduced to the bull trout's range, it has negatively impacted the bull trout through replacement and hybridization. Both species spawn in the fall when stream temperatures drop below about 48 °F (9 °C),

mainly in September and October, and both select small tributary streams for spawning. Since the two species have no evolutionary history of coexistence, bull trout lack innate reproductive behavior that would segregate them from brook trout during spawning. Thus hybridization between the two species is common where they occur together.

Bull trout and Dolly Varden occasionally hybridize, but where hybridization occurs the two species maintain their identities, as occurs, for example, when pink salmon and chum salmon hybridize. The two do not homogenize into a hybrid swarm, as typically happens where rainbow trout are introduced into populations of native cutthroat trout.

However, hybridization with brook trout often results in the replacement of bull trout by brook trout and hybrids. Although adult bull trout are larger than adult brook

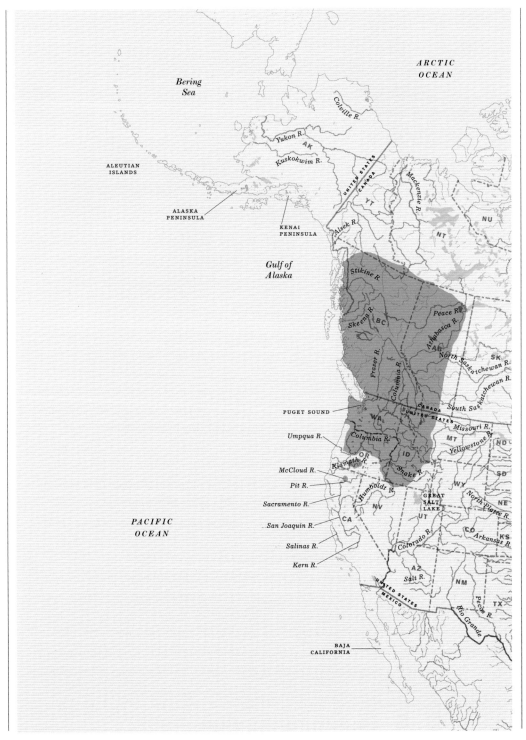

trout and thus would be dominant over brook trout in interactions between the species, brook trout have an advantage in their greater reproductive potential. Brook trout in small streams typically mature sexually in their second or third year, while bull trout do not mature until their fourth or fifth year, or later. Brook trout can be much more abundant than bull trout where they occur together, and this distorted ratio of abundance can lead to mass hybridization.

The main environmental factor limiting distribution of bull trout is water temperature. They prefer temperatures of about 50 to 54 °F (10–12 °C), with maximum summer temperatures not above about 59 to 60 °F (about 15 °C). In rivers draining from the Cascade Range to the Columbia River in Washington, bull trout are typically found only in the coldest headwater tributaries, often associated with the native westslope cutthroat trout. Downstream, as the water warms, brook trout occur first and then the native redband trout *(O. mykiss gairdneri)*, both as resident populations and as juvenile steelhead.

Bull trout are eliminated from streams when excessive livestock grazing or clear-cut logging removes shade-producing riparian vegetation. In the unshaded streams, water

The precise boundaries of the historic range of the bull trout are not known with certainty because of its frequent confusion in the past with Dolly Varden and Arctic char. However, bull trout are known from the headwaters of the Mackenzie and Yukon Rivers in the north and south to a small portion of north-central Nevada. Included in this range is the Columbia River basin west to Montana, the Klamath River basin, Puget Sound, and coastal drainages of British Columbia.

Bull × Brook Trout Hybrid
S. confluentus × *S. fontinalis*

5–12"

temperatures can increase beyond the tolerance of bull trout.

Bull trout, like cutthroat trout, are highly susceptible to angling. Because bull trout may live for 10 years or longer, they can easily be overexploited; most of the older, larger bull trout are caught with even light fishing pressure (10 to 20 hours of angling per year per surface acre of stream or lake). Because of this susceptibility to angling, officials in the United States and some parts of Canada have imposed no-kill fishing regulations for bull trout populations. Where protected, all bull trout must be released.

DISTRIBUTION The northernmost distribution of bull trout occurs in the headwaters of the Yukon and Mackenzie River basins of Alaska and Canada. In Pacific Coast drainages, they occur in rivers of British Columbia southward to around Puget Sound. Bull trout are not native to Vancouver Island or other islands off the Pacific Coast of Canada and southern Alaska. The Skagit River has the highest known incidence of bull trout × Dolly Varden hybrids, probably stimulated by its human-induced modified environment. Native distribution includes the upper parts of the North and South Saskatchewan River drainages of Alberta, Canada (the Hudson Bay basin). Bull trout occur in the coldest waters of the Columbia River basin, typically where temperatures rarely exceed 59 to 60 °F (about 15 °C).

To the south, a few bull trout populations persist in cold headwater tributary streams in the Upper Klamath Lake basin of Oregon.

The southernmost population of bull trout once occurred in the McCloud River, in California. However, those bull trout rapidly declined in the 1940s after Shasta Dam blocked access to large runs of anadromous Chinook salmon and steelhead, and bull trout were extinct there by the 1970s. It is likely that juvenile salmon and steelhead were the major food source for McCloud River bull trout, and when this food supply was lost, the bull trout could not maintain the abundance necessary for long-term survival. The introduction of nonnative brown trout and brook trout into the McCloud River probably hastened the demise of the bull trout.

It is interesting to speculate on the routes followed by ancestral bull trout to reach the Upper Klamath Lake basin and the McCloud

River of the Sacramento River basin. Some bull trout populations can live in marine waters, and it is possible that ancestors came along the coast and moved up the Klamath and Sacramento Rivers. However, it is more likely that the bull trout ancestors came via inland connections. Virtually all the fishes native to Upper Klamath Lake came from inland, not coastal, sources. The headwaters of the Pit River drainage of the Sacramento basin are contiguous with tributaries of the Upper Klamath Lake basin, and the study of several species of fish clearly points to past connections between the Upper Klamath basin and the Pit River. Because bull trout cannot tolerate water warmer than 60 °F (15 °C), all the connecting-link populations from the Columbia basin to Upper Klamath Lake and to the McCloud River would have been lost during postglacial warming. The upper McCloud River is fed by large, cold springs. Only in this environment did bull trout find a postglacial refuge in the Sacramento basin, where they persisted until human intervention—in the form of Shasta Dam and nonnative trout introductions—eliminated them about 30 years ago.

There is a possibility that bull trout once occurred in the Bonneville basin. Fossil fragments of trout identified as bull trout have been found in the Bonneville basin, and in 1834 the naturalist J. K. Townsend recorded men catching trout (Bonneville cutthroat trout) and "char" in the Bear River. However, except for Townsend's observation of "char" in the Bear River, there is no evidence that bull trout, if they once occurred in the Bonneville basin, persisted into modern times.

EVOLUTION AND CLASSIFICATION

Genetic data shows that the bull trout is a valid species and is well differentiated from other char species of North America. Chromosome number, especially total "arm" number, is a relatively stable characteristic in the evolution of different lines in the genus *Salvelinus*. The chromosomes of brook trout and lake trout (their "karyotype") denote an ancient evolutionary branch of the genus established in North America. Brook trout and lake trout both have 84 chromosomes with 104 arms. A V-shaped (metacentric) chromosome has two arms: 10 metacentric chromosomes would have a total of 20 arms. Dolly Varden and Arctic char have 98 chromosomal arms. Arctic char and the northern subspecies of Dolly Varden have a total (diploid) number of 78 chromosomes, and the southern subspecies of Dolly Varden has a total diploid number of 82. All have a total arm number of 98, denoting they are derived from the same ancestral evolutionary line. Bull trout have 78 chromosomes with 100 arms. The only other two char with the bull trout's karyotype of 100 arms are the white-spotted char (*S. leucomaenis*) of the Far East and the "stone char" of Kamchatka. (The proper scientific name of the "stone char" is unresolved.) Thus the probable closest relationships of bull trout are with Far Eastern species, rather than with Dolly Varden and Arctic char.

Throughout its range the bull trout is a "stable" species. It exhibits little intraspecific differentiation in different geographical regions that might be recognized as sub-species, except for the long-isolated bull trout of the Upper Klamath Lake basin, and, most likely, the now extinct population of the McCloud River, California.

When the bull trout was recognized as a species distinct from Dolly Varden in 1978, a problem arose over its correct scientific name because several inadequately defined species of char and trout named in the nineteenth century might have been bull trout. The question was: What was the first valid name used for the bull trout? George Suckley, a surgeon-naturalist with the Pacific Railroad Surveys of the 1850s, named several species of trout and salmon, among them "*Salmo confluentus*," described in 1858 from a specimen running up the Pullayup River from Puget Sound. However, Suckley's description is imprecise and cannot be used to associate the description with bull trout. During Ted Cavender's research on bull trout, he examined the specimen collected by George Suckley—which had been preserved in the U.S. National Museum—and determined it to be a bull trout. Thus the bull trout officially became *Salvelinus confluentus* with the publication of Cavender's paper in 1978.

There is no "code of nomenclature" for determining common names of fish species. This lack of formality simplifies the continued usage of the common name Dolly Varden for the species *Salvelinus malma*. When the bull trout was recognized as a species separate from the Dolly Varden, a new "official" common name was called for. The name bull trout has a long history, especially in Idaho and Montana, and is the common name chosen by Cavender. It has been recognized by the American Fisheries Society.

When Livingston Stone went to the McCloud River in 1872 to set up a salmon hatchery for the U.S. Fish Commission, he wrote about a species of "salmon-trout" called *wye-dar-deekit* by the local Native Americans. Stone mentioned that European American anglers from the lodge at Soda Springs, on the upper Sacramento River, would hike over to the McCloud River to catch large "salmon-trout" which the anglers called Dolly Varden. They named them for a character of that name in Charles Dickens's novel *Barnaby Rudge.* The character, familiar to most Americans at that time,was associated with a green calico cloth with red dots, called the Dolly Varden pattern. The colors and spots of the salmon-trout of the McCloud River suggested this pattern, and the common name Dolly Varden was first used for what were later recognized as bull trout in the McCloud River. Since there are no formal rules for associating common names with particular species of fish, no rule was broken when Dolly Varden continued to be the common name for *S. malma,* and the original Dolly Varden of the McCloud River became the bull trout. (The possibility that *S. malma* also occurred in the McCloud River in 1872 is discussed in the Dolly Varden account.)

CONSERVATION Bull trout are especially vulnerable to human-induced factors that increase water temperatures and sediment loads, change flow regimes, block migration routes, and establish nonnative trout, especially brook trout in streams and lake trout in lakes. These impacts have caused a great decline in bull trout abundance and distribution as well as the extinction of the bull trout in the McCloud River.

In 1992, environmental groups petitioned the U.S. Fish and Wildlife Service to list bull trout existing in the 48 contiguous states for protection under the Endangered Species Act. In 1998, bull trout specifically of the Columbia River basin and the Upper Klamath Lake basin were listed as a threatened species. In 1999, bull trout of the Puget Sound basin and of the St. Marys–Belly River drainage (the headwaters of the South Saskatchewan River basin) in Montana were added, in the threatened category. Protection and restoration efforts include habitat improvements, improved land-use management to maintain and restore riparian vegetation and thus cold water temperatures, and an end to the stocking of nonnative trout in waters with bull trout.

Arctic Char
Salvelinus alpinus

Arctic Char
Salvelinus alpinus

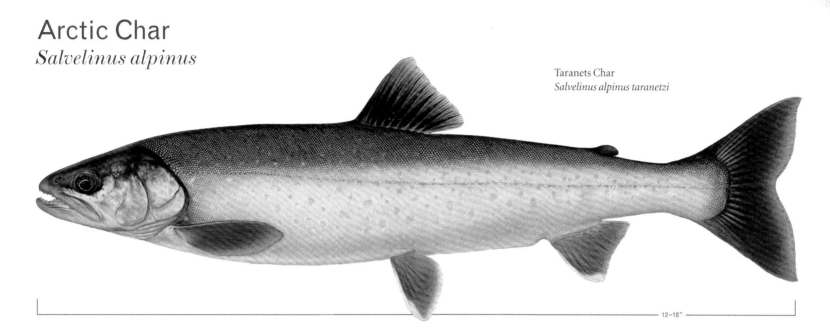

Taranets Char
Salvelinus alpinus taranetzi

12–18"

The beautiful and mysterious Arctic char has fascinated laymen and scientists for centuries. Despite its minor commercial importance, no other fish species has generated and sustained such intense interest, enthusiasm, and controversy among fishery scientists, who have made it the subject of extensive research and analysis.

The Arctic char is the most complex and controversial of all North American salmonids. Biologists often refer to the "Arctic char species complex," because no general agreement exists on how the enormous range of variation in morphological and life history traits found in Arctic char throughout the northern regions of the world should be classified. Should the Arctic char be considered as a single species with several subspecies or as many separate species? There is much that is unknown about the Arctic char and gaps in information are filled with speculation. The classification controversy is ongoing and not likely to result in consensus anytime soon.

For this book, three subspecies of Arctic char are recognized. Over the past 30 years, I have published several papers on the evolution and classification of the species. Despite the fact that my opinions have often been in strong disagreement with those of some of the world's leading char experts, we have maintained a strong bond of friendship in the fraternity of Arctic char fanatics.

DESCRIPTION   If any species of fish could be characterized as defying description, it is the Arctic char. The great range of variation in size, shape, coloration, and life history truly defeats any attempt to arrive at a general description.

Can a population of dull grayish char in an Arctic lake, where reproduction occurs

TARANETS CHAR

SCIENTIFIC NAME
Salvelinus alpinus taranetzi

OTHER COMMON NAMES
Arctic char

HABITAT
Deep cold pools and runs of medium to large rivers; lakes; possibly anadromous in North America

LENGTH AND WEIGHT
Typically 12–18" (30–46 cm) and rarely over 2 lb (0.9 kg); maximum known 12 lb (5.4 kg); dwarf form typically 9–10" (23–25 cm)

LIFE SPAN
Typically 6–8 years; 20–30 years in more northern populations

DIET
Aquatic invertebrates, fish eggs, other fishes, especially sockeye salmon fry when available

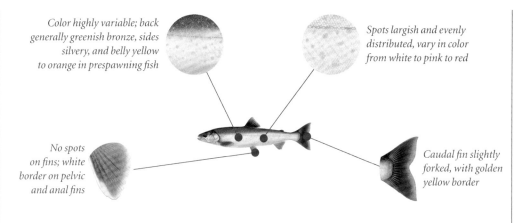

Color highly variable; back generally greenish bronze, sides silvery, and belly yellow to orange in prespawning fish

Spots largish and evenly distributed, vary in color from white to pink to red

No spots on fins; white border on pelvic and anal fins

Caudal fin slightly forked, with golden yellow border

TARANETS CHAR

when the fish are 4 to 6 inches (10–15 cm) long and weigh less than an ounce (about 25 g), be the same species as a group of brilliant red, anadromous char that attain lengths of more than 36 inches (91 cm) and weigh 20 pounds (9 kg) or more? In a single lake, can large predatory char and "dwarf" char on which the predators feed both be members of *Salvelinus alpinus*?

My answer is yes. These highly divergent life histories are part of the highly variable species *S. alpinus.* There are many examples of two, three, or four populations of Arctic char—each filling different niches, each with distinctive morphological and life history traits—coexisting in the same lake with reproductive isolation. These coexisting (sympatric) populations are valid biological species in that they occupy different niches and do not hybridize. From an evolutionary perspective, however, the evidence is convincing that this diversity has evolved since the retreat of glacial ice some 10,000 to 12,000 years ago. If all the populations of Arctic char that conform to the definition of valid biological species were to be described

as separate species, the number of species would multiply beyond coherence.

Subspecies are assumed to classify geographically distinctive groups that are derived from preglacial branchings that became isolated in different glacial refugia. From these refugia the ancestral lines began to disperse in the Holarctic region when the last ice age ended. Different subspecies came in contact in transition areas where the diagnostic traits of subspecies intergrade, indicating that hybridization occurred between two ancestral lines. On the basis of this scenario I divide the Arctic char of North America into three subspecies.

The char native to northern New England and southeastern Canada, *S. alpinus oquassa,* probably represents the first evolutionary line of Arctic char established in North America before the last glacial epoch (more than about 60,000 years ago). Most likely the common ancestor survived the glaciation in a refuge south of the maximum extent of the glacier and moved northward as the glacial ice retreated. Most of the waters available in New England for Arctic char in the

postglacial era were occupied by brook trout. With postglacial warming, Arctic char persisted only in a relatively few deep, colder lakes with suitable temperature and oxygen regimes. This same form of char persisted in many lakes in Quebec, New Brunswick, Nova Scotia, and Newfoundland. The ancestor was undoubtedly anadromous, dispersing from river to river via the sea, but all historical populations of *oquassa* have, until recently, been thought to be resident lake populations. In 1999, a paper demonstrated that some char in a lake tributary to the Gulf of St. Lawrence had fed in marine waters.

The coloration of *S. a. oquassa* is variable from lake to lake and at different stages of sexual maturity. Yellow and orange colors on the sides and ventral region are common, but in many lakes red is more characteristic of the *oquassa* group known as Quebec red trout. The basic background body coloration is silvery gray, tinted with blue. Toward the dorsal region, coloration darkens. These color variations have given rise to such local common names as golden, silver, blueback, and red trout. Spots on the body range from pale white to bright red. This subspecies averages about 20 to 21 gill rakers, the lowest number found in Arctic char. Their number of vertebrae averages about 64, also at the low end of the range. Typical pyloric caecal counts are about 35 to 40.

S. a. oquassa, contains the relict char of northern New England and southeastern Quebec—Sunapee trout, blueback trout, and Quebec red trout. Formerly recognized as three separate species, these groups, historically called trout, now technically have become one subspecies of char, but their

Dwarf Arctic Char
Salvelinus alpinus taranetzi

9–10"

well-established common names continue to be used.

The char of the high Arctic region, the subspecies *S. alpinus erythrinus,* has a broad distribution from the Ob River basin eastward across Siberia and North America in Arctic Ocean drainages on both sides of northern Hudson Bay around northern Quebec and Labrador. West of the Ob River, the characteristics of char indicate intergradation between the subspecies *erythrinus* and *alpinus.* Southward in Labrador, the Arctic char populations show intergrading characters between *erythrinus* and *oquassa.*

In northern Quebec and Labrador the range of the Arctic char overlaps with that of the lake trout and the brook trout. Despite the fact that in the genus *Salvelinus,* the lake trout and the brook trout are the species that are most distantly related to the Arctic char, hybrids between Arctic char and lake trout

and Arctic char and brook trout are known from Labrador. Hybrids between Arctic char and lake trout are found frequently in Labrador lakes and the Northwest Territories where both species occur. Arctic char × brook trout hybrids are documented in Labrador, but this hybrid is rarer than the lake trout × Arctic char hybrid. The closest interspecific relationships are between Arctic char and Dolly Varden, but no hybrids between these two species are known. Evidently, life history distinctions act to completely segregate them during spawning.

In North America the range of *erythrinus* overlaps with northern Dolly Varden from the Mackenzie River westward across northern Alaska. In this region of overlap, as far as we know, Arctic char occur only as resident lake populations and the Dolly Varden are mainly anadromous.

The Arctic char and Dolly Varden are well

differentiated. The subspecies *erythrinus* typically has from 25 to 30 gill rakers (versus 20–23 in *S. malma malma*) and 40 to 50 pyloric caeca (versus 25–30 in Dolly Varden). The spots are relatively larger in Arctic char compared to Dolly Varden. Brilliant red colors on the sides and ventral region commonly develop, especially in sexually mature anadromous populations.

The Taranets char, *S. a. taranetzi,* occurs from northwestern Alaska southward to the Alaska and Kenai Peninsulas and in lakes on Kodiak Island and the Shumagin Islands, south of the Alaska Peninsula. In Asia, this subspecies occurs on the Chukchi Peninsula, southward to the Kamchatka Peninsula, where it occurs as resident lake populations. On the Chukchi Peninsula, *taranetzi* has both anadromous and resident lake populations. In Alaska, where *taranetzi* is known from resident lake populations, the Arctic char and the Dolly Varden have long been confused by both anglers and fishery scientists. Thus anadromous populations of *taranetzi* char in Alaska have likely been confused with Dolly Varden. However, recent analysis of the otoliths of Arctic char from Becharof Lake on the Alaska Peninsula indicates that some fish in this population had spent some time in marine waters.

The *taranetzi* char differs from the subspecies *erythrinus* in their lower number of gill rakers, which average 23 to 25 in *taranetzi* and 25 to 30 in *erythrinus*. In addition, the gill rakers of *taranetzi* char tend to be shorter, thicker, and more blunt compared to the long, fine, acute gill rakers of *erythrinus*. The *taranetzi* char differs from northern Dolly Varden in gill raker characteristics: Northern Dolly Varden typically have 20 to 23 long, fine gill rakers. Taranets char have 40 to 50 pyloric caeca, as compared to 25 to 30 in Dolly Varden. South of the Alaska Peninsula, the southern Dolly Varden is more sharply differentiated from the Tarenets char. In areas where the two species coexist, southern Dolly Varden typically have only 15 to 20 gill rakers.

The spots on the Taranets char are considerably larger and fewer compared to the profusion of small spots characteristic of Dolly Varden. As with all subspecies of Arctic char, coloration is highly variable. Red, yellow, and orange may predominate in sexually mature char of various lakes. In some lakes the entire body becomes bright red, resembling the spawning colors of sockeye salmon.

BIOLOGY   The Arctic char of North America have two basic life history types: lake-resident (lacustrine) and anadromous. As far as is known, anadromy commonly occurs only in the subspecies *erythrinus* in North America.

The anadromous *S. a. erythrinus* of the Arctic region is the typical form of Arctic char known to anglers seeking trophy-size char. The late Al McClane, a well known and widely traveled angling author, wrote that the Arctic char (referring to the anadromous form of *erythrinus* of northern Canada) "may be quite literally the strongest fish that swims. It is unquestionably the strongest salmonid." Many anadromous populations attain maximum weights of 15 to 18 pounds (6.8–8.2 kg), but the largest of any form of Arctic char is the anadromous *erythrinus* of the Tree River, in Northwest Territories, Canada, where the angler-caught world-record Arctic char was landed in 1981, weighing 32 pounds, 9 ounces (14.8 kg).

What is there about the Tree River that allows its char to attain such a great size? Throughout the range of the Arctic char, the species could be called (almost) obligatorily lacustrine. They occur as lake-resident populations or as anadromous populations in rivers with lakes in the drainage, and it's in those lakes that the anadromous char spend most of their lives. In Arctic regions, it typically takes from four to eight years before a smolt size of about 7 to 10 inches (18–25 cm) is attained, and the char then make annual migrations to the sea for about 30 to 60 days for intensive feeding. Virtually all growth takes place during these brief excursions for marine feeding. The Tree River has a barrier

falls about 7 miles (11 km) from the sea that blocks access to upstream lakes. Evidently the lower Tree River serves as a lake for its native char. The access to brackish water at the mouth of the river during most of the year (that is, when the char are not feeding in marine waters) likely extends the feeding and growth period of Tree River char beyond the brief period of intensive marine feeding of other anadromous populations.

High Arctic populations of Arctic char are well adapted to extreme conditions. They enter the sea in June, when the sea ice is breaking up and the sea-water temperature is below the freezing point of fresh water (about 30 °F or –1 °C). They feed voraciously and opportunistically on fishes and larger invertebrates during this 30- to 60-day period of marine feeding in extremely cold water and grow rapidly. At temperatures of about 39 °F (4 °C) and lower, brook trout, brown trout, and rainbow trout will continue to feed, at reduced levels, but they do not grow and will eventually lose weight. Arctic char have physiological adaptations that allow them to thrive under the most extreme conditions. They exist in some lakes that remain ice-covered throughout some years.

A long life span is another adaptation to high Arctic conditions. The maximum age of *erythrinus,* based on interpretation of otoliths, is 33 years, but individuals in most anadromous populations rarely exceed about 20 years, during which time they have probably spawned three times. The char generally attain sexual maturity only after several marine migrations—at ages of 10 to 12 and lengths of about 18 to 24 inches (46–61 cm) or more. It generally takes two to four years

Sunapee Trout
Salvelinus alpinus oquassa

10–15"

between spawnings for sufficient energy to be accumulated for redevelopment of the gonads for the next spawning; under the most extreme Arctic conditions, it may take up to five years. Some populations do not go to sea in the year they spawn, remaining in fresh water for about 21 months without feeding before the next marine migration. During this time they lose up to 35 percent or more of their body weight.

Among different populations in different regions there is variation on this generalized life cycle in which anadromous Arctic char manifest site-specific adaptations that allow members of the species to survive and even flourish under the most extreme climatic conditions.

S. a. oquassa exists almost entirely as lacustrine populations. However, a 1999 study of Arctic char of Davidson Lake, tributary to the Gulf of St. Lawrence, indicated

that about 10 to 15 percent of the fish had fed in marine waters. Evidently, at least some populations of *oquassa* have retained the ability to utilize salt water. In lakes, the char mainly feed on invertebrates, both bottom-dwelling organisms and especially crustacean zooplankton, though they may opportunistically feed on small fish. In Sunapee Lake, New Hampshire, after smelt were introduced and became abundant, the native char fed on the smelt and attained a larger size (to 8–9 pounds, or about 4 kg) than before smelt became established. This is about the maximum size known for *oquassa,* and overall, *oquassa* is the smallest in maximum size and the least predatory of the Arctic char subspecies.

The blueback form of *oquassa* in the Rangeley Lakes of Maine rarely reached more than 10 inches (25 cm) in length. The Rangeley Lakes blueback char were the prey

SUNAPEE TROUT

SCIENTIFIC NAME
Salvelinus alpinus oquassa

OTHER COMMON NAMES
Blueback trout, Quebec red trout, golden trout, silver trout

HABITAT
Deep, cold lakes and ponds; rarely in salt water

LENGTH AND WEIGHT
Typically 10–15" (25–38 cm) and 7–16 oz (198–454 g); maximum known up to 9 lb (4.1 kg)

LIFE SPAN
7–8 years

DIET
Aquatic and terrestrial invertebrates including crustacean zooplankton; fishes, especially smelt

The historic native distribution of North American subspecies of Arctic char included a large area of New England. Highly susceptible to pollution and competition from stocked nonnative fishes, the Arctic char has been extirpated from most of its native range in the United States. Overfishing has effected its abundance in many other areas, especially in more populated regions.

species for large brook trout, similar to the predator-prey relationship between brown trout and Arctic char in European lakes.

In the Chukchi Peninsula, in Russia, anadromous populations of *taranetzi* char have a life history similar to that of *S. a. erythrinus*. In Alaska, nothing is known of anadromous populations of the *taranetzi* char, but lake populations are numerous. In most of these populations, maximum weight rarely exceeds more than 2 pounds (0.9 kg), but if forage fishes, such as juvenile sockeye salmon, are available—especially when the sockeye smolt and prepare to migrate in schools from a lake—the *taranetzi* char becomes predacious and can grow to 10 or 12 pounds (4.5–5.5 kg). In earlier times, when it was not understood that the Dolly Varden and the Arctic char are two separate species, the Dolly Varden took the blame for this predation on sockeye young.

The maximum life spans among Arctic char populations are associated with temperature regimes and length of the growing season. The colder the water and shorter the growing season, the longer the life span. At the southern extreme of the species' range, seven or eight years is the general maximum life span of *oquassa*, whereas in the high Arctic, *erythrinus* populations can live for more than 30 years.

DISTRIBUTION   The northernmost occurrence of any fish species in fresh water is found in the Arctic char of Lake Hazen, on the northern part of Ellesmere Island of the Canadian Arctic, at 82° N latitude.

The distributions of the three North American subspecies are given above, with their description. In Europe, the southernmost natural distribution of the Arctic char occurs in Alpine lakes in drainages tributary to the Rhine, Rhône, and Danube Rivers. It occurs in many lakes of Great Britain and Ireland, especially lakes of Scotland, and in numerous lakes of Norway, Sweden, and Finland. Anadromous populations are found in northern Norway and in Arctic Ocean drainages of Europe, Asia, and North America. Westward from continental Europe the Arctic char is native to Iceland and Greenland. The species is also found on all islands within its area of distribution that maintain freshwater habitat throughout the year.

Although all studies indicate that anadromous Arctic char remain near shore during their 30- to 60-day period of ocean feeding, more distant, open-ocean migration must have occurred in the past. Arctic char are found on Spitsbergen Island, about 500 miles (800 km) from Norway, and on Jan Mayen Island, which lies about 600 miles (960 km) from Spitsbergen and 400 miles (640 km) from Iceland. It was via this Atlantic Ocean route that, in preglacial times, the ancestor of the subspecies *oquassa* probably reached North America. The Atlantic salmon likely also used this route to extend its range to North America. The brown trout, which also has anadromous populations, was able to extend its range only to Iceland.

EVOLUTION AND CLASSIFICATION
Because of the great diversity in size, shape, coloration, and life history found in Arctic char, many species were described after the first description of *"Salmo" alpinus* in 1758. For the char of Great Britain and Ireland, 15 species were described. In the twentieth century, a trend for simplification and lumping resulted in grouping all of this diversity into a single species, which often included the Dolly Varden.

According to the hypothesis guiding the classification used in this book, the ancestor of the subspecies *S. a. oquassa* was the first form of Arctic char to become established in North America. In postglacial times its distribution was greatly reduced and limited to lakes in the southern part of the range of the species.

All populations of *oquassa* are derived from an anadromous Arctic char ancestor that moved northward following the retreat of the glaciers from about 10,000 to 12,000 to about 7,000 years ago. Thus, none have been isolated from a common ancestor for more than about 5,000 years. The virtual identity of all populations of *oquassa* in their taxonomic and genetic characteristics confirms that they have not been isolated for a long time in evolutionary terms and that, most logically, all should be classified as a single subspecies.

The description of the name *oquassa* was published in 1854 for the blueback trout of Lake Oquassa, one of the Rangeley Lakes of Maine. (By the early 1900s, the native char of the Rangeley Lakes was extinct.) The "golden trout" of Sunapee Lake, New Hampshire, was named *aureolus* in 1888 (it became

extinct in Sunapee Lake about 1950 but persists in Floods Pond in Maine), and the Quebec red trout was named *marstoni* in 1893. Because *oquassa* was the first name published, it becomes the present subspecies name for this group of Arctic char, which occur at the southernmost natural distribution of the Arctic char. The closest relationships of *oquassa* are probably with the subspecies *S. alpinus alpinus* of northern Europe rather than with other North American subspecies.

The subspecies *erythrinus* has great variation in Siberia, indicating that differentiation occurred in several glacial refugia. In North America, the characteristics of this subspecies are highly stable, except for areas of Labrador where their distribution overlapped with the *oquassa* evolutionary line and hybridization occurred. This lack of significant variation in its taxonomic characteristics suggests that in postglacial times only one ancestor came to North America from Asia. In North America, the Arctic char is much less diverse than in Europe and Asia, and it can be classified as three subspecies that are relatively valid, at least compared to the taxonomic problems of European and Asian Arctic char.

The earliest name used to describe any form of Arctic char with 25 to 30 or more gill rakers is *"Salmo erythrinus."* It was published in 1775 for the char of Lake Frolikha and the Frolikha River, tributary to the northeastern part of Lake Baikal in Siberia. Although *erythrinus* is a "stable" subspecies in North America—meaning it exhibits little variation in its taxonomic characteristics among anadromous and resident populations—in Asia there is great variation among populations occurring in the same lake. The taxonomic status of this subspecies is in need of further research and revision.

The *taranetzi* char is associated with drainages tributary to the Chukchi Sea, Bering Sea, Bristol Bay, and Gulf of Alaska. This distribution indicates that its ancestor survived the last glaciation in Beringia, an unglaciated refuge associated with the Bering land bridge, which also allowed humans to walk from Asia to North America. In postglacial times the *taranetzi* char dispersed from its refuge to both Asia and North America, maintaining its identity and subspecies status. It coexists with both the southern and northern subspecies of Dolly Varden, and, as far as we know, its distribution does not overlap with that of the subspecies *erythrinus.* The subspecies name *taranetzi* was first used to describe this form of Arctic char from the Chukchi Peninsula.

The evolution and diversification of the Arctic char is very complex. Attempts to unravel this species complex through modern genetic analysis and to better delineate species and subspecies is an ongoing process, one that will probably continue indefinitely. In particular, one organization, the International Society of Arctic Char Fanatics, has been established at the Institute of Freshwater Research, Drottningholm, Sweden, to promote the international exchange of information. However, no general consensus is likely to be reached in the foreseeable future among international char devotees, whose strong opinions are based on different philosophies of classification.

CONSERVATION   Particularly in the southern parts of their range, Arctic char are susceptible to extinction through pollution that depletes oxygen in the deeper zones of lakes and by introductions of nonnative species. In the nineteenth century the Rangeley Lakes char was abundant and sustained commercial and subsistence fisheries, but the bluebacks of all of the Rangeley Lakes became extinct in the early 1900s after Atlantic salmon and smelt were introduced. In Sunapee Lake and two other lakes in New Hampshire and Vermont, the Sunapee char became extinct after lake trout were introduced.

A problem facing at least some populations of Arctic char concerns the fact that they are highly esteemed for their excellent flavor. In the seventeenth century, once a market for Arctic char developed in London, the char population in Lake Windermere, in the English Lake District, was rapidly depleted. Historically, anadromous Arctic char were a major source of food for the Inuit of the Arctic regions of Canada. When human population was sparse and people took char mainly with hand-crafted spears, overexploitation was not a problem. However, an increasing human population that can now sell to an expanding export market uses motorized boats and sleds and nylon gill nets. These methods can rapidly overexploit Arctic char populations and reduce them to a small fraction of their prior abundance.

As with lake trout, which also have a long life span consisting of three- or four-year intervals between spawning and a low annual production or replacement rate, Arctic char populations of the Arctic region are extremely susceptible to overfishing. Consider this highly simplified scenario, based on a synthesis of what is known of the size-age structure of anadromous populations of Arctic char: An annual run from the sea into a river consists of fish from 10 to 20 years old. Of these, no more than one-third will spawn. Maximum size of about 15 pounds (6.8 kg) is attained by char of 16 to 20 years of age. If the annual rate of natural mortality of an unfished population averages 15 percent, and there are 1,000 10-year-old fish in the run, the total number of 10- to 20-year-old char would be more than 6,000 and include about 1,300 of the largest size group of 16 to 20 years of age. If this population is exploited at an annual rate of 45 percent, the total annual mortality would be 60 percent (15 percent natural, 45 percent fishing). At a 60 percent annual mortality rate, this hypothetical population would "crash" within a few years. Fewer than 10 char would exceed 15 years of age. Many years without fishing would be needed before the abundance of this population would be restored. This hypothetical scenario has been found time and again to accurately reflect the actual consequences of exposing anadromous Arctic char populations to a rapid increase in rates of exploitation. Fortunately, unlike a hydropower dam that blocks a spawning run, overfishing is a problem that can be reversed by imposing restrictions and by dispersing fisheries so that exploited populations are given several years of "rest" between exploitation.

The highest value of wild Arctic char is manifested in sport fisheries, where anglers spend considerable amounts of money to be flown to a remote river to fish for large char. Most of the Arctic char sport fisheries are "catch-and-release," so that all char caught are released.

Arctic char are becoming increasingly popular as a gourmet food fish in the United States. This greater demand can be supplied only by cage-cultured Arctic char, as with the Atlantic salmon and the various Pacific salmon. To date, the efficiency of the "farming" of char, which is newer and on a much smaller scale, has not matched that of salmon culture. One problem in marine waters has been that Arctic char (like brook trout and Dolly Varden) evidently have an annual physiological rhythm that, regardless of the temperature of the water, causes the char to become impaired and suffer high mortality when they are held in saline water through the winter. There is considerable intraspecific variation, however, among different populations of Arctic char in the degree of winter impairment.

As demand for Arctic char increases and as selected, domesticated strains of char are developed to increase the efficiency and economics of cultured char production, Arctic char will become a more common menu offering. Depending on a population's diet, the flesh color of the Arctic char can range from white to vivid red; those that are marketed in North America have flesh that is typically deep red, as red as that of the sockeye salmon.

In the southern parts of the range in Europe and in New England, the cold-adapted niche of Arctic char has become squeezed into the deeper, colder zones of lakes during the warmer, postglacial period. In Europe, brown trout typically occupy the other, warmer habitat zones; in North America, the brook trout fills this niche. Under these conditions, relict Arctic char populations are vulnerable to extinction from pollution that increases nutrients in lakes, which results in oxygen depletion in the deep zones, and from the introduction of nonnative species.

Loch Leven, Scotland, lost its char in the 1830s after agriculture developed in its watershed, though the brown trout of Loch Leven continued to flourish, as they are not dependent on deep-water habitat. Many other char populations of Great Britain, Ireland, and on the European mainland have become extinct or have been reduced to small remnant populations.

In New England, three of the four original populations of char that were considered to be Sunapee trout—in Sunapee Lake and Dan's Hole Pond in New Hampshire, and Averill Pond, Vermont—became extinct after lake trout were introduced. The remaining population of Sunapee char, in Floods Pond, Maine, persisted because no lake trout were introduced into Floods Pond. However, Floods Pond serves as the water supply for the city of Bangor. In dry years, and because of an increasing demand for water in general, the level of Floods Pond can be drawn down during the fall spawning season, exposing the only natural spawning site. An artificial spawning bed has been created in deeper water to help ensure the continued existence of the char of Floods Pond.

In the 1920s, eggs of the Sunapee Lake char were shipped to Idaho. The resulting fry were stocked into five lakes in the Sawtooth Mountains. Brook trout were later stocked, and only one population is known to have persisted, but it includes brook trout × Sunapee char hybrids. In this cold mountain lake in Idaho, unlike the conditions in most New England lakes, the Sunapee char reach a greater length— to 18 to 19 inches (46–48 cm)—than the brook trout, which grow to only 9 to 10 inches (23–25 cm).

The most abundant populations of the Maine blueback form of *S. a. oquassa* occurred in the Rangeley Lakes. In the late nineteenth century, Atlantic salmon and smelt were introduced, and the blueback char was extinct in all of the Rangeley Lakes by the early 1900s. Several other blueback populations persisted in inland lakes in Maine, and biologists have made some transplants to establish new populations.

In the modern era of increased environmental awareness and appreciation of nature's biodiversity, the remaining relict populations of Arctic char are regarded as a precious part of our natural heritage that should be protected from further tampering.

Dolly Varden
Salvelinus malma

Dolly Varden
Salvelinus malma

Dolly Varden
SPAWNING MALE

14–18"

The Dolly Varden is also called Dolly Varden trout and Dolly Varden char. Listing the many other common names for the species that have appeared in popular and scientific literature would only be confusing, for those names—as well as the name Dolly Varden itself—reflect the considerable historical complexity of the search for the true identities of the three distinct species we now call Dolly Varden, bull trout, and Arctic char. All three share characteristics in some areas and at some stage of their life history that can make them nearly indistinguishable.

As one example, for many years a "Dolly Varden" of 32 pounds (14.5 kg) from Lake Pend Oreille, in Idaho, was recognized as the world record. We now know that Dolly Varden do not occur in the Columbia River basin, and in 1978, when the bull trout was recognized as a separate species, the former world-record "Dolly Varden" became the world-record bull trout. In another instance, the former Alaska state record for Arctic char (19 lb/8.6 kg) was, in reality, a Dolly Varden, and now that 19-pound fish from Alaska is the world-record Dolly Varden.

The story of how this fish came to be known as Dolly Varden is another tale of misidentification. Dolly Varden is a coquettish character from the 1841 novel *Barnaby Rudge* by Charles Dickens. In this now rather obscure novel, the young woman named Dolly Varden favors brightly colored dresses, "the very pink and pattern of good looks." Subsequently, this character inspired popular patterns of colorful cloth that were milled for dressmaking and called Dolly Varden.

DOLLY VARDEN

SCIENTIFIC NAME
Salvelinus malma

OTHER COMMON NAMES
Dolly Varden trout, Dolly Varden char

HABITAT
Deep runs and pools of streams and rivers; lakes; nearshore marine waters

LENGTH AND WEIGHT
4–5" (10–13 cm) and 1 oz (28 g) in small streams; typically 14–18" (36–46 cm) and 1–2½ lb (0.45–1.1 kg) in rivers; typical maximum 15–20 lb (6.8–9.1 kg); angler record 19¼ lb (8.7 kg)

LIFE SPAN
7–8 years; maximum 10–12 years

DIET
Aquatic and terrestrial invertebrates including snails; salmon eggs in fresh water; fishes and large invertebrates in salt water

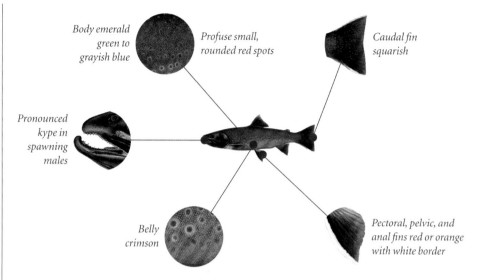

Body emerald green to grayish blue

Profuse small, rounded red spots

Caudal fin squarish

Pronounced kype in spawning males

Belly crimson

Pectoral, pelvic, and anal fins red or orange with white border

SPAWNING MALE

In 1872, Livingston Stone mentioned that anglers from Soda Springs Lodge came to the McCloud River in California to catch large "salmon-trout," which they called Dolly Varden. However, the native char in the McCloud River is the bull trout, so it is highly unlikely that the colorful fish would have been what we know today as Dolly Varden. Nevertheless, the name has persisted as the common name for *S. malma* and it is appropriate of this beautifully colored and often misidentified fish.

Identifications in media photos commonly confuse the Dolly Varden, the bull trout, and the Arctic char, as do submissions for records to the International Game Fish Association. New records continue to be submitted, genetic analysis is ongoing, and the Dolly Varden's complete distribution is yet to be determined. There is still much to be understood about this species.

DESCRIPTION There are two quite distinct forms, or subspecies, of Dolly Varden. The northern subspecies occurs from the Alaska Peninsula northward in North America and from the Kamchatka Peninsula northward in Asia. The southern subspecies occurs in North America south from the Alaska Peninsula to Puget Sound, and in Asia south of Kamchatka to Hokkaido, Japan.

Typical gill raker counts are about 16 to 19 for the southern subspecies and 20 to 24 for the northern. Vertebrae counts are generally in the range of 62 to 65 for the southern subspecies and 66 to 70 for the northern. Both northern and southern Dolly Varden have approximately the same number of pyloric caeca, an average of about 25 to 30. Southern Dolly Varden have 82 chromosomes, and northern have 78.

Where northern Dolly Varden overlap with Arctic char, the Arctic char can be identified by their higher numbers of gill rakers (about 23–30) and pyloric caeca (about 40–50), and by their larger, sparser spots. In marine waters, however, the silvery coloration of the Arctic char can mask or distort the spotting pattern.

Like most char, Dolly Varden can develop brilliant, gaudy colors that can vary greatly depending on the individual's age, sex, and environment. The body, covered with a profusion of small red spots, has a background coloration that can range from emerald green to grayish blue. The ventral region, particularly in large males, can be crimson. The lower fins typically are red or orange, with a white anterior border. In Dolly Varden that live in marine waters the colors on the body, fins, and spots are obscured by the silvery coloration.

BIOLOGY There is no absolute distinction in life histories between northern and southern Dolly Varden. However, while both have anadromous and stream-resident populations, lake-dwelling populations are common in southern Dolly Varden but are very rare in the northern subspecies. Lakes in river basins within the range of northern Dolly Varden are almost always inhabited by Arctic char, and in northern areas Dolly Varden occur mainly as anadromous and stream-resident populations. In these northern areas, Arctic char occur almost exclusively as resident lake populations so the two species rarely come into contact with each other.

Cutthroat trout and sometimes rainbow trout occur in lakes along with southern Dolly Varden. In these lakes, Dolly Varden are mainly restricted to bottom feeding and

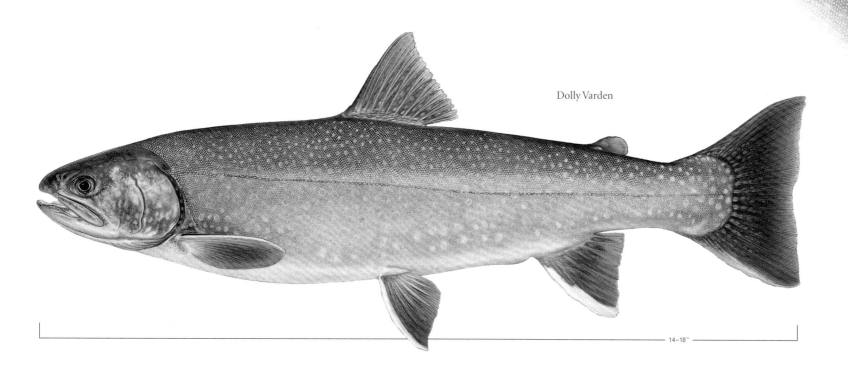

Dolly Varden

14–18″

rainbow or cutthroat trout monopolize the forage organisms in the littoral (shallow, inshore areas) and near-surface zones of the lake. Behaviorally, the southern Dolly Varden is the subdominant species where it occurs in lakes with rainbow or cutthroat trout. In the coastal region of southeastern Alaska, where there are numerous offshore islands, the anadromous form of southern Dolly Varden uses lakes for overwintering.

Dolly Varden typically spawn in streams in September and October, and young hatch the following spring. A stream-resident population, especially if isolated in a head-water above a waterfall, can live out its entire life of seven or eight years while moving upstream or downstream no more than a few hundred yards. Individuals in these small-stream populations typically spawn first

at about four years of age when they are only 4 or 5 inches (10–13 cm) long.

Stream-resident populations spawn annually, but anadromous populations, especially in the range of the northern Dolly Varden, spawn in alternate years. In larger fish and in areas where there is a short growing season, it takes two years to accumulate sufficient energy reserves for a subsequent maturation of the gonads.

Individuals in anadromous populations generally live in rivers for their first three or four years and, in late spring or early summer, migrate to sea for the first time in their fourth or fifth year, when they are typically 5 or 6 inches (13–15 cm) long. After their first summer of marine feeding, southern Dolly Varden enter lakes in late summer to early fall for overwintering; they

do not mature sexually and spawn for the first time until after their second summer of marine feeding. For spawning, Dolly Varden return to their home river drainage. In non-spawning years, they typically overwinter in lakes outside their home watershed. If lakes are not available for overwintering, northern Dolly Varden utilize sections of rivers influenced by springs or groundwater as a refuge until the next year's ocean migration.

Spawning runs of anadromous Dolly Varden returning to their home waters are made up predominantly of first-spawning fish (about 80 percent); about 20 percent of the run is made up of fish spawning for a second or, rarely, a third time.

The typical size range in fish returning to spawn is about 14 to 18 inches (36–46 cm), but individuals of some populations can attain a much larger size. The largest Dolly Varden are from anadromous populations of the Kivalina, Wulik, and Noatak Rivers north of the Seward Peninsula near the northern perimeter of Kotzebue Sound, Alaska. These Dolly Varden can reach maximum sizes in the 15- to 20-pound (6.8–9.1 kg) range; the angler-caught record Dolly Varden, caught in 1998, is 19 pounds, 4 ounces (8.7 kg).

Research on Dolly Varden of the Kivalina, Wulik, and Noatak Rivers has revealed some previously unknown aspects of the species' life history. Anadromous Dolly Varden foraging along the southeastern Alaskan coast and associated islands may travel more than 100 circuitous miles (160 km) but, based on our current knowledge, they do not venture far offshore. By contrast, Dolly Varden that were tagged for identification purposes in these three rivers of northwestern Alaska were later found overwintering far up the Anadyr River in the Russian Far East. From their home waters, these Dolly Varden would have had to move westward in the Chukchi Sea, then south through the Bering Strait into the Bering Sea, west to the Anadyr River, and upstream for overwintering, a distance of 1,000 miles (1,600 km) or more.

In marine waters, Dolly Varden forage opportunistically on large crustaceans and a variety of small fishes. In fresh water, Dolly Varden feed on invertebrates, mainly insects, but will consume snails when available. Dolly Varden are more benthic, or bottom-oriented, in their feeding compared to cutthroat and rainbow trout.

In streams with spawning runs of salmon, Dolly Varden will feed on salmon eggs that become available when successive waves of spawning salmon disturb previous redds. Dolly Varden also feed on bits of flesh from disintegrating salmon carcasses and occasionally prey on salmon fry, although they are not a serious predator. Studies of predation on juvenile salmon show that, in a ranking of salmon predators, the Dolly Varden is a distant third behind cutthroat trout and yearling coho salmon.

As noted, great confusion has attended biologists' attempts to distinguish between the bull trout, the Arctic char, and the Dolly Varden. In salmon rivers, the true Dolly Varden is more a scavenger than a predator. However, for two decades in the early twentieth century it was persecuted because it was thought to be a predator on commercially valuable young salmon. From 1921 to 1939 officials in Alaska paid a bounty ranging from 2 to 5 cents for tails of Dolly Varden in the belief that for each one killed, hundreds of young salmon would be saved. The goal was the destruction of the Dolly Varden as a species, which, it was thought, would greatly increase the survival of juvenile salmon. Today we know that Dolly Varden are not highly predatory and that, in fact, bull trout do not occur in Alaskan salmon rivers. That foolish bounty, which resulted in more than 6 million tails being turned in for payment, was finally ended in 1939 when 20,000 bounty-paid tails were critically examined: 71 percent came from coho salmon, 19 percent from rainbow trout, and only 10 percent from Dolly Varden.

DISTRIBUTION   The sorting and identification of Dolly Varden, bull trout, and Arctic char populations is an ongoing process. In one example, until recently the range of the Dolly Varden was given as eastward in Arctic Ocean drainages up to but not including the Mackenzie River. But, after genetic analysis of char in the Peel River drainage, a major tributary to the Mackenzie, near its mouth, fish previously considered to be Arctic char turned out to be Dolly Varden. In fact, until the 1980s and even into the 1990s much of published scientific literature classified the northern subspecies of Dolly Varden as Arctic char. As it turned out, the Alaskan state angling records for Arctic char were, in reality, Dolly Varden from the Wulik, Kivalina, and Noatak River populations.

The northern Dolly Varden occurs—predominantly as anadromous populations—on both sides of the Alaska Peninsula northward around Alaska, north of the Alaska Range, to the Peel River of the Mackenzie River basin, in Canada. Northern Dolly Varden also occur in at least some parts of the Susitna River basin, which is tributary to Cook Inlet of the Gulf of Alaska south of the Alaska Peninsula. Stream-resident populations in the Arctic are limited to rivers influenced by springs and groundwater that provide overwintering habitat.

In Asia, northern Dolly Varden occur in Kamchatka (the type locality for the name *malma*) northward around the Chukchi Peninsula to Chaun Bay. The precise demarcation between the distribution of northern and southern Dolly Varden is yet to be

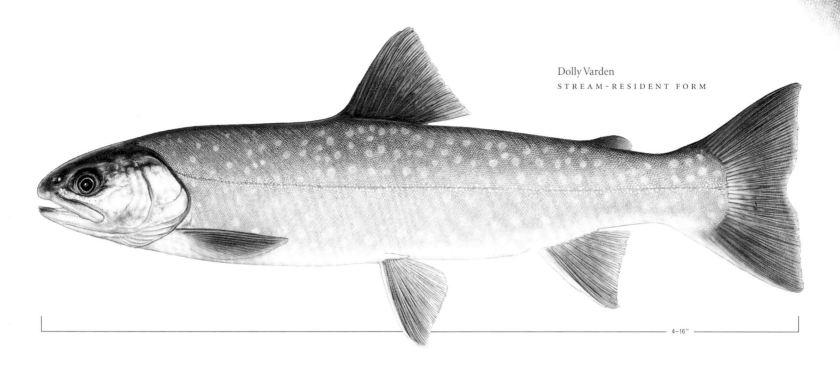

Dolly Varden
STREAM-RESIDENT FORM

4–16"

determined, especially in regard to possible areas of overlap. The basic question is whether there are any areas where northern and southern Dolly Varden coexist with reproductive isolation.

The southern Dolly Varden occurs south of the Alaska Peninsula along the coast of southeastern Alaska and British Columbia to tributaries to Puget Sound. Inland, populations of southern Dolly Varden occur sporadically in headwater areas of the Yukon and Mackenzie River basins. These inland distributions are the result of headwater transfers from coastal drainages.

Southern Dolly Varden are found on all the islands of southeastern Alaska and British Columbia large enough to have perennial streams. Distribution also includes islands, such as Kodiak Island, south of the Alaska Peninsula, and numerous islands in the

Aleutian chain. In Asia, distribution is more or less continuous from the Aleutian Islands to the Commander Islands and south along the Kuril Islands to Hokkaido. Dolly Varden also occur on Sakhalin Island and the Asiatic mainland from south of the Amur River southward to Korea.

Anadromous, stream-resident, and lacustrine life history forms are all represented throughout most of the range of the southern Dolly Varden. Because of the confusion of this species with the bull trout, the southern limit of anadromous populations in North America is not yet documented. Large, silvery char known from Puget Sound that run up tributary rivers are probably bull trout. Inland, Dolly Varden in the Puget Sound basin appear to be all stream-resident populations.

There is an intriguing possibility that Dolly Varden historically occurred in the

McCloud River with bull trout. This is based on Ted Cavender's examination in 1978 of museum specimens during his study to demonstrate that bull trout and Dolly Varden are two separate species, as discussed above in the bull trout account. The fish collection of the U.S. National Museum contains five silvery specimens, in poor condition, listed as from the McCloud River, in California; they are assumed to have been collected by Livingston Stone in the early 1870s during the time he operated the U.S. Fish Commission's salmon hatchery on the McCloud. But in the nineteenth century, shipments of western fish collections to eastern museums were frequently mixed and mislabeled. Cavender identified the specimens as Dolly Varden and believed the silvery coloration indicated they had recently returned from the sea. It is highly improbable that Dolly Varden,

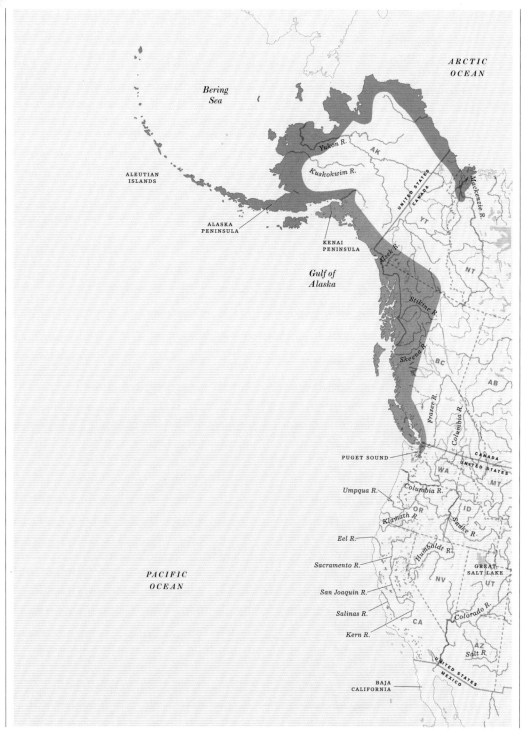

which are even less tolerant of warmer water (about 60 °F, or 15 °C, and higher) than bull trout, could have existed as an anadromous population that migrated through the lower Sacramento River and San Francisco Bay. If a Dolly Varden ancestor reached the McCloud River during the last glacial period, it would be expected that other remnant populations would have historically occurred south of Puget Sound, such as in the vast Columbia River basin. The detailed reports of Livingston Stone on the McCloud River give no indication that more than a single species of char occurred in the McCloud River in the 1870s. The Wintun tribe of Native Americans called the char found in the McCloud River *wye-dar-deekit*. Anglers called them Dolly Varden but it is now known they were, in fact, bull trout.

EVOLUTION AND CLASSIFICATION

Dolly Varden and Arctic char appear to represent a branching in an evolutionary lineage of char after a common ancestor separated from the bull trout–white-spotted char evolutionary line. This may have occurred in early Pleistocene times, or more than 1 million years ago. Southern Dolly Varden have a total number of 82 chromosomes and northern Dolly Varden and Arctic char have a total of 78. This might indicate that the northern Dolly Varden is more closely related to the Arctic char than it is to the southern Dolly Varden, or that the reduction from 82 to 78 chromosomes occurred independently in both the northern

The Dolly Varden is separated into two distinct populations, northern (purple) and southern (gray).

Dolly Varden and the line leading to Arctic char. Again, there is much to learn about the evolution of these fish.

There is no reasonable doubt that the Dolly Varden is a valid biological species. Anadromous populations of southern Dolly Varden coexist with resident lacustrine populations of Arctic char in lakes on Kodiak Island. The northern Dolly Varden (typically as anadromous populations) coexists with resident lake populations of Arctic char in virtually all river basins from the Alaska Peninsula to the Mackenzie River.

The life histories of both northern and southern Dolly Varden differ from Arctic char to the extent that the two species do not spawn at the same time in the same place. They maintain reproductive isolation. No hybrids between Dolly Varden and Arctic char are known; however, because of identity confusion, hybrids likely would be overlooked if they did exist.

"Salmo malma" was described by Johann Walbaum in 1792 and, like the scientific names for Pacific salmon and rainbow trout, was based on the colloquial name used by the native people of western Kamchatka. (The Kamchatkan malma is essentially identical to the northern Dolly Varden of North America.) Therefore, if subspecies status is given to northern and southern Dolly Varden, the northern Dolly Varden is Salvelinus malma malma.

The subspecies name for southern Dolly Varden, which would become the species name if the southern form is elevated from a subspecies to a full species, is not so clear. The southern Dolly Varden of Asia is highly similar to the southern Dolly Varden of North America. In this regard, a single subspecies name could justifiably be applied to both Asian and North American populations similar to S. m. malma for the northern form of North America and Asia.

The oldest scientific name that might apply to southern Dolly Varden as a species or a subspecies is "Salmo curilus," a name published in 1811 for char of the Kuril Islands. A problem with the name curilus is that both Dolly Varden and white-spotted char occur in the Kuril Islands, its potential type locality, and it is not known for which species curilus was intended. The earliest scientific name that might apply to the southern Dolly Varden of North America is "Salmo lordi," a name published in 1866 for a char from the Skagit River of Washington and British Columbia. The Skagit River has both bull trout and Dolly Varden. The 1866 description of lordi cannot be positively identified as to species, but S. malma lordi is commonly used in the literature for the southern Dolly Varden of North America. The Russian literature recognizes their southern Dolly Varden with the tongue-twisting name of S. malma krascheninnikovi, a name with a publication date of 1939. As is only too obvious, the correct scientific name for southern Dolly Varden is not a clear-cut issue.

CONSERVATION   During the past 30 years or so, the public perception and agency attitudes concerning Dolly Varden have undergone an astonishing transformation. The Dolly Varden's image has changed from that of a despised predator whose extermination would increase the abundance of "better" species of trout and salmon to that of a beautiful fish that needs to be maintained as an integral part of its ecosystem.

In Alaska, where a 20-year extermination campaign was waged with bounty payments, the Dolly Varden is now managed as a popular sport fish, and anadromous Dolly Varden are important in the subsistence fisheries of many Inuit villages of Alaska and Canada.

However, the Dolly Varden is highly susceptible to angler catch and overexploitation. In popular fishing waters around Juneau, Alaska, over an eight-year period, as fishing pressure increased, the catch rate of Dolly Varden declined by twentyfold (from 4 to 0.2 fish per hour of angling). The Alaskan Board of Fisheries closed these "overfished" waters to angling to allow the populations to recover. Other popular sport fisheries for Dolly Varden are managed with restrictive regulations, such as limiting the take to two fish per day.

Fortunately, overfishing in sport and subsistence fisheries is not an irreversible threat comparable to environmental alteration and habitat destruction. It can be avoided with sound fishing regulations based on an understanding of life histories and the size-age structures of populations. Where overexploitation occurs, it can be corrected in the short term with proper catch regulations if the environment on which Dolly Varden populations depend remains intact.

Like bull trout, Dolly Varden are temperature-sensitive, preferring temperatures lower than 55 °F (13 °C) and avoiding waters where temperatures reach 60 °F (15 °C) or higher. They also require streams with low sediment loads for successful spawning. Logging, road construction, and urbanization can eliminate or greatly reduce the abundance of Dolly Varden. Watersheds in most of the range of the southern Dolly Varden, in southeastern Alaska and British Columbia, remain intact or have recovered from past logging operations that were unregulated in relation to environmental protection. Badly degraded watersheds and extinctions of populations are localized problems that are in need of correction, but these problems do not pose a broadscale threat throughout the range of the southern Dolly Varden.

No Dolly Varden population is listed under the Endangered Species Act. The watersheds in the range of the northern Dolly Varden are mostly remote from civilization, though some remote watersheds have felt the impact of energy exploration and development, such as the construction of oil fields and the pipeline at Prudhoe Bay, Alaska. Overall, however, throughout its range, the distribution and abundance of the Dolly Varden has not suffered significant decline comparable to those of bull trout and cutthroat trout. One reason is that in the 48 contiguous states, Dolly Varden occur in only a few streams tributary to Puget Sound in Washington and thus have not been exposed to human-induced impacts on the scale that has led to the decline of the bull trout and the cutthroat trout.

Other Salmonids
of North America

Arctic Grayling
Thymallus arcticus

Arctic Grayling
Thymallus arcticus

Arctic Grayling

Its large, sail-like dorsal fin makes the grayling entirely distinct from trout, salmon, char, and whitefishes. Several other characteristics set the graylings (subfamily Thymallinae) off from the other subfamilies of the family Salmonidae: the trout and salmon (Salmoninae) and the whitefishes (Coregoninae). The Thymallinae contains four recognized species worldwide. Two species have restricted distributions in Asia, and two others—the European and the Arctic grayling—are widely distributed.

The genus name *Thymallus* is associated with the herb thyme. According to European folklore, grayling eat "water thyme" and have a thyme-like odor. In reality, it takes considerable imagination to sense an odor of thyme on or in a grayling.

Only the Arctic grayling occurs in North America. The Montana grayling and the extinct Michigan grayling represent populations that live in the southernmost portion of the species' range, long isolated from northern populations.

Like lake trout, grayling cannot live in water in which the salinity is more than about 7 to 8 parts per thousand of salt. As a result, their distribution is limited to freshwater routes of dispersal.

DESCRIPTION   Compared to trout and salmon, Arctic grayling have smaller mouths with tiny teeth, larger scales (from about 80 to 98 in the lateral line), and a deeply forked tail. Coloration can range from iridescent blues and lavender to dark, blackish blues. The dorsal fin has rows of pink and lavender spots and a red or

ARCTIC GRAYLING

SCIENTIFIC NAME
Thymallus arcticus

OTHER COMMON NAMES
Montana grayling (southern populations);
Michigan grayling (extinct)

HABITAT
Clear, cold streams and rivers; lakes

LENGTH AND WEIGHT
11–12" (28–30 cm) and 8–11 oz (227–312 g); southern populations typical maximum 15" (38 cm) and 1 lb (0.45 kg); northern populations typical maximum 24" (61 cm) and 4 lb (1.8 kg); angler record 30" (76 cm) and 5 lb, 15 oz (2.7 kg)

LIFE SPAN
4–5 years for southern populations; 10–11 for northern populations; maximum known 18 years

DIET
Aquatic and terrestrial invertebrates, salmon eggs, and fishes

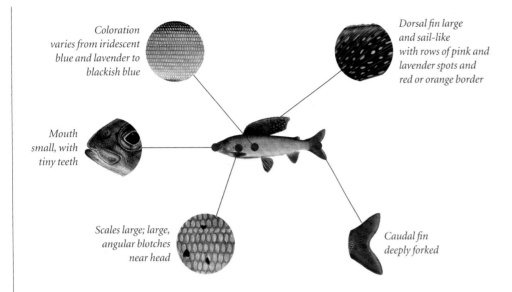

Coloration varies from iridescent blue and lavender to blackish blue

Dorsal fin large and sail-like with rows of pink and lavender spots and red or orange border

Mouth small, with tiny teeth

Scales large; large, angular blotches near head

Caudal fin deeply forked

orange border. Spots, which mainly occur on the body toward the head, appear as large, angular blotches.

The European grayling closely resembles the Arctic grayling. The main distinguishing characteristic is the number of gill rakers: typically 21 to 28 in European grayling and 16 to 21 in Arctic grayling. The teeth on the jaws of European grayling tend to be even more feeble than in Arctic grayling.

The only strictly lake-adapted grayling is the Kosogol grayling whose distribution is restricted to Lake Kosogol, a large lake in the northernmost part of Mongolia. This grayling is distinguished by its high number of gill rakers, which range from 26 to 32.

The most distinct grayling species is the Mongolian grayling of internal drainages of northwestern Mongolia (the Mongolian "Great Basin"). Compared to other graylings, the Mongolian grayling has a smaller dorsal fin, more well-developed teeth, and a larger mouth, and is more trout-like in

appearance. The most predatory grayling in its feeding, it attains the largest size, to about 10 pounds (4.5 kg).

BIOLOGY Mainly an insectivore, the Arctic grayling feeds on aquatic and terrestrial insects on or near the surface in streams and in shallow areas of lakes. However, like most salmonid fishes, the grayling feeds opportunistically on available food. In the northern parts of the species' range, Arctic grayling living in rivers where salmon spawn will consume salmon eggs and small juvenile salmon.

In northern regions, grayling can live 10 or 11 years. Under optimal feeding conditions, they can attain a maximum size of about 24 inches (61 cm) and 4 pounds (1.8 kg). The world-record Arctic grayling—about 30 inches (76 cm) long and weighing 5 pounds, 15 ounces (2.7 kg)—was caught from the Katseyedie River, a tributary to Great Bear Lake, Canada, in 1967.

The southern population known as the Montana grayling has a shorter life span, rarely more than four or five years, and it rarely exceeds about 15 inches (38 cm) in length and 1 pound (0.45 kg) in weight.

Grayling spawn in the spring, from April to June, according to water temperature. Spawning begins when water temperature is in the range of 45 to 50 °F (7.5–10 °C). Like lake trout, grayling do not construct a redd; instead, they spawn over gravel and rocky areas, and the eggs drop between crevices.

The mature eggs of grayling are about $\frac{1}{10}$ inch (2.5 mm) in diameter, less than half the diameter of trout and salmon eggs, and graylings lay a proportionally smaller volume of eggs. However, grayling have a higher relative fecundity than trout and salmon: about 5,000 to 6,000 eggs per pound of female body weight (11,000–13,000 eggs per kg) versus an average of 800 to 1,000 eggs per pound of female trout and salmon (1,800–2,200 eggs per kg). Compared to trout and salmon, grayling embryos have more rapid development, hatching after about 15 days at a water temperature of about 50 °F (10 °C), versus about 30 days for spring-spawning rainbow and cutthroat trout.

Newly hatched grayling are about $\frac{3}{10}$ inch (8 mm) in length, versus about $\frac{3}{4}$ inch (20 mm) in trout and salmon, and they absorb the yolk sac and begin active feeding about 8 days after hatching, versus 20 to 30 days in trout and salmon. This rapid early development allows grayling to live in ponds and lakes and to successfully reproduce in small, ephemeral tributary streams that may flow for only five or six weeks during the spring.

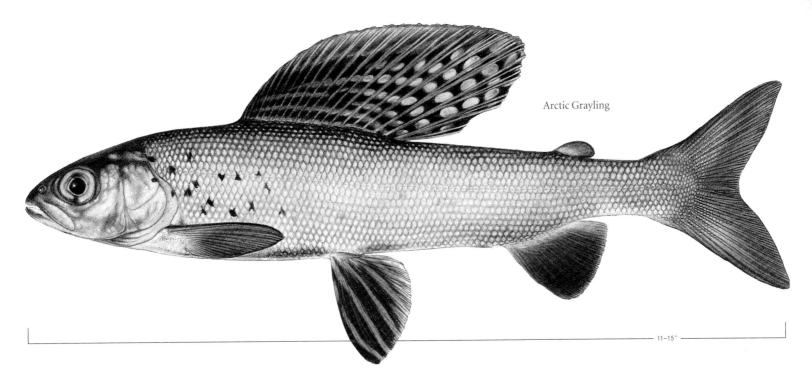

Arctic Grayling

11–15"

DISTRIBUTION   In North America, Arctic grayling occur in most of Alaska and northwestern Canada eastward to drainages tributary to the northern part of western Hudson Bay. Grayling occur throughout the vast Yukon and Mackenzie River basins. Because grayling cannot disperse in marine waters, they are absent from coastal rivers of southeastern Alaska and British Columbia, except for the Stikine River, where grayling gained access via a stream transfer from the Mackenzie basin. Grayling are native to the upper Missouri River basin above Great Falls, Montana.

It is assumed that grayling occurred in western Hudson Bay drainages prior to the last glaciation. During glaciation, which completely covered the Hudson Bay region and almost all of Canada, some grayling moved southward and gained access to the upper Missouri basin. As the glaciers retreated, grayling returned to Hudson Bay from northern glacial refugia but only occupied drainages to about halfway down the west side of the bay.

In postglacial times, a large geographical gap remained between the grayling of Canada and the Montana grayling of the upper Missouri basin. As the melting glaciers retreated northward, a connection formed between the upper Missouri basin and the newly formed Great Lakes, allowing grayling access to the Great Lakes, where they persisted into historical times—though only in Michigan—as the Michigan grayling.

In Montana, the grayling coexisted with cutthroat trout, but grayling distribution was less ubiquitous than that of the cutthroat.

Arctic grayling are stocked in some western lakes as a sport fish. This strikingly colored specimen is from Zimmerman Lake in Colorado.

In 1805, Lewis and Clark did not encounter grayling until they got to the Beaverhead River. They called the grayling "white trout."

Nonnative brown and rainbow trout have largely replaced grayling in their former habitats in the upper Missouri basin. In Michigan, grayling occurred with brook trout in Otter Creek (tributary to Lake Superior) in the Upper Peninsula and in the Jordan River in the northern part of the Lower Peninsula. South of the Jordan River, in tributaries to Lakes Michigan and Huron, brook trout did not naturally occur. Brook, brown, and rainbow trout were introduced in the late nineteenth century and devastating

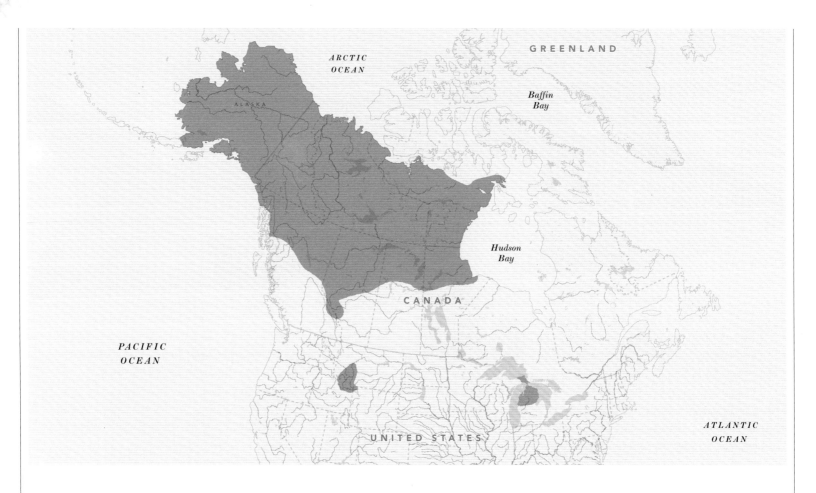

The historic range of Arctic grayling populations in North America includes the Lower and Upper Peninsula of Michigan, the Missouri River basin to above the Great Falls in Montana, and north to a much larger continuous distribution in western Canada and throughout Alaska.

clear-cut logging, beginning in the 1860s, caused the streams to warm and become silted. Grayling rapidly disappeared in Michigan; the Lower Peninsula populations were gone by the early 1900s and the very last of all the Michigan populations of grayling were extinct from their last refuge, Otter Creek, by the mid-1930s.

Montana grayling have long been artificially propagated and widely distributed outside their native range. Populations now occur in many mountain lakes in western states.

In Asia, the Arctic grayling ranges from the Pechora River of northwestern Russia eastward in Arctic Ocean drainages of Siberia, and southward to the Amur River basin, the upper Yalu River of North Korea, and the Kamchatka Peninsula.

EVOLUTION AND CLASSIFICATION

The family Salmonidae represents an array of evolutionarily primitive fishes whose roots extend back into the Cretaceous period, perhaps about 100 million years ago. Since that time, salmonid evolutionary lines have undergone much divergence, radiation, and extinction. A surviving common ancestral evolutionary line eventually initiated divergences that gave rise to the present three subfamilies, probably during the early Cenozoic era, more than 50 million years ago.

Compared to the subfamilies Salmoninae and Coregoninae, Thymallinae contains little diversity: one genus and four species. It appears that there have been considerable extinctions in Thymallinae along the evolutionary pathways that eventually gave rise to the four extant species.

The most divergent, most trout-like grayling is the Mongolian grayling. Despite its predatory feeding and more trout-like appearance, the Mongolian grayling is probably not the primitive ancestral species, but rather a highly specialized grayling. All of its distinctive characteristics are "derived"; that is, they have been modified from the basic evolutionary "plan" of *Thymallus*. For example, the greatly enlarged, predator-like teeth of Mongolian grayling are precisely in the same positions as found in the other species of the genus, but they are greatly enlarged.

The internal drainage basins of northwestern Mongolia have several species of minnows but no relatively large predatory fish, except for the grayling. A logical evolutionary scenario is that a grayling ancestor was the only salmonid species to gain access to the internal basins. Under strong natural selection, modification of typical grayling characteristics occurred so that the Mongolian grayling now fills the niche as the top predator.

As an interesting footnote, a grayling specimen from Mongolia was collected in 1897, preserved in salt, and taken to the British Museum of Natural History. The ichthyologist there was unaware that Mongolian grayling had been described as *T. brevirostris* in 1879, and in 1898 he described a new genus and species, *Phylogephyra altaica.* The genus name indicates a "bridge" between trout and grayling. The locality given for the 1897 specimen—"south slope Altai Mountains on Chinese territory"—adds a bit of mystery to the story. The internal basins of Mongolia where *T. brevirostris* is found drain from the northern slopes of the Altai Mountains. Most of the south-slope rivers drain to the Gobi Desert (to the west, drainages are part of the Arctic Ocean basin). No grayling nor any salmonid species is known to inhabit any river draining to the Gobi Desert. Does the specimen of *"Phylogyphera altaica"* in the British Museum of Natural History represent an even more divergent grayling species? If so, it awaits rediscovery.

CONSERVATION   Arctic grayling at the southern extreme of the range are vulnerable to replacement by nonnative trout and to environmental changes that warm the water, deplete flows in rivers, and increase sediment loads. The Michigan grayling rapidly declined to complete extinction after watersheds were clear-cut and nonnative trout were introduced. The Montana grayling has been largely replaced in its original habitat by brown and rainbow trout. This replace-

ment is enhanced by environmental changes, but it can also occur under pristine environments. For example, the only salmonid species native to the upper Madison River in Yellowstone National Park are (or were) grayling and westslope cutthroat trout. By about 1915, the grayling and cutthroat trout were gone from the upper Madison River, replaced by brown and rainbow trout.

In Montana today, the grayling is a "high profile" species in fisheries programs. Determined efforts by state and federal agencies to protect and restore the native grayling have been under way for several years. A propagation and stocking program maintains grayling populations in many Montana lakes where the species did not occur naturally. Fishing regulations for grayling in Montana are catch-and-release; all grayling caught must be released. On this basis, grayling in Montana can be said to be abundant and widely distributed.

In regard to preserving a range of the original diversity of Montana grayling, however, fluvial populations—those directly descended from grayling that once occupied rivers in the upper Missouri basin—are rare. Recently, the emphasis has been on protecting and restoring fluvial grayling as an important component of the biological legacy of the state.

Mountain Whitefish
Prosopium williamsoni

Mountain Whitefish
Prosopium williamsoni

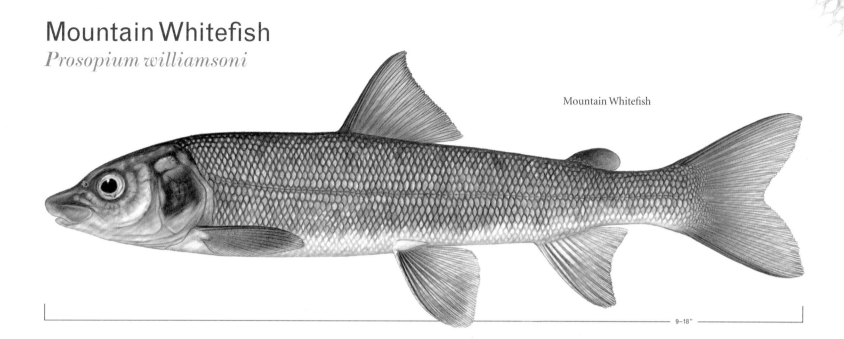

Mountain Whitefish

9–18"

Many anglers who encounter fish actively feeding on the surface of a pool believe they have found the dry-fly angler's dream. The typical response is disappointment when an angler discovers the fish on the end of the line is not a trout, but "merely" a whitefish. Although whitefishes are generally more bottom-oriented, they will feed opportunistically on hatching aquatic insects. Those with a better understanding of the mountain whitefish know they are a species that is to be admired, not dismissed. They are worthy sport fish, can be caught all through the winter months, and are good to eat, especially when smoked.

The mountain whitefish looks somewhat like a sucker and is the most trout-like whitefish in its habitat and feeding. An inhabitant of most of western North America's most popular trout rivers, it is the whitefish species most frequently caught by anglers.

DESCRIPTION The mountain whitefish—with its rounded body form and a small mouth that lacks teeth—typifies the genus *Prosopium,* the most primitive genus of whitefishes. Species in this genus are the only whitefishes in which juveniles have parr marks on the body, as in the subfamily Salmoninae. Also like trout and salmon, *Prosopium* species have a single nostril flap. All other whitefish species have a double nostril flap.

The subfamily Coregoninae consists of about 30 species classified in three genera. In the genus *Prosopium,* there are three widely distributed species of whitefishes, only one of which, the round whitefish, might be confused with the mountain whitefish. The ranges of

MOUNTAIN WHITEFISH

SCIENTIFIC NAME
Prosopium williamsoni

OTHER COMMON NAMES
Whitefish

HABITAT
Streams, rivers, and lakes

LENGTH AND WEIGHT
9–12" (23–30 cm) and 6–11 oz (170–312 g); typical maximum 18" (46 cm) and 2 lb (0.9 kg); angler record 5½ lb (2.5 kg)

LIFE SPAN
8–9 years; maximum known 18 years

DIET
Aquatic and terrestrial invertebrates, fish eggs (including their own), and fishes

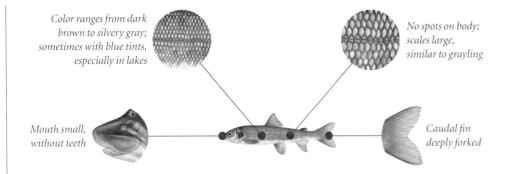

Color ranges from dark brown to silvery gray; sometimes with blue tints, especially in lakes

No spots on body; scales large, similar to grayling

Mouth small, without teeth

Caudal fin deeply forked

the two species are almost mutually exclusive, though there is a small area of overlap in the upper Mackenzie River basin of Canada. The round whitefish has fewer gill rakers, averaging about 17 to 19, versus 20 to 22 in the mountain whitefish.

Whitefishes are not colorful fish, lacking the bright reds, oranges, and golds that are found on cutthroat trout. Body coloration generally ranges from dark brown to silvery gray, though some blue tints may be expressed, especially on whitefish living in lakes. Whitefishes lack spots on the body. Their scales are large, similar to those of grayling. The mountain whitefish typically has 80 to 85 scales in the lateral line.

BIOLOGY   Mountain whitefish spawn in the fall, typically in October and November, but extend into January and February in lake-spawning populations that spawn where winter temperatures are more stable. Embryos develop over the winter, and fry typically hatch in March and April.

Like grayling and lake trout, whitefishes do not dig redds for spawning. The eggs the female releases are fertilized by a male and then disperse into a rocky, gravel substrate selected as a spawning site. Most

populations spawn in streams, but some lake-dwelling populations spawn on the lake bottom in rocky areas with upwelling. Both stream-spawning and lake-spawning populations exist in some large lakes, such as Kootenay Lake, in British Columbia.

Whitefish eggs are small, similar to grayling eggs; variable in size, they average about 1/8 inch (3 mm) in diameter. Relative fecundity is also highly variable, averaging about 5,000 eggs per pound of female body weight (11,000 per kg).

Most whitefish species are specialized to feed on zooplankton and bottom-dwelling organisms in lakes. In a shared habitat, mountain whitefish and trout feed on more or less the same invertebrates, but subtle differences in their diets reduce competition for food. The small mouth of whitefishes limits the size of the food items they can consume, but the inconnu or sheefish, a member of the subfamily Coregoninae, is a large (to 50 pounds/23 kg), predatory species. Also, whitefishes are typically more oriented near the bottom. As noted, mountain white-fish will feed opportunistically on the surface like trout, stimulated by a hatch of aquatic insects, especially in open pools and deep channel areas where the current runs slowly.

Whitefishes are not likely to feed in "pocket water" among boulders in riffles and rapids. In contrast to trout, especially brown trout, mountain whitefish do not seek cover, such as along deep undercut banks, instead preferring deeper water or open channel areas.

In larger river systems, mountain whitefish may exhibit an annual pattern of movement. Feeding is localized to a generally small area in their habitat. In the fall, the fish migrate to sites for spawning, after which they migrate to overwintering sites. In the spring they return to their "home" feeding grounds.

Mountain whitefish and Arctic grayling have similar age-growth characteristics. The whitefish mature at three to six years of age at lengths from about 9 to 12 inches (23–30 cm); in most populations, maximum life span is about eight or nine years. Maximum size is generally about 18 inches (46 cm) and slightly more than 2 pounds (1 kg). The oldest mountain whitefish on record is 18 years old, and the record weight is 5 pounds, 8 ounces (2.5 kg) for a fish caught in the Elbow River, in Alberta (the Hudson Bay basin) in 1995.

DISTRIBUTION   Some species of whitefish in Arctic regions of Asia and North America forage in marine waters. However, all species in the genus *Prosopium* live only in fresh water and their distribution is only via fresh-water routes of dispersal. Ancestral movement between drainage basins came about as the result of interbasin stream transfers.

In North America, the mountain white-fish is a western species. Its southern limits

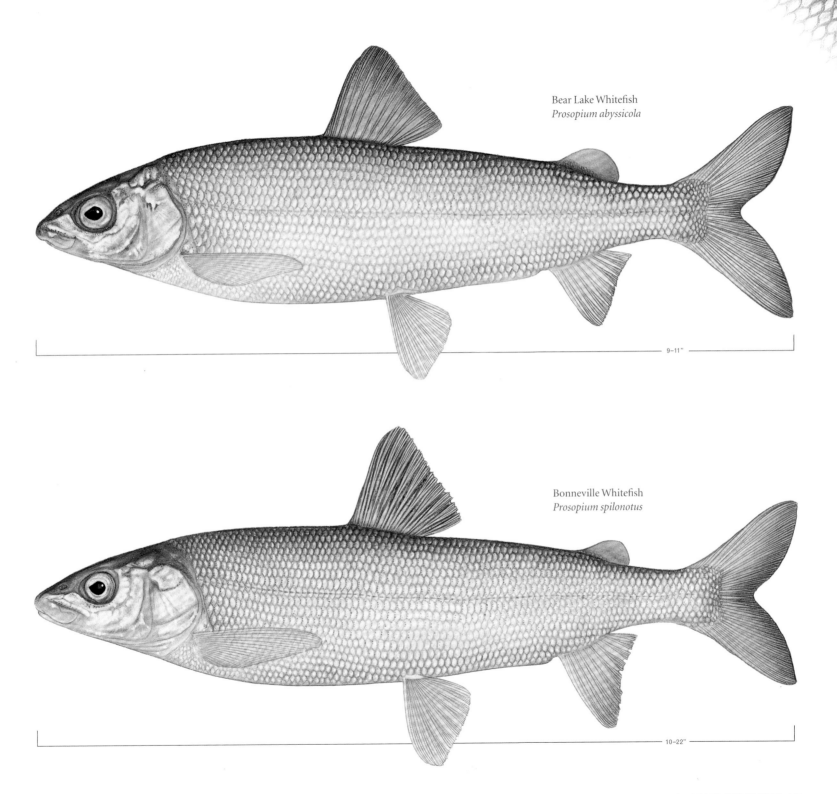

Bear Lake Whitefish
Prosopium abyssicola

9–11"

Bonneville Whitefish
Prosopium spilonotus

10–22"

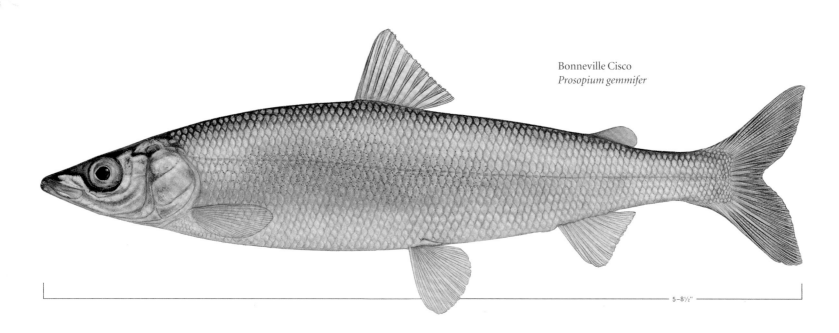

Bonneville Cisco
Prosopium gemmifer

5–8½"

are in the Lahontan and Bonneville basins of the Great Basin and in the Green River drainage of the Colorado River basin. It occurs in the Columbia and Fraser River basins, and reaches its northern limit of distribution in headwater tributaries of the Mackenzie River basin of Canada. It is not native to the Yukon basin nor to Alaska. South of Alaska, mountain whitefish are native to some of the larger Pacific Coast rivers, such as the Stikine, Skeena, Nass, and Bella Coola. It is native to the North and South Saskatchewan Rivers, tributary to Hudson Bay, and in the upper Missouri River basin.

Mountain whitefish distribution in the Missouri basin is more extensive than that of the grayling (and also that of cutthroat trout) as mountain whitefish tolerate warmer and more turbid water than grayling (and

cutthroat trout). Whitefish are native to the Yellowstone River drainage, except for its headwaters above the large barrier falls in Yellowstone National Park. Cutthroat trout entered the Yellowstone drainage from the top, via a stream connection at Two Ocean Pass; the whitefish ancestor entered from the bottom, from the Missouri River.

EVOLUTION AND CLASSIFICATION

Within the whitefishes subfamily, the genus *Coregonus* has "species complexes" similar to that of the Arctic char that have long fueled controversies and diversity of opinions on their evolution and classification. Classification of the species in the genus *Prosopium* is much less controversial. *Prosopium* fossils dated to about 5 million years ago appear to be highly similar to the present mountain and round whitefishes. Thus we might

surmise that *Prosopium* whitefishes are evolutionarily stable—that is, resistant to change through long periods of time. However, three lake-specialized species of *Prosopium* found only in the Bonneville basin's Bear Lake, in Utah and Idaho, indicate that rapid change in morphology and ecology can occur in *Prosopium* under the right conditions and with strong natural selection, in order to fill new niches.

Three of the six recognized species in the genus *Prosopium* occur in a single lake. In a probable scenario, an ancestral mountain whitefish gained access to the Bonneville basin during the last glacial epoch from the Snake River drainage of the Columbia River basin. At its maximum extent, ancient Lake Bonneville had a surface area of about 20,000 square miles (51,800 sq km) and a maximum depth of about 1,100 feet (330 m). In this great

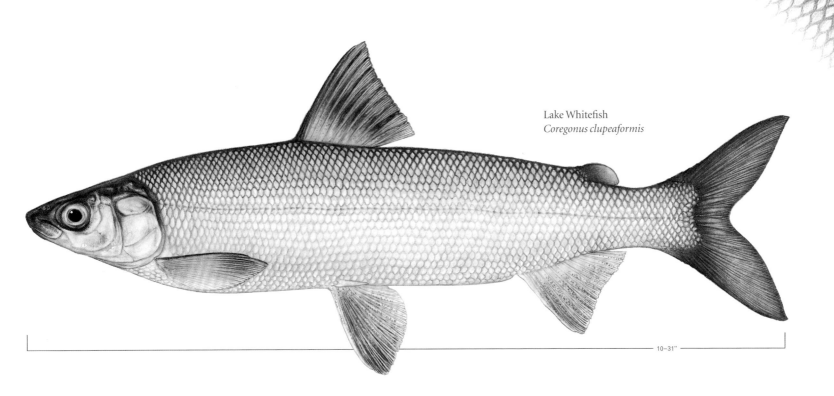

Lake Whitefish
Coregonus clupeaformis

10–31"

lake, there would have been strong natural selection for the ancestral whitefish to diverge to fill unoccupied whitefish niches—deep-water bottom feeder, deep-water pelagic feeder, and open-water pelagic feeder. In postglacial times, Bear Lake was the only body of water in the Bonneville basin with suitable habitat, temperature, and oxygen regimes where these species could persist.

The whitefish fauna of Bear Lake was first described in 1919. At that time, the most distinctive species, the Bonneville "cisco," was believed to be derived from the ciscos of the Great Lakes (pelagic, herring-like whitefish species) and thus was classified in a different genus. There is no doubt, however, that the Bonneville cisco, the Bonneville whitefish, and the Bear Lake whitefish (all endemic only to Bear Lake) are whitefishes of the genus *Prosopium*. All genetic analyses have shown they have extremely close relationships to each other and to mountain whitefish, indicating that their evolutionary divergences from one another and from a common ancestor is a matter of thousands, not millions of years.

A peculiar and little-understood form of diversity has long been known in the mountain whitefish in many areas of its range, especially in the Columbia and Fraser River basins. Along with "normal" mountain whitefish, there is a form with an elongated snout. The whitefish with the elongated snout was described as a new species, *"Coregonus oregonensis,"* in 1911 from the McKenzie River, in Oregon (the Columbia River basin). Impressed by this long-snouted fish, David Starr Jordan created a separate genus, *Irillion,* for it in 1918, as well as the common name "chiselmouthjack."

Then the matter was largely forgotten, until in November 1999, J.D. McPhail of the University of British Columbia, an authority on northern fishes, presented preliminary findings on the long-snouted whitefish at a conference on the ecology and management of northwest salmonids held in Canmore, Alberta.

The long-snouted whitefish has been observed to use its snout to root around in the substrate for feeding on aquatic insect larvae, whereas "normal" whitefish take their food in the drift or on the surface. Genetic analysis of the two forms from the Fraser River basin, in British Columbia, revealed that about half of the long-snouted fish possessed a genetic marker that was absent in all of the "normal" mountain whitefish. The two forms were not hybridizing, at least in the streams where they were sampled.

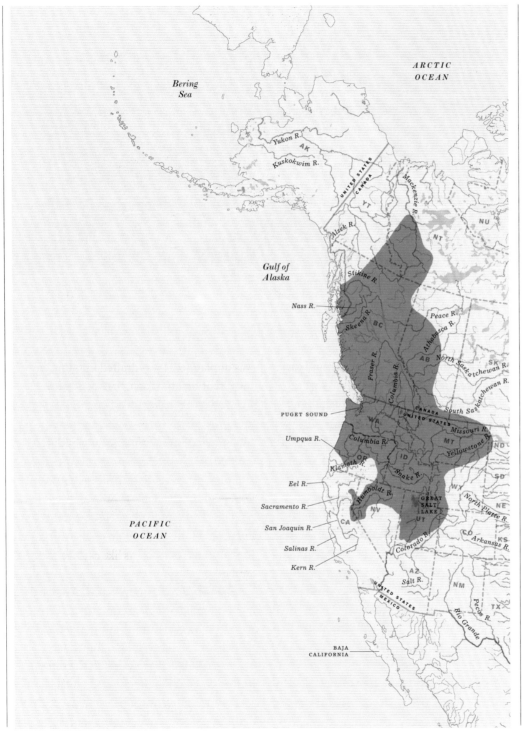

The question is whether all long-snouted whitefish can be traced to a common ancestor, an evolutionary lineage that is distinct from that of the mountain whitefish. If so, then the chiselmouthjack or whatever common name might be used (McPhail calls them "Pinocchios") would be a valid species, *P. oregonensis*. This intriguing phenomenon is worthy of further research.

CONSERVATION   The whitefish fauna of the Great Lakes suffered great declines and extinction from human-induced impacts. Besides the widely distributed "lake herring," seven other species of ciscos have been recognized from the Great Lakes. Four of these are now extinct.

A hardy species, the mountain whitefish occurs in a wide range of habitats and, compared to trout, is more tolerant of warmer, more turbid water. Historically, it has not been generally perceived to be a popular sport fish by anglers or fishery management agencies. Thus there has generally been little expressed concern for its conservation except in the larger context of the conservation of all native biodiversity.

Because larger whitefishes of 12 to 16 inches (30–41 cm) are probably five to eight years of age, a population can be rapidly overexploited with increased fishing pressure. Where such pressure occurs, restrictive regulations, like those used to protect trout populations from overexploitation, should be applied to whitefish. ◂━

The mountain whitefish is a western North American species of the genus Prosopium. *It ranges from the Colorado River basin in the south to the MacKenzie River drainage in northwestern Canada.*

Epilogue

Visits to an old Connecticut millpond are among my earliest memories. The fact that life existed underwater, a completely different kind of world, captivated my imagination. The first fishes I caught on crude, hand-me-down tackle were sunfishes and yellow perch. But to me, trout were the most elegant, mysterious, and most desirable fish. There was only a small window of opportunity to catch a trout in the Rippowam River as it meandered through my neighborhood in Stamford, Connecticut. Stamford was founded in 1641. Early in its history dams were constructed to power mills, and the watershed was converted to agriculture and livestock grazing; numerous industrial enterprises polluted the river, and its native brook trout were gone long before I was born. Each spring, however, enough relatively clean, cold water flowed, and the state fish and game agency would stock a few hundred hatchery brook trout. One spring day, I dangled a worm in a pool below the crumbling mill dam and yanked out a six-inch brook trout, fresh from a hatchery. I was ecstatic. Back then if someone had tried to explain a distinction between wild trout in their native environment and a hatchery-produced imitation, it would have been incomprehensible to me. It would not have dampened my enthusiasm at catching my first trout. I ran home with my precious prize and gently placed it in a pan of water where it revived and swam around to my awe and wonderment. I thought it was the most beautiful thing I had ever seen and I was hooked for life. Ralph Waldo Emerson once wrote that nothing great can be accomplished without enthusiasm and I became a committed trout enthusiast. My transformation to an advocate for wild, native trout was a gradual process. I had no epiphany, no sudden revelation. In the value system of my youth, a trout was a trout, no matter its origin, similar to Gertrude Stein's opinion on roses. Many people might share this notion, but rose fanciers with a deeper understanding of the rose species appreciate and delight in the range of diversity in the various configurations of sizes, shapes, and colors. In a somewhat similar way, those who appreciate distinctions in wines are experiencing the intraspecific diversity found within a single species of grape. Rose fanciers and wine connoisseurs experience pleasure from the varieties of roses and grapes based on learning and experience.

My formal learning or higher education was unplanned: I was drafted into the Army. I was sent first to Japan, then to Korea. Along with a rifle, I carried a fly rod. In my free time, I explored mountain streams of Japan where I encountered two fish that were new to me: the *yamame* (stream-resident form of masu salmon) and the *iwana* (white-spotted char). What were these beautiful little fish that lived in such lovely mountain valleys? How are they related to North American species? It was like catching my first trout all over again: the wonderment, curiosity, and enthusiasm to learn more.

When I was discharged from the Army, I was unemployed and I went to the Veterans Administration for testing and counseling. When I was told I could go to college and pursue my interest to learn more about fishes in general—trout, salmon, and char in particular—I found it difficult to believe.

When nearing graduation from the University of Connecticut in 1957 (where, for an honors project, I published a paper on the freshwater fishes of Connecticut, an update of the last such work published in 1844), I was contacted by Professor Paul Needham of the University of California, Berkeley. Needham had a grant to continue his study of rainbow and cutthroat trout. He offered me a position as his graduate research assistant for the study. If I accepted, I would go to California, and immediately we would leave on a trip through the western states, western Canada, and Alaska to collect specimens (mostly with a fly rod). A fantasy dream come true.

At the time, little was known about cutthroat trout, except that the stocking of nonnative trout had largely replaced them throughout their native range. Thus, cutthroat trout became my first focus of attention. What was the total diversity in the species? How should this diversity be classified into subspecies? How many subspecies were extinct? What was the status of the extant diversity?

Professor Needham had established a research station on Sagehen Creek in the Sierra Nevada of eastern California. Research at the station focused on demonstrating that wild trout in a good environment could sustain a quality fishery without the stocking of hatchery trout. The brook, brown, and rainbow trout of Sagehen Creek were "wild" trout, in that they were self-sustaining, but they were not native trout. The native trout of Sagehen Creek was the Lahontan cutthroat trout, which, at the time, was thought to be extinct throughout the entire Lahontan basin.

The Lahontan basin covers a vast area including many remote mountain streams. I thought there surely must be a few isolated streams that had never been stocked with nonnative trout. I checked out leads, one of which resulted in a backpack trip into the headwaters of the East Carson River, where I found pure populations of Lahontan cutthroat trout existing above waterfalls in two small tributary streams. Such an experience is "reinforcement learning"— an experience that reinforces and renews enthusiasm to learn more.

By this time (around 1960), I had accumulated the learning and experience to become a true believer in the preservation of native trout—what was left of them. The great loss of diversity within our native species of trout and salmon was the direct result of ill-conceived government policies and programs beginning in the last half of the nineteenth century and extending into recent times. The overriding goal of exploitation of natural resources was economic development. By 1900 environmental degradation on a vast scale was apparent from unregulated logging, uncontrolled grazing, and pollution from mining and other industries. President Theodore Roosevelt and his chief forester, Gifford Pinchot, attempted to halt and reverse the trend of environmental degradation. Large tracts of federal land were set aside as forest preserves and national forests. Pinchot defined conservation as the greatest good for the greatest number for the longest time. In modern terms, this would be called sustainability. There is nothing wrong with Pinchot's definition of conservation, but problems

arose over how the definition was interpreted and implemented into government policies and programs. Soon after Roosevelt left office Pinchot was fired and natural resource exploitation returned to business as usual. The "greatest good" or "highest use" of water was for irrigation, power generation, and as a medium to dilute and transport pollution away from its source. The greatest good of vegetation on watersheds was as livestock feed. The greatest good of trees was lumber. Under prevailing federal programs, the greatest good became the only good, without regard to any other values or to the long-term consequences of environmental degradation on a massive scale. Federal programs promoting resource exploitation created subsidized water, subsidized power, subsidized grazing, subsidized logging, and subsidized mining, resulting in subsidized environmental destruction. This, in turn, led to dramatic declines in our native trout and salmon.

A more pervasive influence resulting in further loss of intraspecific diversity resulted from a naive faith in technology to solve problems. It was believed that artificial propagation of great numbers of trout and salmon in hatcheries could maintain abundance despite the building of dams, pollution, and overfishing. For example, salmon hatcheries had to be large to be efficient. In the early 1900s, Chinook salmon of different races were spawned in hatcheries together from all over the Columbia River basin and from other rivers. This forced mixing initiated the breakdown of reproductive isolation maintained in the wild among different races of fish. State and federal agencies made considerable investments in the building of hatcheries, and an entrenched hatchery establishment was created that was devoted to an ever-expanding hatchery program. Despite all findings to the contrary, spokespersons for the U.S. Fish Commission in the 1920s denied that there was a genetic or hereditary basis for intraspecific diversity. Thus the hatchery programs of forced mixing of stocks continued and did so for years. Many of the present problems faced in restoration of anadromous species are the result of a failure to understand how a species is structured. Trout and salmon are not composed of equal and interchangeable parts conducive to mass production of a generic hatchery fish. Their diversity consists of many locally adapted races and the maintenance of this variation determines sustained total abundance. Wild trout and salmon of a particular stock are adapted in many ways to a life history in tune with their specific environment. Once these stocks are mixed in a hatchery, many of the unique characteristics of a race of fish are lost forever.

In recent years, laws and policies governing natural resource management, have become more environmentally enlightened, at least compared to the past, recognizing the values associated with maintaining biodiversity and ecological health.

The late William E. Ricker, perhaps the most influential fisheries biologist of the twentieth century, published a landmark paper in 1972: *Hereditary and environmental factors affecting certain salmonid populations.* This paper was an updated version of an unpublished manuscript he wrote in 1959, 100 copies of which were circulated for review and comment. As a graduate student, I had the opportunity to obtain, read, and re-read Ricker's manuscript. At the time, the fact that anadromous salmonid species in the same river basin consisted of several discrete groupings of populations—each with different life histories, adapted to local conditions maintaining reproductive isolation by homing to their natal spawning streams—was still not widely understood and implemented in management programs. Hatchery operations and regulations largely ignored the reality of intraspecific differentiation and its significance for maintaining abundance.

In Ricker's paper, great amounts of information and data accumulated over many years is brought together, synthesized, and critically analyzed, and the evidence is presented in a convincing manner. I was impressed and greatly influenced in forming my own views and opinions on the values of preserving intraspecific diversity.

Since Ricker's work was published, much research has accumulated verifying that native races of salmon and steelhead have a much higher (up to 10 times greater) survival rate from smolt to returning fish compared to nonnative hatchery fish. In this book examples are given of the "world's largest" of several species: the world's largest Chinook salmon of the Kenai River, Alaska; the world's largest steelhead of the Skeena River, British Columbia; the world's largest rainbow or redband trout, the Gerrard race of Kootenay Lake; the world's largest cutthroat trout of Pyramid Lake, Nevada; the world's largest Arctic char of the Tree River of the Northwest Territories. These record-size fish are not characteristic of the species or subspecies as a whole, but represent single populations that have evolved subtle differences in life histories that allow them to attain such sizes.

I call attention to Ricker's classic work because there is a need to recognize and understand the hereditary basis for life histories. In recent years, modern technology in the form of molecular genetics has erroneously raised doubts similar to those expressed 75 years ago on the hereditary basis of life history distinctions. I consider the doubts raised by molecular genetics to be examples of the "illusion of technique," whereby data derived from the most refined techniques or sophisticated computer models are substituted for critical thinking based on knowledge and experience.

Where different populations of trout and salmon coexist in the same river basin— resident rainbow trout, steelhead, and Pacific salmon—complete isolation among all life history forms of a species during spawning is rare. Occasional mixing and hybridization can occur. This rare hybridization is not sufficient to break down the hereditary basis for distinct life histories. However, the small amount of genetic interchange can be sufficient to prevent unambiguous genetic separation of populations representing different life histories even by the most refined genetic analysis, and this can lead to wrong conclusions. Papers published in leading scientific journals have concluded that there is no genetic or hereditary basis between winter-run and summer-run steelhead or between steelhead and resident rainbow trout. I consider these conclusions erroneous and examples of authors who have never read or comprehended Ricker's great work published 30 years ago. As Ricker discussed in his paper, when many explanations are possible for delineating a complex phenomenon, we typically select the simplest explanation (that there is no genetic or hereditary basis), but when dealing with the complexities of nature, the simplest explanation is usually wrong. Referring to the hereditary basis for the diversity in life histories of salmonid fishes, Ricker wrote in his epilogue: "My strong opinion is that we should avoid any appeal to simplicity or conservatism in such questions. Time and again it has been discovered that nature is more complex than anyone dreamed possible."

Progress on environmental protection and the preservation of biodiversity is neither rapid nor continuous. Some conservation issues can cause divisiveness, and in such situations, lobbying groups and some politicians resort to the traditional rhetoric of "greatest good" in attempts to influence public opinion and public policy. Issues are simplistically phrased in terms of all or nothing; spotted owls or salmon versus people and jobs. Some of the dire predictions made in the 1990s on the consequences of invoking and enforcing the Endangered Species Act to preserve some remnants of old-growth forest included: "we'll be up to our necks in owls and every mill worker will be out of a job"; "it will lead us to the bottom of a black hole"; and will "create a permanent underclass" (of unemployed workers in the timber industry). Such rhetoric reflected a lack of understanding that times and economies change. The facts of the matter were that the timber industry had long over-harvested old-growth forest at rates far in excess of replacement. It could simply not be sustained. Also, the timber industry modernized and became less labor intensive. The greatest loss of jobs in the timber industry occurred during the 1940s through the 1960s.

By 1988, only 3.6 percent of employment in Oregon and Washington was associated with the timber industry. In the 1990s, there was a rapid change in the economies of Oregon and Washington driven by employment in the high technology sector. Despite the prophesies of doom that would result if remnant old-growth forests were protected, from 1990 to 1999, total employment in Oregon and Washington increased by 31 percent and per capita income grew by 26 percent.

From this bit of current history we should learn to be skeptical of the doomsday prophecies commonly used to attack and weaken the laws and policies of environmental protection. The preservation of the remnant diversity of salmonid fishes depends on these programs. The future of trout and salmon can at least be hopeful if we can learn from past mistakes that have caused today's problems.

Artist's Note
Joseph R. Tomelleri

All of the fish illustrations in this book were drawn from nature, and except for several of the rarest trout, which I chose not to keep, were done with a preserved specimen in my studio. Most of the trout and salmon I caught from their native waters. On occasion, I enlisted the help of biologists or other friends to procure and photograph specimens for me, if the logistics of a collecting trip were too difficult to surmount. But mostly I have gone to great and sometimes absurd lengths to see and touch wild fish. These experiences made me poorer in pocket, but surely have led to better knowledge of the subject. There is no substitute for the real thing.

Whenever possible I try to observe and study a half-dozen members of a specific population in order to record variability and to choose the "best" for illustrating. A species is often so variable as to warrant more than one illustration to best describe its appearance. For example, there are dozens of distinct populations of rainbow trout, and many trout, char, and especially salmon look dramatically different during spawning season. The best rule of thumb for describing a population's appearance: Catch one and you know what they look like, catch two and you don't.

Once captured, the fish is photographed as soon as possible to help preserve the colors on film before the hues of the fish begin to change and fade. For some species, I take notes to help capture some of the subtleties of color that photography often misses. Photography is an imperfect medium, and color is affected by the time of day, blue sky, altitude, cloud cover, angle of the sun, depth of shade, or even by the clothes of the handler. For these reasons, though representative of a population, each illustration in this book really represents one specimen captured under specific conditions.

Specimens are either preserved in a chemical solution or frozen for transportation.

Most illustrations are drawn proportionally to 13 inches, which is a comfortable size for working the tiny scales and is an ideal size for reproducing the original prints. Char are typically drawn a bit larger because the scales would otherwise be too tiny to render effectively. Salmon are drawn at life-size or as small as two-thirds life-size, thus the larger illustration lets me use a different technique to produce the relatively larger scales on the sides of the fish.

The specimen is carefully measured and drawn freehand on a 6-ply, 100 percent cotton-rag museum board. Unlike painting, which often requires the colors to be mixed on a palette before application, color pencil drawing requires that the colors be mixed right on the drawing itself, being applied one color at a time until the proper match is achieved. I use two types of color pencils: Prismacolor, vibrant, softer pencils that are used to block in almost all of the color, and Verithin, a harder lead pencil that is good for some details. I also use standard graphite drawing or drafting pencils of varying degrees of hardness for some of the detail work that requires a point of the finest taper.

Prismacolor pencils can be layered one color at a time with each succeeding layer covering a bit more of the grain in the illustration board. Each layer must be applied softly with a sharp pencil so as not to destroy the fine grain of the board. Once the pencil pigments are "burnished" into the board, adjustments to color are more difficult, and sometimes downright impossible. It is the slow, time-consuming process of building colors with pencil that gives the medium its beautiful depth. Once the colors are built to the correct hue, the grain of the board is "removed" from the picture by burnishing or "smoothing" the pigments with a light colored pencil. This technique sometimes requires that the color-building be a bit darker than intended for the finished piece, because burnishing will lighten the colors overall.

On most of the trout illustrations in this book, the scales are too small to be rendered in a typical fashion with colored pencil. Hence the colors of the body are blocked in with Prismacolor pencils and burnished to a smooth finish. The scales (particularly those on the upper sides and back) are then etched into the fish one at a time using an Exacto knife. This technique creates shiny scales on a darker background color that can then be colored in if necessary. A finely pointed pencil or a tinted wash of acrylic paint is then used to achieve higher contrast between the scales and the background color of the back of the fish. Where the body color is lighter, such as the lower sides and belly, a combination of effects is used including drawing the scales over the burnished Prismacolor pencil with a graphite pencil.

Once the drawing is finished it is sprayed with a fixative to protect the piece and prevent a waxy bloom from forming on the pencil pigments. In most instances, the image is then photographed or a digital image might be made using a flatbed scanner.

Acknowledgments

ROBERT J. BEHNKE

Since 1957 when I entered graduate school and embarked on my career of learning all I could about salmonid fishes, so many have supported and contributed to my efforts that a fittingly complete acknowledgments would go on interminably. I can only say to those who have contributed in one way or another, your help is not forgotten.

The late Paul R. Needham provided the opportunity and direction to initiate my career as a graduate student at the University of California, Berkeley. After Needham's death in 1964, the late A. Starker Leopold became my major advisor for the completion of my doctoral studies. Starker loved wild trout and he inherited his father's "land ethic" as it applied to management of natural resources. He was an inspiration to many fishery and wildlife students at Berkeley. One such student influenced by the Leopold family tradition was Phil Pister. After graduating from Berkeley, Phil became a fisheries biologist for the California Department of Fish and Game during the "hook and bullet" era of fish and wildlife management when species of animals were commonly divided into "good species" (species of fish and wildlife sought by hunters and anglers), "bad species" (predators and competitors of the good species), and "worthless species." Phil took the Leopold tradition to heart. To him, all species were good because they were "natural," native species that make up the complexities of nature. Through his persistent efforts, the remnant diversity of desert pupfishes of the Death Valley area was saved from extinction. Phil's example reinforced my beliefs in the values associated with preservation of native trout. Phil Pister became a nationally and internationally reknowned conservationist and has been an inspiration for many fisheries and wildlife biologists of the modern era.

The study of the world's diversity of salmonid fishes makes clear that learning is a lifelong pursuit. The more one knows, the more one realizes how much remains unknown. The more questions that are answered, the more questions that are raised. With this understanding, in 1964, I took part in a 10 month postdoctoral exchange program between the U.S. National Academy of Science and the Academy of Sciences of the then USSR, to further my learning of the salmonoid fishes of the world. I gratefully acknowledge the kindness, assistance, and hospitality shown to me and my wife that made for a rewarding experience. I have continued to maintain contact and information-exchange with old and new Russian colleagues. They have been an important part of my learning process despite (or because of) disagreements on classification.

Because of the enormous geographical areas involved, keeping abreast of new information on the states of various trouts and char of the world requires a network of people who are infused with passion and enthusiasm for these fish. Many are amatuers, that is, they have no formal education in fisheries biology or ichthyology; they are self-taught. Their learning has been driven by their curiosity and enthusiasm to learn more. Among these, the late Bob Smith began a second career after retirement to fulfill his goal of catching all of the species and subspecies of trout and char native to North America. Bob's persistence culminated in a widely acclaimed book, *Native Trout of North America*. This book made an important contribution to increasing public awareness and appreciation of wild, native trout.

For current status on rare and little known salmonoids of Europe, Asia, and North

America, I depend on Johannes Schöffmann of Austria. Although a baker by profession, Johannes is a self-taught ichthyologist of considerable competence who publishes his findings in an Austrian fisheries journal. The most comprehensive, up-to-date, and sometimes the only source of information on the distribution and states of brown trout native to North Africa and the Tigres River of Turkey, the easternmost natural distribution of *S. trutta* in Ama Darya drainage of Kyrgyzstan, the marble trout and species of the genus *Salmothymus* in the former Yugoslavia, *S. ishchan* of Lake Sevan, Armenia, and the Mongolian grayling is found in Schöffmann's publications. In recent years, artist and author James Prosek has joined Schöffmann on expeditions to remote areas of the world in quest of new information on rare and unusual trout.

Kent Andersson who writes on fishes and fishing for a newspaper in Gothenburg, Sweden, keeps me informed on trout and Atlantic salmon of the Baltic Sea region.

Amateurs with a love and enthusiasm for the subject matter can discover new information and make significant contributions to a better understanding of native trout. I seriously doubt that anyone will discover living populations of the extinct yellowfin or Alvord cutthroat trout, but several questions raised in the book await answers. For example, how many ancestral trout gave rise to the present diversity of trout occurring on the mainland of Mexico? Are trout native to river drainages south of the Río del Presidio of Mexico? If so, they would be the southernmost natural distribution of the family Salmonidae. Might cutthroat trout be native to the Río Conchos in remote headwater tributaries of the Sierra Madre Occidental of Mexico? Can anadromous populations of the Faranets char be documented in Alaska? Can northern and southern subspecies of Dolly Varden be found existing together in the same river drainage? If so, the Susitna River basin of Alaska is a likely candidate.

Finally, it is common to acknowledge the support of one's spouse. In my case, it is a true recognition. Last year the building on the Colorado State University campus where I had an office was under reconstruction. To complete the writing of this book, I relocated my office to my home. This meant that I finally had to have a personal computer to keep lines of communication open. I long resisted owning a computer, not because of any antipathy to modern technology, but because I can be characterized as technologically disadvantaged—the problem of an old dog learning new tricks. My wife Sally assumed the duties of computer operator and without her assistance this book could not have been completed in a timely or fully satisfactory manner.

JOSEPH R. TOMELLERI

Many people have helped me procure trout or salmon specimens for the illustrations in this book, but I am especially indebted to the late Frank Cross of the University of Kansas, who spent many hours of his free time helping me to learn the many subtleties of fish identification. Also thanks are due to Bill Stark, Thomas Wenke, and Mark Eberle of Fort Hays State University for their tireless teaching and advice on how to collect fishes, and to Guy Ernsting for his assistance and expertise on many a collecting trip. Drs. Rick Mayden, Binky Kuhajda, and Herb Boschung provided much needed advice and help in collecting specimens. Dr. Dean Hendrickson was indispensable for his help in locating all of the Mexican trout. Others who helped with the Mexican trout were Hector Espinosa, Lloyd Finley, Buddy Jensen, Leslie Ruiz, Kelly Meyer, Albert van der Heiden, Miguel Molina, Azael Salazar, John Hatch, Miguel Molina, Angelica Daza, Jose Luis Villalobos, Charles Nix, George Scott, and Hector Plascenscia. Many thanks to my dear friends Ralph and Lisa Cutter of Truckee, California, who not only taught me how to fly-fish, but also guided me to many of the hard-to-access California native trout. Special thanks to Michael Hatch who took the time to help me catch some of New Mexico's rarer trout, and to Phil Howell, who took me on a whirlwind tour of Oregon in 1991 in search of native Oregon trout. Many other biologists and anglers have assisted me over the years, including Doug Markle of Oregon State University, Stan Gregory, Dave Burns and Don Anderson of McCall, Idaho. Murray Fenton, Dan Bosch, Maggie Lindsey, Ken Morgan, Tom Fliger, Rob Massengal, Ed Jones, Jeff Breakfield, Fred DeCicco, and Jack Dean all helped me with catching and otherwise locating salmon and char in Alaska. Other valuable assistance has been rendered by Dave Winters of the U.S. Forest Service, Sue Swift-Miller, Craig Springer, Glen McFaul of Mesa, Arizona, Paul James, Scott Tollentino, and Kent Sorenson of the Utah Division of Wildlife, Bruce Rosenlund, Eric Gerstung, Stan Stephens, Rob Gipson, Tom Johnson, Fred Kircheis, Henry and Joan Trial, Don Ratliff, Mark Buktenica, Richard Stallings, Bill Kalishek, Ted Halpern, Jon Budge, Stewart Reid, Bill Tinniswood, Sharon Shiba, Theresa Pusteovsky, Paul Chappell, Bill Berg, Mark Wade, Ron McCullough, Bill Taylor of the Atlantic Salmon Federation, Dick Ford, Kevin Rogers, and Dr. John Knaus of Northfield, Illinois.

GEORGE SCOTT

The idea for a comprehensive illustrated book about trout and salmon occurred to me while I was working on a book about birds. At the time I was part of a small publishing army devoted to the creation of a new field guide, the *National Audubon Society: The Sibley Guide to Birds*. For several years, thousands of watercolors created by David Sibley flowed in and out of Chanticleer Press, the product of his life-long interest in birds. I wondered if a similar book could be created about the many types of trout and salmon of North America. While looking through a flyfishing magazine in 1998, a jewel-like illustration caught my eye. It was a native golden trout from the mountains of California. I'd never seen one in real life and I thought, if such a book is possible, this artist is the one to illustrate it. A letter to the art director of the magazine put me in touch with Joe Tomelleri. While looking for a writer to accompany Joe's illustrations, all roads invariably led to Robert Behnke, described to me by many as the foremost expert on native trout and salmon. I also needed someone who could design the book as beautifully as I could imagine it, and luckily, I knew Charles Nix, a good friend, who shares my passion for trout and salmon, and who is a gifted art director, typographer, and teacher. Another requirement was a publishing house to sell and distribute the book. Stephen Morrow at the Free Press saw what we all wished to create, took the chance on the idea and invested his faith in our abilities.

Many people assisted with the editing and research for this book. They generously offered their knowledge and experience by reading manuscript pages and providing data, current scientific papers and reports, range maps, and other material. These contributors include Pat Trotter, Steve Stone, David Moe Nelson, Richard Allen Oswald, Joan G. Trial, George Liles, Mark Minton, Dean Hendrickson, Robert A. Jones, John Kocik, Keith Peterson, Carter Gilbert, Wayne Bowers, and many others.

Special thanks go to freelance editors Anne O'Connor, Pat Fogarty, Pamela Nelson, and Lisa Lester for their careful and intelligent work on the manuscript. Steven Arcella worked tirelessly and artfully to help create the maps. Michelle Bredeson organized and made sense of the many maps in the book and read and made excellent comments on layouts with the able assistance of Annie Lok. Alicia Mills and Arthur Riscen skillfully arranged for the printing and binding. Kate Thomason color corrected the book and traveled to the Far East to oversee the printing process.

After nearly four years of work, the result of our mutual obsession is in your hands. This book is not a field guide in the strict sense. It is not a book to be carried in fishing vests or in bags of wet waders. It is a master guide for anyone who is interested in the history and diversity of the trout and salmon of North America. Many populations of these fish are in trouble, as this book testifies in account after account. Learning about the diversity of the natural world—the birds enumerated in David Sibley's field guide or the fishes illuminated by Joe Tomelleri in this book—is an important step in the path toward responsible conservation of living things. We hope this book informs and inspires others to help maintain and preserve the diversity of our native fishes.

CHANTICLEER PRESS, INC.

Paul Steiner
FOUNDING PUBLISHER

Andrew Stewart
PUBLISHER

STAFF FOR THIS BOOK:

George Scott
EDITOR-IN-CHIEF

Alicia Mills
ASSOCIATE PUBLISHER

Michelle Bredeson
EDITOR

FREELANCE EDITORS:
Anne O'Connor, Patricia Fogarty,
Pamela Nelson

EDITORIAL INTERNS:
Annie Lok, Flynne Wiley

Arthur Riscen
PRODUCTION ASSOCIATE

Alyssa Okun
PRODUCTION INTERN

Sui Ping Cheung
OFFICE MANAGER

Steven Arcella
MAP PRODUCTION

Katherine Thomason
COLOR CORRECTION

The line drawings on pages seven and eight are by John Norton.

Address all editorial inquiries by mail to:

CHANTICLEER PRESS, INC.
665 BROADWAY
SUITE 1001
NEW YORK, NY 10012
ATTN: GEORGE SCOTT, *Editor-in-Chief*

or via e-mail: trout@chanticleer.net

website: http://www.troutsalmon.com

Species List

The following is a listing of the common and scientific names of all the fishes discussed in this book. North American salmon, trout, char, graylings, white fishes, and ciscoes of the family Salmonidae are grouped by genera and appear in the order as described in the text.

A supplemental list, arranged by family, of other fishes mentioned in the book follows the main listing.

GENUS *ONCORHYNCHUS*

Chinook salmon, *Oncorhynchus tshawytscha*

coho salmon, *Oncorhynchus kisutch*

pink salmon, *Oncorhynchus gorbuscha*

chum salmon, *Oncorhynchus keta*

sockeye salmon, *Oncorhynchus nerka*

rainbow trout, *Oncorhynchus mykiss*

coastal rainbow trout, *Oncorhynchus mykiss irideus*

redband trout of the Columbia River basin, *Oncorhynchus mykiss gairdneri*

redband trout of the Northern Great Basin, *Oncorhynchus mykiss newberrii*

Northern Sacramento River redband trout, *Oncorhynchus mykiss stonei*

Sheepheaven redband trout, *Oncorhynchus mykiss* subspecies

Eagle Lake rainbow trout, *Oncorhynchus mykiss aquilarum*

South Fork Kern and Golden Trout Creek golden trout, *Oncorhynchus mykiss aguabonita*

Little Kern River golden trout, *Oncorhynchus mykiss whitei*

Kern River rainbow trout, *Oncorhynchus mykiss gilberti*

rainbow trout of Mexico, *Oncorhynchus mykiss* subspecies

Gila trout, *Oncorhynchus gilae gilae*

Apache trout, *Oncorhynchus gilae apache*

Mexican golden trout, *Oncorhynchus chrysogaster*

cutthroat trout, *Oncorhynchus clarki*

coastal cutthroat trout, *Oncorhynchus clarki clarki*

westslope cutthroat trout, *Oncorhynchus clarki lewisi*

Yellowstone cutthroat trout, *Oncorhynchus clarki bouvieri*

Snake River finespotted cutthroat trout, *Oncorhynchus clarki behnkei*

Bonneville cutthroat trout, *Oncorhynchus clarki utah*

Colorado River cutthroat trout, *Oncorhynchus clarki pleuriticus*

greenback cutthroat trout, *Oncorhynchus clarki stomias*

yellowfin cutthroat trout, *Oncorhynchus clarki macdonaldi*

Rio Grande cutthroat trout, *Oncorhynchus clarki virginalis*

Lahontan cutthroat trout, *Oncorhynchus clarki henshawi*

Paiute cutthroat trout, *Oncorhynchus clarki seleniris*

Alvord cutthroat trout, *Oncorhynchus clarki alvordensis*

Whitehorse Basin cutthroat trout, *Oncorhynchus clarki* subspecies

Humboldt cutthroat trout, *Oncorhynchus clarki* subspecies

GENUS *SALMO*

Atlantic salmon, *Salmo salar*

brown trout, *Salmo trutta*

GENUS *SALVELINUS*

brook trout, *Salvelinus fontinalis*

lake trout, *Salvelinus namaycush*

bull trout, *Salvelinus confluentus*

Arctic char, *Salvelinus alpinus*

Taranets char, *Salvelinus alpinus taranetzi*

Sunapee trout, *Salvelinus alpinus oquassa*

Dolly Varden, *Salvelinus malma*

OTHER SALMONIDS

Arctic grayling, *Thymallus arcticus*

mountain whitefish, *Prosopium williamsoni*

Bear Lake whitefish, *Prosopium abyssicola*

Bonneville whitefish, *Prosopium spilonotus*

Bonneville cisco, *Prosopium gemmifer*

lake whitefish, *Coregonus clupeaformis*

OTHER FISHES

Family Petromyzontidae
sea lamprey, *Petromyzon marinus*

Family Acipenseridae
pallid sturgeon, *Scaphirhynchus albus*
shovelnose sturgeon, *Scaphirhynchus platorynchus*

Family Clupeidae
alewife, *Alosa pseudoharengus*

Family Cyprinidae
common carp, *Cyprinus carpio*
Alvord chub, *Gila alvordensis*
tui chub, *Gila bicolor*
humpback chub, *Gila cypha*
bonytail, *Gila elegans*
roundtail chub, *Gila robusta*
northern pikeminnow, *Ptychocheilus oregonensis*
longnose dace, *Rhinichthys cataractae*
speckled dace, *Rhinichthys osculus*
redside shiner, *Richardsonius balteatus*

Family Catostomidae
Utah sucker, *Catostomus ardens*
longnose sucker, *Catostomus catostomus*
Sacramento sucker, *Catostomus occidentalis*

mountain sucker, *Catostomus platyrhynchus*
shortnose sucker, *Chasmistes brevirostris*
cui-ui sucker, *Chasmistes cujus*
June sucker, *Chasmistes liorus*

Family Osmeridae
European smelt, *Osmerus eperlanus*
rainbow smelt, *Osmerus mordax*

Family Salmonidae
European cisco, *Coregonus albula*
cisco, *Coregonus artedi*
masu salmon, *Oncorhynchus masou*
round whitefish, *Prosopium cylindraceum*
white-spotted char, *Salvelinus leucomaenis*
inconnu, *Stenodus leucichthys*
Mongolian grayling, *Thymallus brevirostris*

Kosogol grayling, *Thymallus nigrescens*
European grayling, *Thymallus thymallus*
taimen, *Hucho taimen*
Danube huchen, *Hucho hucho*

Family Cottidae
mottled sculpin, *Cottus bairdi*
Paiute sculpin, *Cottus beldingi*
slimy sculpin, *Cottus cognatus*
Bear Lake sculpin, *Cottus extensus*
deepwater sculpin, *Myoxocephalus thompsoni*

Family Centrarchidae
Sacramento perch, *Archoplites interruptus*

Selected Bibliography

A comprehensive bibliography for the subject matter of this book would require many more pages than are possible. The citations selected are to general works that contain comprehensive bibliographies and to publications directly pertaining to the subjects discussed in the book.

THE ATLANTIC SALMON ASSOCIATION. 1980. *Atlantic Salmon Rivers of North America.* Rolph McNally Ltd, Canada.

BALON, E.K. (ED.). 1980. *Charrs: Salmonid Fishes of the Genus* Salvelinus. Dr. W. Junk, the Hague, Netherlands.

BEHNKE, R. J. 1968. *A New Subgenus and Species of Trout,* Salmo (Platysalmo) platycephalus, *from Southcentral Turkey, with Comments on the Classification of the Subfamily Salmoninae.* Mitteilungen aus dem Hamburgischen Zoologischen Museum und Institut 66:1–15.

———. 1972. *The Salmonid Fishes of Recently Glaciated Lakes.* Journal of the Fisheries Research Board of Canada 29:639–671.

———. 1989. *Interpreting the Phylogeny of* Salvelinus. Physiology and Ecology of Japan, Special Volume 1:35–48.

———. 1992. *Native Trout of Western North America.* American Fisheries Society Monograph 6.

CAVENDER, T.M. 1978. *Taxonomy and Distribution of the Bull Trout,* Salvelinus confluentus (Suckley) *from the American Northwest.* California Department of Fish and Game 3:139–174.

ELLIOT, J.M. 1994. *Quantitative Ecology and the Brown Trout.* Oxford University Press, Oxford.

GRESSWELL, R.E. (ED.). 1988. *Status and Management of Interior Stocks of Cutthroat Trout.* American Fisheries Society Symposium 4.

GROOT, C. AND L. MARGOLIS (EDS.). 1991. *Pacific Salmon Life Histories.* University of British Columbia Press, Vancouver.

JOHNSON, L. AND B. BURNS (EDS.). 1985. *Biology of the Arctic charr: Proceedings of the International Symposium on Arctic Charr.* University of Manitoba Press, Winnipeg.

JORDAN, D.S. 1891. *Report of Explorations in Colorado and Utah During the Summer of 1889, with an Account of the Fishes Found in Each of the River Basins Examined.* U.S. Fish Commission Bulletin 9:1–40.

JORDAN, D.S. AND B.W. EVERMANN. 1896. *The Fishes of North and Middle America.* U.S. National Museum Bulletin 47, part 1.

———. 1902. *American Food and Game Fishes.* Doubleday, Page, New York.

JORDAN, D.S., B.W. EVERMANN, AND H.W. CLARK. 1930. *Checklist of Fishes and Fishlike Vertebrates of North and Middle America North of the Northern Boundary of Venezuela and Colombia.* U.S. Fish Commission Report for 1928, part 2.

KARAS, N. 1997. *Brook Trout.* Lyons Press, New York.

LICHATOWICH, J. 1999. *Salmon Without Rivers, a History of the Pacific Salmon Crisis.* Island Press, Washington, D.C.

MILLER, R.R. 1950. *Notes on the Cutthroat and Rainbow Trout with a Description of a New Species from the Gila River, New Mexico.* Occasional Papers of the Museum of Zoology University of Michigan, 529.

———. 1972. *Classification of the Native Trouts of Arizona with the Description of a New Species,* Salmo apache. Copeia 1972:401–422.

NEEDHAM, P.R. AND R. GARD. 1964. *A New Trout from Central Mexico:* Salmo chrysogaster, *the Mexican Golden Trout.* Copeia 1964:169–173.

———. 1959. *Rainbow Trout in Mexico and California with Notes on the Cutthroat Series.* University of California Publications in Zoology 67:1–124.

NOAA. 1987. *Bering, Chukchi, and Beaufort Seas— Coastal and Ocean Zones Strategic Assessment: Data Atlas.* Pre-publication edition. Strategic Assessment Branch, NOAA/NOS, Rockville, MD.

———. 1990. *West Coast of North America Strategic Assessment: Data Atlas. Invertebrate and Fish Volume.* Pre-publication edition. Strategic Assessment Branch, NOAA/NOS, Rockville, MD.

RICKER, W.E. 1972. Hereditary and Environmental Factors Affecting Certain Salmonid Populations. Pages 27–160 in *The Stock Concept of Pacific Salmon.* H.R. MacMillan Lectures in Fisheries. University of British Columbia, Vancouver.

ROBINS, C.R. AND SIX COAUTHORS. 1991. *Common and Scientific Names of Fishes from the United States and Canada.* 5th edition. American Fisheries Society Special Publication 20.

SMITH, R.H. 1994. *Native Trout of North America.* Second edition. Frank Amato Publications, Portland, Oregon.

STOLZ, J. AND J. SCHNELL. 1991. *Trout.* Stackpole Books, Harrisburg.

TROTTER, P.C. 1987. *Cutthroat: Native Trout of the West.* Colorado Associated University Press, Boulder.

WATSON, R. 1999. *Salmon, Trout, and Charr of the World.* Swan Hill Press, Shrewsbury, England.

WILLERS, B. 1991. *Trout Biology.* Revised edition. Lyons and Burford, New York.

Glossary

adaptive interspecific diversity   Variation found between two or more species that is the result of adaptation to a particular environmental condition or interaction with other organisms.

adaptive intraspecific diversity   Variation found within a species that is the result of adaptation to a particular environmental condition or interaction with other organisms. For example, the ability of trout that evolved in warmer climates to tolerate higher water temperature versus tolerance to extreme cold in the same species of trout that evolved in colder climates.

adfluvial   A life history characterized by regular migrations between a lake and a stream or river.

aerial stocking   The release of fish—usually fry—from a small airplane or helicopter over a body of water.

anadromous   Describes a migratory fish born in fresh water that spends part of its life cycle in marine environments before returning to fresh water to spawn.

arroyo   A streambed found in drier climates, often deserts, that may or may not contain flowing water.

basibranchial teeth   Minute teeth in the base of the throat at the back of the tongue between the gill arches; not readily detected by the naked eye. Basibranchial teeth are present in some species of trout and char and absent from others.

benthic   Living in the area at or near the bottom of a body of water.

biomass   The total weight of organisms in a specific area or volume, expressed as a unit of weight per unit of area—usually pounds per acre or kilograms per hectare.

carotenoid pigments   Red or yellow pigments that impart coloration to plants and animals. Carotenoid pigments in trout and salmon are responsible for the pink or reddish color of the flesh, as well as red and yellow coloration on the outside of the body.

caudal fin   The tail fin, located at the posterior end of the fish.

caudal peduncle   The narrow region of the fish just before the tail fin.

chromosomal arm   Arm-like projections on chromosomes radiating from a central connection point.

circuli   Concentric rings on the scale of a fish that reflect growth over time.

cline   Consistent change in characteristics in contiguous populations occurring over a geographic area.

convergent evolution   The independent evolution of a similar physical or behavioral attribute in unrelated species or separate evolutionary lineages.

crustacean   A typically aquatic invertebrate of the diverse class Crustacea; crustaceans commonly have a segmented body covered by a shell and paired antennae.

DNA (deoxyribonucleic acid)   The molecules in cells that contain the genetic code.

degree of differentiation   The amount of physical difference between two or more groups of organisms.

diploid   Having two sets of each chromosome per individual; the normal condition of chromosomes in a cell nucleus. In sexually reproducing organisms, one set comes from the female and one from the male.

distinct population segment (DPS)   A term used in the Endangered Species Act (ESA) enacted by the United States government in 1973, which mandates the protection and conservation of species, subspecies, and races. See *evolutionarily significant units* below.

dorsal   Referring to the back or upper parts of an animal.

evolutionarily significant units (ESU)   A term proposed to define a "distinct population" under the Endangered Species Act; a group of populations inhabiting a specific geographic area that comprises a unique segment of the species.

family   A taxon that is a subset of an order and that contains one or more genera. The family Salmonidae includes trout, salmon, char, whitefishes, ciscoes, inconnu, and graylings in North America and several more genera from Europe and Asia.

fin rays   Segmented structural elements of the fins that may be spiny or soft; all trout and salmon have soft rays.

flow   The amount (volume) of water passing a given point per unit of time; generally expressed as cubic feet per second or cubic meters per second.

fluvial   Of or pertaining to flowing water; describes a migratory freshwater life history within a river system.

fry   The early life history stage of a fish soon after hatching.

genus (plural: genera)   A taxon that is a subset of a family and that contains one or more species.

gill arches   A series of four V-shaped structures in the back of the skull beneath the gill cover; comprised of several small rod-shaped bones. Gill arches are the structural support for gill rakers and gill filaments.

gill cover   The outer covering of the gill chamber. The gill cover, or operculum, is a collection of four flat bones attached by cartilage to allow flexibility. It opens and closes to allow water to pass over the gills for respiration.

gill rakers   Fine bones of the gill arches similar in appearance to the teeth of a comb. Gill rakers strain small food items, such as zooplankton.

glacial refugia   Areas free of glaciers during the Pleistocene epoch that served as refuges for living organisms.

habitat   The physical environment of an organism.

hybrid   The offspring of two different species, sometimes applied to the offspring of two different subspecies or races of fish.

hybrid swarm   An interbreeding population derived from hybridization of two different species.

karyotype   The number and general features of chromosomes in a cell.

kype (sometimes: kypes)   The hook-like jaws developed by some mature male salmonids.

lacustrine   Living in or related to lakes.

lateral line   A sensory receptor system that runs along the sides and head of some fishes that detects movement and objects in the surrounding water.

main stem   The larger channel of a river or stream.

meristic   Describes features that may be counted. Meristic characteristics in fishes include the number of scales along the sides, number of vertebrae, number of gill rakers, etc.

microhabitat   A specific portion of a larger habitat.

monophyletic   Having a single common ancestor.

niche   The ecological role of an organism; all of the resources, such as habitat and food sources, that an organism uses to survive.

ocean productivity   The amount of life in a particular region of the ocean, resulting from a complex mixture of sunlight, upwelling of nutrient-rich water from great depths, and ocean currents.

osmoregulation   The maintenance of proper water and salt balance in the body.

otoliths   Tiny bones located in the inner ear chambers of all fish; studied by scientists to determine age, growth rate, and other characteristics.

parr marks   Dark, oblong, or oval markings along the side of the body of most trout and salmon. Particularly prominent in juvenile fish (as camouflage for avoiding predators); typically reduced or absent in adult salmonids.

parr   The stage in sea-going trout and salmon prior to the smolt stage and migration to salt water.

pelagic   Living in or pertaining to the open waters of the oceans (or large lakes), as opposed to coastal waters.

phyletic   Pertaining to a line of descent, implying evolutionary relationship.

phylogeny   The relationships among evolutionary lines of living things.

piscivorous   Fish-eating.

primitive   A relative term used in biology to describe an attribute or characteristic of a species or subspecies, which is evolutionarily older.

pyloric caeca   Small, finger-like projections located at the beginning of the intestines just below the stomach that aid in digestion by secreting enzymes; used in classification of species and subspecies of some fishes.

polyphyletic   Belonging to a group derived from different ancestors.

population   A group of interbreeding organisms found in a particular area.

redd   The spawning nest of some salmonids, created by digging a depression in the substrate.

residual steelhead   A juvenile male steelhead that matures sexually before it smolts and goes to sea, or any steelhead that remains in fresh water and does not migrate to the sea.

salmonid   A fish that is a member of the family Salmonidae.

Salmoninae   A subfamily of the family Salmonidae.

sexual dimorphism   A feature of the anatomy that is variable between different sexes of the same species. For example, male salmon develop hook-like jaws (kype) when spawning, females do not.

sediment load   The amount of particles suspended in the water column of flowing water.

siltation   The accumulation of fine particles on the bottom of a stream, river, or lake.

smolt   A young trout or salmon that has begun its migration from fresh water to the sea. Smoltification is the process whereby young fish lose parr marks, change coloration to a more silvery appearance, and physiologically adapt in order to migrate to marine environments.

spawning   The release and fertilization of eggs in water.

species   A taxon that is a subset of a genus.

steelhead   A rainbow trout that migrates to the sea then returns to fresh water to spawn.

stock   A group of a particular region that shares a similar life history.

subfamily   A taxon that is a subset of a family.

subspecies   A taxon that is a subset of a species; usually describes a population or group of populations that are geographically isolated.

sympatric   A term used to describe two or more species that occupy the same geographic region or habitat; co-occurring. For example, rainbow trout and cutthroat trout are sympatric when they occupy the same stream.

tailwater   The area of a river or stream that is immediately below a man-made reservoir. Many tailwater environments are artificially cool and rich in nutrients because of the temperature of the water and abundant organisms released from the reservoir.

taxon (plural: taxa)   A taxonomic category, such as a family, genus, species, or subspecies, that refers to a distinct natural group.

triploid fish   A sexually sterile fish that has three sets of chromosomes, instead of the normal complement of two (diploid). Fertilized eggs in hatcheries are exposed to heat to create triploid fish in an attempt to prevent reproduction in the wild after stocking.

type specimen   The specimen on which the name of a species or subspecies is based.

ventral   Refers to the bottom or "belly" portion of an animal.

vomer   A narrow bone in the roof of the mouth.

vomerine teeth   Teeth attached to the vomer bone.

year class   A group of organisms of the same species born in the same year; also sometimes referred to as an "age class," when a specific age is known.

Index

Page numbers in bold type refer to the main account of a particular fish or group of fishes. Page numbers in italic type indicate an illustration of the fish is reproduced on that page.

Colophon

The text of this book is set in $^{10.5}/_{14}$ point *Minion,*
designed by Robert Slimbach.
The heads are set in *Monotype Grotesque*
and *Monotype Scotch Roman*
from The Monotype Corporation.
Subheads are set in *Gothic 725 Black*
from Bitstream, Inc.

All files for production were prepared
on Macintosh computers.

Color separations were prepared by
Bright Arts, Hong Kong.
It was printed and bound in Singapore by Imago, Inc.
The paper is 128 gsm Neo Matt Art Shinmoorim and
it is bound in Brillianta cloth.

It was designed by Charles Nix.